Forty years ago I dreamed of teaching *gurukula* students with Śrīla Prabhupāda's *Śrīmad-Bhāgavatam* serving as the central text. Toward realizing that goal, I had compiled the *Bhāgavatam* into its essential stories, for I trusted Śrīla Prabhupāda's words that such study would truly educate and prepare my students on every level for a satisfying and worthwhile life.

But Kṛṣṇa had a more wonderful plan. The opportunity to fulfill Śrīla Prabhupāda's desire – like a fragrant lotus in the form of this *Śrīmad-Bhāgavatam: A Comprehensive Guide for Young Readers* – has been carefully placed in the open hands of Mātājī Aruddhā Devī Dāsī and her team of parents and educators. May the fortunate children who take advantage of their love-laden offering gain a taste for this sweet, potent literature. May those children continue throughout their lives to taste and distribute to others what they have relished in their childhood and youth. May the *Śrīmad-Bhāgavatam* safeguard their rapid journey to the lotus feet of Śrī Kṛṣṇa. And may Śrīla Prabhupāda bless those who have sought to fulfill his desire by compiling this offering and placing it into his lotus hands.

BHŪRIJANA DĀSA

Śrīmad-Bhāgavatam: A Comprehensive Guide for Young Readers, to our reading, and from all reports, is an unsurpassed resource for teachers of *Śrīmad-Bhāgavatam,* both in families and in schools. The variety of materials and amount of work that went into producing the book as a gift to Śrīla Prabhupāda are astonishing.

HANUMATPREŚAKA SWAMI (PROF. H. H. ROBINSON)

As I travel around the United States, I get to personally witness how much devotee families have benefitted from Aruddhā Devī Dāsī and her homeschooling methods, which are completely based on Śrīla Prabhupāda's books and teachings. I am an ardent supporter of her and the models of education which she develops and promotes through her books and various homeschooling seminars.

It is very pleasing to note that she and her team have come up with a second project, *Śrīmad-Bhāgavatam: A Comprehensive Guide for Young Readers.* The series' main objective is to provide children with a *Bhāgavatam*-centered education, with lots of activities created by parents and teachers that are geared toward different learning styles, while meeting devotional, cognitive and language objectives of a growing child in Kṛṣṇa consciousness. This innovative and systematic compilation of various activities in book form is a great resource for any homeschooling parents who want their children to go deeper into the messages of *Śrīmad-Bhāgavatam.*

ROMAPĀDA SWAMI

From my reading of Aruddhā Devī Dāsī's book on studying *Śrīmad-Bhāgavatam*, it is evident that she is fulfilling Śrīla Prabhupāda's desire that our children get the best Kṛṣṇa conscious education. As Śrīla Prabhupāda said in a lecture on *Śrīmad-Bhāgavatam* 1.5.13 given in New Vrindaban in 1969: "When one can understand *Śrīmad-Bhāgavatam* in true perspective, then it is to be understood that he has finished all his educational advancement. *Avadhi. Avadhi* means 'this is the limit of education.' *Vidyā-bhāgavatāvadhi.*"

This book gives the highest knowledge in an interesting way, so that children may access the *Bhāgavatam* on many levels, including higher-level thinking and application to their lives, as well as artistic, dramatic and journalistic approaches. I recommend this book for all parents who want to give their children a higher taste for reading Śrīla Prabhupāda's *Śrīmad-Bhāgavatam*.

NĀRĀYAṆĪ DEVĪ DĀSĪ

ŚRĪMAD BHĀGAVATAM

A Comprehensive Guide for Young Readers

CANTO 6

ŚRĪMAD BHĀGAVATAM

A Comprehensive Guide for Young Readers

CANTO 6

COMPILED BY

Aruddhā Devī Dāsī

Krishna
Homeschool

Library of Congress Cataloging-in-Publication Data

Srimad Bhagavatam: a comprehensive guide for young readers, Canto 6 /
compiled by Aruddha devi dasi.
356 pages
ISBN 978-1-7369610-1-8
1. Puranas. Bhagavatapurana–Textbooks. 2. Hinduism–Textbooks.
I. Aruddha, devi dasi.
BL1140.4.B436S745 2014
294.5'925--dc23
2014005526

Cover and book design:
Eight Eyes
www.eighteyes.com

Cover illustration: by Prithvi Kumar

For more information, contact:

Krishna
Homeschool

Contact the author at aruddha108@yahoo.com

CONTENTS

This book is a tribute to the spiritual master of the entire world, His Divine Grace
A.C. Bhaktivedanta Swami Prabhupāda, who gave us the invaluable gift of *Śrīmad-
Bhāgavatam*. Śrīla Prabhupāda spent many hours at night translating this vast literature
from Sanskrit to English and promised that anyone who studies his books will be
liberated from the miseries of material life and directly connected to Kṛṣṇa.

ACKNOWLEDGMENTS

This book is a tribute to the spiritual master of the entire world, His Divine Grace A.C. Bhaktivedanta Swami Prabhupāda, who gave us the invaluable gift of *Śrīmad-Bhāgavatam*. Śrīla Prabhupāda spent many hours at night translating this vast literature from Sanskrit to English and promised that anyone who studies his books will be liberated from the miseries of material life and directly connected to Kṛṣṇa.

My humble obeisances and gratitude to my spiritual master, His Holiness Gopal Krishna Goswami, a dear and dedicated disciple of Śrīla Prabhupāda, who is untiring in his efforts to preach Kṛṣṇa consciousness throughout the world. He always encourages me to share my experiences of Kṛṣṇa conscious parenting with devotees.

My gratitude to my husband Anantarūpa Prabhu, my sons Rādhikā Ramaṇa and Gopāla Hari, and my daughters-in-law Amṛta Keli and Devī Mūrti, who greatly supported my efforts in completing these series of books.

My profound thanks to all the contributors of this book who spent many hours studying the topics in Canto 6 and creating suitable resources for children. They hail from countries around the world. I offer my heartfelt gratitude to the following contributors for their committed and excellent efforts in specific areas:

India
- Prithvi Kumar for the front cover artwork and beautiful book illustrations.
- Pūrṇeśvarī Rādhā Devī Dāsī for critical-thinking, analogy, introspective, and science activities.
- Śyāmeśvarī Prīti Devī Dāsī for action, writing, and language activities.

South Africa
- Nikuñja Vilāsinī Devī Dāsī for chapter summaries, themes, higher-thinking questions, and art suggestions.

United States

- Amṛta Sundarī Devī Dāsī for action, language, artistic, and theatrical activities.
- Amala Nāma Dāsa for adding diacritics and reviewing the text.

My profuse thanks to Nikuñja Vilāsinī Devī Dāsī (Nirvana Kasopersad) for her excellent editorial work. Her expertise in checking content, correcting grammar, and proofreading, with constant attention to quality and detail, proved to be a great blessing as we put together this voluminous work.

Many thanks to Raghu Consbruck and Govinda Cordua of Eight Eyes for their excellent design and layout and the cover design, which makes the book polished, attractive, and friendly to children.

I am also grateful to Amala Nāma Dāsa (Amol Bakshi) for reviewing the content with care and attention, for his valuable feedback, and for spotting minute errors with an eye for detail.

This book is the product of many hands, and it would not have existed without the dedication of all these devotees. I am deeply indebted to them for taking time from their busy schedules to create a valuable resource for children everywhere.

INTRODUCTION

While conducting seminars on homeschooling and Kṛṣṇa conscious parenting throughout the world during the last seven years, I met many parents who wanted to teach their children *Śrīmad-Bhāgavatam* but who needed more guidance on how to do it. It was then that I started doing workshops, during which we would sit together with their children and I would demonstrate how to guide a discussion in a way that evoked the child's curiosity about the nature of the world, God, the self, and the purpose of life. Together, we would read the translations of a chapter of *Śrīmad-Bhāgavatam* and discuss the stories, main themes, and great personalities. We would talk about the relevance of *Śrīmad-Bhāgavatam* in our own lives – how it provides spiritual solutions to material problems. Both the children and parents were thoroughly enlivened and absorbed in the discussions.

When I explained at seminars how I taught my boys *Śrīmad-Bhāgavatam* through interactive reading and discussion, hundreds of parents were inspired to follow. However, many parents who wanted to study the *Bhāgavatam* with their children were uncertain about how to do it. They needed a formal curriculum, *and* I pondered how I could help. I decided to start a collaborative project, involving devotee parents from around the world. I formed an online group in which approximately 15 parents – from Australia, New Zealand, India, South Africa, the United Kingdom, and the United States – worked together to create study resources for each chapter of Canto 1. Every parent would send their creations to others in the group, who would use the material with their own children and offer feedback.

All the parents brought special skills – our team included English teachers, musicians, artists, and computer professionals. With children of their own, they were highly motivated to give them a *Bhāgavatam*-centered education. The result? An innovative collection of material on every chapter of Canto 1. The creators used the curriculum with their own children as they designed it, seeing the results firsthand.

However, having all this material in email

attachments was beneficial only to a certain extent – it had to be edited, organized, and compiled. So we began the painstaking task of systematically compiling a book for use by parents and teachers anywhere, which was published as *Śrīmad Bhāgavatam: A Comprehensive Guide for Young Readers, Canto 1*. We then went through a similar process for Canto 2, Canto 3, Canto 4, ,Canto 5, and now we are pleased to present to you Canto 6. This book is primarily geared for children between the ages of 12 and 18, but much of the material can be adapted for children younger than 12, or older than 18.

WHY STUDY ŚRĪMAD-BHĀGAVATAM?

Śrīla Prabhupāda said that from the very beginning, children "should be taught Sanskrit and English, so in the future they can read our books. That will make them MA, Ph.D. Because the knowledge in these books is so advanced, children would be well-educated, happy, satisfied, and even go back home, back to Godhead." (Jagadīśa, April 6, 1977)

As is evident in many of his lectures, Śrīla Prabhupāda desired that children in his *gurukula* schools read *Śrīmad-Bhāgavatam*. In 1974, speaking on *Śrīmad-Bhāgavatam* (1.16.22), Śrīla Prabhupāda emphasized that the *Bhāgavatam* would equip one to know any subject: "So in *Śrīmad-Bhāgavatam* you will find everything, whatever is necessity, for the advancement of human civilization, everything is there described. And knowledge also, all departments of knowledge, even astronomy, astrology, politics, sociology, atomic theory, everything is there. *Vidyā-bhāgavatāvadhi.* Therefore, if you study *Śrīmad-Bhāgavatam* very carefully, then you get all knowledge completely. Because *Bhāgavatam* begins from the point of creation: *janmādy asya yataḥ.*" (July 12, 1974, Los Angeles)

If we give children this foundation, they become confident of their spiritual identity and also do well academically. Śrīla Prabhupāda's books inspire critical reasoning and creative thinking, which are the main elements of academic education. In addition, *Śrīmad-Bhāgavatam* is pure and perfect and can equip them with the highest knowledge, both material and spiritual.

Parents and teachers who have taught their children *Śrīmad-Bhāgavatam* from their early lives have experienced how easily they pick up English language skills, especially reading, comprehension, and analytical reasoning. *Śrīmad-Bhāgavatam* is full of analogies, allegories, figurative speech, and metaphors. Even a seven-year-old child can grasp difficult concepts because the subject matter of *Śrīmad-Bhāgavatam* encourages higher-thinking skills.

Śrīmad-Bhāgavatam is a wonderful book to teach from because it gives the philosophy of the *Bhagavad-gītā* through stories, and children love stories. These stories are not fictitious; rather, they are the lives of great saintly personalities and the pastimes of Kṛṣṇa and His *avatāras*. By reading these, they directly associate with the great personalities and their teachings and begin to emulate the character of these personalities. As children grow older, they learn to appreciate the instructions given by Queen Kuntī, Prahlāda Mahārāja, Dhruva Mahārāja, Kapiladeva, and so many others. In fact, many of the devotees described in the *Bhāgavatam*, such as Prahlāda and Dhruva, are children themselves, so our children have perfect examples and heroes to follow.

The scriptures tell us that Śrī Caitanya Mahāprabhu heard the stories of Dhruva Mahārāja and Prahlāda Mahārāja hundreds of times while growing up, and still he was never bored. The example and instructions of these saints are so valuable that no other moral book can compare with them. Children develop good character, saintly qualities, and pure *bhakti* by reading *Śrīmad-Bhāgavatam*. Indeed, *Śrīmad-Bhāgavatam* is the very essence of Lord Caitanya's *saṅkīrtana* movement.

(A) *Discussion*

In my book, *Homeschooling Kṛṣṇa's Children*, I emphasize the necessity of giving our children a Kṛṣṇa conscious education based on Śrīla Prabhupāda's books. I discuss the methodology of studying *Śrīmad-Bhāgavatam* through interactive reading and discussion – the most important element of the process. We sit in a circle and take turns reading only translations, pausing frequently for discussion. (For children who cannot read, they can listen as their parents read and paraphrase the translations). This method has been followed for thousands of years by the great sages of Vedic India as we see in the *Bhāgavatam* itself.

Discussion is an important part of reading. For children it breaks up the monotony of reading and can add both interest and challenge. By using *Śrīmad-Bhāgavatam* as their basic text, children can learn all aspects of language skills: composition, comprehension, vocabulary, critical thinking, and analytical reasoning. The children often drive the discussion by asking questions, raising doubts, or making observations about what they read. By expressing themselves, children understand the material better, gain self-confidence, and learn communication skills. Parents can pick up on their children's cues and ask questions of their own to encourage deeper understanding. Parents can also present their own realizations, play devil's advocate, and relate the stories to practical life, thus making the *Bhāgavatam* study a dynamic learning experience.

Reading and discussion also lead to good speaking, debate, and logical thinking. The nature of *Śrīmad-Bhāgavatam* is such that it encourages a person to ask questions, think critically, and work creatively because the *Bhāgavatam* is full of analogies, metaphors, and figurative speech. For example, the analogy of the car and the driver that Prabhupāda uses to describe the difference between the body and the soul is practical and simple, but it allows a child to appreciate a foundational principle of Kṛṣṇa consciousness. Some analogies may be difficult for a four- or five-year-old, but as he or she grows older, these analogies will become the basis for strong reasoning skills.

Before reading a chapter (translations) with their children, parents should read the chapter and purports on their own and go through the discussion (higher-thinking questions) provided in this book. These questions give parents ideas of how to inspire discussion as they read with their children. Please remember, however, that the discussion questions are only for the purpose of stimulating ideas, not to create a highly structured "oral exam" atmosphere while reading. The key is to keep the discussion dynamic and student-driven, using the sample questions when needed and adapting/rephrasing them appropriately for the age and personality of the child. During a vibrant discussion, you and your child will, no doubt, come up with questions and topics that were not mentioned in this book, and we encourage you do so. Here are some suggestions for raising interesting and thought-provoking questions:

- Take turns reading the translations, going in a circle. This keeps the child's attention because children eagerly await their turn. If your child cannot read, you should read and pause frequently to paraphrase the story at the child's level. Ask your child to tell the story in his or her own words.
- Whenever possible, ask "why" and "how" questions rather than "what" (factual) questions, thus encouraging your child to think and reason.
- Don't be afraid to ask open-ended questions that do not have a clear-cut answer. These questions often lead to beneficial discussions.
- Discuss the many analogies and metaphors in Śrīla Prabhupāda's purports, which are

good opportunities to connect the *Śrīmad-Bhāgavatam* to your child's experience and imagination.

- Frequently encourage your child to make comments and raise questions. When your child raises a question for which you don't know the answer, don't be afraid to say so. Discuss his or her question thoroughly, read through purports to find guidance, and you will see many fresh realizations arise.
- Try to relate the story to daily life: "Why did Parīkṣit Mahārāja not retaliate against the boy's curse?" or "What can we learn from Parīkṣit Mahārāja's behavior?" However, don't put your child on the spot by pointing fingers: "How should you have behaved with your friend Johnny the other day?" Such finger-pointing destroys the discussion and intimidates the child.
- Draw connections with other stories from the scriptures that your child may already know: "The boy Śṛṅgi showed anger in an inappropriate way, but when is it okay to feel angry? Can you give an example from other stories in the scriptures?"
- Continue reading until you come to a translation that raises a question or comment. Don't worry if a particular section doesn't raise discussion – some sections will be more interesting to a child than others.
- Have a "realizations session" at the end of a chapter where your child can tell you what they learned from the chapter, and you can tell your child what you learned. Or bring the family together and ask your child to give a short class on the chapter.
- If you have not read *Śrīmad-Bhāgavatam* before, that is okay. As a parent (or teacher), you have more life experience, and you know your child, which will allow you to lead a discussion and engage your child.
- When you read with an older child (the specific age will vary based on the maturity of the child), take the stance of a fellow reader and learner. This will help your child open up and feel comfortable. Of course, as the teacher, you will still need to correct a mistaken line of reasoning or raise points that are important but try to do it as a partner rather than as a master.
- Consider these readings/discussions as your time with *Śrīmad-Bhāgavatam*. Stay focused and become absorbed in *Śrīmad-Bhāgavatam*. Just because your study partner is a seven-year-old child does not mean that you will gain any less from studying *Śrīmad-Bhāgavatam*.

(B) *Written and Oral Exercises*

Once you have read a chapter of the *Bhāgavatam* translations together, you can use a variety of exercises provided in the book to teach language skills – including writing, comprehension, and vocabulary – which will help in understanding the chapter. This book provides comprehension questions, key themes and messages, language puzzles, arts and crafts, and many other activities. In this volume we have eliminated some language activities and extra resources to not make it too thick and unwieldy for children. We also encourage you to use your creativity to compile interesting new activities that would stimulate your child. To decide which verses children can memorize, please use the verse references under the key messages. Our goal is to provide you with practical tools to make *Śrīmad-Bhāgavatam* a central part of your children's education. Regardless of whether you are homeschooling or sending your children to school, we hope these tools will inspire you to create other innovative ways to help your children.

Here are the different sections you will find in this book:
- Story Summary
- Themes and Key Messages
- Discussion and Higher-Thinking Questions
- Analogy Activities

- Critical-Thinking Activities
- Introspective Activities
- Science Activities
- Writing and Language Activities
- Crossword Puzzles, Games, and Action Activities
- Arts, Crafts, Drama, and other Hands-On Activities
- Answers (includes answers to specific questions and puzzles)

The instructions for each activity are addressed directly to the child, but if your child is younger, we encourage you to explain and supervise the activities.

LEARNING OUTCOMES

The book's main objective is to provide children from the ages of 12–18 with spiritual knowledge from the *Śrīmad-Bhāgavatam* and the opportunity for personal realization.

The primary process for doing this is by reading chapter translations with the children, discussing the stories and philosophical content of the chapter, and providing the children with the opportunity to make their own inquiries and share their personal experiences.

In addition, the activities in this book develop the key themes and philosophical points presented in each chapter by accommodating different learning styles in a range of learning modes (visual, auditory, and kinesthetic). The activities also meet the following cognitive and language objectives:

Developing thinking skills (based on Bloom's *Taxonomy of Educational Objectives*)
- Developing comprehension skills
- Acquiring knowledge
- Applying knowledge
- Using knowledge to be creative
- Analyzing information
- Promoting self-evaluation

Language objectives:
- Written language (includes reading and writing)
- Visual language (includes communicating through the visual arts, such as drama and static imagery)
- Oral language (includes communication through speaking)

This book also supplements any existing curriculum that parents or teachers may use to teach language skills. This is not a course designed to teach reading and writing in itself, but it can work together with a formal curriculum to further develop language skills, while providing children with a resource for studying *Śrīmad-Bhāgavatam*.

Śrīmad-Bhāgavatam lies at the heart of Śrī Caitanya Mahāprabhu's philosophy and movement. I pray that this book will help children and their parents develop a lifelong love for this great literature, following in the footsteps of Śrīla Prabhupāda and our previous *ācāryas*. *Śrīmad-Bhāgavatam* is very profound, and this book only skims the surface. I humbly request you to forgive any faults and shortcomings in our humble endeavors.

Aruddhā Devī Dāsī
March 2023

1

Parīkṣit Mahārāja's heart felt heavy. He had just heard about the terrible suffering that sinful people had to endure in hell. He wanted to ask a question for their benefit.

Mahārāja Parīkṣit folded his palms and glanced at the Gaṅgā, which shone like tiny diamonds on a turquoise velvet robe. The cool breeze carried the aroma of white lotuses that danced on the river's waves. The King took a deep breath, the sacred air invigorating him. The air had become more sacred from the narrations of Śukadeva Gosvāmī, who sat facing the King with a serene smile on his lips.

The King bowed his head and asked, "My dear lord, you have described the path of liberation, *nivṛtti-mārga* [in the Second Canto]. By following this path, one goes to Brahmaloka from where one goes to the spiritual world, a place of no birth and death.

"The conditioned souls have material desires and act accordingly, influenced by the modes of nature. These souls therefore act piously and sinfully. They walk the *pravṛtti-mārga* and

experience both happiness and distress. They go either to heaven [as described in the Third Canto] or hell [as in the Fifth Canto]. You've already nicely described this material universe with its planets, stars, rivers, oceans, mountains, and trees in the upper, middle, and lower planetary systems. You've also described the various living beings that occupy each part of this vast universe based on their *karma*.

"O greatly fortunate and opulent Śukadeva Gosvāmī, how can human beings be saved from going to hell in which they suffer terrible pains?"

Śukadeva Gosvāmī smiled, noting the compassion of his disciple. One might think that the King would have been focused on himself since he was soon to die. But no. He was concerned with how to liberate others.

Whispers broke out throughout the assembly. The sage put his finger to his lips, and the audience was again silent, drinking in every word with their ears.

Śukadeva Gosvāmī replied, "My dear King, if one has performed sinful acts in this life,

The assembly of learned *brāhmaṇas* this time broke out in startled whispers. Was the King challenging his *guru*?

Parīkṣit Mahārāja respectfully bowed his head and continued, "Even one who is careful not to sin again becomes a victim of sin. It is like the bathing of an elephant. Even after the elephant takes a clean bath, he throws dirt all over his body again. So, I consider this process of atonement useless."

Śukadeva Gosvāmī lifted his hand to silence the assembly. Little did they know that the sage had been testing his disciple.

"You are right," said Śukadeva Gosvāmī, smiling. He was delighted that the King had been absorbing and realizing much of what he had been explaining thus far. "Since acts of atonement (*karma*) also give fruitive results, it will not free one from fruitive work. People who follow the rules and regulations of atonement are not at all intelligent; they are in the mode of darkness. In ignorance, how can you try to counteract one action with another action? It's useless because it will not uproot your sinful desires, and thus you will continue to act impiously.

"Real atonement is to become enlightened in perfect knowledge, when one understands the Absolute Truth."

"Jaya!" cheered the assembled *brāhmaṇas*, now understanding that Parīkṣit Mahārāja had indeed understood his *guru's* instructions. They now looked reverentially upon the King.

Śukadeva Gosvāmī continued, "My dear King, if a sick person follows the pure diet prescribed by a doctor, he is gradually cured. Similarly,

one has to atone for one's sins according to the instructions of the Manu-saṁhitā and other *śāstras*. Otherwise one will certainly enter the hellish planets after death and suffer terribly as I've described to you. Just like a doctor treats a disease according to the seriousness of the disease, one should atone according to the severity of one's sins."

Parīkṣit Mahārāja thought for a moment and said, "A sinner may know that it is not good to sin; after all, he sees that a criminal is punished by the government and rebuked by the people. He also hears from *śāstra* that you go to hell in the next life for committing sinful acts. But in spite of knowing this, he commits sins again and again even after atoning for them. So what is the use of such atonement?"

if one follows the regulations of knowledge (*jñāna*), he gradually becomes free from material contamination."

"So what exactly should the person do?" asked Parīkṣit Mahārāja.

"One has to focus one's mind by observing celibacy, austerity, self-control, charity, truthfulness, cleanliness, and nonviolence. One should follow the regulative principles and chant the holy name of the Lord. However, for one who is cultivating knowledge, he is only temporarily purified of all sins. These sins are like the dry leaves of creepers beneath a bamboo tree. Even burned by fire, their roots remain and then grow at the first opportunity."

Parīkṣit Mahārāja smiled. He had known that *jñāna* was not the answer to his question. He asked, "So what can uproot the desire for sinful actions completely and truly liberate such a person?"

"Only a rare person who develops complete and pure devotion to Kṛṣṇa can uproot the weeds of sinful desires with no possibility of their ever reviving. Just as the sunrays immediately dissipate the fog, devotional service can totally remove sinful desires, the root cause of sinful acts."

Parīkṣit Mahārāja's face glowed as his *guru* confirmed what he had been thinking.

"A person can become completely purified by serving the bona fide spiritual master and dedicating his life to the lotus feet of Kṛṣṇa," continued Śukadeva Gosvāmī. "One cannot become completely purified by doing austerity, penance, celibacy, and the other methods of atonement I have described. The path followed by pure devotees is certainly the most auspicious path.

"As a liquor pot cannot be purified even if washed in the waters of many rivers, nondevotees cannot be purified by the processes of atonement even if they perform them very well. Yet, those who haven't even fully realized Kṛṣṇa but who have just once surrendered completely to Kṛṣṇa

and are attracted to His name, form, qualities, and pastimes are completely free from all sinful reactions. Even in dreams, they do not see Yamarāja, the lord of death, or his order carriers, the Yamadūtas, who bind the sinful person with ropes.

"I will tell you an old historical incident that proves this. It involves a discussion between the order carriers of Viṣṇu, the Viṣṇudūtas, and those of Yamarāja, the Yamadūtas."

"Please enlighten us, my lord," implored Parīkṣit Mahārāja, eager to hear how devotional service can save one from the ropes of the Yamadūtas.

Śukadeva Gosvāmī began narrating the story.

Ajāmila, a *brāhmaṇa*, lived in the city of Kānyakubja. He married a prostitute and lost all his brahminical qualities because of associating with this low-class woman. He cheated people in gambling and even plundered them to maintain his wife and sons. His years of abominable sinful life passed quickly, and at the age of 88 he had his tenth son named Nārāyaṇa who became the life

of the mother and father. Ajāmila was enchanted by the child's broken language and awkward movements. When Ajāmila ate and drank, he called Nārāyaṇa to eat and drink with him. He wouldn't let the boy out of his sight. "Nārāyaṇa! Nārāyaṇa!" he would constantly call out. But the old man did not realize that death was upon him. He was completely infatuated by his son, so much so that when he was on his deathbed, he thought only of his son Nārāyaṇa.

Pain ravaged his body at the time of death, and just as he was about to leave his body, he saw three persons approaching him. But they weren't ordinary. Their fierce twisted faces terrified the dying Ajāmila, and when he saw their horrifying deformed figures with ropes in their hands, he thought he would die just from the fear of seeing them.

Ajāmila saw his little son playing nearby. Only thoughts of his son comforted him. In desperation and confusion, with tears in his eyes, Ajāmila shouted, "Nārāyaṇa! Nārāyaṇa!"

The Viṣṇudūtas heard the cry of their master's holy name. They rushed to the side of the dying Ajāmila, who had chanted without offense because he had chanted in complete anxiety.

The Yamadūtas were snatching the soul from the core of Ajāmila's heart. "Stop! Stop!" the Viṣṇudūtas yelled with voices of thunder, "We forbid you to take this soul!"

The Yamadūtas were caught by surprise. No one had ever hindered them in their duty to their master, Yamarāja. Sweat poured from their brows, and they clenched their teeth in anger. But when they saw the glittering crowns on the heads of these effulgent four-handed personalities, they stopped in their tracks and calmed down.

"Who are you, sirs?" one Yamadūta asked firmly. "How dare you challenge the jurisdiction of Yamarāja?"

The glowing Viṣṇudūtas simply smiled, their peaceful demeanor and beautiful faces dissipating the anger from the servants of Yamarāja.

"Dear sirs, whose servants are you, and where are you from?" asked another Yamadūta, his shrivelled frowning face sending shivers through Ajāmila. "Why are you forbidding us to touch Ajāmila's body? Are you demigods or sub-demigods?"

Then looking closer at the radiant personalities, he asked, "Or are you the best of devotees?"

The third Yamadūta said, "You have eyes like lotus petals, yellow silk garments, lotus garlands, and glittering crowns and jewels. Your four long arms hold bows and arrows and other weapons, conchshells, discs, and lotuses. Your blazing effulgence has completely removed the darkness of this place. Now, sirs, why are you obstructing us?"

"What nonsense are they speaking?" the Viṣṇudūtas thought. "If they are actually Yamarāja's servants they should know that Ajāmila is not a suitable candidate for them to take."

The Viṣṇudūtas challenged the Yamadūtas with voices as deep as the sound of rumbling clouds: "We are the messengers of Lord Viṣṇu. If you are actually Yamarāja's servants, explain to us the meaning of religious principles and the symptoms of irreligion. What is the process of punishing others? Who actually should be punished? Should all *karmīs* be punished, or only some of them?"

One of the Yamadūtas replied, "We've learned from our master, Yamarāja, that religious principles, *dharma*, are that which are prescribed in the *Vedas*. The opposite of that is *adharma*, irreligion. The *Vedas* are nondifferent from the Supreme Personality of Godhead, Nārāyaṇa, who is the supreme cause of all causes. All living beings are given different duties according to their nature and qualities, and they have to follow the religious principles prescribed in the *Vedas*. If they don't, they have to be punished."

"But then who witnesses their activities?" asked a Viṣṇudūta, challenging them to see if they really knew what they were talking about. "Surely, their wrongdoings have to be seen by others so that their fate can be decided?"

The Yamadūta quickly responded, "The sun, moon, night, day, directions, water, land, and the Supersoul are all witnesses to the activities of the living beings. These many witnesses confirm the candidates for punishment – those who have deviated from their regulative duties and who have engaged in sinful acts."

Another Yamadūta folded his palms and said, "O inhabitants of Vaikuṇṭha, you are sinless, but all those in the material world are *karmīs*, whether pious or impious. They are contaminated by the three modes of nature and act accordingly. They have accepted a material body, so they cannot be inactive. And acting sinfully is inevitable for anyone under the modes of material nature. Therefore all the living beings in this world are punishable."

The other Yamadūta added, "Oh, yes! One must enjoy or suffer in the next life in proportion to one's religious or irreligious actions in this life. Just as springtime in the present indicates the nature of spring in the past and the future, so happiness and distress and the mixture of both in this life indicates a person's religious and irreligious activities in the past and future lives."

The first Yamadūta continued, "Our master Yamarāja is as great as Lord Brahmā. Like the Paramātmā, he knows the past activities of living beings and thus understands how they will act in future lives as well.

"The subtle body of the soul has very strong material desires and therefore causes the soul to transmigrate from one body to the next in human life, animal life, or life as a demigod. In the body of a demigod one is very jubilant, in a human body one is always lamenting, and in an animal's body one is always fearful. But in all conditions, one is actually miserable. The soul is like a silkworm that creates its own cocoon and becomes trapped in it."

The Viṣṇudūtas nodded. They knew well the plight of the living being in the material world.

"But!" the Yamadūta continued, "If these pitiful souls are taught to associate with the Supreme Personality of Godhead or His pure devotee, they can overcome their condition.

"You will be surprised to know that Ajāmila was once a great saintly person. He strictly followed the Vedic injunctions and was very pure. In fact, he was humble, gentle, truthful, non-envious, kind and benevolent, and very respectful to his *guru,* guests, and the elderly. He was actually a perfect *brāhmaṇa*!"

"Then what happened?" asked one Viṣṇudūta.

"Oh, it's a sad story. Once, while picking fruit and flowers in the forest, young Ajāmila saw a lusty *śūdra* embracing a prostitute. They were both drunk. When Ajāmila saw the prostitute's loose clothes and hair and the *śūdra* embracing her, the dormant lust in his heart awakened and he could not stop thinking of this lady. He tried

to remember the instructions of the *śāstras* to not even see a woman. He tried to control his lusty desires, but alas, he failed to control his mind. He lost all sense and took the prostitute as a servant in his house. Very soon he fell from his position and began spending his inheritance money on the prostitute just to satisfy her. He gave up his beautiful young wife, and he earned money, somehow or the other, to maintain the prostitute and her children. He lived extravagantly and broke all the rules and regulations of the scripture."

The sad expression of the Viṣṇudūtas did not dissuade the Yamadūtas from their goal. They were here to take this sinner's soul, no matter what.

Scowling, the Yamadūta said, "This man is full of sins. He did not atone for his sins, so we must take him to Yamarāja, our master and the judge of his fate! To purify him, we must punish him! This is for his own benefit. So don't stop us!"

Themes and Key Messages

Please go through this table of themes and key messages, with corresponding verses, and discuss each topic further.

THEMES	REFERENCES	KEY MESSAGES
A compassionate devotee wants to free others from the *pravṛtti-mārga* and lead them to the *nivṛtti-mārga*.	6.1–2, 6	Parīkṣit Mahārāja, out of compassion for the souls wandering in different bodies from the hellish planets to the heavenly planets, asks Śukadeva Gosvāmī how these souls can be delivered from the *pravṛtti-mārga*, the path of pious and sinful activities, to the *nivṛtti-mārga*, the path of liberation. A Vaiṣṇava is *para-duḥkha-duḥkhī*, very unhappy to see others unhappy and always thinking of how to save them from hellish life.
One can remove suffering due to sinful reactions not by the path of *karma* (atonement) or *jñāna* (acquiring knowledge) but by *bhakti* (devotional service).	6.1.7–15	Śukadeva Gosvāmī first tells Mahārāja Parīkṣit that one can remove suffering due to sinful reactions by atoning for one's sins. Parīkṣit Mahārāja counteracts this by saying that atonement (*karma*) does not remove the root of sin because one commits the sin again and again. Then Śukadeva Gosvāmī agrees and explains that by cultivating knowledge (*jñāna*) of the Supreme one can counteract sinful reactions because one can understand why one should not sin. Yet, this process also has a temporary effect because it doesn't remove the root of sin. Śukadeva Gosvāmī concludes that only devotional service (*bhakti*) can uproot the weeds of sinful actions with no possibility of their reviving. One automatically develops a distaste for material activities when one is Kṛṣṇa conscious, which completely uproots sin, just as the sun alone has the power to dissipate fog.

THEMES	REFERENCES	KEY MESSAGES
One who surrenders to Kṛṣṇa and serves His pure representative becomes automatically freed from all sinful reactions. This is the true method of atonement.	6.1.16–19, 55	The path followed by the pure devotee of Kṛṣṇa is most auspicious. When one serves such a pure devotee and surrenders to Kṛṣṇa, one's sinful life is vanquished automatically. We don't need to separately endeavor to destroy our sinful reactions. Devotional service is necessary not to drive away an insignificant stock of sins but to awaken our dormant love for Kṛṣṇa. In the process one's heart is automatically cleansed and one stops sinning. Therefore, devotional service is the true method of atonement. Such surrendered souls do not see Yamarāja or the Yamadūtas at death.
The power of offenseless chanting of the holy names can deliver one at the time of death even if chanted unintentionally.	6.1.20–29	Because Ajāmila, a sinful *brāhmaṇa*, was attached to his son Nārāyaṇa and called his name all the time, he received *ajñāta-sukṛti*, unknowingly chanting the name of Nārāyaṇa and getting spiritual benefit. Thus, at death when he saw the Yamadūtas coming for him, he chanted the name of Nārāyaṇa with tearful eyes, which would save him from going to hell. He did not know that by constantly chanting the name of Nārāyaṇa, even unintentionally, he was becoming purified.
All livings beings are accountable for every one of their acts.	6.1.42–54	Those who have deviated from *dharma*, religious principles, have to suffer for their sinful activities. No one can be inactive; all beings act according to the modes of material nature that control them. They suffer and enjoy the reactions to their *karma*, religious and irreligious, in their next lives. And there are many witnesses to one's acts. So one's happiness and distress in this life indicates one's past lives and one's future lives. The gross and subtle bodies in all lives are created according to one's desire.
Through bad association one can fall from one's spiritual position and must face the consequences of sinful activity.	6.1.56–68	Ajāmila was a learned and pure *brāhmaṇa*, but by thinking of a prostitute and then associating with her, he fell from his position and engaged in sinful activities. He lost all his good qualities, and because he didn't atone for his acts, the Yamadūtas wanted to take him to Yamarāja to be punished. In this way he would also become purified.

Higher-Thinking Questions

Now try to deepen your understanding of this chapter by delving into Śrīla Prabhupāda's purports and reflecting on the following questions:

1. In verse 6 purport Śrīla Prabhupāda quotes Prahlāda Mahārāja who says that he has no personal troubles. How is this? What problem does a Vaiṣṇava like Prahlāda Mahārāja have?

2. Why doesn't Śukadeva Gosvāmī immediately recommend *bhakti* to stop one's sinful reactions? What does he recommend for those who are not devotees? (See verse 7 purport.)

3. Atonement is recommended for a sinful person. In verse 8 purport Śrīla Prabhupāda explains that capital punishment for a murderer should not be stopped. What reason does he give? Do you think that this is a valid reason? Explain.

4. When one takes to devotional service, explain the phases of sinful reactions that are vanquished. (Refer to verse 15 purport.)

5. Give two reasons why the Viṣṇudūtas appeared when Ajāmila chanted Lord Nārāyaṇa's name even though he had been sinful and had only meant to call his son Nārāyaṇa. Refer to purports 29 and 30.

6. Why did the Viṣṇudūtas challenge the Yamadūtas by asking them to explain the meaning of the symptoms of religion. (See verse 38 purport.)

7. Who is punishable and not punishable according to Śrīla Prabhupāda in verse 39 purport?

8. Why is Arjuna considered a person of *dharma*? What is actual *dharma* as explained in verse 40 purport?

9. According to verse 54, what is the unseen cause of a person taking birth in a particular family, receiving a body either like that of his mother or father? Reflect on your situation. Do you think that this unseen cause is the reason that you have the good fortune of practicing Kṛṣṇa consciousness? Why or why not?

10. Why did the Yamadūtas say in verse 68 that the sinful person has to be punished? How do you think this comes about? Reflect on what you learnt about punishment from Canto 5.

ACTIVITIES

In this section you will find many exciting things to do. These activities
will get you thinking, moving, drawing, and having loads of fun.

Analogy Activity

... to bring out the scholar in you

DOES ATONEMENT WORK WITHOUT BHAKTI?

In this chapter Parīkṣit Mahārāja, for the benefit of others, asks Śukadeva Gosvāmī about how people can become free from sinful reactions so that they don't have to suffer in hell.

Śukadeva Gosvāmī presents to him the process of atonement. Let's see whether atonement can remove the tendency to commit sin as well as the reactions to sinful activities (one's bad *karma*).

Jahnavi is trying to create an "Atonement Ladder" to present the power of *bhakti* through the analogies in this chapter. She is trying to create an ascending sequence of steps a living entity may take to atone for sins. She also highlights how each step leads to a higher level of purification for the living entity. Finally, she wants to highlight how *bhakti* automatically frees one from sin and sinful reactions.

Jahnavi is trying to make the game fun by putting an analogy on each rung of the ladder. Looking at the appropriate verse, the audience is supposed to work out the significance of each analogy and why it is placed in that position. As the ladder progresses upwards, they understand the depth of purification *bhakti* can bring about.

The ladder Jahnavi has created is given to the right. Can you look up the explanation to each analogy by referring to the verse number provided? Discuss these analogies with your class.

The sun can immediately dissipate fog. (15)
A pot of liquor remains impure even when it is washed well. (18)
A bamboo tree burns down in a forest fire, but the roots remain. (14)
After an elephant takes a bath, it comes to the bank and puts sand on its body. (10)
One should treat a disease according to its severity. (8)
A silkworm wraps itself in a cocoon made of its own saliva. (52)

Then in your notebooks, explain the progression of the conditioned soul in relation to atonement from the bottom rung to the topmost rung.

Once Jahnavi has completed the activity, what should she say to present her conclusion strongly?

Theatrical Activity

... to bring out the actor in you 

ROLE PLAY: FROM PRAVṚTTI-MĀRGA TO NIVṚTTI-MĀRGA

In verses 1 and 2, Parīkṣit Mahārāja asks Śukadeva Gosvāmī how one can progress from the *pravṛtti-mārga*, the path of pious and sinful activities, to the *nivṛtti-mārga*, the path of liberation.

Parīkṣit Mahārāja is surprised that the souls in the material world generally do not accept the path of liberation, devotional service, instead of suffering in so many hellish conditions. They also choose to worship the demigods to maintain and fulfill their material desires. Thus they continue in the *pravṛtti-mārga*, in countless material bodies and different realms in the universe, suffering and enjoying the results of their activities.

Everyone is accountable for their acts and achieves a certain result or destination.

Draft a role play (group activity)

- With your group, draft a short script for a role play or skit, which clearly shows how the path you choose leads you to a particular destination. For example, persons engaging in sinful activities without worrying about consequences do receive the appropriate negative consequences; people worshiping the demigods or ancestors achieve a specific destination; and those who worship Kṛṣṇa and are focused on the path of liberation achieve a certain result. You may include Yamarāja as one of your characters who judges the different kinds of conditioned souls.
- Be creative in your plot corresponding to the topic. Show how one is accountable for one's acts and receives a certain result or destination on the *pravṛtti-mārga* and the *nivṛtti-mārga*.
- You may use various dramatic techniques and effects, expressions, and figurative language (similes/metaphors, etc.) to make it more dramatic and comprehensive even to those who may not realize the importance of following the *nivṛtti-mārga*.
- Enact your drama/skit in class or on stage.

Critical-Thinking Activity

IS THE MODE OF GOODNESS NOT GOOD ENOUGH?

Ajāmila was initially a pure *brāhmaṇa*, trained and situated in the mode of goodness. Still, he fell from his position.

1. Why do you think being in the mode of goodness did not protect him from falldown?

2. Can you find any verse from the *Bhagavad-gītā* to support what you think?

3. What lesson do you think we can learn from Ajāmila's falldown? In other words, how can we try our best to protect ourselves?

Introspective Activity

ATONING FOR YOUR MISTAKES

Śrīla Prabhupāda says in his purport to verse 8 that "atonement (*prāyaścitta*) is required, and atonement must be undergone according to the gravity of one's sinful acts."

We all make mistakes, from which we can learn. We should not try to hide from them or feel overly ashamed, but it is important to objectively atone for them in the proper way.

Imagine that you took an attractive piece of stationery (color pencil/pen/eraser/markers) from your friend's bag without his or her permission and accidentally damaged it. Your friend is very upset with your behavior, and your teacher has asked you to reflect on your action.

You may also choose any other mistake that you have done or could do.

Discuss with your class and teacher
- Do you think taking someone else's belongings without permission was a good thing to do? Why or why not?
- What would have been the right thing to do?
- How can you confess your mistake and make sure your friend is no longer upset with you?

Write a confession letter to Kṛṣṇa

- Write a letter to Lord Kṛṣṇa confessing your mistake and telling Him how you would like to atone for your mistake.
- Keeping in mind that Kṛṣṇa is very merciful and forgiving, open your heart and share all your ideas in the letter: what you would do and how you would ask for forgiveness from your friend and make him or her feel better.
- Also explain the lesson you learned and how it taught you not to make this mistake again.

Now reflect on how devotional service, trying to love and serve Kṛṣṇa, can purify your heart from all materialistic or negative tendencies and is the ultimate means of atonement.

Writing and Language Activities

... to help you understand better

POSTER: TAKING SHELTER

Verses 16 to 19 and verse 55 describe why we should take shelter of Kṛṣṇa and His pure representative.

Step 1: Take notes

Read the purports to these verses and write down some points of why we should take shelter of Kṛṣṇa or the spiritual master. (You may refer to the answer section for more points.)

Step 2: Make a Mind Map

Using your notes make a mind map of the important words and phrases related to taking shelter of Kṛṣṇa.

You can use one of the examples of mind maps below:

Step 3: Create a Poster

With the help of the mind map, design a poster with the key phrases and words describing why and how we should take shelter of Kṛṣṇa and the spiritual master.

Use the following features to design your poster:

1. Eye-catching design

2. Large fonts

3. Key heading

4. Catchy slogan

5. Powerful vocabulary

6. Information based on this chapter

7. Other details: pictures/images/supporting *ślokas*, etc.

You may display your poster in your classroom or in your home.

DIALOGUE: YAMADŪTAS EXPLAIN RELIGION AND IRRELIGION

In his purports to verses 28 and 29, Śrīla Prabhupāda states that the Yamadūtas, the order carriers of Yamarāja, came to snatch the soul from Ajāmila's heart, because, according to them, he had committed the most abominable sins.

With a partner write the following dialogue and then read it out in class:

- Imagine yourself as one of the three Yamadūtas, who, on Yamarāja's orders, have come to snatch the soul of Ajāmila. Four Viṣṇudūtas suddenly appear to restrict you and your team from taking away the soul of Ajāmila.
- Think, plan, and frame a short dialogue between you and the Viṣṇudūtas on why you are rightfully taking away the soul of Ajāmila. According to the arguments of the Yamadūtas in this chapter regarding what is religion (*dharma*) and irreligion (*adharma*), try to convince the Viṣṇudūtas in your own words why they should not be restricting you.
- Use persuasive language to convince them about your intentions of following the orders of your master, Yamarāja.

THE IMPORTANCE OF FOLLOWING INSTRUCTIONS

The importance of following the Lord's instructions as presented in the *śāstra* is emphasized in this chapter. Just as one has to follow the laws of the state and is punished if one breaks the laws, one is punished if one disobeys the laws of religion, or *dharma*.

A. Discuss with your teacher and class the importance of following instructions:
- Who gives you instructions?
- Do you follow instructions?
- Why must we always follow instructions given by our teachers and parents?
- What do instructions help you in?

B. Write at least five instructions of Vaiṣṇava etiquette and behavior in your class or school.
    Example: 1. Be respectful of your teacher, so listen attentively to the class.
              2. Keep your bag and books in the correct place.

C. Now write down the immediate consequences of not following three of these instructions and then write down the long-term effects of disobeying these instructions.

Example:

Immediate consequence: If I do not keep my bags and books in the correct place, they may get lost. Long-term consequence: If I do not take care of my belongings, I will become irresponsible and lose things easily.

WRITE A DESCRIPTION: DHARMA

In the box below write a suitable description of "Dharma" beginning with each letter of the word. See example.

D	H	A	R	M	A
		Accepting the authority of the Supreme Personality of Godhead.			

NARRATIVE ESSAY – GOOD AND BAD ASSOCIATION

In this chapter we learned how Ajāmila was affected by his association.

Write a narrative essay on either of the following topics in third person (from someone else's perspective) or first person (from your perspective):

1. Good association lifts you up.

How did someone's good association evolve or change you positively? Who was the person in your life? How did you meet them? What about them inspired you to change your behavior or outlook of life?

2. Bad association brings you down.

How did the bad association affect your life? Did it teach you any lessons? Did it give you an opportunity to value the importance of good association?

CHAPTER 1 ANSWERS

Does Atonement Work without Bhakti?
(52) The uncontrolled living being is trapped in the network of sin without atonement; (8) The sinful person undergoes atonement according to the severity of his sins; (10) *Karma-kāṇḍa* atonement: one sins and atones and continues to sin and atone in a cycle; (14) *Jñāna-kāṇḍa* atonement: it burns the sins of the body, mind, and words with knowledge, but the roots of sinful desires remain; (18) Atonement by any method other than *bhakti* cannot fully purify us because the tendency to sin remains; (15) Atonement by *bhakti*: one's sinful reactions as well as the tendency to sin are burnt – this is the real atonement.

Conclusion: Bhakti by itself is sufficient to destroy sinful desires, sinful activity, and sinful reactions, which means a person can become fully purified. However, *bhakti* does more than that because it reconnects us to Kṛṣṇa. The results of genuine atonement is therefore a byproduct only of *bhakti*.

Is the Mode of Goodness not Good Enough?
1. The mode of goodness is purifying, but not permanent. Someone can also become conditioned by the mode of goodness because they begin to feel that they are advanced in knowledge and are better than others. Depending on what mode one associates with, one can fall or rise to that mode. Becoming attracted to the mode of passion and ignorance, Ajāmila fell to the lower modes from goodness; 2. *Bhagavad-gītā* (14.10): "Sometimes the mode of goodness becomes prominent, defeating the modes of passion and ignorance, O son of Bharata. Sometimes the mode of passion defeats goodness and ignorance, and at other times ignorance defeats goodness and passion. In this way there is always competition for supremacy." 3. We too can fall down at any moment; therefore we should be vigilant to follow the instructions of the Lord and pray to Him for protection. Following the instructions of the *śāstra*, the spiritual master, and the pure devotees is the safest path to elevate oneself to the topmost destination.

Taking Shelter (*Potential Answers*)
Results of taking shelter of Kṛṣṇa: We become purified of sinful desires; We become inspired to follow the path of the pure devotee; We receive the mercy and blessings of Kṛṣṇa and His pure devotee to progress on the path of *bhakti*; We acquire all good qualities; We are automatically freed from sinful reactions; We do not see Yamarāja or the Yamadūtas at death, which means that we will not take birth again or suffer in hellish conditions in the next life; We get a spiritual body and thus the association of Kṛṣṇa.

2

AJĀMILA DELIVERED BY THE VIṢṆUDŪTAS

The Yamadūtas surely had sound arguments. Ajāmila had been a sinner, according to their definition of religion and irreligion, and had not atoned for his sins; therefore he needed to be punished.

The Viṣṇudūtas had listened attentively. As far as they were concerned Ajāmila had already atoned for his sins in a most effective way.

One of the Viṣṇudūtas finally addressed the servants of Yamarāja: "You are supposed to be in charge of maintaining religious principles. But what a shame that you are unnecessarily punishing a sinless, unpunishable person. How painful it is to see you being irreligious yourselves!"

The Yamadūtas glared at the servants of Lord Viṣṇu, speechless.

The first Viṣṇudūta continued, "You are supposed to be followers of Yamarāja, the master of justice, and follow in his footsteps. The king or leader is supposed to be like a father to the citizens and give them protection out of love. The general people believe in their master's protection. They are not very learned. They don't know what's religion or irreligion; they simply follow the example of their leaders. So if such leaders are impartial and punish innocent people, where will the citizens go for shelter?"

The Yamadūtas looked at each other, frowning in disbelief.

The second Viṣṇudūta explained, "Ajāmila has already atoned for his sins – not only for sins performed in this life but in millions of lives. This is because in a helpless state he called out the holy name of Nārāyaṇa. Even though he didn't chant purely, he chanted without offense. And now he is purified and eligible for liberation."

The third Viṣṇudūta added: "Even before the time of death, Ajāmila used to call out to his son, 'Nārāyaṇa, come here; Nārāyaṇa, do this.' He had constantly uttered the four purifying syllables nā-rā-ya-ṇa, which was sufficient to eradicate the sinful reactions of millions of lives. It did not matter that he was calling his son; the holy name alone is effective."

The dying Ajāmila could not believe his

good fortune. Or perhaps it was all a dream, he thought. But what he heard next made him believe that he was indeed witnessing a debate between the servants of Viṣṇu and those of Yamarāja.

"The chanting of Lord Viṣṇu's holy name is the best process of atonement for any kind of sinner: for a thief, a drunkard, a killer of a *brāhmaṇa*, a murderer of women, a cow slaughterer, and for all other sinful people. Just by chanting the holy name of Viṣṇu, they attract the attention of the Lord, who considers, 'Because this person has chanted My name, I must give him protection.' "

Ajāmila's eyes welled up with tears, and the Yamadūtas still stared, astounded.

"You see," continued the Viṣṇudūta, "even if sinful persons atone by following the Vedic ritualistic ceremonies, they do not become as purified as by chanting the holy name of Lord Hari even once. Even though ritualistic atonement may free one from sinful reactions, it does not awaken devotion for the Lord. But the holy names remind one of the Lord's fame, qualities, attributes, and pastimes. This is because of the Lord's omnipotence – He is nondifferent from His name."

Ajāmila could feel the effects of the Lord's mercy in His holy name. He simply wanted to hear more and more about the Lord.

"In fact," added the fourth Viṣṇudūta, "These ritualistic methods of atonement cannot completely clean the heart because after atoning, one's mind still runs after material activities. But the holy name works differently – it completely removes the dirt from the heart."

Pointing to Ajāmila, the Viṣṇudūta continued, "This Ajāmila helplessly and very loudly chanted the holy name of Lord Nārāyaṇa at the moment of leaving his body. This utterance of the holy name, along with all the previous utterances, has freed him from the reactions of all sinful life." Bowing his head to the Yamadūtas, he said, "Therefore, O servants of Yamarāja, do not take him to your master for punishment."

A Yamadūta opened his mouth to reply, but the first Viṣṇudūta cut him off: "The holy name is so powerful that even if one chants indirectly or jokingly, for musical entertainment or even neglectfully, one is immediately freed from the reactions of unlimited sins. Even if a sinful person dies from some misfortune or accident and chants the name of the Lord, he is absolved from entering hell. The effects of all kinds of sins – heavy or light – are all pardoned. This is accepted by the scriptures and all learned scholars.

"Austerities, charity, vows, and other such methods may neutralize the reactions of sinful life, but they cannot uproot material desires from the heart. However, service to the lotus feet of

gone. Looking around desperately, he called out to them, but they did not return. Now all that Ajāmila was left with were his thoughts. He thought of how fortunate he had been, not just to be saved from death but to have been given divine knowledge. He could now understand the irreligious principles that act under the three modes of material nature, and religious principles, which are above the modes. He could understand his loving relationship with the Supreme Lord. Having heard the Lord's glories from the Viṣṇudūtas, Ajāmila's heart became filled with love for his Lord.

But then he remembered his past actions. Tears flooded his face. The remorse he felt was like a dagger striking his chest. His words were muffled amid his pitiful sobs: "Alas! I was a servant of my senses. How degraded I became! I was a qualified *brāhmaṇa* and yet had children from a prostitute. How condemned I am! I acted so sinfully that I degraded my family. I gave up my beautiful chaste wife to be with a prostitute accustomed to drinking wine. I even gave up my old parents who had no one to take care of them. I deserve to be thrown into hell."

Ajāmila's head began to spin. He looked around frantically again: "I saw frightful men with ropes in their hands coming to drag me away. Where have they gone? Was it all a dream? Where are the four beautiful, dazzling persons who saved me from hell?"

Drowning his hands in his palms, Ajāmila wept again. "I am most abominable," he cried.

Then Ajāmila remembered the effulgent Viṣṇudūtas with their warm smiles and

the Lord immediately frees one from all such contamination. In fact, the holy name of the Lord, chanted knowingly or unknowingly, burns to ashes all sinful reactions just as fire burns dry grass to ashes. It's like taking a certain medicine for a disease. Whether you take the medicine willingly or not, or whether you are aware of its potency, it doesn't matter; the medicine will still act."

The Yamadūtas slackened their grasp on the noose that had captured Ajāmila. The Viṣṇudūtas smiled as they saw the Yamadūtas' anger dissipate. Leaving the fortunate Ajāmila behind, the servants of Yamarāja vanished. They rushed to inform their master of what had happened and to find out how his unstoppable order could have been overturned.

Ajāmila sat up straight and bowed his head to the Viṣṇudūtas, who had saved him from imminent death. He didn't know whether to laugh or cry. His heart fluttered in bliss. He felt rejuvenated. All his fear had vanished. His life had been extended by the mercy of the Lord. He now had a second chance.

Folding his palms, he started to thank the Viṣṇudūtas, but when he lifted his head, they were compassionate glances. Amid his sobs, he began to smile and then laugh: "I actually saw those four exalted personalities! Just by thinking of their visit I feel so happy!"

Wiping the tears from his eyes, Ajāmila continued, "It is because of my past spiritual activities that they had come. Were it not for my past devotional service, how could I, a most unclean keeper of a prostitute, have gotten a chance to chant the holy name of Viṣṇu at the time of death?" Shaking his head, he said, "No, it wouldn't have been possible.

"Still, I am a shameless cheater who has killed the brahminical culture. I am sin personified. What is my position compared to the all-auspicious chanting of Lord Nārāyaṇa's holy name?"

Ajāmila's face then lit up with a glimmer of hope. He said to himself, "I cannot lose this opportunity, this new life that I've been given. I must completely control my mind, my life, and my senses now and always serve my Lord so that I don't fall into material life again."

Looking at his old and shriveled body, he exclaimed, "I am not this body! Thinking that I was this body, I had a desire to enjoy with it. This is how one gets trapped into pious and impious

action. This is material bondage. But no more! I will disentangle myself from this bondage, which was caused by the Lord's illusory energy in the form of a woman. I will now give up lust and free myself from such illusion."

Smiling, he said, "I shall become a merciful, well-wishing friend to all living beings and absorb myself in service to my Lord. I know I shall not fall victim to the enticements of this material world again because my heart is becoming purified from chanting the Lord's holy name. I just want to fix my mind on the lotus feet of Kṛṣṇa."

With renewed faith and determination, Ajāmila left for Hardwar to perfect his life. Such is the result of a moment's association with the Lord's devotees.

In Hardwar, he took shelter of a Viṣṇu temple where he practiced *bhakti-yoga*. He followed his resolution to control his senses and engage his mind in serving the Lord.

When he became absorbed in thinking of the Lord's form, Ajāmila again saw the four celestial beings before him. He fell to the ground in obeisance. He readily gave up his body on the banks of the Ganges and attained a spiritual body like that of the Viṣṇudūtas. They led him into a golden airplane, which then soared into space above the material realms to the spiritual abode of Lord Viṣṇu, where the Lord was waiting for him with open arms.

"Just see," said Śukadeva Gosvāmī to Mahārāja Parīkṣit, "the power of chanting just a glimpse of Lord Nārāyaṇa's holy name. A *brāhmaṇa*, because of bad association, had become most fallen and was destined to be dragged to hell by the Yamadūtas yet was saved by the holy name.

"Therefore if one wants the same result as Ajāmila, one should chant the holy names and glorify the name, fame, form, and pastimes of the Supreme Personality

of Godhead. Nothing else – not *karma*, *jñāna*, or mystic *yoga* – can give the same benefit; by these processes one will simply become overcome by passion and ignorance again."

Parīkṣit Mahārāja closed his eyes and softly chanted "Nārāyaṇa, Nārāyaṇa . . ." These four syllables had the power to deliver anyone. He meditated on each syllable, feeling invigorated after hearing the glories of the holy name.

"Hearing this historical narration with faith and devotion has the potency to vanquish all sinful reactions, regardless of how sinful anyone can be," said Śukadeva Gosvāmī. "Indeed, the Yamadūtas do not approach such a person. If one follows in the footsteps of Ajāmila by chanting the holy names faithfully and offenselessly, there is no doubt that one will go back home, back to Godhead."

Themes and Key Messages

Please go through this table of themes and key messages, with corresponding verses, and discuss each topic further.

THEMES	REFERENCES	KEY MESSAGES
When leaders punish blameless people, the people lose faith in their leaders.	6.2.1–6	It is the government's duty to spiritually guide and nourish the citizens. The Viṣṇudūtas explain that the citizens follow the example of their leaders. Whatever the leader accepts and does, they also accept. So they express that the Yamadūtas, who are in charge of maintaining religious principles, should not break religious principles themselves by punishing a blameless person who didn't deserve to be punished.

THEMES	REFERENCES	KEY MESSAGES
Chanting of the holy names of the Lord without offense burns to ashes the results of sins performed in millions of lives.	6.2.7–10, 18	Although Ajāmila had performed many sinful activities, he was considered pure because he chanted the name of Nārāyaṇa at the time of death offenselessly. According to Śrīla Viśvanātha Cakravartī Ṭhākura, he remembered the Lord. As a result, all past sinful reactions were removed and he became a fit candidate for liberation. Even while unconsciously calling his son Nārāyaṇa, he was atoning for the sinful reactions of millions of lives. The Lord considers that because a person has chanted His name, His duty is to protect that person.
Chanting the holy name and glorifying the name, fame, qualities, and pastimes of the Lord is the best method of atonement even for the greatest sins and also awakens one's love for the Lord.	6.2.11–13	Chanting the name of the Lord even once is more effective than the ritualistic ceremonies of atonement. This is because the holy name purifies the heart of sinful desire, the root of sin, and awakens pure devotion to the Lord. Thus the Viṣṇudūtas pleaded to the Yamadūtas not to take Ajāmila to be punished by Yamarāja, for he had chanted the name of Nārāyaṇa and had become purified of his sins.
One should give up one's past sinful habits and always regret one's past sinful acts.	6.2.26–35	Ajāmila lamented and regretted his past sinful acts and considered himself fallen. Śrīla Prabhupāda explains that when one becomes elevated to pure devotional service by the grace of the Lord and the spiritual master, one first regrets one's past sinful activities, which helps him to advance more in spiritual life. Śrīla Prabhupāda therefore advises that we should always appreciate the opportunity that we are given to advance in spiritual life and use our good fortune to chant Kṛṣṇa's holy names.
The association of pure devotees saves one from going to hell and also plants the seed of *bhakti* in the heart.	6.2.34, 36–39	The Viṣṇudūtas had saved Ajāmila from hellish conditions and reminded him of the Supreme Personality of Godhead and his relationship with the Lord. The *guru* and the Vaiṣṇavas also do the same by being compassionate to the fallen souls. Vaiṣṇavas are determined to be free from *māyā* and are also compassionate to those who are in *māyā's* clutches. Their association gives people the opportunity to awaken their relationship with the Lord and to be thus saved from hellish life. Therefore one should always keep company with devotees to become free from the bodily concept of life.

THEMES	REFERENCES	KEY MESSAGES
If one constantly, faithfully, and inoffensively chants the holy name of the Lord, he is guaranteed to go back home, back to Godhead.	6.2.45–49	If one chants the holy names loudly and distinctly, always conscious of not committing offenses to the holy name, at the time of death it is possible to chant the holy name of the Lord with love and faith. Even by a glimpse of chanting the holy name purely, in the clearing stage (*nāma-ābhāsa*), as Ajāmila did, one can mature to the pure stage of chanting and go back to Godhead.

Higher-Thinking Questions

Now try to deepen your understanding of this chapter by delving into Śrīla Prabhupāda's purports and reflecting on the following questions:

1. According to Śrīla Prabhupāda in verse 3 purport, how can the Kṛṣṇa consciousness movement create actual peace and prosperity in the state? How do you think this can happen? (Refer to verse 4 and purport.)

2. Why did the Viṣṇudūtas feel that Ajāmila did not deserve to be punished? In other words, why did they call him "sinless" and "unpunishable" in verse 2 when we know that he lived most of his life in sin? (See verse 7 and purport.)

3. How do you think the holy name purifies the heart as mentioned in verse 11? (Hint: The name of the Lord and the Lord are identical, so what do you think the Lord's association can do?)

4. Why do you think ritual atonement is not recommended in verse 11?

5. What practical evidence does Śrīla Prabhupāda give in verse 19 purport that the holy name can purify anyone?

6. How do we know that the Lord never forgot Ajāmila even when he took to sinful life? What does this tell you about the mercy of the Lord and His love for us? Refer to verse 32 purport.

7. According to verses 33 and 34, give two reasons why Ajāmila was saved from his abominable condition?

8. How have Vaiṣṇavas in the Kṛṣṇa consciousness movement help save sinful people from going to hell? See verse 34 purport.

9. What does Ajāmila pray for in verse 37 now that he had been saved by the Viṣṇudūtas? Why should we not only save ourselves but also help save others as explained by Śrīla Prabhupāda in the purport.

ACTIVITIES

In this section you will find many exciting things to do. These activities
will get you thinking, moving, drawing, and having loads of fun.

Analogy Activity

... to bring out the scholar in you

PRESCRIBE THE HOLY NAME, DR. DEVOTEE!

"If a person unaware of the effective potency of a certain medicine takes that medicine or is forced to take it, it will act even without his knowledge because its potency does not depend on the patient's understanding. Similarly, even though one does not know the value of chanting the holy name of the Lord, if one chants knowingly or unknowingly, the chanting will be very effective." *SB* 6.2.19

In Ajāmila's case, we see exactly how the holy name acted as a medicine even though he chanted unknowingly. But because he chanted offenselessly, he got the full result of chanting the holy name.

Śrīla Prabhupāda knew that the holy name acts whether or not a person is aware of its glories. Therefore, he tried to give the chanting of Hare Kṛṣṇa even to people who did not understand its effects.

A. In the image below Śrīla Prabhupāda is giving a prescription of the holy name to different people. Draw at least five kinds of people on the seats below that Śrīla Prabhupāda is giving the prescription to; for example, religious leaders, professors, businessmen, etc.

B. Below is a close-up image of Śrīla Prabhupāda's "prescription" of the holy name. From what you learned from this chapter, complete each prescription as follows:

- Fill in the "patient name," one kind of person that the holy name can be given to.
- Fill in possible symptoms of their material condition, which the holy name can cure.
- Tick which mode the person is under the influence of.
- Fill in simple instructions of how to chant the holy name to get the desired effect.
- Then fill in the "Recovery Signs," the results the patient will receive, and then the additional benefits of chanting as you've learned in this chapter.

PRESCRIPTION

Patient name: _______________________________________

Symptoms of material condition: _______________________________
____

Modes: goodness   passion   ignorance

Remedy: Chant Hare Kṛṣṇa.
Hare Kṛṣṇa Hare Kṛṣṇa Kṛṣṇa Kṛṣṇa Hare Hare/ Hare Rāma Hare Rāma Rāma Rāma Hare Hare

Instructions for chanting: _____________________________________
____
____
____

Recovery signs:_______________________________________
____

Additional benefits: ___________________________________
____
____
____

Do you think this prescription would work for the persons you drew in Part A of this activity? What can you conclude about the effects of the holy name on different people?

Artistic Activity

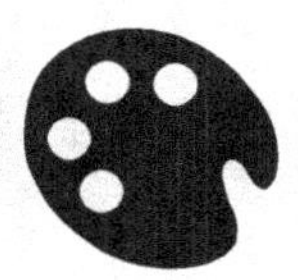

THE HOLY NAME TIPS THE SCALE OF SIN!

Let us make a balance (scale) and see how Ajāmila's chanting the holy name tipped the balance in his favor!

What you will need: two paper cups; some thread; a clothes hanger; the following eight labels: Ajāmila's sin (four labels), Nārāyaṇa, Ajāmila, Hellish Punishment, Back to Godhead; four small pebbles; one big pebble/rock heavier than all four pebbles put together.

Directions:

1. Take the two paper cups. Punch two holes on opposite sides from each other on the top of the cups as shown in the diagram.

2. Thread some string (each 40 cm in length) into each punched hole of the paper cup and tie the string on each side of the punched hole. The cup can now be hung.

3. Take a clothes hanger. Hang a paper cup on each end of the hanger as shown. The Holy Name Balance is now ready!

4. Now attach the different labels to the balance and the pebbles:
   a) On the top middle of the hanger, paste the "Ajāmila" label.
   b) On the left cup, paste the "Hellish Punishment" label.
   c) On the right cup, paste the "Back to Godhead" label.
   d) On each of the small pebbles, paste one "Ajāmila's sin" label.
   e) On the big pebble, paste the "Nārāyaṇa" label.

5. You are now ready to see how chanting the holy name purely even once can carry one back to Godhead, despite many sins!
   a) Place the small pebbles on the left cup. Ajāmila now has so many sins that he is going to hell! No wonder the Yamadūtas came to get him.
   b) Ajāmila chanted just one holy name of Nārāyaṇa at the time of death. Put the "Nārāyaṇa" pebble in the right cup now. Lo and behold! The balance tipped! Just by chanting the holy name purely once, Ajāmila is now going back to Godhead!

That is how powerful the Lord's holy name is!

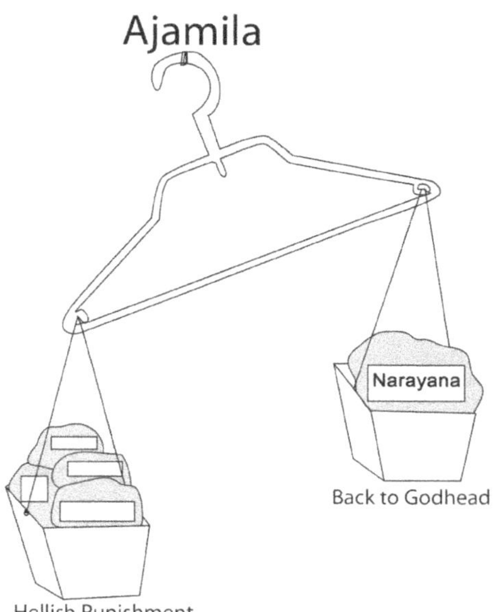

Introspective Activity

SECOND CHANCES: THE BEST ATONEMENT

We all like getting second chances. If we make a mistake or don't do well in a test or exam, we would love a second chance. And in this story of Ajāmila, we see how Ajāmila was given a second chance by the Lord and the Viṣṇudūtas just because he chanted the holy name of the Lord.

Similarly, if we sincerely try to connect with the Lord through chanting His holy names and serving Him with love, He will overlook our mistakes and give us a second chance to improve. Such is the Lord's mercy.

When Ajāmila was given a second chance, he first repented and felt sorry for all his past mistakes. He then resolved never to make such mistakes again, and his faith and determination became stronger.

Imagine that you were given a second chance after you committed a big mistake or failed at something. How would you feel? How would you react? What would your next steps be? Do you think you will strive harder to achieve whatever goal you were set on in the beginning?

The same applies in our Kṛṣṇa consciousness. If we are not successful in reaching our spiritual goals or if we become weak in our practices, Kṛṣṇa is always giving us a second chance to improve ourselves until we are successful. The human form of life itself is a chance to come closer to Kṛṣṇa.

So whenever we fail in our practices or actions, we can repent and atone by chanting the holy names as the Viṣṇudūtas suggested.

Now, from what you learned in this and the last chapter, write a few lines on why chanting the holy names is the best atonement?

Critical-Thinking Activity

OFFENSES TO THE HOLY NAME

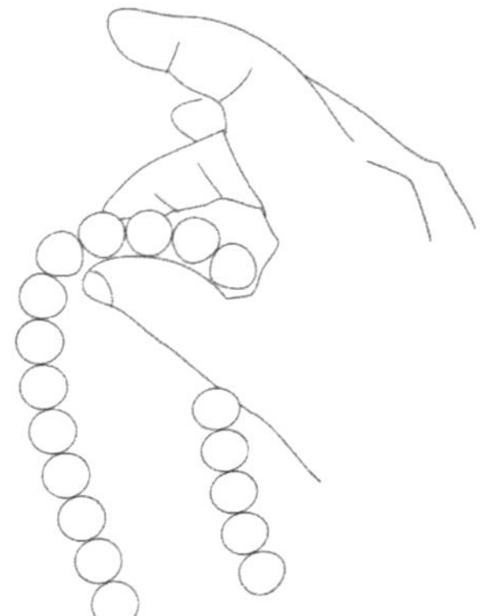

Śrīla Prabhupāda comments that Ajāmila's chanting of the holy name may be called pure chanting. How is this so when we know that a) Ajāmila did not even call Lord Nārāyaṇa at the time of death; he called for his son; b) Ajāmila committed sinful activities; c) Ajāmila was attached to a sinful woman, with whom he was living.

We learn from the *ācāryas* that our chanting becomes pure when we don't commit the ten offenses to the holy name.

Let us evaluate if Ajāmila chanted without offenses, and then we can conclude whether or not his chanting was pure.

The Holy Name Machine below has a list of the ten offenses. (Śrīla Bhaktivinoda Ṭhākura adds the eleventh offense, which is also important to avoid.)

Let us put Ajāmila's chanting of Nārāyaṇa's name at the time of death into this machine.

Read each offense. If Ajāmila knowingly committed that offense, put "Y" for "yes" against the space beside it, or else put "N for "no." After checking his chanting for each of the ten offenses, write down a conclusion in the final output box.

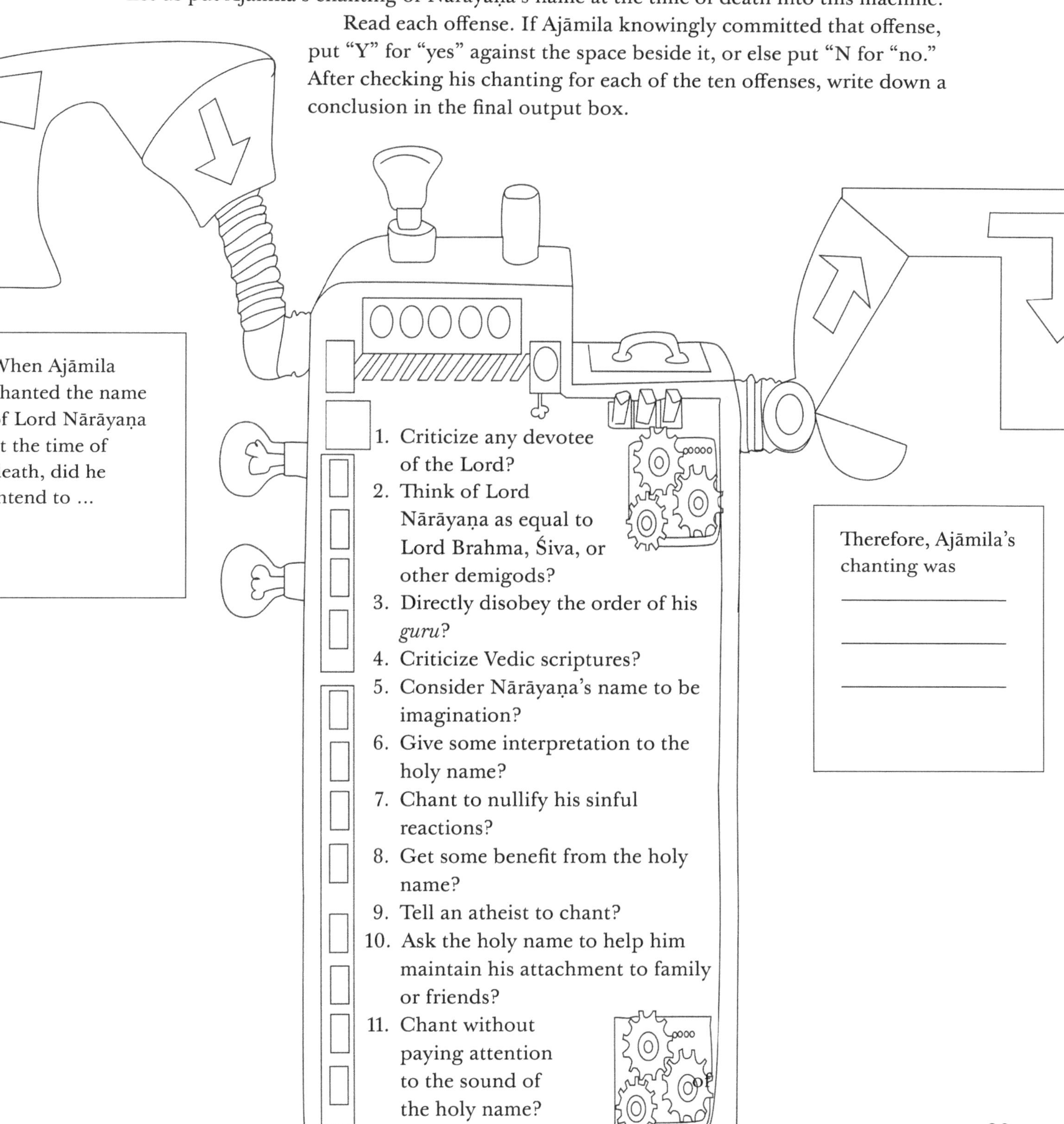

Remember, Ajāmila was able to chant offenselessly because:

1. His only motive was to call out to his son in fear. He did not commit any of the ten offenses. Which offense did he especially not commit related to his sinful activities?

2. Due to his past devotional nature and activities, he had named his son after the Supreme Lord. He was trained in his childhood in devotional service. What can you understand about childhood training in devotional service from this?

3. In verse 10, the Lord says, "Because this man has chanted My holy name, My duty is to give him protection." Ajāmila's deliverance proves that the Lord never gives up on His devotee. In the *Varāha Purāṇa*, the Lord states, "If My devotee is unable to remember Me at the time of death because of disturbances felt within the body at that time, then I shall remember My devotee and take him back to My supreme abode."

As a result, according to Śrīla Viśvanātha Cakravartī Ṭhākura, Ajāmila remembered Lord Nārāyaṇa when he chanted Nārāyaṇa's name even though he had intended to call his son. What personal lesson can we draw from this?

Writing and Language Activities

... to help you understand better

INVITATION LETTER/POSTER: KIRTANA FESTIVAL

In his purport to verse 11, Śrīla Prabhupāda states, "What cannot be achieved through performance of Vedic rituals can be easily achieved through the chanting of the Lord's holy name."

The temple in your community is hosting a grand three-day *kīrtana* festival. They are inviting famous *kīrtaniyas* (*kīrtana* singers) from around the world to sing at the festival. The temple president has asked you to write a short appealing invitation letter to devotees in your community to register for the event.

Choose a few attractive points that you learned from this chapter about the potency of the holy name to include in your letter, which will be posted on social media and the temple's website. Use catchy phrases and words, preferably verbs, that will inspire devotees to attend the event.

Examples:
- **Cleanse your heart and mind** and feel spiritually rejuvenated.
- **Experience the power** of the holy name.

- **Feel the bliss** of chanting the holy name.
- **Uplift your spirits**

Alternatively, you could design an attractive poster highlighting some of the benefits attendees will receive at the event. Include illustrations or pictures. This poster will be sent to various temples in your country to advertise on their bulletin boards. You may use a graphics program on your computer to do this.

Remember to also include the date, time, venue, a short schedule of what attendees can expect, highlights (names of prominent singers), and registration details.

NARRATIVE ESSAY: VAIṢṆAVAS ARE VIṢṆUDŪTAS

Śrīla Prabhupāda in his purport to verse 22 states that Vaiṣṇavas are also Viṣṇudūtas because they carry out the orders of Kṛṣṇa to save the conditioned souls. Vaiṣṇavas plant the seed of *bhakti* in their hearts and remind them of Kṛṣṇa, just as the Viṣṇudūtas reminded Ajāmila of his relationship with Kṛṣṇa.

Śrīla Prabhupāda is one such Viṣṇudūta who inspires us in many ways to develop our relationship with Kṛṣṇa and also become Viṣṇudūtas ourselves by spreading Kṛṣṇa's message.

Choose one of the following assignments to show the wonderful qualities of Vaiṣṇavas and the importance of their association:

A. Write a narrative describing how Śrīla Prabhupāda was a Viṣṇudūta to so many Ajāmilas in the world. Highlight his qualities and what actions he took to give Kṛṣṇa to everyone through the holy names.

B. Write a short story beginning with the following words: "It was a major turning point of my life when . . ."

Show how a Vaiṣṇava/Viṣṇudūta played a prominent role in cleansing your heart and transforming your life.

C. Vaiṣṇavas do not always have four arms and a form like the Lord's, but they have compassion like the Lord. By giving someone the holy name, they free the greatest of sinners from their bad *karma* and give them an opportunity to go back to Godhead. Therefore someone who receives such mercy from the Lord's devotees should see how their sinful reactions are diminishing, that whatever difficulties they are going through is just a token reaction for what was supposed to happen.

Begin a story with the following: "While cutting vegetables, the knife slipped and nicked my finger. As I watched the blood oozing from my cut, I thought how fortunate I was that I hadn't sustained a more serious injury." Narrate the good fortune you received from a devotee that diminished your sinful reactions and protected you from having a worse reaction. (You may use another hypothetical incident.)

SETTING THE EXAMPLE

The Viṣṇudūtas express that the Yamadūtas should set an example and not punish a blameless person, because whatever a leader does the followers accept and follow. But the Yamadūtas didn't consider themselves to be breaking any principles; in fact, they thought that they were right.

Let's see whose arguments were stronger in the case of Ajāmila.

On the next page are some of the arguments the Yamadūtas posed in the last chapter. For each argument, provide a counter-argument the Viṣṇudūtas give in this chapter (use the corresponding numbers of each speech bubble).

What can you conclude after analyzing these arguments? Would the Yamadūtas be setting the right example if they arrest Ajāmila and take him to hell? Explain.

1. All persons have to follow the religious principles mentioned in the Vedas. If they don't, they have to be punished.
2. Ajāmila is full of sins and must atone for them.
3. Everyone is contaminated by the three modes of material nature, so they are prone to act sinfully and have to accept material bodies.
1.
2.
3.

CHAPTER 2 ANSWERS

Prescribe the Holy Name, Dr. Devotee (*Potential Answers*)
Patient name: students, scholars, businessmen, singers, householders, etc. Anyone can receive the holy name if they are receptive.

Symptoms of material condition (corresponding to patient): attachment to sense enjoyment; tendencies toward impersonalism; vices such as lust, greed, anger, envy.

Instructions for chanting: Chant at least sixteen rounds every day; follow the four regulative principles (no meat eating; intoxication; gambling; or illicit sex); chant and hear with attention; avoid the ten offenses to chanting; chant in the association of devotees.

Recovery signs: development of detachment – one gives up sinful activities, speculative/imaginative or impersonal ideas about the Lord, negative qualities, etc. (Fill out the prescriptions in a specific way for each case.)

Additional benefits: Your sins get destroyed by chanting; your reactions to past sinful acts diminish; you feel closer to Kṛṣṇa; you become more peaceful, content, and happy; you ultimately attain love of Godhead.

Conclusion: Yes; the holy name benefits every person provided that the person accepts the prescription and follows its directions.

Second Chances (*Potential Answers*)
It cleanses our heart of dirt (negative tendencies and qualities), so we are less likely to commit any sin or undesirable act again; we will develop our love for Kṛṣṇa, which automatically frees us from past sinful reactions and allows us to go back to Godhead.

Offenses to the Holy Name
Answers to Holy Name Machine: "N" for all the offenses; Ajāmila's chanting was pure.
1. The seventh offense of committing sinful activities and then thinking that chanting the holy names would nullify his sinful reactions; 2. Practicing Kṛṣṇa consciousness from childhood can give us a strong foundation that we can build on from any point in our lives; 3. We should perform devotional service attentively to attract the mercy of the Lord. We do not know what our condition at the time of death will be, but if we please the Lord, He can deliver us even if we fail to remember Him.

Setting the Example
Answers of the Viṣṇudūtas:

Speech bubble 1: Yes, that's true, but Ajāmila chanted the name of the Lord offenselessly and not because he was trying to be relieved of sinful reactions. Hence he was excused. This is because the Lord protects anyone who takes shelter of Him and His names even unknowingly.

Speech bubble 2: The greatest form of atonement is to chant the Lord's holy names, which destroys the roots of sin – the tendency to sin and all contamination from the heart.

Speech bubble 3a: Chanting the holy names of the Lord without offense burns to ashes the results of sins performed in millions of lives.

Speech bubble 3b (also corresponding to point 3): If one constantly, faithfully, and inoffensively chants the holy name of the Lord, one ends the cycle of getting material bodies and goes back home, back to Godhead.

The Viṣṇudūtas arguments are stronger because they explain why chanting the holy name without offense can deliver even a sinful person. No, the Yamadūtas would not be setting a proper example because if they arrest Ajamila and take him to hell, people would incorrectly consider devotional service or chanting the holy names to be incapable of removing all sins and sinful reactions.

3

YAMARĀJA INSTRUCTS HIS MESSENGERS

Mahārāja Parīkṣit was curious to know what had happened when the Yamadūtas dashed back to Saṁyamanī-purī to question their master Yamarāja. Never had their lord's order been foiled. Śukadeva Gosvāmī related what had happened.

The three Yamadūtas bowed their heads to the lord of death. Yamarāja frowned. His large helmet and golden ornaments sparkled against his dark face. As he casually wielded his mace behind his head, his bulging muscles rippled. "So? What is the reason for this audience?" he asked, his thunderous voice echoing through the hall.

One of the Yamadūtas cleared his throat and said, "Er . . . er . . . as you know, our dear lord, we have been unable to bring Ajāmila, the sinful *brāhmaṇa*, to justice."

Yamarāja raised an eyebrow. The Yamadūtas tried to avoid his reddish eyes. "Oh?" he sneered.

"The Viṣṇudūtas stopped us from arresting Ajāmila," the Yamadūta blurted out.

Yamarāja sat on his majestic throne, a grin forming on his lips.

The second Yamadūta stepped forward with his head held high. He could not conceal his anger anymore. Raising his voice, he asked, "Dear lord, how many controllers are there in this world? If there are many authorities giving contradictory judgments, someone may be wrongly punished or wrongly rewarded. Since there are many different *karmīs* there may be different judges or rulers to give them justice. But there must be one supreme controller to guide all the judges."

"Hmmm . . ." said Yamarāja.

The third Yamadūta came forward and said, "We thought that you are the master of all living entities, the supreme authority who discriminates between the pious and impious activities of humans. But now, to our surprise, we see that your order is no longer effective, since it has been transgressed by four wonderful, perfect persons.

"Those beautiful beings from Siddhaloka cut the knots of the ropes with which we were arresting Ajāmila. You see, as soon as the sinful Ajāmila uttered the name Nārāyaṇa, these men immediately arrived and reassured him, 'Do not fear. Do not fear.' Please tell us who they are."

The Yamadūtas were startled to see Yamarāja stand up and smile from ear to ear. Were there tears in his eyes? They could not tell, but something had changed his whole demeanor.

"Nārāyaṇa! Nārāyaṇa!" Yamarāja chanted loudly, raising his hands in the air. Having heard his Lord's name from the lips of his servants had made him even more happy. How he wished he had told them of Nārāyaṇa.

"Yes, there is one supreme controller above all else," he replied.

The Yamadūtas shot glances at each other, wondering what their lord meant.

Yamarāja continued, "My dear servants, you've accepted me as the Supreme, but factually I am not. Above me, and above all other demigods, is the one supreme master and controller. Lord Brahmā, Viṣṇu, and Śiva are just His partial manifestations. He is like the two threads that form the length and breadth of a woven cloth. He controls the entire world just as a farmer controls a bull by a rope in its nose. In this way the Supreme Personality of Godhead binds all men through the ropes of His words in the *Vedas* and controls them through the *varṇāśrama* system."

The Yamadūtas twisted faces became even more distorted in disbelief.

"None of us can understand the Supreme Lord, not the greatest of demigods nor the great *ṛṣis*," said Yamarāja. "Even we, in the mode of goodness, cannot understand Him. What to speak of others who are under illusion and just speculate about God?

"Just as the limbs of the body cannot see the eyes, the living beings cannot see the Supreme Lord, who is the Supersoul in everyone's heart. He cannot be understood by any material

means. Lord Nārāyaṇa is self-sufficient and fully independent."

"Then who are those effulgent beings who dared stop the mission of our lord?" asked one of the Yamadūtas.

"They are the order carriers of Lord Viṣṇu, the Viṣṇudūtas," said Yamarāja, smiling. "They are worshiped even by the demigods, because they are Vaiṣṇavas who are just as beautiful and transcendental as their Lord. They are rarely seen, and they move where they please. The Viṣṇudūtas protect the Lord's devotees from the hands of enemies, from envious persons, from natural disturbances, and even from my jurisdiction."

"But you have entrusted us to protect religious principles," said the first Yamadūta, "and Ajāmila's escape from our custody has spoilt our efforts. If there are different views of piety and sin, then there are no true religious principles."

Yamarāja sat down again and spoke, "You think that the topmost religious principles are the ritualistic ceremonies recommended in the *Vedas*. These are not transcendental; they are only meant to keep peace and order among materialistic persons.

"Do you know what is *bhāgavata-dharma*, or real religious principles?"

The Yamadūtas shook their heads.

"Not even the sages or demigods know what real religious principles are, to say nothing of the *asuras* and ordinary human beings. However, only I know, along with Lord Brahmā, Nārada, Lord Śiva, the four Kumāras, Lord Kapila, Svāyambhuva Manu, Prahlāda Mahārāja, Janaka Mahārāja, Grandfather Bhīṣma, Bali Mahārāja, and Śukadeva Gosvāmī."

"So what are the real religious principles, dear lord?" asked the second Yamadūta, bowing his head. All the Yamadūtas now looked at their master with newfound reverence.

"My dear servants," said Yamarāja, pleased with his servants' questions and eagerness to know about the Lord, "the transcendental religious principle, known as *bhāgavata-dharma*, is exclusive surrender to the Supreme Personality of Godhead in love. It is completely pure, confidential, and difficult to understand. But if you are fortunate to understand it, you are immediately liberated and will go back to the Lord's spiritual abode."

The Yamadūtas were speechless.

Yamarāja got up and walked towards the Yamadūtas. Looking at them in the eyes, he said, "Devotional service to the Lord, beginning with chanting His holy name, is the ultimate religious principle for the human being."

"Aha!" thought the Yamadūtas, "So this is why Ajāmila was delivered!"

"O my dear servants, you are as good as my sons," said Yamarāja softly. "Just see how glorious is this chanting of the Lord's holy name. The sinful Ajāmila chanted only to call his son, but by chanting the holy name he remembered Lord Nārāyaṇa and thus was saved from the ropes of death.

"Therefore, you should know that one is relieved from all sinful reactions simply by chanting the holy name, qualities, and activities of the Lord without offenses. Even if chanted imperfectly, with improper pronunciation, the holy name will give the result.

"So, my dear servants, do not get swayed by the ritualistic ceremonies in the *Vedas*, which are aimed only for temporary material benefits. Even the compilers of the religious scriptures, like Yājñavalkya and Jaimini, do not know the confidential religious system of the twelve *mahājanas* I mentioned. They do not understand the value of devotional service or of chanting the Hare Kṛṣṇa *mantra* because their minds are attracted to worldly things. In fact, their intelligence has become dull."

Looking at his servants with compassion, Yamarāja continued, "So don't be unintelligent like them. Intelligent men solve all problems by serving the Lord with devotion and chanting His holy name. And who is this Lord? He is situated in your heart; He is a mine of all auspicious qualities. Therefore I have no jurisdiction over His

devotees. They are always protected from sinful reactions because they chant the Hare Kṛṣṇa *mantra*."

The Yamadūtas were wonderstruck. They wished they could learn to chant the holy names. Even their lord was a devotee of Lord Nārāyaṇa, and not just any devotee; he was one of the twelve *mahājanas*, one of the topmost devotees. They understood that he was the best person from whom to learn about the Lord.

Yamarāja came closer and suddenly stuck his finger in the chest of the Yamadūta in front of him. The others winced and took a step back. Yamarāja then glared at all of them and warned, "My dear servants, do not approach such devotees! They are surrendered to the lotus feet of the Supreme Personality of Godhead and are always protected by His club. So do not even go near them! Do you understand?"

The Yamadūtas nodded fervently.

"Exalted persons are always drinking the honey of the Lord's lotus feet. Neither Lord Brahmā, the time factor, nor I can chastise them. So don't bring them to me!

"My dear servants, bring to me for punishment only persons who are averse to the Lord, who do not associate with exalted devotees, and who are attached to family life and worldly enjoyment. Bring to me those sinful persons who do not use their tongues to chant the Lord's holy name and qualities, and whose heads do not bow before Lord Kṛṣṇa. Send me those who do not perform their duties to Viṣṇu. Please bring me all such fools and rascals!"

The Yamadūtas immediately fell to the ground in obeisance and exclaimed, "Oh yes, our lord!"

Yamarāja paced the floor as his servants sat on their knees staring at him. "What could be troubling him now?" they thought.

Yamarāja threw his arms in the air and exclaimed, "O my Lord! O Nārāyaṇa, please forgive us! My servants have committed a great

offense by arresting Your devotee, Ajāmila. Because of our ignorance, we did not recognize Ajāmila as Your servant."

Going down on his knees, Yamarāja said, "Therefore, my Lord, with folded hands we beg Your pardon."

Parīkṣit Mahārāja put his arms in the air after hearing this narration from Śukadeva Gosvāmī. "All glories to Lord Nārāyaṇa and His holy names!" he exclaimed.

Śukadeva Gosvāmī smiled and folded his palms: "My dear King, I heard this confidential history from the great sage Agastya when I approached him in the Malaya Hills while he was worshiping the Supreme Personality of Godhead.

"Certainly, this story teaches us many valuable lessons. We've learned that the chanting of the holy names can uproot the reactions to even the greatest of sins. One who constantly hears and chants about the Lord's activities can very easily come to the platform of pure devotional service and cleanse the dirt from the heart. People cannot become purified merely by observing vows and performing Vedic ritualistic ceremonies as acts of atonement. Such people will be incompletely purified and will perform sinful activities again and again.

"Yet, devotees never give up the lotus feet of Kṛṣṇa. They always lick the honey from His lotus feet. They do not care for material activities performed under the three modes and which bring only misery."

Clearing his throat, Śukadeva Gosvāmī continued, "After hearing from Yamarāja, the Yamadūtas never approached a devotee at the time of death. Since then, as soon as they see a devotee, they fear him and dare not look at him again."

Parīkṣit Mahārāja chuckled and exclaimed, "How wonderful!"

Śukadeva Gosvāmī concluded the narration and said, "Therefore, O King, the chanting of the *saṅkīrtana* movement is the most auspicious activity in the entire universe. Please try to understand this so others will take it seriously."

Themes and Key Messages

Please go through this table of themes and key messages, with corresponding verses, and discuss each topic further.

THEMES	REFERENCES	KEY MESSAGES
Kṛṣṇa is the one supreme controller over everything and is the supreme judge.	6.3.4–13	The Yamadūtas were confused because it was the first time that they had seen a sinner escape death and the judgment of Yamarāja. They therefore doubted Yamarāja's superior position, thinking that there must be a higher authority. Yamarāja explained that he is not the supreme controller or judge; there is one supreme master and controller who is greater than him and who is the Lord of all the other demigods as well. He is the Supreme Personality of Godhead, Kṛṣṇa, the essence of creation and the controller of all beings. He controls human society through the *varṇāśrama* system.
Even though the Lord is everywhere and controls everything, He remains unknowable even to the great sages and demigods.	6.3.14–16	Because Kṛṣṇa is above the three modes of material nature, He and His actions are not known to those under the control of the modes, even to the sages and demigods who are in the mode of goodness. Not by the senses, the mind, the life air, or by thoughts, words, or any other material means can the Supreme Lord's position be known. As Kṛṣṇa says in the *Bhagavad-gītā* (7.3 *manuṣyāṇāṁ sahasreṣu . . .* and 18.55 *bhaktyā mām abhijānāti . . .*), only His devotees, who are engaged in devotional service, which is transcendental to the material modes, can understand the Lord and His purpose.

THEMES	REFERENCES	KEY MESSAGES
The real religious principles, *bhāgavata-dharma*, are enacted by the Supreme Personality of Godhead and His representatives.	6.3.17–21	Since Ajāmila had escaped their custody, the Yamadūtas were doubtful of what true religious principles are. The Yamadūtas thought that religious principles are those enacted in the Vedic literature, which include Vedic ritualistic ceremonies. However, Yamarāja explained that the real religious principles, or *bhāgavata-dharma*, are above the modes of material nature. The real *bhāgavata-dharma* is to give up all other duties and surrender to Kṛṣṇa, which is understood by the Lord's representatives, such as the twelve *mahājanas,* who imbibe this principle fully.
Devotional service, beginning with chanting the Lord's holy name, is the ultimate religious principle for human society.	6.3.22–24, 31–33	The supreme religion is that which teaches its followers how to love the Supreme Personality of Godhead. Such a religious system begins with the chanting of His holy names. After becoming purified by chanting the holy name, one gradually sees the Lord's form, pastimes, and divine qualities. The holy name chanted offenselessly gives relief from sinful reactions and gives liberation even if chanted imperfectly. The history of Ajāmila is sufficient proof of the power of the holy name and the exalted position of a devotee who chants the holy name incessantly. Simply by devotional service, and not by Vedic ritualistic ceremonies, one can understand everything about the Supreme Lord, and upon leaving the body go back home, back to Godhead.
By chanting the holy name, a devotee is saved from Yamarāja's jurisdiction whereas nondevotees are not.	6.3.26–29	Yamarāja instructs the Yamadūtas not to bring to him devotees of the Lord, because they are protected from sinful reactions by the chanting of the holy names. Even if they sometimes commit sinful acts, they are excused. This is the value of the *saṅkīrtana* movement. Death himself (Yamarāja) and his servants revere even such aspiring devotees. Lord Viṣṇu personally protects them with the club in His hand. However, materialistic persons who forget Viṣṇu's service should be brought to Yamarāja for punishment.

Higher-Thinking Questions

Now try to deepen your understanding of this chapter by delving into Śrīla Prabhupāda's purports and reflecting on the following questions:

1. In what ways does the Lord control the living beings? (Refer to verses 12 and 13.)

2. Although the Lord is unknowable to everyone except His devotees, how does Yamarāja describe the Lord in verse 17 to make some of His qualities known?

3. Why are the Viṣṇudūtas above the Yamadūtas, explained by Śrīla Prabhupāda in verse 17 purport?

4. In verse 18 purport Śrīla Prabhupāda describes that the Viṣṇudūtas and the Lord always protect the surrendered devotee from danger. However, we see that devotees also become victims of danger through disease, natural disasters, and other material calamities. How can we understand that they are still protected?

5. In verse 24 purport what does Śrīla Prabhupāda recommend to those who chant offensively? Why? Does this encourage you to continue chanting even if the quality of your chanting is not good?

6. Why does Śrīla Prabhupāda consider *saṅkīrtana* more important and valuable than Vedic ritualistic ceremonies? (Refer to verse 25 and purport.) Why does he discourage Vedic ritualistic ceremonies in verse 32 purport?

7. Why is Deity worship also important as explained by Śrīla Prabhupāda in verse 25 purport? How should we see *saṅkīrtana* in relation to Deity worship?

8. In verse 31 purport Śrīla Prabhupāda explains that the Lord excuses a devotee who accidentally performs some sinful activity. What does he warn devotees not to do? Why do you think avoiding this offense to the holy name is important to follow?

9. Why do you think that a devotee is dangerous for the Yamadūtas as explained in verse 34 and purport? (Refer to verse 27 purport.)

ACTIVITIES

In this section you will find many exciting things to do. These activities will get you thinking, moving, drawing, and having loads of fun.

Analogy Activity

THE INVISIBLE DIRECTORS

"As the different limbs of the body cannot see the eyes, the living entities cannot see the Supreme Lord, who is situated as the Supersoul in everyone's heart. Not by the senses, by the mind, by the life air, by thoughts within the heart, or by the vibration of words can the living entities ascertain the real situation of the Supreme Lord." *SB* 6.3.16

In this analogy the eyes are compared to the Supersoul, and the different parts of the body that are directed by the eyes are compared to the living entity, the soul.

Let us first understand the comparison clearly before analyzing the position of the Supersoul.

Look at the boxes below. In the left column, the limbs of the body are trying to understand and appreciate the position of the eye although none of them can perceive the eye. The right column relates each of their points to the soul or Supersoul. Study the statements in both columns and answer the questions that follow:

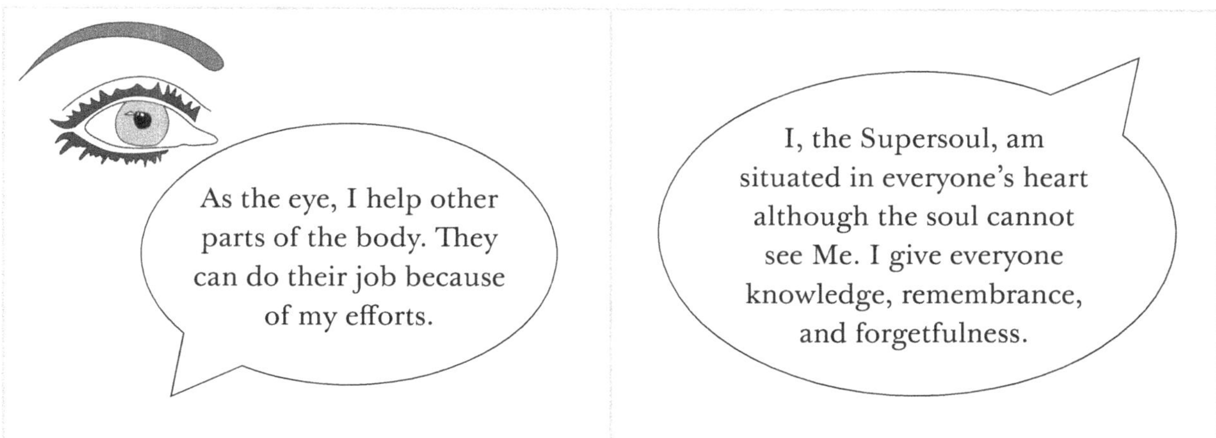

Notice that in the above analogy each organ has a different understanding of the presence and function of the eye – some organs barely can understand anything at all, while others can understand things they can experience but not sense directly. In the same way, we see in the corresponding boxes for the soul and Supersoul that some *jivas* do not understand much of the Supersoul even after experiencing His presence, while others understand that seeing is not the only proof of His existence – He can be perceived in other ways too.

Think about and discuss:

- Each pair of opinions in the analogy reflect a certain thought process. Can you identify each?
- Which thought process do you agree with?
- What conclusive point are they trying to make?

Śrīla Prabhupāda writes in the purport, "Although one cannot see the Supersoul in one's heart through sensual activities, His direction is necessary."

Using the analogy of the eye, explain in two to three sentences why the direction of the Supersoul is necessary for the soul and how the conditioned soul should receive and follow these instructions.

Artistic Activity

... to reveal your creativity

MAHĀJANA KEYCHAIN

Let's make a *mahājana* keychain!

What you will need: cardboard; pencil; pen; color pencils or paints; pictures; Mod Podge or similar brand all-in-one craft glue, sealer, and finish; metal keyring

Directions:
Look at verses 20 and 21, which tells us the names of the twelve *mahājanas*. Śrīla Prabhupāda explains that these *mahājanas* are the authorities of devotional service and we should follow their example and teachings to attain love of God.

These twelve great personalities are Brahmā, Nārada, Śiva, Kapila, Manu, Prahlāda, Janaka, Bhīṣma, Bali, Śukadeva, and Yamarāja. Let's make our own keyring cards to remember them!

- On cardboard outline 12 rectangular shapes and cut them out. Alternatively you can design the shapes on a computer program.
- On each shape/card draw or glue a picture of one of the *mahājanas*. Label each *mahājana*.
- If using a computer program design the 12 shapes and insert pictures of the *mahājanas* on them. Cut them out. You could also print your shapes and draw the pictures (see images 1, 2, and 3).
- Keep a space on the top of each card to punch a hole.
- After making a hole on all the cards, laminate them, or with a brush apply a layer of Mod Podge so they have a varnished finish (optional).
- Then through the hole insert all the cards onto a keyring (see image 4). Can you learn all the names?

Now you have a keychain that you can use and at the same time remember the *mahājanas*. After all, they give us the key to spiritual knowledge and enlightenment!

Image 1

Image 2

Image 3

Image 4

Theatrical Activity

... to bring out the actor in you

THE FEARLESS PATH OF BHĀGAVATA-DHARMA

With a partner enact the following skit:

Player 1:

nehābhikrāma-nāśo 'sti
pratyavāyo na vidyate
svalpam apy asya dharmasya
trāyate mahato bhayāt

Player 2: Oh, *Bhagavad-gītā* 2.40! "In this endeavor there is no loss or diminution, and a little advancement on this path can protect one from the most dangerous type of fear."

What reminds you of this **śloka** today, dear friend?

Player 1: The story of Ajāmila that we are learning in class. Yamarāja, the controller of death, has revealed the fearless path of devotional service to Lord Kṛṣṇa.

Player 2: So true! Mahārāja Parīkṣit was worried after hearing the description of hell. The path of atonement given in the *dharma-śāstras* is too difficult to follow, nor does it destroy the desire to sin. But by chanting the holy names of Nārāyaṇa, even unknowingly, Ajāmila was freed from all sins and was offered divine protection by the Viṣṇudūtas.

Player 1: The most dangerous type of fear is to fall into the lower species of life. Here Ajāmila was not only saved from the hands of the Yamadūtas but was also given a chance to perfect his devotional service even in the same body.

Player 2: What is the need to fear when we follow the principles of *bhāgavata-dharma*, beginning with hearing and chanting the name and fame of Lord Kṛṣṇa?

Player 1: Where will you find a kinder master then Lord Hari, who is full of love for His parts and parcels? Even if you chant His names unknowingly, He is willing to give you all protection.

Player 2: When chanted with attention, the chanting of the holy names gives us love of Godhead. It is the goal of life, the most confidential knowledge hidden in the *Vedas*.

Player 1:
> *harer nāma harer nāma*
> *harer nāmaiva kevalam*
> *kalau nāsty eva nāsty eva*
> *nāsty eva gatir anyathā*

Player 2: What a wonderful verse from the *Bṛhan-nāradīya Purāṇa*. "In this Age of Kali there is no other means, no other means, no other means for self-realization than chanting the holy name, chanting the holy name, chanting the holy name of Lord Hari."

    This narration of Ajāmila has inspired me to take to the chanting of the Hare Kṛṣṇa *mahā-mantra* with all my heart and soul. My faith has increased manyfold!

Player 1: Śrīla Prabhupāda and his dear servants have given us everything we need to succeed: the powerful holy names, the process of chanting, Vaiṣṇava association, and the scriptures to guide us.

Player 2: All we have to do is to accept their gifts and follow their instructions!

Players 1 and 2: (with raised arms) Hare Kṛṣṇa Hare Kṛṣṇa, Kṛṣṇa Kṛṣṇa Hare Hare/ Hare Rāma Hare Rāma, Rāma Rāma Hare Hare

Critical-Thinking Activity

... to bring out the spiritual investigator in you

COMPARE AND CONTRAST: VEDIC RITUALS AND BHĀGAVATA-DHARMA

In this chapter Śrīla Prabhupāda has emphasized the importance of the *saṅkīrtana* movement's activities compared to Vedic rituals. Use the table below to understand and document the characteristics of both, referring to verses 19 to 33 and their purports. The first column introduces the topic and gives the verse reference. The first attribute is done for you. Please complete the rest of the table.

		VEDIC RELIGIOUS PRINCIPLES AND RITUALS	SANKIRTANA MOVEMENT (BHĀGAVATA-DHARMA)
1	The three modes of nature (*SB* 6.3.19 purport)	These are affected by the three modes and are meant to keep peace and order among materialistic persons.	Real religious principles are *nistraiguṇya*, above the three modes of material nature, or transcendental.

		VEDIC RELIGIOUS PRINCIPLES AND RITUALS	**SANKIRTANA MOVEMENT (BHĀGAVATA-DHARMA)**
2	Purpose (*SB* 6.3.19)	These are given to gradually elevate people to *bhāgavata-dharma,* to the transcendental platform of knowing Kṛṣṇa.	
3	Knowledge of Kṛṣṇa in relation to the twelve *mahājanas* (*SB* 6.3.20–21, 25)	Because they are bewildered by the illusory energy of the Lord, Yājñavalkya and Jaimini and other compilers of the religious scriptures cannot know the secret and confidential religious system of the twelve *mahājanas.*	
4	Benefits and destination (*SB* 6.3.25 verse and purport)		One attains the highest success of love for Kṛṣṇa and the Lord's spiritual abode by chanting the holy names of the Lord without offense.
5	Process of liberation in Kali-yuga (*SB* 6.3.23)	In this age of Kali, no one can perform all the ritualistic ceremonies for becoming liberated; that is extremely difficult.	
6	Desire to enjoy matter (*SB* 6.3.33)		Devotees who always lick the honey from the lotus feet of Lord Kṛṣṇa do not care at all for material activities, which are performed under the three modes of material nature and which bring only misery.
7	Candidates for punishment (*SB* 6.3.26)	Nondevotees engaged in religious activities for show are neglecting their religious duty and are punishable by Yamarāja.	

Action Activity

INTERVIEW GAME: WHO UNDERSTANDS KRSNA?

In this chapter we learn that those who are controlled by passion and ignorance cannot understand Kṛṣṇa. Even those in the mode of goodness, like the many demigods and great *ṛṣis*, cannot understand the activities of the Supreme Personality of Godhead. Only His devotees, who are engaged in devotional service, which is transcendental to the material modes, can understand the Lord and His purpose to a greater extent.

Directions:

With a partner choose one demigod or sage who you think doesn't understand the Lord fully. Then choose one devotee, such as one of the *mahājanas* mentioned in this chapter, who knows the Lord more.

Alternatively, it could be anybody of your choice. You can research some personalities and choose someone you are interested to know about.

You and your partner can choose the personality that you would like to enact or pretend to be.

Now prepare some questions for each other, using some of the action words (verbs) below to formulate your questions. You can also create your own list of action words.

- Engage
- Decide
- Explain
- Offer
- Prefer
- Understand

- Control
- Value
- Consider
- Know

Make five questions using some of these verbs to see how well each personality understands the Supreme Lord, Kṛṣṇa. Each question will have a different verb.

For example: Questions for Sūrya, the sun-god

- How did you **decide** to become the sun-god? Who assigned the task to you?
- Do you **know** about the qualities of the person who assigned the task to you?
- Would you like to **control** the whole cosmic manifestation since you are so powerful?
- Would you **prefer** to remain as the sun-god or would like to try some other services for Kṛṣṇa?
- Can you **explain** why Kṛṣṇa comes to the material world?

Similarly, create questions for the other personality.

Taking turns, now pose the questions to each other to see how well each personality understands Kṛṣṇa and His purposes. Can you conclude who understands Kṛṣṇa more?

Introspective Activity

... to bring out the reflective devotee in you

TRANSFORMATION OF THOUGHT

The Yamadūtas went through a huge internal transformation due to the events triggered by the Viṣṇudūtas' association:

- Initially, without really knowing who they were and due to being stopped from performing their duty, they went through **frustration** and **anger**.
- Then, when they accused Yamarāja of being a bad master, they noticed that Yamarāja remained **calm** without getting angry at them.
- Yamarāja pacified them by explaining elaborately who the Viṣṇudūtas were, why Ajāmila rightly deserved to be let off, and based on what religious principles this decision was correct. This **amazed** the Yamadūtas, for they had never really heard of the transcendental religious system, which was beyond the material.
- The Yamadūtas likely returned home feeling **grateful** to have one of the *mahājanas* as their own master, since they could now learn and practice the injunctions of *bhakti-yoga* under Yamarāja's guidance.

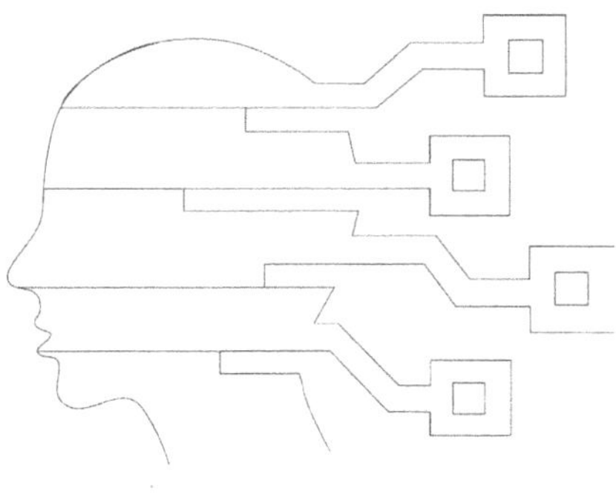

Reflect on one of the following topics and write down a diary entry of about 100 to 150 words expressing your transformation. Use the prompts above to help you. Read out your diary entry to your group.

Choose either A or B:
A. Imagine you are one of the Yamadūtas who had gone to arrest Ajāmila and who later heard Yamarāja at the assembly that day.

You go home and reflect on the events of the day and think about how it has changed your life and understanding of religion forever.

B. Reflect on an incident or occasion that caused your thoughts or emotions to transform. It could be an incident that triggered your anger or frustration and which later transformed into peace or gratitude.

Writing Activities

... to bring out the writer in you

ESSAY: THE HEART OF A MAHĀJANA

Yamarāja is the superintendent of justice, but his order was transgressed by the Viṣṇudūtas. How Yamarāja deals with the Yamadūtas' anger and disappointment and instructs them in the science of *bhāgavata-dharma* reveals his glorious position as a *mahājana*, a great devotee who surrenders to Lord Kṛṣṇa.

All the twelve *mahājanas* have this quality of surrender. From the list of the *mahājanas* given in verses 20–21, choose three *mahājanas* and briefly describe their story of surrender to the Lord.

Directions:

1. Introduce the topic of *mahājanas* in the first paragraph and what it means to be a *mahājana*.

2. In three separate paragraphs show how each were *mahājanas*.

3. Conclude by explaining how the Lord and His devotees enact *bhāgavata-dharma*, the principle of surrender and loving service to the Lord, setting the example for others to follow.

LETTER: DON'T TOUCH THE LORD'S DEVOTEES!

In this chapter Yamarāja instructs the Yamadūtas to stay away from devotees, for they have fully surrendered to the lotus feet of the Supreme Personality of Godhead. They are always protected by the club of the Supreme Lord, and therefore even Lord Brahmā, Yamarāja, or the time factor cannot chastise them.

Directions:
Imagine yourself as one of the Yamadūtas who received instructions from Yamarāja about whom to approach for punishment. You need to explain to your friend and co-Yamadūta, named Maraṇakāla, to stay away from the devotees, as they are dangerous (refer to verse 34).

Write a letter to your Yamadūta friend explaining why devotees are considered

dangerous and why your friend should never approach such devotees but only bring nondevotees for punishment. Explain how he should differentiate between the devotees and the nondevotees. Give clear instructions for him to follow. (Refer to verses 26 to 29 purports.)

Note: For writing a friendly letter, mention the name of the person you are addressing and your name to sign out.

Example:

Dear Maraṇakāla,

xxx

Your friend,

____

(your name as one of the Yamadūtas)

Language Activities

COMIC STRIP: KṚṢṆA, THE SUPREME JUDGE

Yamarāja revealed to his servants that he is not the supreme judge; Kṛṣṇa is the supreme controller and the supreme judge. Not just Yamarāja, but we ourselves may sometimes think that we can judge someone for their behavior or situation.

Prepare a comic strip, showing how Kṛṣṇa is the supreme judge of everyone's activities. Look at examples of comic strips online.

Directions:

1. First brainstorm some ideas with your class and teacher. Some ideas:

- You could illustrate a conversation between two friends who are debating about whether Kṛṣṇa (God) is the supreme witness and judge.
- You could show how someone was judged wrongly. For example, a new student comes to the class, and because he looks different or acts strangely, the other students judge and make fun of him according to his looks or external behavior. Then the teacher reminds them that the students shouldn't judge, because only Kṛṣṇa in the heart can truly understand the intentions of someone.
- You can show how judging someone wrongly can have disastrous or embarrassing results.

2. With a pencil first make a draft of your comic strip, planning how many frames (scenes) would be necessary.

3. Prepare your dialogue between your characters. For any narration, use captions either on the top or bottom of each box. Write your dialogue in speech bubbles after you draw your characters in each scene.

4. If you wish, you may color in your comic strip.

NO OTHER WAY, NO OTHER WAY, NO OTHER WAY

In the first three chapters of Canto 6, you've learned that chanting the holy name of Lord Hari is the recommended process for achieving spiritual perfection in this age of Kali.

Memorize the verse below from the *Bṛhan-nāradīya Purāṇa* quoted by Śrī Caitanya Mahāprabhu in *Caitanya-caritāmṛta Ādi* 17.21:

> *harer nāma harer nāma*
> *harer nāmaiva kevalam*
> *kalau nāsty eva nāsty eva*
> *nāsty eva gatir anyathā*

"In this Age of Kali there is no other means, no other means, no other means for self-realization than chanting the holy name, chanting the holy name, chanting the holy name of Lord Hari."

Now above the speech bubbles below, write down one thing that supports or elaborates on the point. For example, *harer nāma*, "chant the holy names," is mentioned three times. So for each time it is mentioned, write down why we should chant the holy names. Similarly, for *nāstyeva*, "no other means" or "no other way," mentioned three times, write down three other processes that do not have the same effect as chanting the holy names to show there is no alternative means for achieving spiritual perfection in this age.

CHAPTER 3 ANSWERS

The Invisible Directors

Discussion: Each pair is progressively making a point about the eye or the Supersoul – the first set discusses from the viewpoint of the eye/Supersoul about how they are real and perform specific useful functions; the second set explores the possibility of their existence by mere observation or experience; the third set begins to establish their existence by some inference; and the final set explains the principle based on their existence as a fact. Śrīla Prabhupāda also makes an important point in the purport that one cannot understand the Supersoul or the Supreme Personality of Godhead by *pratyakṣa* or *anumāna pramāṇa*. One can experience His activities, and one should accept His presence based on the teachings of the *śāstra* and *ācāryas*.

Why direction is necessary: It is because the soul cannot understand anything without the presence of the Supersoul. An advanced devotee may receive instructions directly from the Supersoul in the heart, but a neophyte should receive instructions from the scriptures and the spiritual master and follow them.

Compare and Contrast

2. The principles of *bhāgavata-dharma* are given by the Supreme Personality of Godhead, which are meant to give up all other duties and surrender to Kṛṣṇa. (The *saṅkīrtana* movement was established by Lord Caitanya for this purpose.)

3. The twelve *mahājanas* know and realize the real religious principle of surrender to Kṛṣṇa.

4. At best, the fruitive ritualistic activities elevate one to the higher planets.

5. All *śāstras* and *ācāryas* have recommended that in Kali-yuga chanting the holy name is the only means of deliverance.

6. Vedic rituals do not remove the root of sin, and thus those who atone in this way are not completely purified and return to sinful activities again and again.

7. Intelligent men, or devotees of the Lord, who chant the holy name of the Lord, are not within Yamarāja's jurisdiction even if they accidentally commit sinful acts due to previous bad habits.

No other way, no other way, no other way (*Potential Answers*)

1. It cleanses the heart from all vices; 2. It uproots the desire to sin; 3. It gives love for Kṛṣṇa.

Other alternatives: it gives the association of Kṛṣṇa; it gives the highest bliss; it takes you back to Godhead.

4. *Karma* or pious acts; 5. *Jñāna* or speculative knowledge; 6. Atonement or ritualistic activities

Other alternatives: worship of the demigods; mystic *yoga*; chanting of other *mantras*

4

THE HAMSA-GUHYA PRAYERS

The forest of Naimiṣāraṇya was silent. It seemed that even the birds were listening to Sūta Gosvāmī as he narrated the discussion between Śukadeva Gosvāmī and Mahārāja Parīkṣit to the assembly of sages seated beneath the trees.

Sūta Gosvāmī said, "O great sages, blessed King Parīkṣit wanted to hear more about the creation during the reign of Svāyambhuva Manu, which Śukadeva Gosvāmī had explained earlier (in the Third Canto). He wanted to know about the Lord's potency which brought about the secondary creation. Śukadeva Gosvāmī was very pleased with King Parīkṣit's inquiry."

Sūta Gosvāmī began to describe what Śukadeva Gosvāmī told Parīkṣit Mahārāja. In fact, Śukadeva Gosvāmī had related this incident previously (in the Fourth Canto), but now the King was ready to hear more details.

Śukadeva Gosvāmī said, "As I explained before, the ten sons of King Prācīnabarhi, the Pracetās, were immersed in their austerity of meditating on the Supreme Lord under water. As

you remember, Nārada Muni, out of compassion, instructed Mahārāja Prācīnabarhi to stop his Vedic rituals in which animal killing was taking place. The King then renounced his kingdom to perform austerities in the forest, but alas, there was no king to rule the kingdom since his ten sons were still performing their austerities. So when the ten sons emerged from the waters, they saw that the earth had been neglected. Its entire surface was covered by trees.

"This is not what they had been expecting. 'How dare these trees block our path! We'll teach them a lesson,' they thought. After their long and severe austerities they felt powerful, but they couldn't control their anger. Fire and wind burst forth from their mouths, burning the trees to ashes.

"My dear King Parīkṣit, when Soma, the moon-god, saw the trees burning, he felt very sorry because he is the maintainer of all herbs and trees. He appeared before the Pracetās to appease their anger. He said, 'O greatly fortunate ones, you should not kill these poor trees. Instead, your

duty is to be the well-wishers and protectors of all your citizens. In fact, the Supreme Lord, the master of all living beings, has created all these trees and vegetables for other living entities. By nature's arrangement one kind of living entity is food for another living entity. Your father has ordered you to generate population, so how can you burn these trees and herbs, which are needed to maintain your subjects and descendants?'

'Your father, grandfather, and great-grandfathers have always followed the path of goodness by maintaining their subjects, including the men, animals, and trees. So you should follow the same path. Don't become unnecessarily angry. Control your anger!'

'Just as the parents are the friends and maintainers of their children, just as the eyelid is the protector of the eye, as the husband is the maintainer and protector of his wife, as the householder is the maintainer and protector of beggars, and as the learned is the friend of the ignorant, so the king is the protector and giver of life to all his subjects. The trees are also your subjects, so you should give them protection.

'Why do you distinguish between different living entities. Don't you know that the Supreme Personality of Godhead is within the core of everyone's hearts. You should consider every body a temple of the Lord. If you have this vision, you will satisfy the Lord.

'If you inquire about self-realization your powerful anger will be subdued. The modes of material nature won't be able to touch you.

'Leave alone whatever trees remain. Let them be happy, and you too should be happy. I want to give you a gift from these trees; it is their daughter Mārisā. She is an Apsarā girl who was abandoned by her mother, Pramlocā, and raised by the trees; so accept her as your wife.'

"The words of Soma extinguished the burning fire of anger within the Pracetās. They married the exquisite heavenly girl according to the religious system, and in time they got a son from her whose name was Dakṣa. He was able to fill the three worlds with living entities."

"Wait!" Parīkṣit Mahārāja blurted out, "Is this Prajāpati Dakṣa? Wasn't he punished for offending Lord Śiva and received a head of a goat?"

Śukadeva Gosvāmī smiled and said, "Yes, this is the same Prajāpati Dakṣa. He had appeared during the reign of Svāyambhuva Manu, the *manvantara* in which he offended Lord Śiva. Then he gave up that body with the head of a goat, and in the Cākṣuṣa *manvantara* he was born as the son of the Pracetās to continue with the task of populating the universe."

"Aha!" Parīkṣit Mahārāja exclaimed. "Please tell me more!"

Śukadeva Gosvāmī continued, "Prajāpati Dakṣa created many kinds of living beings through his semen and through his mind. With his mind, he first created the demigods, demons,

humans, birds, animals, aquatics, and so on.
But then he realized that he wasn't properly
generating all kinds of living beings. So he went
to the Vindhya Mountains and performed severe
austerities there to please the
Supreme Lord, Hari."

"Then what happened?"
asked Mahārāja Parīkṣit with
great anticipation.

"Dakṣa recited the Haṁsa-
guhya prayers to the Supreme
Lord. I shall explain those
prayers to you and how the
Lord was pleased with Him for
those prayers."

"Oh, that's
wonderful!" exclaimed
Parīkṣit Mahārāja.

"The Lord is most
merciful and relishes
the prayers of His
devotees."

Śukadeva Gosvāmī
then described how Prajāpati
Dakṣa, with bowed head and
folded palms, recited the
Haṁsa-guhya prayers from the *Vedas*. With eyes
closed and in a faltering voice he said:

I offer my obeisances to you, my Lord
Who is beyond illusion
Self-sufficient, the causes of all causes
the controller of this creation

I offer my obeisances to you, my Lord
The supreme controller and master
The conditioned souls do not see
their senses led by the supreme director

I offer my obeisances to you, My Lord
Who is omniscient and unlimited
We may know our body, senses, and life airs
But can't see or understand You, even if elevated

I offer my obeisances to You, my Lord
Who can only be seen in a purified state
When our mind and consciousness are in trance
You reveal Yourself and Your qualities so great

I offer my obeisances to You, the Paramātmā
Who from us is never apart
Just as *brāhmaṇas* can extract fire from wood
Your devotees can find You in their heart

When we are eager to be liberated
We can see the Supersoul
Not by the contaminated mind and senses
But by Your loving service, life's goal

When will You be pleased with me, My Lord
Who is inconceivable and beyond this creation
You are the supreme source and resting place
The ultimate doer, the Supreme Brahman, and
object of meditation

I offer my obeisances to You, my Lord
Between philosophers you cause dissension
You direct them from within the heart
So they can't come to a conclusion

The theists and the atheists argue
They offer opposing statements
Yet they are both focused on You
The ultimate cause of existence

You are especially merciful to Your devotees
Loving worship they perform
According to one's desires and mood
You manifest Yourself in a particular form

You may appear as a demigod, not in your
    original form
But what's the use of this
May my desires be fulfilled by the original You
the ultimate source of bliss

Dakṣa opened his eyes. A golden effulgence

blinded him. He shaded his eyes with his hands only to see the same Supreme Personality of Godhead, the object of his prayers, before him. The same Lord Hari who had appeared to his fathers, the Pracetās, was now smiling, standing on His carrier, Garuḍa. Dakṣa's loving prayers had attracted Him to this place known as Aghamarṣaṇa.

At first Dakṣa winced in fear, but then when he saw the smiling face and eyes of the Lord, His heart raced in excitement. The Lord's long eight arms each held a disc, conchshell, sword, shield, arrow, bow, rope, and club. His yellow garments dazzled against His deep bluish complexion, and from His neck to His feet hung a garland of flowers. Decorated with various ornaments, a gorgeous round helmet on His head, and shark-shaped earrings, He enchanted Dakṣa's mind.

Dakṣa fell to the ground like a stick to offer respects. He could not move or say anything; all his senses were erupting in bliss. Although he had initially approached the Lord with desires for procreation, now he couldn't ask for anything.

The Lord smiled, and in a voice that melted Dakṣa's heart, He said, "O most fortunate Prācetasa, because of your great faith in Me, you've attained devotional ecstasy. Indeed, because of your austerities combined with exalted devotion, your life is now successful. You've achieved complete perfection."

Dakṣa gradually got up, his limbs trembling in divine happiness. He sat on his knees with folded palms, captivated by the Lord.

"My dear Prajāpati Dakṣa," the Lord continued, "you've done extreme austerities for the welfare of the world. I also desire that everyone in this world be happy, so I am pleased with you because you are trying to fulfill My desire.

"Lord Brahmā, Lord Śiva, the Manus, all the other demigods, and you *prajāpatis,* who are increasing the population, work for the benefit of all beings. Therefore you are incarnations of My various qualities.

"Listen, my dear *brāhmaṇa;* austerity in the form of meditation is My heart; Vedic knowledge in the form of hymns and *mantras* is My body, and spiritual activities and ecstatic emotions are My actual form. The ritualistic ceremonies and sacrifices are My various limbs, the good fortune resulting from pious or spiritual activities is My mind, and the demigods who execute My orders are My life and soul.

"I alone existed before the creation, I am a reservoir of unlimited potency, and I am all-pervading and unlimited. The creation appeared from within Me, and then the chief being, Lord

Brahmā, appeared. He is your source and is not born of a material mother. When Lord Brahmā, the secondary creator, was trying to create, he felt incapable, so I instructed him to perform austerities. Because of these austerities he was able to create nine personalities, including you, to help him with creation.

"My dear son, Dakṣa, I offer you the daughter of Prajāpati Pañcajana, Asiknī, as your wife. Now beget hundreds of children with her to increase the population. After you have many hundreds and thousands of children, they will also be captivated by My illusory energy and have many children. But because of My mercy to you and them, whatever they do will be offerings of devotion to Me."

Śukadeva Gosvāmī continued, "After the Supreme Personality of Godhead, Hari, spoke to Dakṣa, He immediately disappeared. Dakṣa looked around, wondering if he had been dreaming, but because of the joy he still felt in his heart, he knew that it was certainly no dream."

Themes and Key Messages

Please go through this table of themes and key messages, with corresponding verses, and discuss each topic further.

THEMES	REFERENCES	KEY MESSAGES
A devotee does not become angry when put into difficulty.	6.4.5, 14	The Pracetās became angry at the trees after undergoing long austerities. Śrīla Prabhupāda comments that a devotee is a *sādhu* and therefore does not get angry when put into difficulty. Rather, a devotee who undergoes austerity is forgiving. Caitanya Mahāprabhu recommends that those who preach the Lord's glories should not become angry when preaching but should chant the holy names of the Lord in a humble state of mind, be more tolerant than a tree, and offer all respect to others. One who can subdue one's anger can transcend the influence of the material modes of nature. This is only possible when one engages in the service of the Lord.
All living entities, including animals, trees, and plants should be protected.	6.4.7–13	Lord Soma reminded the Pracetās that the trees and vegetation were created by the Lord to provide food for other living beings, so therefore the Pracetās should protect them. If the Pracetās killed them, then their own subjects would suffer without food. Cow killing is particularly condemned. Therefore Soma instructed the Pracetās that the king should be the protector of all his subjects, including the trees. He also reminded them that the Lord is situated in the hearts of all living beings and therefore they should consider all bodies a temple of God. By such vision they could satisfy the Lord.

THEMES	REFERENCES	KEY MESSAGES
The Lord can only be seen and known by those whose consciousness is pure and who engage in His loving service.	6.4.24–29	The Lord, who is the supreme controller, immeasurable and unlimited, cannot be seen by the conditioned soul although He resides in the heart of every living being as the Supersoul. This is because the heart is covered by the three modes of material nature, the fourteen material elements, and the ten senses, which are the Lord's external energy. The Lord can neither be seen through the material senses or mind. The Lord can only be seen when one's mind and consciousness are cleansed of all contamination by engaging in the Lord's loving service. Ultimately, one can realize Kṛṣṇa by His mercy even though He is inconceivable.
Although the devotees (theists) and the impersonalists (atheists) argue over the existence or nonexistence of the Lord or His form, they both focus on the ultimate cause of existence, Kṛṣṇa.	6.4.30–32	Philosophy means finding the ultimate cause of everything. Kṛṣṇa is the cause of everything, but various philosophers invent their own philosophy and speculate about the origin of everything and therefore contradict each other. As a result, many controversies arise. Such philosophers are offenders and are envious of the Lord; therefore the Supreme Lord keeps them bewildered. Nevertheless, although they fight with one another they focus on the same Absolute Truth.
The Supreme Personality of Godhead is especially merciful to His devotees who worship His lotus feet. He appears to different worshipers according to their desire and worship.	6.4.33–34	The Lord reciprocates with His worshipers according to how they worship Him and what they want. To the impersonalists and speculators, He does not reveal Himself, but to His devotees who know that His form is completely spiritual, He reveals Himself fully. Thus He shows His greatest mercy to His devotees. For those who think that Kṛṣṇa has no form and no work, He comes to the material world to show that He indeed works (performs pastimes and manages the material world through His potencies), has a supreme spiritual form, and is affectionate and merciful to His devotees.

| A devotee has the same desire as the Lord – to benefit all living beings by giving them Kṛṣṇa consciousness. | 6.4.44–45 | Prajāpati Dakṣa was trying to beget children so that they could have a chance to become liberated from material life. The Lord was pleased with him, the Manus, and the demigods for working for the benefit of all living beings. Similarly, the Kṛṣṇa consciousness movement is working for the welfare of all conditioned souls because it elevates everyone to the platform of surrender to Kṛṣṇa. If one gives others a chance to become Kṛṣṇa conscious, the Lord is very pleased because this is what He desires. In the Lord's service it is not that only Lord Brahmā is considered very great while an ordinary human being preaching the Lord's glories is considered low. Anyone engaged in the Lord's service is very dear to Him. |

Higher-Thinking Questions

Now try to deepen your understanding of this chapter by delving into Śrīla Prabhupāda's purports and reflecting on the following questions:

1. Why does Śrīla Prabhupāda mention in verse 6 purport that we cannot accept that there are no trees or vegetation on the moon? What does this prove of the scientists' moon expeditions?

2. Why did Soma try to convince the Pracetās that it wasn't a good idea to kill the trees? (Refer to verses 8 to 10.)

3. In verse 13 Soma tries to convince the Pracetās that they should see the Lord in everyone's hearts and should thus consider their bodies a temple of God and protect them. By not protecting them they would displease the Lord. Why do you think this argument could work to convince the Pracetās? (See verse 13 purport.)

4. What is the secret to controlling anger as explained by Śrīla Prabhupāda in verse 14 purport?

5. In verse 23 purport Śrīla Prabhupāda raises the question that if the Absolute Truth is beyond measurement, how can one realize Him? What do you think is the answer?

6. Explain in your own words how one can eventually see the Lord as described in verse 26.

7. Although the personalists and impersonalists fight with one another, how are they approaching the same Supreme Lord as described in verse 32? (Refer to the first and second paragraphs of the purport.)

8. Why is Kṛṣṇa called *anāma*, or nameless, as described in verse 33 purport? How do we know that Kṛṣṇa's name is not an ordinary mundane name? (Hint: Give an example that you've just learned about.)

9. Why does Śrīla Prabhupāda describe a devotee as the best philosopher at the end of verse 34 purport?

10. Why does the Lord compare Dakṣa to Lord Śiva, Lord Brahmā, or the Manus, even though he is not on their level? Refer to verse 45 purport.

ACTIVITIES

In this section you will find many exciting things to do. These activities will get you thinking, moving, drawing, and having loads of fun.

Analogy Activity

... to bring out the scholar in you

THE CONTROLLER AND THE CONTROLLED

"As the sense objects [form, taste, touch, smell and sound] cannot understand how the senses perceive them, so the conditioned soul, although residing in his body along with the Supersoul, cannot understand how the supreme spiritual person, the master of the material creation, directs his senses." *SB* 6.4.24

In the last chapter we saw how the soul cannot perceive or understand the Supersoul even though the Supersoul is so close to the soul. This analogy further explains the same idea.

In this purport Śrīla Prabhupāda explains that the soul cannot see or understand the Supersoul by material means. He gives several examples to help us understand this fact:

- Example 1: Two friendly birds are sitting on the same branch of a tree. One bird is busy eating the fruit of the tree without noticing the other bird. The second bird is watching the first bird and simply directing him. The first bird is so busy enjoying that he hardly notices that he is being directed.

- Example 2: Ordinary citizens are governed by the king or the ruler, although the king or ruler is not directly present before them always. The citizens can understand they are being ruled over (through laws) but cannot see how the king is directly in control of them.
- Example 3: Every company has a managing director and employees. The managing director controls the employees, even though the employees do not directly see him every day or come under his direct instructions.

Can you think of two or three more examples from everyday life of "hidden" controllers? How do these analogies of hidden controllers help us appreciate the presence of the Supersoul and His control over us?

Action Activities

SHADOWING SAṄKĪRTANA LEADERS

Soma reminded the Pracetās to act in a way that the Supreme Lord is pleased with them; they should see everybody as a temple of the Lord in whose hearts He resides, and they should thus give up their anger by engaging in devotional service.

To successfully chant the holy names and preach the glories of Lord Kṛṣṇa one must subdue anger.

In this activity you are requested to go out on book distribution for three to five days (or as many days as you can) with senior members of your community. The book distributors may be misunderstood, ignored, or met with hostility during their preaching services. Observe how they respond to such situations and control their senses. Record how they treat each individual, regardless of their situation or background, as a dear child of Kṛṣṇa, trying to engage them in Kṛṣṇa's service. Study their behavior when they are confronted with unpleasant situations. What motivates them to rise above their emotions and act on the platform of spiritual knowledge?

Śrīla Prabhupāda states in verse 14 purport: "One is always a servant of lusty desires, anger, greed, illusion, envy and so forth, but if one obtains sufficient strength in spiritual advancement, one can control them. One who obtains such control will always be transcendentally situated, untouched by the modes of material nature. This is only possible when one fully engages in the service of the Lord."

After shadowing the *saṅkīrtana* leaders, ask at least two of them the following:

1. What are their daily spiritual practices?

2. Who are their heroes and what goals do they have in spiritual life?

3. What are their most rewarding and challenging experiences?

4. How did the rewarding experiences motivate them?

5. How did the challenging experiences make them stronger?

6. What is their advice to other book distributors and devotees in general?

After the interview, read their responses and write your understanding of how regulated and consistent spiritual practice helps one rise above the modes.

MEMORIZE AND RECITE

Verses 27 and 28 explain how we are covered by different gross and subtle elements (27 in number). These elements are various energies of Lord Kṛṣṇa. Being covered by material nature, we are unable to perceive the Lord's presence in our heart. The Supersoul is only realized by those who are eager to become liberated and who engage in the Lord's loving service.

From the purport to verses 27–28, select verses that Śrīla Prabhupāda quotes from the *Bhagavad-gītā* that highlight the process of devotional service and inspire your practice. Memorize at least three verses and their meanings and present them before your family and friends.

Some other examples from *Bhagavad-gītā*: 3.43; 7.4; 7.13; 7.14; 9.29; 9.32; 9.34; 10.8–11

Critical-Thinking Activity

... to bring out the spiritual investigator in you

SPECULATIVE CONFUSION MISTAKEN FOR SPECULATIVE CONCLUSION

The Haṁsa-guhya prayers were recited by Dakṣa to please the Supreme Lord and gain his favor for creating progeny. In verse 31 Dakṣa points out that the Supreme Lord cannot be understood by those who speculate about Him, for they can never reach a proper conclusion about Him through their material methods. In this purport Śrīla Prabhupāda lists six types of philosophers, most of whom cannot come to the proper conclusion about the Supreme Lord's true form and nature. Śrīla Prabhupāda further stresses in this chapter that the Lord can only be understood by those who follow in the footsteps of pure devotees.

In this activity let us look at the different types of philosophers who try to understand the Supreme Lord, the conclusions they come to, and why these conclusions cannot help them understand the Lord as He is. Elsewhere in his books, Śrīla Prabhupāda lists six systems of philosophy propounded by six different sages, based on their understanding of the Vedic literatures. Look at what each one has to say:

1. Sage Gautama and Kaṇāda: Nyāya and Vaiśeṣika Philosophy

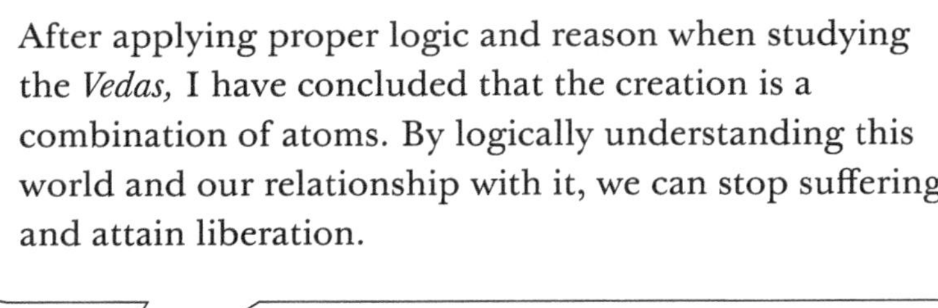

2. Sage Jaimini: Mīmāṁsā Philosophy

3. Sage Kapila: Atheistic Sāṅkhya Philosophy

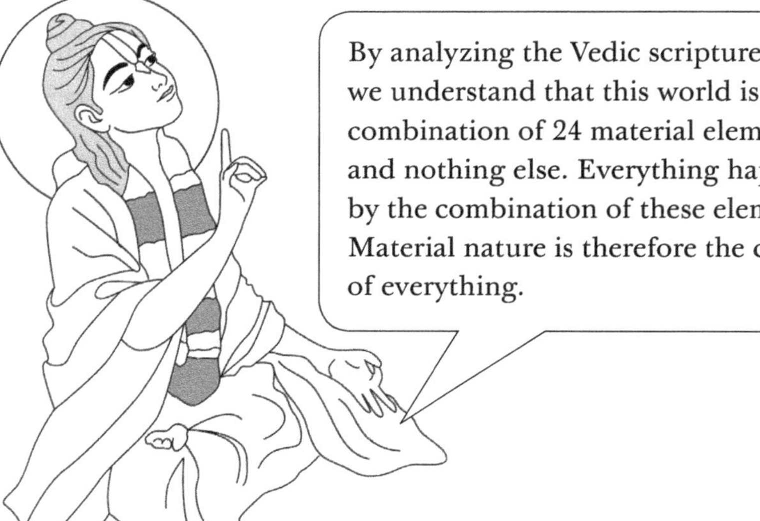

4. Sage Aṣṭāvakra:
Māyāvāda Philosophy

5. Sage Patañjali: Yoga

Vyāsadeva, the sage who propounded the sixth stream of Vedic thought, the Vedānta philosophy, concludes that the Supreme Lord is the original person and the cause of all causes; He is transcendental to material nature and cannot be understood by material methods. This is the philosophy taught in the *Śrīmad-Bhagavatam* and followed by Vaiṣṇavas.

Fill out the following table based on your understanding:

Propounding Sage	System of philosophy	What is the ultimate cause according to them?	Do they understand the Ultimate Truth as He is?
1. Gautama/Kaṇāda	Nyāya/Vaiśeṣika		

Propounding Sage	System of philosophy	What is the ultimate cause according to them?	Do they understand the Ultimate Truth as He is?
2. Jaimini	Mīmāṁsā		
3. Kapila (not the son of Devahūti)	Atheistic Sāṅkhya		
4. Aṣṭāvakra/ Śaṅkarācārya	Māyāvāda		
5. Patañjali	Yoga		
6. Vyāsadeva	Vedānta		

Now, read the purport to verse 31 and discuss:

1. All the philosophers study the same Vedic texts. Why then do they come to different conclusions?

2. Which of the sages was able to find the proper cause of everything? What system of study did he follow to come to the correct conclusion?

3. What is this conclusion? How is this conclusion supported by Kṛṣṇa Himself?

4. Who else supports this conclusion?

5. How can we understand and adopt the same conclusion to find the cause of all causes?

Introspective Activity

LESSONS ON FORGIVENESS FROM THE PRACETĀS

In verses 5 to 15 we see how the Pracetās became so angry with the trees that they burned many of them. Soma, the demigod who nurtures the plants and trees, stopped them.

Śrīla Prabhupāda speaks about the effects of anger and the power of forgiveness in the purports to these verses.

Read the short purports to these verses and complete the following statements in the table below.

Possible effects of the Pracetās' anger:

1. By doing *tapasyā* (austerity), the Pracetās were expected to control lower qualities such as _______________ (5). By not controlling it, their austerity would have been viewed as ineffective.

2. By killing the trees in anger, the Pracetās would have made _______________ (8) also suffer, for trees are also required for food. They would not have been considered good rulers.

3. The Pracetās would have displeased the _______________ (13) by not giving protection to the trees, because trees are also _______________ (12) of the rulers.

Why practicing forgiveness to overcome anger was important for the Pracetās:

1. We may have many tendencies in this world, but in the _______________ (9) we should learn how to curb those tendencies.

2. Practicing forgiveness would help the Pracetās develop _______________ (13) and thus please _______________ (13).

3. Overcoming anger by practice of forgiveness would help the Pracetās transcend the _______________ (14).

4. All this was possible only by _______________ (14).

Do you get upset with others, like the Pracetās did, when things don't go your way? Think of a situation when you reacted in anger at something someone did to upset you.

- What were the consequences of your anger at that time?
- How could you have handled the situation differently by either calming down, thinking, or forgiving the person?
- Would the situation have concluded differently had you worked this way?
- What lessons can you draw from this for next time?

Discuss the effects of anger with your group and come up with a few things you can do to react more calmly the next time you are faced with a situation that makes you angry.

Writing and Language Activities

... to help you understand better

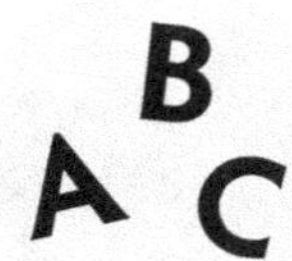

CAN DEVOTEES CONTROL THEIR ANGER EASILY?

In this chapter we learn that a devotee doesn't get angry in difficult situations. Rather, he is engaged in devotional service, which helps him transcend the influence of material nature and thus control his anger.

Directions:

1. Read and think about the statement, "Devotees can control their anger easily."

2. Do you agree or disagree with this statement?

3. Note down some points to justify your viewpoint.
(You can refer to the example of the Pracetās from the chapter. How did they react to a difficult situation?)

You can also take examples from the table below:

AGREE	DISAGREE
<ul><li>Devotees have the knowledge and realization of the Supreme Lord, which help them control their anger.</li><li>Devotees always engage in devotional service and chant the holy name.</li></ul>	<ul><li>Even though the Pracetās were exalted devotees, they couldn't control their anger initially, when they came out of their austerities, what to speak of us!</li><li>We have several examples from the *śāstras* of great devotees who were blinded by anger, like Mahārāja Parīkṣit himself.</li></ul>

AGREE

- Devotees perform severe austerities, which help them transcend the influence of material nature.
- A devotee is humble, compassionate, and tolerant and thus understands that difficult situations are just tests in their service to Kṛṣṇa.

DISAGREE

- Difficult situations momentarily snatch away our intelligence.
- Due to the influence of material nature and the senses, even devotees fall prey to the influence of anger and other negative traits.

4. Now, express your viewpoints with reasoning, either orally or in writing.

Divide your class or group of students into two groups and participate in an oral debate.

What is a debate? A debate is a discussion or an argument on a topic in which different individuals express their viewpoints and reasoning, either by agreeing or disagreeing to a given topic.

Both groups act as opponents, each side choosing one viewpoint and defending it.

(An opponent in a debate is a person who takes the opposite stand and argues against your viewpoints.)

Each person in the group provides a particular argument. Then the persons in the other group present their arguments. At the end, the leader of each group make the conclusive statements.

Use the table below to plan your discussion.

I agree / disagree (select your choice)

My opinion and justification:

1.

2.

3.

4.

5.

Alternatively, you can write an argumentative essay, using your points in the above table. Remember to introduce your topic and the viewpoint you support in the first paragraph and make a strong conclusion in the last paragraph.

POSTER: PROTECT ALL BODIES AS A TEMPLE OF GOD!

Lord Soma advised the Pracetās to protect all living entities because each living body is a temple where the Supersoul resides.

Make a poster to promote the protection of all life on our planet.

Some ideas:
- The present climate crisis by which all life is affected
- Cow protection
- Veganism or vegetarianism
- Any other topic related to animal or environmental protection

A poster is a useful and effective means of making an announcement or an appeal, advertising, or bringing awareness about any issue of people's interest. A poster is usually colorful, attractive, and readable from a distance.

How to make a good poster:

1. Identify the theme.

2. Choose pictures, drawings, or illustrations to portray the theme.

3. You may use bright colors to draw the pictures or outline the poster if you want.

4. You may write short texts or a title to explain the theme (see example).

HAIKU: CAN WE FIND KRṢṆA?

Kṛṣṇa can only be seen and known with a pure consciousness and an attitude of loving devotional service.

Haiku is a form of traditional Japanese poetry. Haiku poems only have three lines, with the pattern 5-7-5. The first line contains five syllables, the second contains seven, and the last line five syllables again. Haiku poems do not usually rhyme.

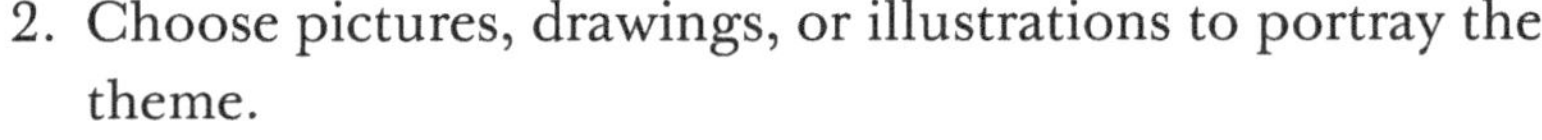

How to write a haiku:

With the help of your teacher, follow the steps below:

Step 1: Brainstorm your ideas

- Choose the topic: in this case "how to find or see Kṛṣṇa."
- Brainstorm words that associate with the topic.
- Note sufficient words which would give you enough ideas for the haiku.

Step 2: Format your haiku

- First line: five syllables
- Second line: seven syllables
- Third line: five syllables
- Write your haiku poem following this format with the help of your word list.

Examples to help you:

Haiku 1:

I | read| ma|ny| books – five syllables
1   2   3   4   5
Fo|llowed| tough| aus|te|ri|ties – seven syllables
1   2   3   4   5 6 7
Could| not| find| Kṛṣ|na – five syllables
  1   2   3   4   5

Haiku 2:

With| pure| con|scious|ness – five syllables
  1   2   3   4   5
And| lo|ving| ser|vice| to| Him – seven syllables
  1   2   3   4   5   6   7
I| can| see| Kṛṣ|na – five syllables
1   2   3   4   5

You may add an illustration at the end of the Haiku to make it more interesting and attractive.

CROSSWORD PUZZLE

Across

1. The king of the trees and predominating deity of the moon.
4. Desiring to burn the trees, the Pracetās generated wind and what from their mouths?
6. Soma asked the Pracetās to control this.
7. Dakṣa executed very difficult austerities near this mountain range.
8. The Lord's eagle carrier.
9. The Supreme Brahman.
10. Kṛṣṇa's earrings resemble this.

Down

1. The Lord within the core of the heart.
2. Prajāpati Pañcajana's daughter.
3. How many sons of Prācīnabarhi performed austerities under the sea?
5. Pleased by Dakṣa's prayers, the Supreme Lord appeared in this holy place.

*Answers spelled with diacritics

CHAPTER 4 ANSWERS

The Controller and the Controlled (*Potential Answers*)
Examples: Video games are pre-programmed and can take decisions as the game progresses, but behind these decisions is the code written by a coding professional. The real decision maker and controller of the game is therefore the professional and not the game character itself; household appliances can function at the press of a button, but they are programmed to function by their inventor in specific ways, so the real controller is not the operator, but the inventor; the internet can help us browse many different websites and go to different spaces virtually at the click of a button, but the browser is not actually the person responsible for all this – the web designers and networking professionals who create and maintain things on the internet are the ones in control of the browser's net experiences.

These and many more examples teach us that there is more to the world than we can see and that we are more controlled than we can imagine, but we think we are more in control of things than we really are. When we accept the reality of our limited control of things even in material aspects, it becomes easy to accept that we are also controlled by the Supreme Lord.

Speculative Confusion Mistaken for Speculative Conclusion
Ultimate cause according to each sage: 1. Atoms and their combinations; 2. Dutiful action; 3. Material nature; 4. Impersonal Brahman; 5. Impersonal Brahman; 6. Lord Kṛṣṇa, the Supreme Personality of Godhead. Except for Vyāsadeva, they all do not understand the Ultimate Truth as He is.

1. Different philosophers come to different conclusions because they study Vedic literatures in their own speculative ways. Some are bewildered about the position of the soul and draw their conclusions, others with a vague idea of the soul may draw another set of conclusions, and others may understand things in yet another way and come to another conclusion. So they differ in opinion because they try to understand the scriptures with their limited and differing mental abilities. Śrīla Prabhupāda points to three more causes why speculative philosophers are not able to understand the Lord through Vedic study: 1) Ignorance 2) Not following authority 3) Envy of the Supreme Lord as He Himself states in the *Bhagavad-gītā* 9.1, 16.18, 18.67, and 18.71.

2. Only Vyāsadeva comes to the correct conclusion, following in the footsteps of authorities and studying the *Vedas* without an envious heart.

3. The conclusion is that the Supreme Lord is the cause of all causes and He is a person transcendental to material nature. Kṛṣṇa supports this conclusion in *Bhagavad-gītā* 10.8: "I am the source of all spiritual and material worlds. Everything emanates from Me. The wise who perfectly know this engage in My devotional service and worship Me with all their hearts."

4. Arjuna supports this conclusion in *Bhagavad-gītā* 10.12–13, and other authorities support this conclusion; e.g., Lord Brahmā in *Śrī Brahma-saṁhitā* 5.1.

5. We can also adopt the same conclusion by understanding the Vedic literature as presented by Śrīla Prabhupāda and the *ācāryas* of the Gauḍīya-vaiṣṇava sampradāya.

Lessons on Forgiveness from the Pracetās
Left side: 1. anger; 2. their subjects and descendants; 3. Supersoul, subjects/citizens.

Right side: 1. human form; 2. equal spiritual vision, Supersoul; 3. modes of nature; 4. devotional service.

Crossword Puzzle
Across: 1. Soma; 4. Fire; 6. Anger; 7. Vindhya; 8. Garuḍa; 9. Kṛṣṇa; 10. Sharks

Down: 1. Supersoul; 2. Asiknī; 3. Ten; 5. Aghamarṣaṇa

5

NĀRADA MUNI CURSED BY PRAJĀPATI DAKṢA

Nārāyaṇa-saras, the great place of pilgrimage on the banks of the river Sindhu, was always filled with the chants of learned sages. Today, the ten thousand sons of Dakṣa, the Haryaśvas, were bathing in the Sindhu's holy waters. They had come to perform austerities and get the Lord's blessings to have children. One by one, they emerged from the river, feeling purified by the water's touch and detached from worldly activities. But their father's order to populate the universe echoed in their minds. They knew they could not escape their duty. They had to fulfill their father's desire.

Nārada Muni watched the Haryaśvas as they performed their austerities and regularly bathed in the river. He could see that they were becoming uninterested in material life. Perhaps he could fan this spark of spiritual awakening, he thought.

One day the Haryaśvas saw Nārada Muni approaching them. They fell to the ground in obeisance, excited to see the great sage. They offered him a seat and then sat around him, eager to hear what had brought him there. Nārada Muni glanced affectionately at the boys – what gentle and kind-hearted souls they all were. "They are ready for liberation," Nārada thought. "Why then should they become entangled in family life?"

Smiling, the revered sage said, "My dear Haryaśvas, you have not seen the extent of this earth. There is a kingdom where only one man lives, and in that place there is a hole. If anyone enters that hole, they will not come out. An unchaste woman, who dresses very attractively, lives there with her husband. In that kingdom there's a river flowing in both directions, a home made of 25 materials, a swan that makes various sounds, and a revolving object made of sharp razors and thunderbolts."

The boys looked at each other, puzzled. Did all this actually exist, or was Nārada Muni trying to tell them something else?

"You haven't seen all this, my dear boys," Nārada Muni continued. "You are inexperienced without much knowledge of how the material nature works. You don't even know your father's actual order, so how will you create progeny?"

system called Pātāla is a hole of hopeless no return. Similarly, if one goes to the Vaikuṇṭha planets, the spiritual world, he does not return to the miserable material world. If there is such a place, what is the use of jumping like monkeys in this temporary material world and not seeing or understanding that topmost place?

The purport of Nārada's words was entering deep into the Haryaśvas' hearts. They began to question the purpose of their existence and their activities.

Nārada Muni had described a prostitute woman. "What could this woman be?" they thought. Then it came to them: the unsteady intelligence. The unsteady intelligence of every living being is like a prostitute who changes dresses just to attract attention. What is the benefit of such foolish intelligence? One should be intelligent enough not to change from one body to another any longer.

And the prostitute's husband? He is the soul who associates with the polluted intelligence. By such association he loses his independence because he follows the intelligence, which brings happiness and distress. This prolongs his materialistic life. If one acts under such conditions, what is the benefit?

It was as if Nārada Muni was revealing the answers to them, one by one. There are four encounters facing the souls who search for pleasure. The first is a river flowing in both directions.

"Now, this is a difficult one," they thought. But the meaning came to them in an instant.

Material nature works in two ways: by creating and destroying. This carries on in a cycle – everything we create for our enjoyment is destroyed, just like this river which flows in one direction and then flows backwards. Someone

The Haryaśvas then understood that Nārada Muni was trying to teach them deep philosophical truths through an allegory. They thought for a while, trying to understand. And then, suddenly, they were able to decipher its meaning.

The "earth" referred to the field of activities. The material body, the result of the living being's actions, is his field of activities. The conditioned soul has received various types of bodies since time immemorial, which has bound him to the material world. If one does not become free from such bondage, what is the benefit of his actions?

The kingdom with only one male referred to the only enjoyer, the Supreme Personality of Godhead. He is independent and observes everything, everywhere, both in the material and spiritual realms. He is beyond this material creation and is full of six opulences. If humans do not care to understand Him through their knowledge and activities but simply work hard day and night for temporary happiness, what is the benefit of their actions?

"The hole of hopelessness – what could that mean?" they thought. Aha! The lower planetary who falls in such a river of *māyā* drowns in the waves and is unable to get out. If he is not able to understand how he is being tossed by the waves but simply engages in activities for sense enjoyment, what is the benefit?

The second encounter is the home of 25 elements, which are the 25 material elements in this world and are part of the Lord's inferior energy. If one is not able to understand the cause of these elements, the Supreme Lord, what benefit will he derive?

The third is the swan. "Now, what can the swan represent?" the Haryaśvas asked themselves. A swan can separate milk from water.

Oh yes! A realized person is like this, who can discriminate matter from spirit. The sounds of the swans refer to exalted persons' explaining the Vedic literatures about bondage and liberation. If one does not study the *śāstras* but engage in temporary activities, what would be the result?

And then sharp razors and thunderbolts? Eternal time moves very sharply, like razors and thunderbolts, and drives the activities of the entire world. If one doesn't study the elements of eternal time and misuses time, what benefit will he derive from performing temporary material activities?

Nārada Muni had asked them how they could defy their own father. They couldn't understand what he had meant. According to them, they were trying to follow the order of their father, Dakṣa. Everything they had been doing was to please their father.

Then it dawned on them. Their first birth was from Dakṣa. But their second birth was having received instructions in the *śāstra* from a bona fide spiritual master. So the *śāstra* was their real father. And what was the *śāstra* saying? They should end their material way of life. If they didn't know the purpose of their father's orders, the *śāstras*, they were ignorant.

They realized that Dakṣa's orders to engage in material activities were not the instructions of their real father.

They gazed at Nārada Muni, who stood smiling in front of them. He strung his *vīṇā*, filling the air with a divine sound. The seven musical notes – *ṣa, ṛ, gā, ma, pa, dha,* and *ni* – originally come from the *Sāma Veda.* Nārada Muni vibrated these notes on his *vīṇā* and sang the Hare Kṛṣṇa *mahā-mantra.* The music captivated his new disciples' minds and hearts. Nārada Muni, with eyes closed, fixed his mind on the Lord's lotus feet. The Haryaśvas could see that he was directly perceiving the Lord. They were convinced of what they now should do. The real purpose of life is to search for and know the ultimate cause of existence, Kṛṣṇa, and engage in His service.

Śukadeva Gosvāmī continued, "My dear King Parīkṣit, the Haryaśvas accepted Nārada Muni as their spiritual master. They deviated from Dakṣa's order. They circumambulated the great sage and followed the path by which one never returns to this world."

"And what about Dakṣa? What did he do when he found out?" asked Mahārāja Parīkṣit anxiously.

"Oh, Nārada Muni himself gave Dakṣa the news, and he just lamented. Lord Brahmā had to come and console him. Thereafter, Dakṣa got one thousand more children, the Savalāśvas, from his wife Pāñcajanī.

"They also went to Nārāyaṇa-saras to perform austerities. They bathed in the holy river, and by its touch their hearts were cleansed. They chanted *mantras* to Lord Nārāyaṇa and drank only water

and ate only air. Nārada Muni observed them and approached them as he had done with their brothers."

Parīkṣit Mahārāja could not bear the suspense any longer. "Did he convert them too?" he asked, the impatience evident in his voice.

Śukadeva Gosvāmī explained that Nārada Muni spoke to them in the same way.

"O sons of Dakṣa," Nārada Muni said, "please hear my instructions carefully. I know you are very affectionate to your elder brothers, so you should follow their path. A brother aware of religious principles should follow the footsteps of his elder brothers and attain the planet of the demigods, and better still, the abode of the Supreme Lord."

Nārada Muni's words pierced their hearts. Just like their brothers, they abandoned the idea of producing children and devoted their lives to Kṛṣṇa. They thus received the Lord's mercy, and just as nights that have gone west, they have not returned till now.

Dakṣa saw inauspicious signs. When he heard that his second group of sons had renounced everything and had followed the path of their brothers according to Nārada's instructions, he almost fainted. He was furious at Nārada.

He confronted the great sage. With lips quivering in rage, he said, "Alas, Nārada Muni, you wear the dress of a saintly person, but you are no saint. Even though I am in *gṛhastha* life, I am a saintly person. By showing my sons the path of renunciation, you've done me a great injustice."

Nārada Muni looked at Dakṣa with eyes of

compassion. He had always intended to deliver Dakṣa from the blind well of household life just as he had delivered King Prācīnabarhi, the Pracetās, and Dakṣa's sons.

"You've induced my sons to neglect their obligations," Dakṣa continued. "Because they haven't fulfilled the three debts – to the demigods, the saints, and their father – you have hindered their good fortune.

"You claim to be an associate of Lord Viṣṇu, but in fact you're defaming the Supreme Lord by committing violence against other living beings. You created a mentality of renunciation in my innocent boys even before they were ready for it. You are shameless and have no compassion!

"All the Lord's devotees are very kind except you! You become enemies of those who are not your enemies. Are you not ashamed of posing as a devotee?"

Nārada Muni simply smiled, which seemed to infuriate Dakṣa even more.

"Don't think that awakening renunciation in my boys will make them detached from the material world," Dakṣa said. "Knowledge, not premature renunciation, will help them become detached from this world."

Nārada continued to smile, knowing well that he had indeed awakened true renunciation in the hearts of Dakṣa's sons through devotional service.

"It's true that material enjoyment is the cause of unhappiness," said Dakṣa, "but one cannot give up enjoyment unless one experiences how much suffering it can give. If you try to change someone's mind to become renounced, it won't work so well. They need to have personal experience of suffering to become renounced."

Nārada Muni grinned and shook his head slightly. He understood that material nature is so strong that although a man suffers at every step, he will never stop trying to enjoy. One can only renounce material enjoyment by the mercy and association of the pure devotee.

"I have performed all kinds of sacrifice and have followed all Vedic injunctions," Dakṣa continued. "Yet, for no reason, you've displeased me by misguiding my sons. Maybe I can tolerate this once, but twice? No! You are simply a rascal who misbehaves toward others."

Nārada grimaced but remained silent.

"I curse you, Nārada!" Dakṣa shouted. "You may travel all over the universe, but you won't be able to reside anywhere."

Nārada Muni bowed his head. With folded palms he said, "*Tad bāḍham* – so be it. I accept your curse."

Nārada Muni could have counteracted the curse, but he didn't. He could have left the place when he was insulted, but he didn't. He tolerated and stayed there for a while, hoping that Dakṣa's anger would dissipate and he would repent. He was hoping that he could still deliver transcendental knowledge to Dakṣa.

But Dakṣa's fault-finding mentality would not make him listen to transcendental knowledge.

Such was the power of the remnants of his offense to the greatest Vaiṣṇava, Lord Śiva.

Seeing that Dakṣa was not inclined to apologize or repent, Nārada Muni lifted his *vīṇā* to his shoulder and darted towards the heavens. He was ready to deliver more souls wherever they may be. In fact, Dakṣa's curse had turned out to be a blessing!

Themes and Key Messages

Please go through this table of themes and key messages, with corresponding verses, and discuss each topic further.

THEMES	REFERENCES	KEY MESSAGES
The living entity is encaged in a body and has no interest in how to become free. One's duty is to release oneself from this bondage.	6.5.11–13	Nārada Muni expressed to the Haryaśvas that they are inexperienced boys and do not understand how the material nature works. The living entities work hard all day and night for sense gratification without knowledge of the soul, which is encaged within the body. Like animals, they blindly act in a particular body for some flickering happiness, which only ends in misery. They try to imitate the Lord's position as the supreme enjoyer and therefore enter the "hole of hopelessness," the hellish life. Therefore, in the human form one should work hard to understand the Supreme Personality of Godhead and become free from the bondage of birth, death, old age, disease and not return to the miserable material world.
The real purpose of life is to search for and know the ultimate cause of existence, Kṛṣṇa, and engage in His service.	6.5.14–17	When one's intelligence is polluted, like that of a prostitute, one does not turn his attention toward Kṛṣṇa but simply changes bodies in the material world. One who follows the dictations of his material consciousness and intelligence cannot be happy because he simply chases after *māyā*. He is thus forced to accept various material bodies. The Haryaśvas realized that they should focus their intelligence and mind on Kṛṣṇa and engage in His loving service if they want to become purified and go back to Godhead.

THEMES	REFERENCES	KEY MESSAGES
One should study and follow the instructions of the Vedic literatures, one's real father, and use one's time for spiritual realization.	6.5.18–20	The material world is comprised of both matter and spirit, and the *Vedas* explain both. But a swanlike person can separate one from the other and accepts only the essence of the *Vedas*, which is spiritual. The *śāstra* is one's real father; therefore, the Kṛṣṇa consciousness movement presents the essence of the Vedic literatures in many languages all over the world to guide people how to end one's material way of life. In this way one should use one's time for spiritual realization and not misuse it. Even a moment cannot be returned in exchange for millions of dollars.
Even if the spiritual master is condemned by others, he does not give up his mission of delivering the conditioned souls in the material world.	6.5.21–24, 36	The Haryaśvas accepted Nārada Muni as their spiritual master and had faith in his instructions and renounced everything. When their father, Dakṣa, heard about this, he lamented, yet Nārada Muni was not affected. He was fixed in his duty to deliver the fallen souls from material life by giving them the holy name. Similarly, as followers of Nārada Muni in the Gauḍīya-Mādhva-sampradāya, we should follow his instructions to chant the holy names, surrender to Kṛṣṇa, and give this knowledge to others. [Like Nārada Muni, Śrīla Prabhupāda was not swayed in his determination to guide others in spiritual life and renunciation despite the protests of his disciples' angry parents.]
One who is fully surrendered to Kṛṣṇa is freed from all debts.	6.5.37	There are three debts that everyone owes: to the great saints, the demigods, and one's father (or parents). Dakṣa accused Nārada of obstructing his son's progress in this world because they were still indebted to these persons. However, Dakṣa did not understand the great service of Nārada Muni to his sons. When one fully surrenders to the Lord, one is freed from all debts to others; when one satisfies the Lord, everyone else is satisfied.
One can only become renounced from material life if one's knowledge is awakened and if one gets the association of a pure devotee.	6.5.40–41	Dakṣa accused Nārada Muni that he had not elevated his sons in knowledge and therefore they had artificially and prematurely renounced everything. But this is not true. Nārada Muni had given them transcendental knowledge and then they automatically renounced the world. Without such knowledge one cannot give up attachment for material enjoyment. Dakṣa also expressed that his sons needed to experience the happiness and distress of this world to renounce, but Śrīla Prabhupāda comments that *māyā* is very strong and one may not stop trying to enjoy even if one suffers. One can only renounce material enjoyment by the mercy and association of a pure devotee.

Higher-Thinking Questions

Now try to deepen your understanding of this chapter by delving into Śrīla Prabhupāda's purports and reflecting on the following questions:

1. Nārada Muni uses an allegory to teach the Haryaśvas valuable lessons just as he did to their great-grandfather, King Prācīnabarhi. Do you think this was an effective method to teach them these valuable truths? Why do you think they could immediately understand the meaning of the allegory unlike their great-grandfather?

2. Why are the scriptures described as one's real father in verse 20? What is a student's second birth?

3. In the purport to verse 30, Śrīla Prabhupāda explains that Nārada Muni instructed Vyāsadeva to write the *Śrīmad-Bhāgavatam*. Why did Nārada do this? How is the *Bhāgavatam* the topmost *śāstra*?

4. Śrīla Prabhupāda frequently comments in his purports in this chapter that parents should not hinder their children from making spiritual advancement and join the Kṛṣṇa consciousness movement. What does this indicate of the struggles Śrīla Prabhupāda faced with his disciples' parents? Is it any different today? Explain.

5. How does Śrīla Prabhupāda defeat Dakṣa's argument in verse 41 that only after experiencing suffering in householder life one can renounce? What, does he say, causes one to become renounced from material life?

6. In the purport to verse 43 Śrīla Prabhupāda expresses that he also had been cursed like Nārada Muni to never have a permanent place of residence. How do you think this worked in his favor and in the favor of Nārada Muni?

7. Why do you think Dakṣa did not repent for his actions and did not become a pure Vaiṣṇava as Nārada Muni had hoped? (See verse 44 purport.)

8. Nārada Muni accepted the curse and stayed in Dakṣa's presence for some time, giving him a chance to give up his anger and repent. What does this indicate about Nārada's character and qualities? What example does Śrīla Prabhupāda use in verse 44 purport to illustrate a pure devotee's compassion?

ACTIVITIES

In this section you will find many exciting things to do. These activities will get you thinking, moving, drawing, and having loads of fun.

Analogy Activity

... to bring out the scholar in you

TEN STATEMENTS THAT CHANGED TEN THOUSAND LIVES

In verses 6 to 20, Nārada Muni again uses an allegory to preach to more descendants of Svāyambhuva Manu. As you've learned, an allegory is a story that can be interpreted to reveal a hidden meaning. The Haryaśvas were learned enough to understand the allegory, and they eventually left for the west, to live a life of austerity to please the Supreme Lord. Let us look at the allegory and try to understand what the Haryaśvas understood.

Nārada Muni spoke in allegorical form on ten subjects to the Haryaśvas.

Ten topics in Nārada Muni's allegory:

1. You have not seen the extremities of the earth.

2. There is a kingdom in which only one man lives.

3. There is a hole from which, having entered, no one emerges.

4. There is an unchaste woman dressing attractively to get attention.

5. The unchaste woman has a husband who is not happy.

6. There is a river flowing in both the directions and flowing swiftly near the banks.

7. There is also a house made of 25 elements.

8. There is a speaking swan that vibrates various sounds.

9. There is an automatically revolving object made of sharp razors and thunderbolts.

10. How will you procreate without knowing your actual father's orders?

The Haryaśvas made the following notes of their understanding. Match each note to each of
the above points. Then write down in simple words what the Haryaśvas understood that helped
them leave to the forest to worship the Supreme Lord.

1
Eternal time revolves
sharply like a shaft
and moves the
activities of the
whole world.

2
The hole is a place
from where there
is no return: either
Pātāla or Vaikuṇṭha.

3
Material nature (*māyā*)
works by creating and
destroying, which is
compared to backward
and forward motion.

4
There is no
end to the false
designations that
the *jīva* accepts in
material bodies.

5
The actual father is
Lord Kṛṣṇa, who
desires liberation of all
jīvas from the material
world even more than
procreation.

6
When intelligence
becomes unsteady like
this, the *jīva* is not
happy even if it changes
bodies and tries to enjoy
in different ways.

7
In the material world,
the *jīva* has unsteady
intelligence, which
tempts a person from
shifting from one
enjoyment to another.

8
The *śāstras* that
discriminate between
matter and spirit and
explain the means
of bondage and
liberation.

9
The Supreme Lord
is the only enjoyer
in all of creation; He
is fully independent
and transcendental.

10
The Supreme Lord
is the reservoir
of 25 elements.
He controls them
and causes their
manifestation.

Artistic Activity

MONOTYPE ART: NĀRADA MUNI

A monotype is a printmaking technique. The artist applies paint or printmaking ink on a flat sheet of metal, glass, or plastic. The painted image is then transferred to paper either manually or by press. In this activity you will create a monotype print of Nārada Muni wandering in the universe for everyone's benefit.

What you will need:
- A hard surface like plexiglass or sturdy cardboard of size 6 inches x 8 inches or slightly larger.
- The template of Nārada Muni. Cut along the lines as shown in Image 1.
- 2 to 3 plastic sheets of the same size as your hard surface.
- Masking tape
- Black paint or black water-soluble ink; e.g., Speedball® block printing ink
- 3 brushes: sizes 2, 4, and 6
- Few earbuds
- Black ink pen
- Scissors
- 2 to 3 good quality drawing paper, same size as the hard surface
- Water to clean the brushes or to wet the paint
- White acrylic paint for corrections or embellishments

Steps:

1. Lay the cut drawing of Nārada Muni on your hard surface (Image 1).

2. Place the plastic sheet over the drawing and secure it with masking tape all around (Image 2).

3. Think about the background of your print. Where is Nārada Muni? Dakṣa's palace, the banks of Nārāyaṇa-saras, or the cosmic sky?

4. Take some paint on a palette or paper plate. Keep your brushes and drawing paper sheets ready. All application of ink must be done within few seconds, and the removal of ink to create the background should also be done very quickly before the paint dries up.

5. Apply black ink around the silhouette of Nārada Muni swiftly, using the appropriate brush (Image 3).

6. With the number 2 brush, quickly mark the *vīṇā*. Now wet the earbuds, and from the black background, start removing some ink to reveal the cosmic sky or whatever background you want to create (Image 4).

7. Place your drawing paper above the painted surface. With your palms, gently press so that the ink transfers on your drawing paper.

8. Gently lift the paper starting from the bottom right corner (Image 5).

9. Let the ink dry completely. It usually takes 5 to 10 minutes. Now you can add the finer details, like the facial features, hair, and *vīṇā* details with a black pen.

10. Use the white acrylic paint to correct any smudged ink or to embellish your art. Trim the print to get clean edges (Image 6).

11. Your Monotype is ready for framing!

Helpful hints:
- You can wipe your hard surface with a wet cloth and use it to make another print.
- If your paint dries before you can pull out your print, try spraying your drawing paper with water before you lay it on the inked surface.
- Printmaking is somewhat unpredictable; you may have to try more than once to get a satisfactory result.

Image 1

Image 2

Image 3

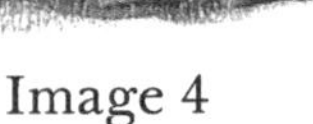

Image 4

Image 5

Image 6

Template

Introspective Activity

THE POWER OF CONTEMPLATION

In verses 6 to 21 we see how Nārada Muni preached to the Haryaśvas and how they contemplated on his instructions and came to a conclusion.

Here is what they did:

(Note: You may create a small story board for the below statements.)

1. They were simple, obedient sons who had come to Nārāyaṇa-saras on the order of their father.

2. They were already performing austerities on the banks of the Sindhu River and had become purified.

3. They were thinking of using the result of their austerity to acquire qualifications to increase the population of the world.

4. In a purified state they received instructions from Nārada Muni about the purpose of their austerity and life itself.

5. They understood, reflected, and concluded about why austerity should be done.

6. They rejected their father's purpose, accepted Nārada Muni's purpose, and became *sannyāsīs*.

Now think about how introspection helped the Haryaśvas change their purpose from material to spiritual. What result did they achieve for the same austerities because of this?

Next, think about the power of spiritual knowledge. Can you think of any incident in your life when you applied spiritual knowledge and it changed your understanding or action, leading to different results? Discuss in turns with your *Bhāgavatam* group.

Action Activity

  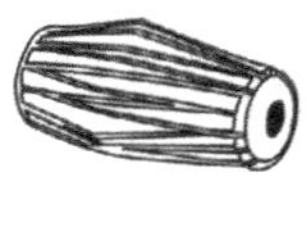    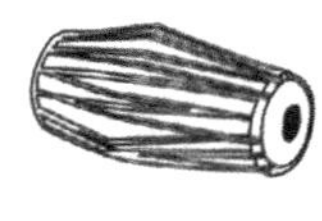 

FOLLOWING IN THE FOOTSTEPS OF NĀRADA MUNI

    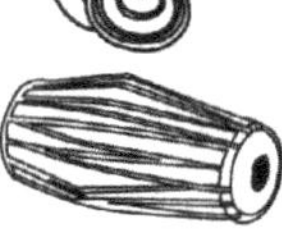 

In this chapter Śrīla Prabhupāda emphasizes that the members of the Kṛṣṇa consciousness movement should follow the footsteps of Nārada Muni by chanting the transcendental vibration Hare Kṛṣṇa, Hare Kṛṣṇa, Kṛṣṇa Kṛṣṇa, Hare Hare/ Hare Rāma, Hare Rāma, Rāma Rāma, Hare Hare and go everywhere to deliver the fallen souls by vibrating the Hare Kṛṣṇa *mahā-mantra* and the instructions of the scriptures. This will please the Supreme Personality of Godhead.

The following activity is to encourage you to have monthy/ yearly goals to increase your desire to chant the holy names and share the gift of the holy name and the scriptures with others. *Nāma ruci* (taste for the holy name) and *jīva dayā* (compassion for the living entities) is the essence of religion.

Discuss with an accountability partner about your goals and note them in a book. Meet with him or her every month to review different checkpoints in the timeline and how to achieve them. You should do the same for your partner's goals. For example, if your partner has a goal to memorize four verses for the month, check to see if their goals were met, and if not, how their goals could be achieved.

For *japa* and *kīrtana*, you can have goals like:

1. Increase concentration on hearing the holy names.

2. Chant with an intention to please Kṛṣṇa.

3. Do *japa* early in the morning.

4. Inquire from senior devotees on how to improve *japa* and *kīrtana*.

For preaching services, the goals could be:

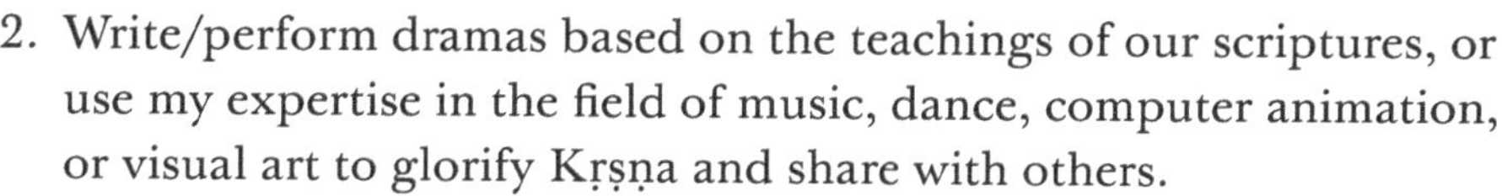

1. Memorize important verses and their translations.

2. Write/perform dramas based on the teachings of our scriptures, or use my expertise in the field of music, dance, computer animation, or visual art to glorify Kṛṣṇa and share with others.

3. Help with book distribution at the local community or temple.

4. Associate with devotees who serve the preaching mission and learn from their experiences.

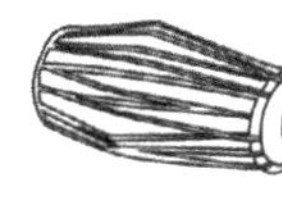

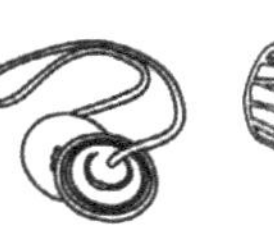
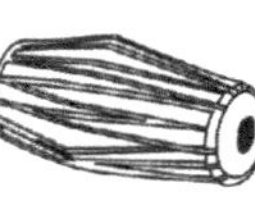

Critical-Thinking Activity

... to bring out the spiritual investigator in you

ONE MASTER, ONE PURPOSE, TWO PATHS

Dakṣa and Nārada represent two missions of the Supreme Lord: to increase the population of the material world, and to liberate the population of the material world. Both these missions, however, have the same purpose – to give the conditioned souls in the material world a chance to understand their relationship with Him and go back to the spiritual world and serve Him.

Nārada Muni understands that both these missions have the same purpose; he also understands that the second mission is dearer to the Lord. He therefore goes all over the universe, looking for candidates to liberate. Dakṣa, however, understands and tries to execute the first mission; he does not understand the purpose of the Lord behind creation. Therefore, he is distressed when Nārada liberates two sets of his sons. So he curses Nārada.

Directions:

- Look at the table on the next page. It contains Dakṣa's statements to Nārada. Each of these statements is rooted in Dakṣa's incomplete understanding of the *śāstric* version and purpose. Nārada's understanding, however, is very clear.

- Divide the class into two groups. Assign to each group a group mentor, who will lead the discussions. The first group will research the purports indicated to find out Dakṣa's misunderstanding which gave rise to these statements, and the second group will research the same purports for the proper understanding of *śāstra*, which Śrīla Prabhupāda, a representative of Nārada, provides.
- Then set up a group discussion with both sides presenting their views. Your group mentor or class teacher should help you come to a proper conclusion that is in line with the disciplic succession.

DAKṢA'S STATEMENTS	DAKṢA'S MISUNDERSTANDING	NĀRADA'S UNDERSTANDING
You are a *sannyāsī*, but you are not a saint. I am a *gṛhastha*, but I am a saint. (36)		
You have obstructed my sons' progress toward good fortune because they are still indebted to the saintly persons, the demigods, and their father. (37)		
You needlessly created a mentality of renunciation in innocent boys, and therefore you are shameless and devoid of compassion. (38)		
Although you wear the dress of a devotee, you create enmity with people who are not your enemies, or you break friendship and create enmity between friends. (39)		
Unless full knowledge is awakened, simply changing dresses as you have done cannot possibly bring detachment. (40)		

DAKṢA'S STATEMENTS	DAKṢA'S MISUNDERSTANDING	NĀRADA'S UNDERSTANDING
Material enjoyment ultimately causes unhappiness, but one can't give it up unless one has experienced the suffering it gives. (41)		
I am known as a *gṛhavrata*. Unfortunately, you have greatly displeased me by misguiding my sons, for no reason, to the path of renunciation. (42)		
You may travel all over the universe, but I curse you to have no residence anywhere. (43)		

Writing and Language Activities

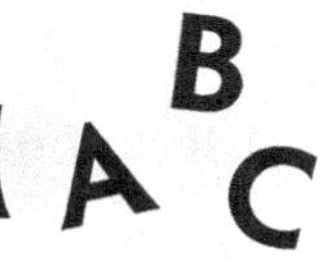

PREACHING STRATEGIES

Nārada Muni delivered many kings from the dynasty of Svāyambhuva Manu: Priyavrata, Uttānapāda, Dhruva, Prācīnabarhi, the Pracetās, and the Haryaśvas and Savalāśvas. Nārada Muni, being an expert preacher, used different approaches according to the time and circumstances. In this chapter, Nārada Muni utilizes three different strategies toward the Haryaśvas, Savalāśvas, and Dakṣa. Nārada Muni speaks an allegory suitable to inspire the Haryaśvas, and he uses the natural family affinity of the Savalāśvas to follow their brothers. To deliver Dakṣa, Nārada Muni takes advantage of a suitable time to give his mercy. He tolerates Dakṣa's accusations and curse, thinking that this would relieve his anger and he would repent. Unfortunately, Dakṣa does not take advantage of Nārada Muni's grace because of his fault-finding mentality, which was the result of his past offense to Lord Śiva.

Write a paragraph describing three other preaching activities of Nārada Muni and his insightful methods you have studied so far. For example: How did he guide Dhruva to achieve the audience of the Supreme Lord? How did he test Dhruva's determination?

Then write another paragraph on Śrīla Prabhupāda's preaching strategies despite all the obstacles he faced. For example: How did Śrīla Prabhupāda first approach the hippies in the USA? How did he inspire and uplift people during that time?

SHAPE POETRY: THE SWAN

Shape poetry is a poem presented in a shape of the thing it describes. It is also called a concrete poem. For example, if you want to compose a poem on a butterfly, you could write the words in the drawing of a butterfly, or you could write the words in a way that it forms the outline of a butterfly.

Nārada Muni has given wonderful instructions in his allegory to the Haryaśvas. The subjects earth, river, time, and swan are suitable for shape poetry. In this activity you will compose a shape poem of a swan mentioned in verse 18 and purport.

Helpful hints:
- The speaking swan is the *śāstras* or persons that describe the Lord.
- The swan depicts bondage and liberation through transcendental talks.
- The swan is able to distinguish spirit from matter.
- The swan depicts grace, beauty, love, and purity.

Directions:

1. Read verse 18 and purport and make some notes on what you like to convey through your poem. It could be a rhyming poem or one that doesn't rhyme.

2. Finalize your composition.

3. In your notebook trace the template of the swan on the next page with pencil.

4. On the pencil outline begin writing the words of your poem so that the words form the outline of the swan (see images on the next page). Alternatively, write your poem within the outline of the swan so that the words form the shape of the swan (research online examples).

5. Now erase the pencil outline to reveal only the words of your poem that make up the swan.

O, beautiful white swan, gliding down the nectar-lake.
...don't...
The Supreme is revealed, on path back home,
sporting in stems of lotuses...
divine sounds you make, reach my heart, doubts and fear depart.
O, beautiful white swan, gliding down the nectar-lake.
...don't...
Supreme, revealed, on path back home,
sporting the nectar-lake.

CHAPTER 5 ANSWERS

Ten Statements that Changed Ten Thousand Lives
point 1 – note 4; point 2 – note 9; point 3 – note 2;
point 4 – note 7; point 5 – note 6; point 6 – note 3;
point 7 – note 10; point 8 – note 8; point 9 – note 1;
point 10 – note 5.

Summary of the Haryaśvas' understanding: The
Supreme Lord is the only enjoyer and the only object
of worship in creation. The *śāstras* help us understand
His personality and ultimate will, which is to liberate
the *jīvas* from the clutches of birth and death. The *jīva*
is caught in this cycle because he wants to enjoy. He
does not realize the power of time or the nature of this
world; with an unsteady intelligence he simply moves
from one form of life to another. We should focus our
mind and intelligence to serve the Lord and please
Him, which will end this cycle of birth and death and
take us back to Godhead.

One Master, One Purpose, Two Paths
Dakṣa: 36: A saint should lead a man to live a full
life, including *gṛhastha* life. One who directly leads
people to *sannyāsa* is not really following the *śāstric*
path; 37: The son of a *brāhmaṇa* must undergo celibacy
(*brahmacarya*) to clear his debts to the saintly persons,
perform ritualistic ceremonies to clear his debts to the
demigods, and beget children to become free from his
debts to his father. One cannot attain liberation unless
one fulfils these obligations; 38: Nārada induced his
sons to prematurely deprive themselves of material
enjoyments and therefore was merciless to them. 39:
Nārada had made himself an enemy of Dakṣa for
influencing the Haryaśvas and Savalāśvas from Dakṣa's
purpose. Nārada was also responsible for breaking the
relationship between Dakṣa and his sons; 40: Changing
dress from white to saffron and doing whatever you
want won't make you renounced; one should enter
the renounced order with full knowledge; 41: While
developing spiritual knowledge, it is better to have
personal experience of the misery of false material
happiness than renouncing everything; in this way one
can become genuinely detached; 42: He did not take

action the first time, but Nārada had done the same
thing twice. He wanted to prove that he was a greater
sādhu than Nārada and that even a saintly person like
him could not tolerate such behavior twice; 43: To a
gṛhastha like Dakṣa, this seemed like a curse as one
cannot enjoy adequately without a proper residence.

Nārada: 36: People of all orders, whether *gṛhastha*
or *sannyāsī*, should perform devotional service. A
gṛhastha also follows the path of renunciation by
giving up many bad habits; therefore Vedic literature
teaches detachment, either gradually by becoming
a *vānaprastha* or directly adopting *sannyāsa* and
performing austerities to please the Supreme Lord; 37:
The *śāstras* also say that if one fully surrenders to Kṛṣṇa,
Mukunda, the giver of liberation, one is freed from all
debts. Even if one does not repay his debts, he is freed
from all debts if he renounces the material world for
the sake of the Supreme Personality of Godhead; 38:
A pure devotee is not interested in yogic perfection,
travel to higher planetary systems, or oneness with
Brahman. He is interested only in rendering service
to the Personality of Godhead, which is the ultimate
goal of life; 39: Nārada never tried to create enemies,
but only showed sincere souls the path back to
Godhead. Devotees are friends of every living entity
but are misunderstood to be enemies; 40: Nārada had
awakened the sense of detachment and renunciation
in Dakṣa's sons through full knowledge, not through
sentiment; 41: It is not a fact that because material
enjoyment involves so many painful conditions one
will automatically become detached. *Māyā* is so strong
that even if someone suffers he will try to enjoy. One
needs the blessings of a pure devotee like Nārada Muni
to become detached; 42: Nārada could do this not
twice but many times more to put souls on the path
of devotional service. He could tolerate many parents
like Dakṣa. His aim was to please the Lord, not parents
like Dakṣa; 43: To a *sannyāsī* like Nārada, this was the
greatest boon because it gave him an opportunity to
preach far and wide.

6

Dakṣa finally did repent, but it was too late. He looked around anxiously but couldn't see Nārada anywhere. What had he done? he thought. He had just cursed one of the greatest devotees of the Lord, the spiritual master and well-wisher of many of his ancestors. How foolish! His fault-finding mentality and pride had made him lose his composure and his respect for Kṛṣṇa's pure devotee. He couldn't go on, he thought.

Lord Brahmā was very concerned. If Dakṣa would not continue to populate the world, what would be the fate of the material universe? Lord Brahmā convinced Dakṣa to continue his duty. This time Dakṣa decided he was not going to lose any of his sons. "So better not to have any sons," he thought. Dakṣa smiled and then laughed to himself: "Yes, I will have daughters,

chaste and devoted daughters, who will not be converted by anyone. In fact, women are not meant for the renounced order of life, so Nārada doesn't stand a chance."

And so, Dakṣa had 60 daughters from his wife Asiknī. How happy and relieved he was that his daughters would continue his dynasty. He knew that nothing could stop his plans now. His daughters loved their father and obeyed him. Dakṣa gave them in marriage to exalted personalities. He gave ten daughters to Yamarāja, twenty-seven daughters to Candra, the moon-god, two to Aṅgirā, two to Kṛśāśva, two to Bhūta, and seventeen to Kaśyapa.

Now Dakṣa was satisfied. He was certain that these great persons would take good care of his daughters and create progeny, which would be Dakṣa's descendants. And sure enough, one by one, they had many children, but not ordinary children. Some of Dakṣa's descendants were kings and even demigods, including the Mauhūrtikas who could deliver the reactions to the living beings' actions at their respective times.

The daughters gave birth to lust, the eight Vasus, Harṣa (happiness), Śoka (lamentation), and Bhaya (fear). They gave birth to various towns and cities, Skanda (Kārttikeya), and Śiśumāra, an expansion of the Supreme Lord. Viśvakarmā, the celestial architect, became their descendant, along with two Manus and their descendants. One daughter gave birth to Pañcayāma, the span of day, who awakens all living entities to material activities.

Śukadeva Gosvāmī continued to describe the progeny of Dakṣa's daughters:

Dakṣa's two daughters who married Bhūta had ten million Rudras, including the eleven principal Rudras and a host of ghosts and hobgoblins. Imagine that!

The descendants of Dakṣa's two daughters with Aṅgirā were the Pitās and the Atharvāṅgirasa Veda.

From Kṛśāśva and two of Dakṣa's daughters came the great sages Dhūmaketu, Vedaśirā, Devala, Vayuna, and Manu.

The 27 daughters who married the moon-god could not bear any children.

"Why was that?" asked Parīkṣit Mahārāja.

"Oh, it's a long story," said Śukadeva Gosvāmī. "Because the moon-god had favored one wife and neglected the others, Dakṣa cursed him with a disease, preventing him from having children. However, afterwards the moon-god pacified Dakṣa with sweet words and he regained the portions of light he had lost during the disease. Thus the moon loses its shining power during the dark fortnight and manifests its light again in the bright fortnight."

"Aha! Fascinating!" thought Parīkṣit Mahārāja. He asked, "And what about Kaśyapa's descendants with the 17 daughters of Dakṣa?"

"Through Kaśyapa, the first four daughters gave birth to different living beings – many kinds of birds, locusts, varieties of serpents, and two very special descendants," said Śukadeva Gosvāmī, widening his eyes.

"Oh, who were they?" asked Parīkṣit, his eyes alight with curiosity.

"Garuḍa, the carrier of Lord Viṣṇu; and Aruṇa, the chariot driver of the sun-god."

"Jaya!" exclaimed Parīkṣit Mahārāja. "And what about the 13 other wives of Kaśyapa? Whom did they give birth to?"

"From their wombs the population of the entire universe has come. They are the mothers of the universe, and their names are very auspicious to hear: Aditi, Diti, Danu, Kāṣṭhā, Ariṣṭā, Surasā, Ilā, Muni, Krodhavaśā, Tāmrā, Surabhi, Saramā, and Timi.

"From Timi all the aquatics took birth, and from Saramā ferocious animals like tigers and lions took birth.

"From the womb of Surabhi the buffalo, cow, and other animals with cloven hooves took birth, and from Tāmrā the eagles, vultures, and other large birds of prey came about. From the womb of Muni the angels took birth.

"From Krodhavaśā came the serpents and the mosquitoes. From Ilā were born various trees and creepers, and from Surasā, the Rākṣasas and bad spirits were born.

"The Gandharvas were born from Ariṣṭā, and animals like horses were born from Kāṣṭhā. From the womb of Danu came 61 sons of whom 18 were prominent. These sons in turn had daughters who got married to suitable husbands and had children. One of their descendants was Rāhu and the one hundred Ketus who attained positions in the influential planets. In this way, the population of the universe grew.

"Lord Brahmā instructed Kaśyapa to marry two of Danu's granddaughters." Seeing Parīkṣit's startled expression, Śukadeva Gosvāmī continued, "I know, how could Kaśyapa marry

his own descendants? Ordinarily it would be considered improper and inappropriate, but his actions cannot be criticized nor imitated because he wasn't an ordinary soul and he was following superior authority. So from these two wives he had 60,000 sons. They were very strong and expert fighters whose aim was to disturb the sacrifices of great sages.

"My dear King, when your grandfather, Arjuna, went to the heavenly planets, he alone killed all these demons, and this is why King Indra became extremely affectionate toward him."

King Parīkṣit raised his eyebrows, surprised by all this information. "And what about Dakṣa's prominent daughters, Diti and Aditi? Who were their progeny?" he asked.

"Aditi had 12 prominent sons, including the sun-god Vivasvān, Pūṣā, whom we've learned about before . . ."

"Oh yes!" exclaimed Parīkṣit Mahārāja, "When Lord Śiva was angry at Dakṣa, Pūṣā had laughed at Lord Śiva and shown his teeth. Therefore he lost his teeth and had to live by eating only ground flour."

"Yes!" said Śukadeva Gosvāmī, smiling. "And Aditi's most prominent son was Urukrama."

"That is Lord Vāmanadeva, the plenary expansion of the Supreme Personality of Godhead Nārāyaṇa!" Parīkṣit Mahārāja exclaimed.

Śukadeva Gosvāmī smiled and nodded. "From Aditi's sons came three Manus along with two sets of twins: Yamarāja and the river Yamunā, and the Aśvinī-kumāras. Aditi's sons also fathered various learned scholars, the human species who are meant for self-examination, and the powerful brothers Sanniveśa and Viśvarūpa, who were born of Prajāpati Tvaṣṭā's marriage with Racanā, the daughter of a demon."

Parīkṣit Mahārāja's eyes opened wide. "How wonderful that the Lord had arranged to populate the universe in this way," he thought.

"Although Viśvarūpa was the son of a demon's daughter," Śukadeva Gosvāmī continued, "the demigods accepted him as their priest on the order of Lord Brahmā. You see, the demigod's spiritual master, Bṛhaspati, had abandoned them when they disrespected him."

Themes and Key Messages

Please go through this table of themes and key messages, with corresponding verses, and discuss each topic further.

THEMES	REFERENCES	KEY MESSAGES
A wife shares the results of her husband's pious activities.	6.6.1	Women are not meant for the renounced order of life; therefore, this time Dakṣa had daughters instead of sons so that Nārada wouldn't be able to convince them to take to the renounced order. A wife who is faithful and chaste to a good husband shares the results of his pious activities. If the husband achieves liberation, she will be liberated with him.

THEMES	REFERENCES	KEY MESSAGES
The secondary creation initiated by the Prajāpatis are under the direction and mercy of the Supreme Lord.	6.6.14, 38–39	Even though the Lord is not directly involved in the secondary creation, He arranges that the creation takes place nicely under the order of Lord Brahmā and the Prajāpatis, including Dakṣa. The Lord Himself descended as a plenary expansion, Lord Vāmana, the son of Aditi, to perform His pastimes and reclaim lost souls. He also appeared as Śiśumāra, an expansion of the Lord.
The union of Dakṣa's 60 daughters with various exalted personalities filled the entire universe with various kinds of living entities.	6.6.21–22, 25–31	The secondary creation, headed by Lord Brahmā and the Prajāpatis, including Prajāpati Dakṣa, brought about various living entities, such as human beings, demigods, demons, beasts, birds, and serpents. The 17 daughters who were married to Kaśyapa became the mothers of the universe because they were mainly responsible for populating the universe with various kinds of living beings. Thus living beings did not evolve as modern science may proclaim, but were created by the daughters of Dakṣa.
Lord Brahmā created the human species, which are endowed with a capacity for self-examination.	6.6.42	From Aditi's descendants came sons who knew what to do and what not to do. From the sons who were interested in pursuing spiritual life, Brahmā produced the human race. Humans have the capacity for discrimination and self-realization.

Higher-Thinking Questions

Now try to deepen your understanding of this chapter by delving into Śrīla Prabhupāda's purports and reflecting on the following questions:

1. In this chapter many of the descendants of Dakṣa's daughters seem fantastical. From your knowledge of Canto 5, how can you understand that the secondary creation described is not fantasy?

2. Why do you think that Dakṣa, despite his faults and material desires, became repentant for having cursed Nārada?

3. According to verse 42, Lord Brahmā created the human race from the sons of Aditi who were pious and knew what to do. What does this indicate about humans and what their goal in life should be?

ACTIVITIES

In this section you will find many exciting things to do. These activities
will get you thinking, moving, drawing, and having loads of fun.

Theatrical Activity

... to bring out the actor in you

VAIṢṆAVA HUMOR: MISSING THE POINT
OF THE HUMAN RACE

Śrīla Viśvanātha Cakravartī Ṭhākura explains that from Aryamā and
Mātṛkā were born sons who knew what to do and what not to do.
From the sons who were interested in pursuing spiritual life, Brahmā
produced the human race. *Puruṣatve cāvistarām ātmā*: the search for
the *ātmā* is manifested only in the human form. (*Aitreya-āraṇyaka*
2.3.2.4)

Śrīla Prabhupāda explains the above verse in his purport
to *SB* 11.9.28 and 11.7.21. Please go through both purports.
Prepare a comic skit based on this theme: If we live like
trees, reptiles, four-legged animals, birds or snakes, what
use is our human life?

Sometimes when we present philosophical truths in a
humorous way, the message becomes easily acceptable.

See example below:

A person walking down the street ignores the Hare Kṛṣṇa devotees doing *saṅkīrtana*.

Devotee: (devotee leader) O fortunate one, would you mind sparing a few minutes?

Nondevotee: (turning back) Okay, since you properly addressed me, I will speak to you for
exactly two minutes. (Says proudly) Did you call me fortunate because I recently won a gold
medal in high jump?

Devotee: No! Kangaroos can jump three meters high.

Nondevotee: A kangaroo? Don't compare me with such funny animals. Am I fortunate because
I live on the top floor of a 50-story building?

Devotee: Not at all, Peregrine falcons can nest 1,300 feet or higher.

Nondevotee: I know, I know; you were appreciating my parental skills.

Devotee: Chimpanzees, elephants, and many animal species are known for their love for their young.

Nondevotee: My organizing skills?

Devotee: Bees are great at that.

Nondevotee: (Defiantly) I am so hard working!

Devotee: Can't beat the ants.

Nondevotee: (Exasperated) Then why am I fortunate?

Devotee: Because you have the intelligence to inquire about who you are and who is God?

Nondevotee: The other species cannot do this?

Devotee: Have you seen them in a temple or a mosque?

Nondevotee: (smiles) No. I get your point! How can I learn more?

Devotee: Take these books by His Divine Grace A. C. Bhaktivedānta Swami Prabhupāda! (Hands him *Bhagavad-gītā*)

Devotees continue their *kīrtana*: Hare Kṛṣṇa Hare Kṛṣṇa Kṛṣṇa Kṛṣṇa Hare Hare . . .

Critical-Thinking Activity

... to bring out the spiritual investigator in you

ŚRĪLA PRABHUPĀDA EMPOWERS WOMEN

In text 1 Śrīla Prabhupāda explains how women need only be chaste wives, and in so doing they will share the credit of their husbands without separate endeavor. While Śrīla Prabhupāda wrote extensively on this subject in his books, he also often encouraged women to perform services and practice Kṛṣṇa consciousness similar to the men.

Look at the lives of the following two women devotees: Devahūti, from *Śrīmad-Bhāgavatam*, and Yamunā Devī, Śrīla Prabhupāda's disciple. How were their lives similar? How were they different?

DEVAHUTI

Devahūti was the daughter of Svāyambhuva Manu and the wife of the great sage Kardama. Having chosen to marry Kardama, she served him with great reverence. She was blessed with Kapiladeva, the Supreme Personality of Godhead, as her son. After receiving instructions from Him, she attained the spiritual world.

YAMUNA DEVI

Yamunā Devī was a disciple of Śrīla Prabhupāda. She met Śrīla Prabhupāda through her sister and was soon initiated by him. Along with her husband, Gurudāsa, and two other couples, she started a center in San Francisco and London. She dedicated 45 years of her life to Śrīla Prabhupāda's service. She is known for her *kīrtanas,* cookbooks, and high standards of Deity worship and cleanliness.

1. In what way was Śrīla Prabhupāda's engaging women in Kṛṣṇa consciousness different from Kardama Muni's?

2. Why did Śrīla Prabhupāda do this?

Science Activity

DARWIN'S THEORY OF EVOLUTION

In this chapter we see that many species of life came from the daughters of Dakṣa, whose duty was to populate the universe.

One of the modern theories of creation is Darwin's theory of evolution. Let us find out more about this theory and analyze it from the Vedic viewpoint:

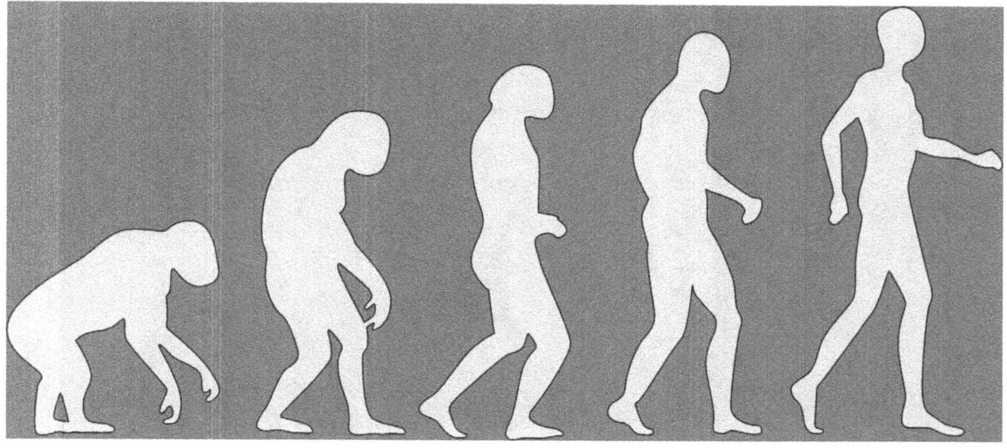

- Using credible online sources, research Darwin's theory. In your notebooks write down three to five points.
- Then, understanding that this is just a theory, use credible sources to look for at least three defects in this theory. You may research some of the works of Śrīla Prabhupāda's spiritual scientist disciples who presented the book *Forbidden Archaeology* and some of their points defeating this theory.
- Then write a conclusion of the Vedic viewpoint of evolution and explain why we accept this viewpoint as fact.

Writing and Language Activities

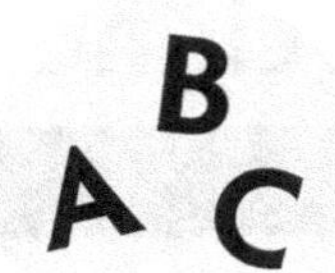

... to help you understand better

CROSSWORD PUZZLE

Across

3. Moon-god's favorite wife.
4. Dakṣa's wife.
6. The span of day, which awakens all living entities to material activities.
8. He lost his teeth due to his offense against Lord Śiva.
9. The 27 daughters who married the moon-god could not get any of this.
10. Dakṣa's two daughters who married Bhūta had ten million ________ .

Down

1. Another name for Lord Vāmanadeva.
2. Aditi's prominent son, the sun-god.
5. Dakṣa resolved his problem by begetting these instead of sons.
7. These took birth from Timi.

REMEMBERING THE SUPREME CREATOR

In previous cantos we've studied the creation (*sarga*) and the secondary creation (*visarga*). In the Second Canto we saw how Brahmājī was empowered by Lord Viṣṇu to create and also how Lord Kṛṣṇa is all pervading; He is the supreme cause of creation, maintenance, and destruction. Dakṣa and his wife, Asiknī, were empowered by the Supersoul for procreation.

In a short paragraph, please write your reflections on how this chapter has brought to your attention the presence of the Supreme Lord directly and indirectly in the material creation. Lord Kṛṣṇa is the generating seed of all existence. When we remember His activities, pastimes, compassion, and opulence, we increase our faith and surrender to Him.

Additional ideas to guide your write-up:

1. There are at least three expansions of Lord Vāsudeva mentioned in the progeny of Dakṣa: Jayanta (6.6.8), Śiśumāra (6.6.14) and Urukrama (6.6.38–39).

2. Lord Kṛṣṇa declares, "Know that all opulent, beautiful, and glorious creations spring from but a spark of my splendor." (*Bg.* 10.41)

3. In *Bhagavad-gītā*, Chapter 10, Lord Kṛṣṇa mentions a few of His *vibhūtis*, or divine opulences. Do you recall any from this chapter? (Garuḍa, the sun, the moon, Arjuna, Lord Brahmā, Aryamā, Yama, Indra, among the Vasus, Agni, etc.)

4. Although this material world is a place where rebellious souls live, still the Lord out of His infinite compassion creates, maintains, and destroys this material realm for eternity.

CHAPTER 6 ANSWERS

Śrīla Prabhupāda Empowers Women

1. They both sincerely served their spiritual masters. Devahūti's example was that of an ideal wife, and simply by serving her husband, she attained glorious results. When Śrīla Prabhupāda went to the West to preach, he noticed that women and men worked as equals, so he encouraged women to also serve in the same way. This was a simple adjustment made according to time, place, and circumstance but brought wonderful results.

2. Śrīla Prabhupāda's intention was to encourage everyone to serve Kṛṣṇa from their own positions, irrespective of whether their life situations or social cultures matched Vedic standards. It is acceptable for an *ācārya* to adjust the application of a Vedic standard to bring people closer to Kṛṣṇa – it does not mean that the Vedic standard can be changed or overridden, but that the higher principle of serving Kṛṣṇa under all circumstances should and could be done. Śrīla Prabhupāda encouraged this with many women disciples, and they all are eligible to attain the same result that Devahūti did through serving her husband. Spiritual chastity, therefore, is important.

Crossword

Across: 3. Rohiṇī; 4. Asiknī; 6. Pañcayāma; 8. Pūṣā; 9. Children; 10. Rudras

   Down: 1. Urukrama; 2. Vivasvān; 5. Daughters; 7. Aquatics

7

INDRA OFFENDS HIS SPIRITUAL MASTER, BṚHASPATI

Parīkṣit Mahārāja pondered for a moment and asked Śukadeva Gosvāmī, "Why did Bṛhaspati reject the demigods, his own disciples? They must have committed an offense toward him. Please tell me what happened."

Śukadeva Gosvāmī looked at the King. His grave expression revealed the seriousness of the offense. "It all started when Indra, the king of the demigods, became proud of his great opulence, which made him transgress the rules of Vedic etiquette."

Śukadeva Gosvāmī continued to describe what had happened.

Indra, the king of heaven, sat on his throne. A white umbrella as effulgent as the full moon hung over his head. He glanced at his servants, who fanned him with yak-tail whisks and offered him items of worship. He smiled at the residents of heaven – the Maruts, Vasus, Rudras, Ādityas, Aśvinī-kumāras, Siddhas, Cāraṇas, Gandharvas,

Seeing that his spiritual master had left, Indra came out of his reverie. He stood up, summoning for the music to stop. The expression on his face changed to utter despair. He slapped his hand on his forehead and exclaimed, "How foolish and proud I've been to have committed such a grave mistake! I've insulted my own *guru* by not welcoming him and showing him respect."

Tears welled up in Indra's eyes. Everyone stared at him, not knowing what to do. Indra looked down in embarrassment and then looked up again to address his followers: "I condemn my wealth and opulence! I became proud of a little opulence and polluted by false ego. Who would accept such opulence at the risk of falling down?"

Gesturing to the demigods, he continued, "I am supposed to be your king, in the mode of goodness, but see what I've done! If a person says

Vidyādharas, Apsarās, Kinnaras, and others – who surrounded him and bowed their heads, offering prayers. Celestial creatures and saintly persons also offered their respects. Indra's smile grew wider. He possessed the opulence of the three worlds!

He glanced at his wife, Śacīdevī, mesmerized by her beauty. The magical sound of musical instruments accompanied by the sweet singing of the Apsarās and Gandharvas enthralled him. He didn't care that the spiritual master of the demigods, Bṛhaspati, had just entered the assembly. His *guru*, who was respected by the demigods and demons alike, just stood there without being offered a seat or a fitting welcome. Indra did not rise to receive him nor did anything to show respect.

Bṛhaspati sighed and tolerated being ignored. He could have cursed the proud king, but he didn't. He could foresee everything that would happen. "This Indra is so puffed up by his material opulence that he has violated basic etiquette. What a shame . . ." thought the revered sage. Shaking his head, Bṛhaspati left the assembly and went home.

that one should not stand up to show respect to another king or a *brāhmaṇa*, he does not know superior religious principles. To follow such a person is like boarding a stone boat that will sink – their instructions will not allow one to cross the ocean of darkness. In fact, such leaders go to hell, and their followers go with them."

Indra paced the floor as the residents of heaven watched him wide-eyed. He suddenly stopped – there was a glimmer of hope in his eyes. He said, "I know what to do! Without duplicity I will bow my head at the lotus feet of Bṛhaspati, our beloved spiritual master. I shall touch his lotus feet and beg for his forgiveness. I will offer my obeisances and certainly try to satisfy him."

While Indra repented in his assembly, Bṛhaspati, the most powerful spiritual master, could understand Indra's mind. He immediately left his home so Indra could not find him. With the other demigods Indra searched frantically for his spiritual master, but, alas, he could not be found.

"Now I am doomed," Indra thought. "My spiritual master is displeased with me, so how can I achieve any good fortune?" The demigods could not pacify his troubled mind.

News spread of Indra's pitiable condition. The demons took advantage of it and got their weapons ready under the instruction of their *guru*, Śukrācārya. They declared war against the demigods.

The demigods were defeated. The demons' sharp arrows had pierced their bodies. With blood oozing from their wounds, they approached Lord Brahmā for shelter and instruction.

Lord Brahmā said, "O best of the demigods, because of your madness that came from your material opulence, you did not receive Bṛhaspati properly. I'm astonished that you've behaved so impudently towards such a saintly person in full control of his senses.

"In fact, because of your offense to your *guru* you've been defeated. Since the demons have always been weak in front of you, how else could they have defeated you now?

"O Indra, because the demons have worshiped

Śukrācārya with great devotion, they have again become powerful. Because of their devotion, they've become so strong that they can even take my abode away from me.

"The demons are not worried about you anymore, but you need not worry. Anyone who has faith in the mercy of the *brāhmaṇas*, cows, and the Supreme Personality of Godhead, Kṛṣṇa, remain strong in their position.

"Therefore, O demigods, I instruct you to approach Viśvarūpa, the son of Tvaṣṭā, who is a pure and powerful *brāhmaṇa*. Accept him as your *guru* and worship him. Being pleased with you, he will fulfill your desires. However, he is inclined to side with the demons, so you will have to tolerate this."

The demigods were relieved. They followed Lord Brahmā's instructions and approached the sage Viśvarūpa. They embraced him and said, "Beloved Viśvarūpa, we've come to your *āśrama* as your guests, so please fulfill our desires. In fact, we are like your parents. The highest duty of a son is to serve his parents, what to speak of a *brahmacārī* son like you.

"The *ācārya*, the spiritual master, is the personification of the *Vedas* because he teaches Vedic knowledge and gives initiation by offering the sacred thread. Similarly, a father personifies Lord Brahmā; a brother, King Indra; a mother, the planet earth; and a sister, mercy. A guest personifies religious principles, an invited guest personifies the demigod Agni, and all living entities personify Lord Viṣṇu, the Supreme Personality of Godhead.

"Dear son, our enemies have defeated us, and so we are very aggrieved. Please fulfill our prayers and become our *guru*. By the power of your austerity we can easily conquer our enemies.

"Do not worry about being criticized because you are younger than us. Such etiquette does not apply to someone like you who is advanced in chanting the Vedic

mantras. So even though you are junior to us, we do not hesitate to accept you as our priest."

Viśvarūpa smiled and said, "O demigods, to become a *guru* or priest is decried because one can lose one's brahminical power due to the sinful reactions of the disciples. But how can I refuse your request? You are all exalted commanders of the entire universe. I am your disciple and must take many lessons from you. So I must agree for my own benefit.

"A true *brāhmaṇa* has no material possessions and lives on a few grains that are left on the field or on the ground in the marketplace. Household *brāhmaṇas* perform austerities and penances and maintain their families. A *brāhmaṇa* who gains wealth by professional priesthood has a very low mind. How can I be such a priest?

"Therefore I accept to be your priest by dedicating my life and my possessions."

Then the exalted Viśvarūpa enthusiastically

performed all the necessary priestly activities on behalf of the demigods.

Śukrācārya continued to protect the demons by his talents and tactics, but the most powerful Viśvarūpa composed a protective prayer, known as the Nārāyaṇa-kavaca, for the demigods. This intelligent *mantra* took away the opulence of the demons and gave it to Mahendra, the King of heaven.

Viśvarūpa spoke this secret hymn to King Indra, which protected the demigods and conquered the military power of the demons.

Themes and Key Messages

Please go through this table of themes and key messages, with corresponding verses, and discuss each topic further.

THEMES	REFERENCES	KEY MESSAGES
We should follow the Vaiṣṇava etiquette of showing respect to superiors.	6.7.9–11, 13	Even though a king like Indra is given all respect by anyone who enters his assembly, he must show respect to his spiritual master, the *brāhmaṇas*, and Vaiṣṇavas by standing up and offering obeisances. Even Lord Kṛṣṇa set the example by offering obeisances to Nārada Muni and bathing the feet of His *brāhmaṇa* friend Sudāmā. We should follow such Vaiṣṇava etiquette, which helps us avoid offending others and allows us to receive affection and blessings from our superiors.
Material opulence often leads to pride and then degradation.	6.7.11–12	Usually when one has material opulence, like wealth, fame, position, strength, or beauty, one becomes proud, which can lead to degradation. Generally, people try to enjoy material comforts and become addicted to wine and women. This usually leads to a criminal society that is lawless and unmanageable. If, however, they take advice from the spiritual master, Kṛṣṇa's representative, they can become happy and ideal members of society.
Those who mislead people go to hell, and their followers go with them.	6.7.14	Indra repented for his behavior and thought of himself as someone who misleads people. Such leaders are leading others onto stone boats, which represent different paths of religious practice. People who blindly follow these leaders will sink and drown on the stone boat. They will be saved only if they take the proper boat offered by Kṛṣṇa, which is to understand the aim of life, understand God, and fulfill the human mission.

| One should respect the spiritual master as the Lord Himself. If one disrespects or offends the spiritual master, one loses everything. | 6.7.15, 21–24 | The *ācārya* is a perfect *brāhmaṇa* and has unlimited intelligence in guiding the activities of his disciples. Therefore, Kṛṣṇa advises in *Bhagavad-gītā* (4.34) that one should render service unto such a spiritual master and inquire from him submissively. In *Śrīmad-Bhāgavatam* (11.17.27), the Lord also says that one should respect the spiritual master as the Lord Himself and never think of him as an ordinary person. Therefore, Lord Brahmā chastised the demigods for offending their *guru*, telling them that because they had offended their *guru*, they had become weak and were defeated by the demons. On the other hand, one who worships the *brāhmaṇas*, cows, and Lord Kṛṣṇa are always strong in their position. |
| If one is advanced in Kṛṣṇa consciousness, regardless of his position in human society, he may become a spiritual master. | 6.7.33, 35–38 | Although Viśvarūpa was junior to the demigods, he became their spiritual master because he was advanced in Vedic knowledge. Usually, such priesthood is not accepted by *brāhmaṇas* because they have to take the sinful reactions of their disciples, but Viśvarūpa agreed for the demigods' benefit and because he had great respect for them. Such *brāhmaṇas* live very austerely and use whatever they get in the Lord's service. |

Higher-Thinking Questions

Now try to deepen your understanding of this chapter by delving into Śrīla Prabhupāda's purports and reflecting on the following questions:

1. Why does Indra condemn his wealth and opulence in verse 12? (Refer to the purport.) Do you think wealth and opulence can always make one degraded? Explain.

2. Why do you think that Bṛhaspati did not curse Indra? (See verse 9.)

3. Indra regretted his mistake and wanted to beg for forgiveness. What does this tell us about Indra, as when he begged forgiveness for other similar mistakes?

4. In verse 12 Indra explains that he, like the demigods, is supposed to be in the mode of goodness. How then should one in goodness act?

5. How is ISKCON providing a proper boat with an expert captain to cross over the material ocean? (Refer to verse 14 purport.)

6. How do you think Bṛhaspati's neglect benefited Indra? In other words, what lessons did Indra learn?

7. In verse 24 Lord Brahmā mentions that whoever worships the *brāhmaṇas*, cows, and the Supreme Personality of Godhead, Kṛṣṇa, are always strong in their position. What other reference do you know of from the scriptures to confirm this?

8. In verse 29–30 why do you think these references are given of the spiritual master, father, mother, sister, and guest? Refer to the purport.

9. Viśvarūpa became powerful through his austerities and advancement in knowledge. Can you think of any other personalities in the *Bhāgavatam* who became powerful through austerities? What is the ultimate purpose of all austerity?

10. Why did Viśvarūpa obey the request of his superiors to be their spiritual master, even though this was against the general etiquette?

ACTIVITIES

In this section you will find many exciting things to do. These activities will get you thinking, moving, drawing, and having loads of fun.

Analogy Activity

... to bring out the scholar in you

THE SMART BOAT ENGINEERS

Verse 14 states that ignorant leaders mislead their followers on the path of destruction, just like a captain of a stone boat leads its ignorant passengers to death at sea. The analogy is meant to explain how people ignorant of higher spiritual values degrade those who follow them.

Let us further understand this analogy of the stone boat and the floating boat. Consider the following:

• Both the stone boat and the floating boat are made of specific materials with specific buoyancies (ability to float in water).
• They each have a designer.
• When the boats are at sea, they each have a captain who directs it.
• Also, boats have navigation, safety, and emergency equipment.

Despite all this, we can easily conclude that the stone boat will sink while the other boat will most likely cross the ocean. Can you explain why?

Read purport 14. Then give appropriate labels to each part of the diagram below, identifying the different elements of the analogy and explaining what each refers to. Finally, write down which "boat" you think will cross this "ocean" and why.

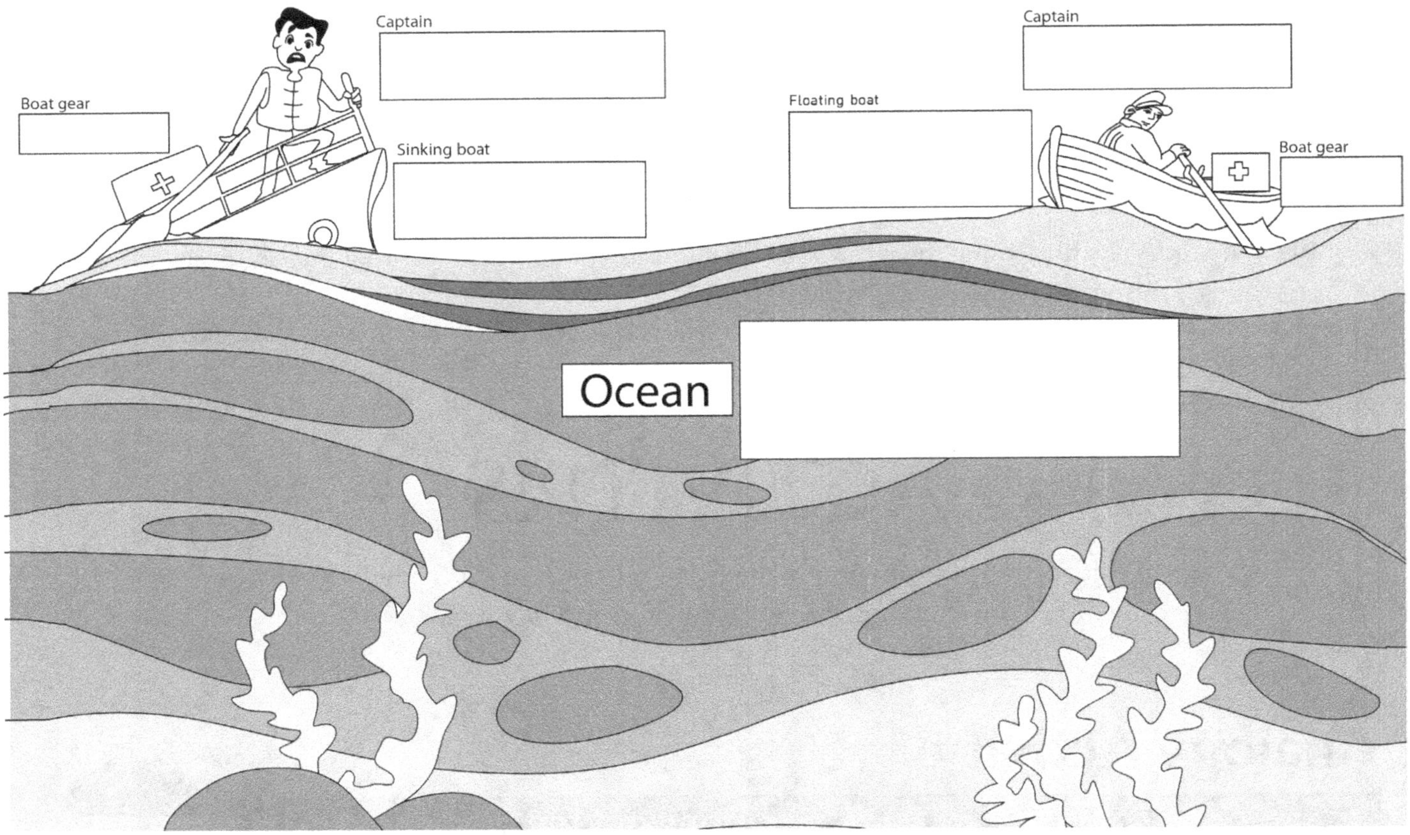

GURU-NIṢṬHĀ PHOTO FRAME

The famous *Śrī Gurvaṣṭakam* prayer by Śrīla Viśvanātha Cakravartī Ṭhākura states: *yasya prasādād bhagavat-prasādo yasyāprasādān na gatiḥ kuto 'pi*: by the mercy of the spiritual master one receives the benediction of Kṛṣṇa; without the grace of the spiritual master, one cannot make any advancement. Many ISKCON devotees have succeeded simply on the strength of following their spiritual master's instructions. Let us glorify their success and understand how they succeeded.

Interview a family member or community leader about their *guru-niṣṭhā*, their firm faith in their *guru* and their *guru's* instructions.

Create a small photo frame using the template at the end of this chapter.

Materials needed: an 8x11" frame, 8x11" card stock paper, scissors, glue, photo of their *guru* or of Śrīla Prabhupāda, ink pen.

Directions: Photocopy or cut out the template, color the border, glue a picture of the devotee's spiritual master in the center and fill out the details. Glue the page on the card stock paper. Then you may frame the page. As a special way to honor this devotee, gift them the frame as a token of gratitude for their service!

Action Activity

SPIN AND SPEAK: THE EFFECTS OF MATERIAL OPULENCE

In this chapter we learned that material opulence can make us proud and can often lead to our degradation if we are not careful.

Directions for the game:

1. First make a spinner. On a piece of cardboard or paper, draw and cut out a circle with equal sized segments (see template).

2. Write various life situations on each segment of the circle or use the examples below.
   a) Winning a beauty contest
   b) Buying an expensive house
   c) Holding a high position in a company
   d) Owning a private jet
   e) Winning a boxing championship
   f) Being voted the most popular student at the school

3. Punch a small hole in the center of the circle. To the hole attach a metal clip and slightly bend the two prongs at the back so that the spinner can spin. Attach a paper clip or an arrow cut from a piece of paper into the center.

4. Spin the spinner, and when it stops, see to which situation of material opulence the arrow points.

5. Think about how the situation would affect one's life and might lead to degradation:
   » One can get puffed up
   » One can be blinded by opulence
   » One can mistreat others

6. Take turns and share your viewpoints with your teacher and friends.

7. Also discuss how one may avoid becoming degraded even with these material opulences.

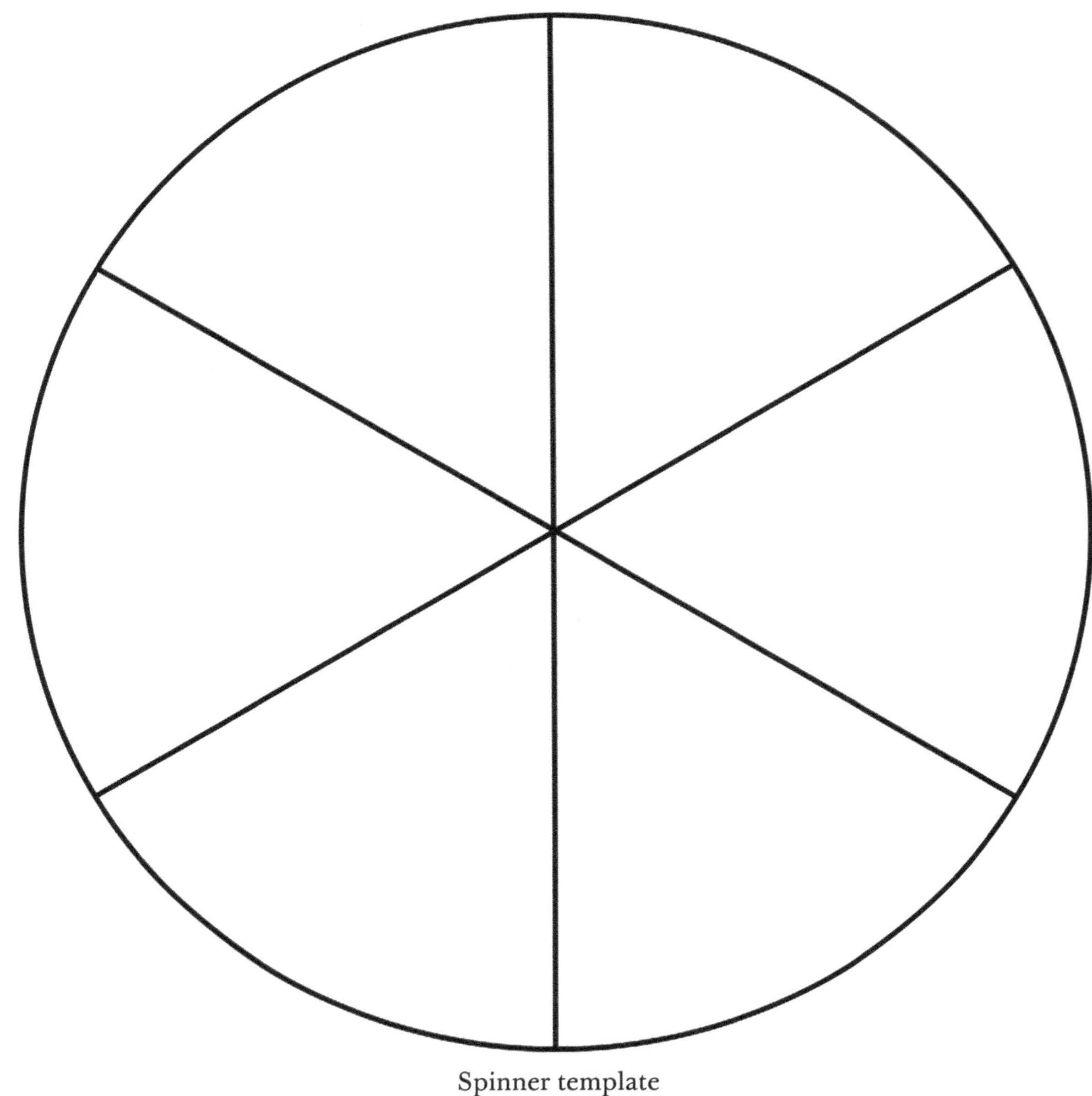

Spinner template

A DROP OF THE GURU'S MERCY

The essential message of this chapter is devotion and service to Śrī Guru. We are dependent on the mercy and blessings of a bona fide spiritual master to progress in our spiritual journey.

Memorize the following Bengali *bhajana* by Śrīla Bhaktivinoda Ṭhākura and learn to sing it. Read the translation and answer the questions to understand how the spiritual master can bestow all qualifications to a submissive disciple.

Gurudeva Kṛpā Bindu Diyā

By Śrīla Bhaktivinoda Ṭhākura from the book *Śaraṇāgati*

gurudev!
kṛpā-bindu diyā, koro' ei dāse,
tṛṇāpekṣā ati hīna
sakala sahane, bala diyā koro',
nija-māne spṛhā-hīna

sakale sammāna korite śakati,
deho' nātha! jathājatha
tabe to' gāibo, hari-nāma-sukhe,
aparādha ha 'be hata

kabe heno kṛpā, labhiyā e jana,
kṛtārtha hoibe, nātha!
śakti-buddhi-hīna, āmi ati dīna,
koro' more ātma-sātha

yogyatā-vicāre, kichu nāhi pāi,
tomāra karuṇā—sāra
karuṇā nā hoile, kāṅdiyā kāṅdiyā,
prāṇa nā rākhibo āra

Translation:

1. Gurudeva! By a drop of your mercy make this servant of yours humbler than a blade of grass. Give me the strength to bear all trials and troubles, and free me from all desires for personal honor.

2. O Lord and master! Invest me with the power to properly honor all living beings. Only then will I sing the holy name in great ecstasy and will all my offenses cease.

3. O Lord and master! When will this devotee be blessed by obtaining your mercy? I am low, fallen, and devoid of all strength and intelligence. Please make me your beloved servant.

4. When I examine myself, I find nothing of value. Your mercy is therefore essential to me. If you are not merciful, I will constantly weep, and I will not maintain my life any longer.

Questions:

1. What are some of the results of the *guru's* mercy to a submissive disciple?

2. Why is the *guru's* mercy essential to the disciple? How is this illustrated in the story of Indra offending Bṛhaspati?

3. The demons were successful because they took shelter of their *guru*, Śukrācārya. Even if the demons were victorious because of their *guru's* blessings, what does this tell you about taking shelter of a *guru* for spiritual reasons?

Introspective Activity

THE GURU DILEMMA

Indra makes the mistake of disrespecting his spiritual master and then regrets it. Bṛhaspati is not available when he wants to beg forgiveness from him for his action. Then, on the advice of Brahmā, he accepts Viśvarūpa as his spiritual master despite knowing his tendency to favor the demons.

Imagine you are Indra who has been advised by Brahmā. You realize it is not the best option to accept Viśvarūpa as your *guru*, but perhaps it is the only option available to you at this point. You desperately want to regain your kingdom, but you have to win the battle within yourself before you win the external battle.

Fill out the thought bubble in a few sentences (you can write in your books if you like). Write down what emotions Indra is going through because of his offense to Bṛhaspati, how he feels about accepting Viśvarūpa instead, and how he thinks this will help his mission of getting back his kingdom. Evaluate and discuss how much introspection he has to do before making a difficult decision for the higher good.

Critical-Thinking Activity

CONSEQUENCES FOR ACTIONS

Given below is a chronological order of events that occurred in this chapter. From the events in this chapter we can learn a lot about how a *guru* should be honored and the consequence of not doing so.

Look at each event and the listed impact. Evaluate the impact, trying to understand how seemingly harmless or small events add up to a larger consequence. The first one has been done for you.

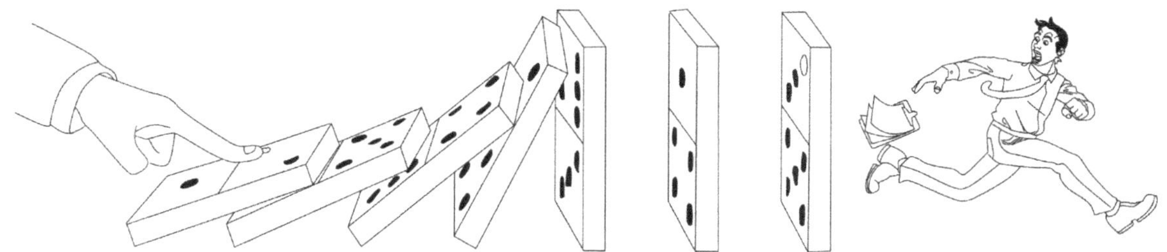

EVENT	POSITIVE IMPACT	NEGATIVE IMPACT	EVALUATION
1. Indra becomes proud of his opulence.		He does not show any respect to his spiritual master, Bṛhaspati, when he enters the assembly.	We should never forget that we receive immense blessings from the spiritual master, and no matter who we become, we should remain humble before the spiritual master – Indra forgot this and that was his grave mistake.
2. Bṛhaspati notices Indra's transgression of etiquette.	He does not curse or punish him although he is capable of it.		
3. Indra realizes his mistake.	Indra regrets his mistake and condemns his wealth and opulence that caused him to behave disrespectfully.	The mistake had already been committed, and Indra would have to face a consequence for it.	
4. Indra and the demigods repent their mistake.	Indra and the demigods decide to go to their spiritual master and beg forgiveness from him.		

EVENT	POSITIVE IMPACT	NEGATIVE IMPACT	EVALUATION
5. Bṛhaspati understands Indra's mind and intentions.		Being dissatisfied with his disciple, Bṛhaspati became invisible and left home so as to be unavailable to Indra.	
6. Demigods do not find Bṛhaspati.		They are neither able to apologize nor rectify their offense at the feet of their *guru*.	
7. Demons serve their spiritual master, Śukrācārya, obediently and respectfully.		They request his blessing to attack the demigods. They receive his blessings because of their faithfulness to him.	
8. The demigods approach Lord Brahmā who advises them to approach Viśvarūpa.	The demigods respectfully approach Viśvarūpa with the purpose of conquering the demons.		
9. Viśvarūpa accepts the request of the demigods to be their *guru* and priest.	He creates the Nārāyaṇa-kavaca to protect the demigods.		

Writing and Language Activities

APPRECIATION LETTER: BE RESPECTFUL TO EVERYONE!

In this chapter we learned that when we follow the Vaiṣṇava etiquette of showing respect to superiors we can receive blessings and affection from them.

An appreciation letter is like an award-letter given to a person for their extraordinary performance in something. It is a good way **to acknowledge their hard work and dedication**. The letter encourages them to work harder in future and get good results.

Directions for writing an appreciation letter:

1. Think of someone you know who is very respectful to everyone. This could be anyone, from someone junior in school to a family member, a worker whom you know, or a boy or girl in your neighborhood.

2. You recognize their Vaiṣṇava quality of showing respect to all seniors and superiors. Note down all their little ways of being respectful.

3. Write an appreciation letter addressed to the individual, acknowledging all their areas of respectful Vaiṣṇava behavior.

4. Use all your praises, affection, and encouraging words to appreciate them.

5. Reach out to them and give them the appreciation letter.

6. Don't forget to say "thank you"!

TWO TRUTHS AND A LIE: THE SPIRITUAL MASTER

This chapter emphasizes that the spiritual master is nondifferent from Kṛṣṇa, in the sense that he represents Kṛṣṇa perfectly and is therefore empowered by Him. Therefore he is not an ordinary person. One must always render service to him and never offend him.

Two truths and a lie is an interesting game to enhance a person's understanding of a concept or someone. It helps us to use logic and reason and recognize the truth among a few lies.

Directions to play the game:

1. On a sheet of paper note down two truths about the theme of the spiritual master discussed in this chapter. Among the truths write a lie to contradict the theme.

» Example: *A spiritual master gives protection from illusion. He guides his disciples on the path back to Godhead. He holds his disciples accountable for all their past sins and then guides their activities.*

2. Fold your sheet of paper and put it in a tray with the pieces of paper from the other students in your class. Then jumble them up.

3. Next, choose one folded sheet from the tray. Read it in your mind.

4. Try to recognize the lie from the set of truths.

5. Correct the wrong statement and read it out aloud for everyone, or identify the wrong statement.

6. Each student takes turns to play the game.

WHO CAN BECOME A SPIRITUAL MASTER?

The demigods accepted Viśvarūpa as their spiritual master although he was younger than them. This was because he was advanced in Vedic knowledge (verse 33). Śrīla Prabhupāda states in the purport that it does not matter whether one is a *brāhmaṇa*, *śūdra*, *gṛhastha*, or *sannyāsī*. These are all material designations. A spiritually advanced person has nothing to do with such designations. Therefore, if one is advanced in the science of Kṛṣṇa consciousness, regardless of one's position in human society, one may become a spiritual master.

Read the following passages and write a few lines in your notebook on how they reflect the above principle:

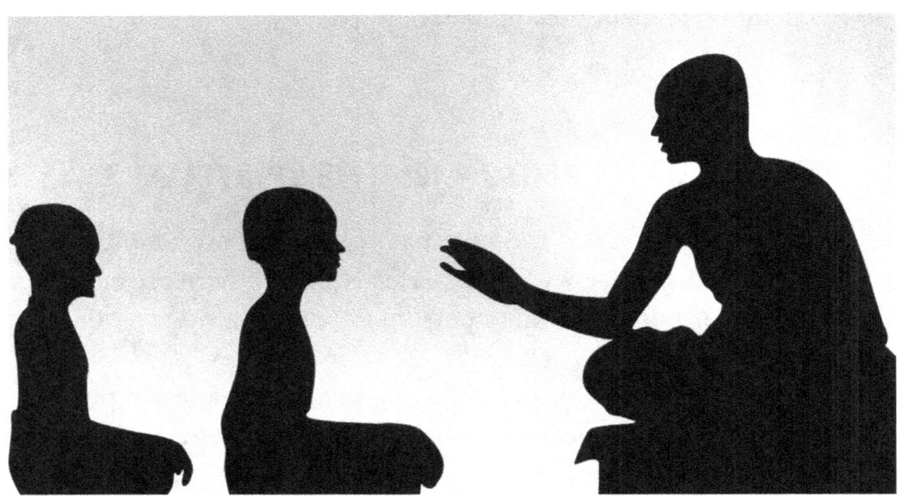

Mukunda dāsa and his glorious son Raghunandana: When Mukunda dāsa ordered Raghunandana to feed their family Deity Śrī Gopīnātha in his absence, Śrī Gopīnātha ate all the offerings, moved by Raghunandana's intense devotion and requests. To test him, Mukunda again gave him an offering of *laddu* and hid to see if Lord Gopīnātha really accepted the *bhoga*. To his great amazement and satisfaction, Lord Gopīnātha ate half the *laddu*. Later, when Mukunda met Lord Caitanya, the Lord asked who is the father and who is the son? Mukunda replied, "Raghunandana is my father, and I am his son." Lord Caitanya was very happy to hear this. He said, "Yes, it is correct. One who awakens devotion to Kṛṣṇa is certainly the spiritual master." (*CC Madhya* 15.117)

Lord Anantadeva in the body of a snake charmer glorifies Śrīla Haridāsa Ṭhākura: One day a snake charmer was glorifying Lord Kṛṣṇa's pastimes at Kālīya-daha. When Haridāsa Ṭhākura heard about Kṛṣṇa's mercy on a cruel snake, he fell unconscious. Seeing the pure ecstatic transformations in the body of Haridāsa when he danced, another envious *brāhmaṇa* began to imitate him. The snake charmer, understanding his duplicity, severely beat the *brāhmaṇa*. When the audience asked him to disclose the reason for his respect towards Haridāsa and his roughness towards the *brāhmaṇa*, Lord Anantadeva spoke through the mouth of the snake charmer. Lord Ananta stated that a Vaiṣṇava may appear in any family or in any class of human society and is still worthy of respect. This is the verdict of the scriptures. Śrīla Haridāsa Ṭhākura was born in a low-class family, but he is a *mahā-bhāgavata*. The demigods desire his touch and even Mother Ganges desires that Haridāsa bathe in her waters. What to speak of his touch, just by seeing Haridāsa, one is released from the bondage of fruitive activities. (From *Caitanya Bhāgavata, Ādi-khaṇḍa* 16.199–250)

The Smart Boat Engineers

Labels: ocean – material ocean; stone boat – material means/methods; stone boat captain – yogis, nondevotee leaders, politicians; stone boat gear – politicking, diplomacy; floating boat – spiritual knowledge; floating boat captain – spiritual master; floating boat gear – holy names, knowledge of self-realization; the spiritual boat can cross the ocean as it has been designed to weather the conditions of the material ocean and has an able captain, the spiritual master. It is also designed intelligently by the Vedic literatures so as not to sink in the material ocean.

A Drop of the Guru's Mercy

1. Becoming humble, getting strength to bear challenges, becoming free of material desires, being able to offer honor to all beings, chanting the holy name in ecstasy, becoming free from all offenses.

2. The *guru* guides the disciple on the path back to Godhead; without his direction, one can become lost. By the *guru's* blessings one can attain all the qualities mentioned in this song and attain love for Kṛṣṇa. When Indra offended Bṛhaspati and displeased him, Indra and the demigods were defeated by the demons. They lost all their power; therefore Brahmā advised them to take shelter of Viśvarūpa, and by doing so they became successful again. The *guru's* blessings and guidance not only give material success but, more importantly, success on the spiritual path.

3. The *guru's* blessings are essential to attain anything in life; therefore one should worship, glorify, and serve the *guru*.

The Guru Dilemma

Answers may vary. Touch upon feelings like repentance because of his pride, regret at having wealth that misled him, personal sense of loss of both *guru* and kingdom, the dilemma of uncertainty versus duty: to obey Brahmā and accept Viśvarūpa, and the uncertainty of regaining the kingdom under Viśvarūpa, etc. It must have been hard for him to work with someone younger in age, especially not exclusively favorable to him, but he makes up his mind for the greater good instead of thinking of his immediate needs and desires. Working for the greater good gives positive results.

Consequences for Actions

2. Being a highly elevated *brāhmaṇa*, Bṛhaspati noted the offense. Being powerful, he could have cursed Indra, but he restrained himself because of his great spiritual wisdom. This did not really help alleviate Indra's problems, because the offense had been a major one already; 3. Indra fortunately realized his mistake, and he was willing to make amends and rectify the situation. Yet, while he was saved from committing more offenses, he could not undo what he had already done and had to face consequences; 4. While Indra's reactions to his offense was right, it was perhaps too late to make amends – the bigger the offense, the harder it is to make amends and the more difficult it is to face the consequence; 5. Dissatisfaction of the spiritual master can have great consequences, even when the disciple later repents and is ready to make amends; one should therefore be very careful not to offend the spiritual master; 6. It may be too late for a disciple to realize the gravity of his offense at the feet of the *guru*; by his *guru* leaving, Indra could realize the seriousness of his offense. 7. The secret to success is pleasing the spiritual master. Both material and spiritual goals can be achieved simply by pleasing the spiritual master; 8. When we repent we may not always become forgiving, but by repenting we can receive mercy and be corrected. Thus the demigods received an opportunity to get the shelter of Viśvarūpa; 9. Without the mercy of *guru* and Kṛṣṇa, we cannot achieve anything in this world.

Presented to: ____

Name of spiritual master: _______________________________________

Instruction of *guru*: _______________________________________

How I attempted to follow: _______________________________________

How I received my *guru's* mercy: _______________________________________

8

THE NĀRĀYAṆA-KAVACA SHIELD

Parīkṣit Mahārāja was struck with wonder. He asked Śukadeva Gosvāmī, "My lord, this Viṣṇu mantra armor is indeed powerful; it protected King Indra and enabled him to conquer his enemies who wanted to kill him. Please tell me more about this Nārāyaṇa armor."

Śukadeva Gosvāmī began to explain how King Indra also inquired about the armor from Viśvarūpa, the priest of the demigods. This armor, known as the Nārāyaṇa-kavaca, was infused with Viṣṇu *mantras* and meditations.

Viśvarūpa instructed Indra: "If you are ever afraid of anything, you should prepare to chant and apply this armor. First, wash your hands and legs and cleanse yourself by performing *ācamana* and chanting this purifying *mantra: oṁ apavitraḥ pavitro vā sarvāvasthāṁ gato 'pi vā/ yaḥ smaret puṇḍarīkākṣaṁ sa bahyābhyantaraḥ śuciḥ/ śrī-viṣṇu śrī-viṣṇu śrī-viṣṇu.* Then you should touch the *kuśa* grass ring on the ring finger of each hand and, facing north, sit silently. First, chant the eight-syllable *mantra oṁ namo nārāyaṇāya* while touching eight parts of your body, starting with the feet and progressing to the knees, thighs, abdomen, heart, chest, mouth, and head. Then you should chant the twelve-syllable *mantra oṁ namo bhagavate vāsudevāya*, placing eight syllables of the *mantra* on your fingers and the remaining four on the joints of your thumbs. In this way, you begin to bind your body with the Nārāyaṇa coat of armor."

Indra was amazed. He certainly was afraid of the demons' newly acquired power and wished to have this divine coat of armor to protect him.

Viśvarūpa continued, "Then chant the six-syllable *mantra oṁ viṣṇave namaḥ* with a meditation, placing each of the syllables on different parts of the body: the '*om*' on the heart, the '*vi*' on the top of the head, the '*sa*' between the eyebrows, the '*na*' on the sikha, and the '*ve*' between the eyes; then the '*na*' on all the joints of the body, and meditate on the syllable '*ma*' as being the weapon. Then chant the fourth *mantra* '*maḥ astrāya phaṭ*' in all directions. In this way the protective armor of the *mantra* will bind all directions."

Lord who rides on Garuḍa and possesses eight mystic powers, protect me at all times.

"May the Supreme Lord in His incarnations of Matsya, Vāmana, and the gigantic form of the Lord, Viśvarūpa, protect me in the water, land, and sky.

"May Lord Nṛsiṁha protect me in all directions and all difficult places, such as the forest and the battlefield.

"May Yajñeśvara, the indestructible Lord of sacrifices and who is Lord Varāha, protect me from rogues on the street. May Paraśurāma protect me on the tops of mountains and Lord Rāmacandra, along with Lakṣmaṇa, protect me in foreign lands.

"May Sanat-kumāra protect me from lusty desires, may Lord Hayagrīva protect me from neglecting to offer respect to the Lord, and may Devarṣi Nārada protect me from my offenses in Deity worship. May Lord Kūrma protect me from falling into hellish planets.

"May Lord Dhanvantari protect me from physical illness, may Lord Ṛṣabhadeva protect me from the fear of heat and cold, may Yajña protect me from defamation, and may Lord Balarāma as Śeṣa protect me from envious serpents.

"May the Vedic scriptures compiled by Śrīla Vyāsadeva protect me from ignorance and may surrender to Lord Buddha protect me from misusing Vedic injunctions. May Lord Kalki, who

King Indra was astonished and excited at the same time. Surely, this was the way to conquer his enemies, he thought. He listened attentively.

"After you've finished this chanting, meditate on the Supreme Personality of Godhead, Nārāyaṇa, who is full in six opulences. Think of yourself one in quality with Him. Then begin to chant the protective prayer, the Nārāyaṇa-kavaca, to Lord Nārāyaṇa."

Viśvarūpa closed his eyes and folded his palms in prayer, meditating on the Supreme Lord. King Indra tried to do the same.

Viśvarūpa's voice echoed and penetrated Indra's heart: "May the all-powerful, eight-armed

the beginning of night, may Lord Hṛṣīkeśa protect me, and in the dead of night may Lord Padmanābha alone protect me. May the Lord who bears the Śrīvatsa on His chest protect me after midnight, and may Lord Janārdana protect me at the end of night. May Lord Dāmodara protect me in the early morning, and may Lord Viśveśvara protect me during the junctions of day and night."

Viśvarūpa took a deep breath and continued, evoking the weapons of the Lord: "May the Lord's Sudarśana *cakra*, with its sharp edges, burn our enemies to ashes.

"O club in the Lord's hands, you produce sparks as powerful as thunderbolts, and you are extremely dear to the Lord. I am also His servant, so please protect me and help me pound to pieces the evil living beings, such as Rākṣasas and Bhūtas. O Pāñcajanya, O best of conch shells who is always filled with Kṛṣṇa's breath and who creates a fearful vibration, drive away all the ghosts and other enemies. O king of sharp-edged

appeared to protect religious principles, protect me from the dirt of Kali-yuga."

Viśvarūpa smiled, meditating on Lord Kṛṣṇa's attractive form, and said: "May Lord Keśava protect me in the first part of the day; may Lord Govinda, who always plays His flute, protect me in the second part of the day; may Lord Nārāyaṇa protect me in the third part of the day; and may Lord Viṣṇu, who carries a disc to kill His enemies, protect me in the fourth part of the day. May Lord Madhusūdana, who carries a fearful bow, protect me during the fifth part of the day, and in the evening, may Lord Mādhava, protect me."

King Indra's eyes stayed shut. A slight smile played on his lips as he meditated on the Lord. How insignificant he felt in front of the all-powerful Lord. He began to feel dependent on Him. Fear began to leave him. He could trust his Lord. He stood up tall, feeling confident in the Lord's hands. The Supreme Lord was protecting him in all parts of the day and night.

Viśvarūpa's voice still resounded: "In

swords who is engaged by the Supreme Lord, cut the soldiers of my enemies to pieces. O shield marked with a hundred brilliant moonlike circles, please cover my enemies' eyes and pluck them out."

King Indra could see the Lord's weapons as if they were before him.

Viśvarūpa opened his eyes and said to Indra: "How wonderful it is to glorify the Lord's divine name, form, qualities, and paraphernalia. Just by doing this we are protected from the influence of bad planets, meteors, envious humans, serpents, scorpions, and animals like tigers and wolves. We are also protected from ghosts, lightning, and the material elements. Even our past sins cannot touch us. We are always afraid of these hindrances and dangers, but they are all completely destroyed by the chanting of the Hare Kṛṣṇa *mahā-mantra*."

Closing his eyes again, Viśvarūpa continued with the Nārāyaṇa-kavaca: "Garuḍa, Lord Viṣṇu's carrier, is as powerful as the Lord Himself. May he protect us from all dangerous conditions, and may Lord Viṣvaksena, the Personality of Godhead, protect us from dangers by His holy names.

"In this way, may the Supreme Lord's holy names, His transcendental forms, His carriers, and His weapons protect our intelligence, mind, senses, and life air from all dangers."

"How wonderful!" thought King Indra.

"Everything connected to the Lord is spiritual and nondifferent from Him, so they are all engaged in His service and capable of giving protection," said Viśvarūpa, opening his eyes. "The Lord can destroy our dangers by any of His potent parts. He is also present everywhere. Everything we see is an expansion of His energy. So may He always protect us everywhere from all calamities."

Viśvarūpa then recited the final prayer: "May

Lord Nṛsiṁhadeva, who roars for His devotee Prahlāda, protect us from all fears of dangers, which come through poison, weapons, water, fire, air, and so on. May Lord Nṛsiṁhadeva protect us in all directions and in all corners, above, below, within, and without."

"Jaya Nṛsiṁha!" exclaimed King Indra. This prayer included all the other prayers before it.

Looking at King Indra's peaceful yet joyful face, Viśvarūpa smiled and said, "O Indra, by wearing this mystical armor, you will certainly conquer the demons. One who is even touched or seen by a person wearing this armor becomes free from all fear, what to speak of the person actually wearing it!

"One who wears it is never disturbed by or put in danger by the government, by plunderers, by demons, or by any type of disease.

"Once, a *brāhmaṇa* named Kauśika used this armor when he chose to leave his body in the desert by mystic power. Citraratha, the King of Gandharvaloka, was passing over the dead *brāhmaṇa's* body in his airplane, and by the power of the armor he was forced to fall there with his airplane. The great sages ordered him to throw the *brāhmaṇa's* bones in the nearby river Sarasvatī before returning to his own abode."

"Such is the power of the Nārāyaṇa-kavaca," said Śukadeva Gosvāmī after relating the story to Mahārāja Parīkṣit. "One who wears this armor or hears about it with faith when afraid is immediately freed from all dangers and is worshiped by everyone.

"King Indra recited these *mantras* and wore the armor confidently. He conquered the demons and once again enjoyed the opulence of the three worlds."

Themes and Key Messages

Please go through this table of themes and key messages, with corresponding verses, and discuss each topic further.

THEMES	REFERENCES	KEY MESSAGES
It is our duty to seek the mercy and protection of the Lord.	6.8.8–11	We should meditate on the Lord and our relation to Him as being equal in quality to Him but minute in quantity, just as water of a river is the same nature as the water of the sea. In this way, when we think of ourselves as subordinate to the Supreme, we will always seek His mercy and protection in all circumstances. The Nārāyaṇa-kavaca, which is an armor of potent *mantras*, guides us to take shelter of the Lord alone and become dependent on Him.
Various incarnations of the Lord, who appear for various purposes, protect the devotee.	6.8.13–26	One can chant the Nārāyaṇa-kavaca prayers to be protected by the various incarnations of the Lord for specific purposes as they had done when they appeared on earth. They also protect the devotee during different times of day and night and in all directions. These prayers act like a shield or protective armor against the dangers of this world. They also evoke the Lord's weapons, which protect the devotee.
The chanting of the Lord's holy names offers the best protection.	6.8.27–28	Everything connected to the Lord, including His names and glories, is nondifferent from Him and can give us shelter at any time and place. We can immediately come in contact with Kṛṣṇa, become fearless, and get His protection by chanting His holy name.

<table>
<tr><td>THEMES</td><td>REFERENCES</td><td>KEY MESSAGES</td></tr>
<tr><td>The Supreme Lord is present everywhere and knows everything; therefore He can protect us everywhere and in all situations.</td><td>6.8.29–34</td><td>As fire in one place can expand its heat and light everywhere, the omnipotent Lord situated in His spiritual abode expands Himself everywhere, in both material and spiritual worlds, by His various energies. Similarly, the ornaments and weapons of the Lord are His expansions, and the holy name is identical with Him; therefore they all have equal power to protect the devotee.</td></tr>
</table>

Higher-Thinking Questions

Now try to deepen your understanding of this chapter by delving into Śrīla Prabhupāda's purports and reflecting on the following questions:

1. According to verse 12 purport, how can we understand ourselves to be qualitatively one with the Supreme Lord?

2. Why are the prayers to the Lord's ornaments, weapons, and carriers not false as explained in verse 33 purport?

3. According to verse 41, what is the result of hearing about and using the Nārāyaṇa-kavaca armor?

4. How should the *mantras* be received to be successful? (See verse 42 purport.)

5. After hearing about the Nārāyaṇa-kavaca shield, Mahārāja Parīkṣit could've easily counteracted Śṛṅgi's curse by reciting these prayers. Why didn't he? Recall or refer to *SB* 1.19.15–16. What does a pure devotee want, which we should aspire for?

6. Sometimes it may seem that a devotee is not protected by the Lord when the devotee faces a calamity or even death. How can we see that the Lord is still protecting such a devotee?

7. Do you think the recitation of the Nārāyaṇa-kavaca is part of surrender. (Hint: Recall the six items of surrender you previously learned about.)

8. Do you think reciting the Nārāyaṇa-kavaca is part of pure devotion? Explain.

9. According to verse 42 purport, why was Indra successful in defeating the demons? Was it because of the *mantras* alone or also how they were received? Elaborate.

ACTIVITIES

In this section you will find many exciting things to do. These activities
will get you thinking, moving, drawing, and having loads of fun.

Analogy Activity

HOW IS THE CAUSE ALSO THE EFFECT?

"As a fire, although existing in one place, can expand its light and heat everywhere, so the omnipotent Lord, the Supreme Personality of Godhead, although situated in His spiritual abode, expands Himself everywhere, in both the material and spiritual worlds, by His various energies. Since both cause and effect are the Supreme Lord, there is no difference between cause and effect." *SB* 6.8.32–33

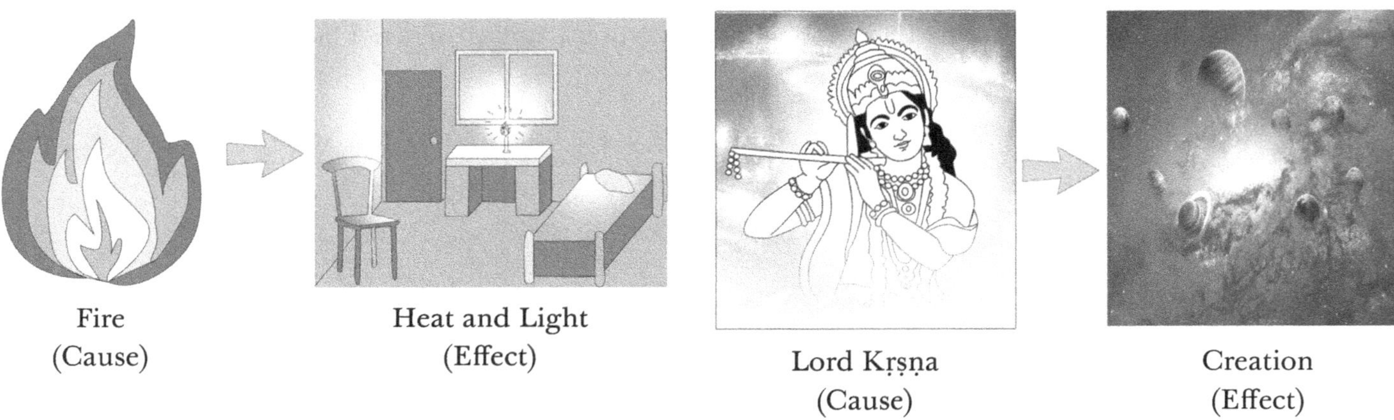

Fire
(Cause)

Heat and Light
(Effect)

Lord Kṛṣṇa
(Cause)

Creation
(Effect)

This analogy explains how the Lord is present everywhere, either directly by His presence or indirectly by His energies. It uses the example of the fire – the fire is physically present in one place, but it is also indirectly present all around the area through its effect: heat and light.

The analogy further says that the cause and effect are nondifferent. Let us understand this deeper.

What this simply means is that fire is the cause of heat and light. We can deduce the presence of fire simply by detecting heat and light even without physically seeing the fire; for example, when we see the above room (in the picture) from a distance. In the same way, we do not have to physically see the Lord to understand His existence – simply by seeing the creation, which comes from Him in the same way that heat and light come from fire, we can understand His presence and His greatness.

In the table below analyze some of the things associated with the Lord, and in a class discussion or with the help of your teacher understand how they are nondifferent from Him. Then fill in the last column.

CAUSE	EFFECT/ENERGY	REASON FOR CREATION	HOW IT IS NONDIFFERENT FROM KRSNA
Kṛṣṇa	Spiritual world	Manifested by the Lord for the living entities who wish to serve Him.	
Kṛṣṇa	Material world	Created by the Lord for the living entities who wish to enjoy separately from Him.	
Kṛṣṇa	Ornaments and weapons	Created by the Lord to assist Him in His pastimes.	
Kṛṣṇa	Holy name	The Lord Himself in sound form for the benefit of the living beings in the material world and which is also glorified in the spiritual world.	

Śrīla Prabhupāda further explains in the purport to verses 32–33 that the worship of the above energies of the Lord is as good as His personal worship. How can you deduce this from the discussion above?

Now reflect on the lesson from this analogy and discuss the following with your class or group: Because the Lord is everywhere, He knows everything and can protect us.

Artistic Activity

SHADING TECHNIQUES: THE LORD'S WEAPONS

In this chapter the demigods glorify the Lord's weapons: the Kaumodakī club, the Vidyādhara sword, the shield, the Pāñcajanya conch, and the Sudarśana *cakra*. These weapons are expansions of the Lord that serve Him. In this activity you will draw and shade a few weapons of your choice. Learn a few shading techniques, which can make your drawings look more realistic.

What you will need: sheets of plain drawing paper; eraser; sharpener; HB, 2B, 4B, and 6B pencils

Shading Techniques:

1. Hatching: In this drawing technique, create a 3-D shading effect by drawing closely spaced parallel lines. Dark areas have darker and more closely packed lines, and lighter areas have light or little shading.

Practice shading a cube using this technique. Use HB pencils to first draw the shape, 2B to shade lighter value, 4B to shade medium dark areas, and 6B to shade the darkest parts.

First draw the cube lightly as in Figure 1. Now shade the lightest part on the left side of the cube first, using 2B pencil and pressing it lightly (Figure 2). Add parallel lines close to each other. Now shade the top part of the cube with 4B pencil (Figure 3). And finally shade the front of the cube with 6B pencil (Figure 4).

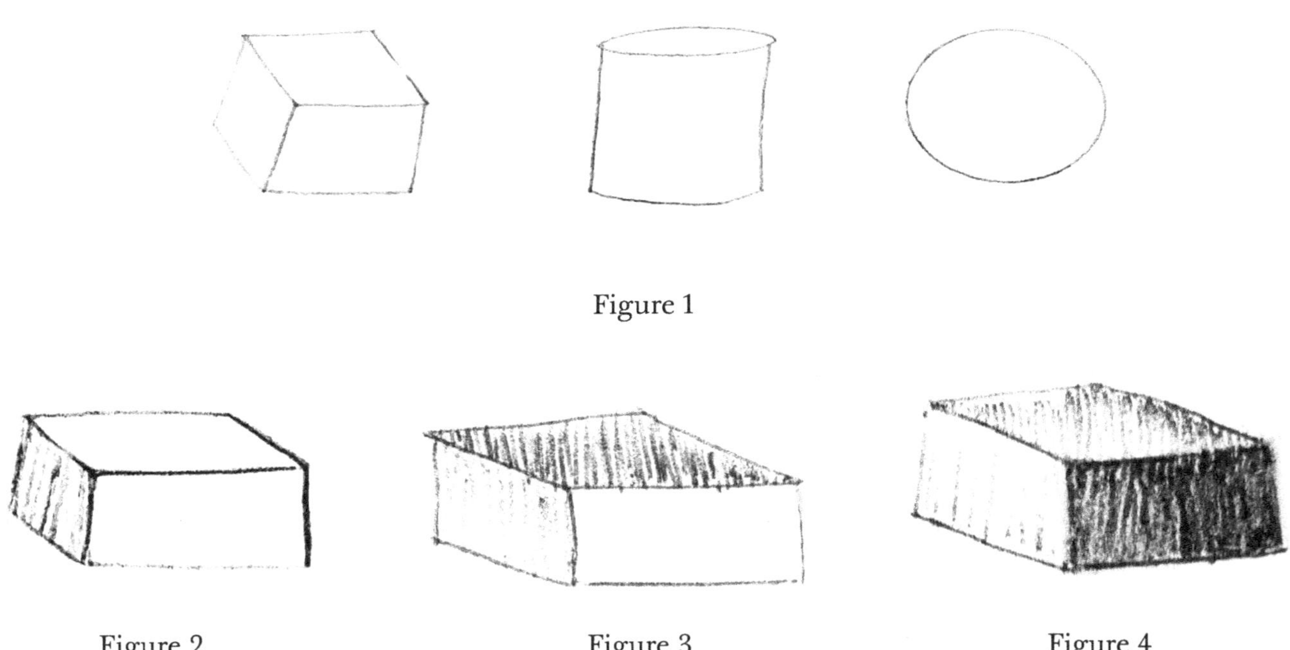

Figure 1

Figure 2   Figure 3   Figure 4

2. Contour shading: This is similar to hatching, but the lines follow the contour of the object. So your lines can be vertical, diagonal, or spherical.

Practice shading a cylinder using contour shading. Begin by drawing the cylinder shape lightly as shown in Figure 1 above. The difference between the cube and cylinder shading is the shape of your strokes. They will be curved unlike the straight parallel strokes in the cube. Begin by drawing curved lines on the left of the cube (Figure 5). Now add the medium dark strokes in the middle (Figure 6). Complete your shading by adding the darkest shading on the right (Figure 7).

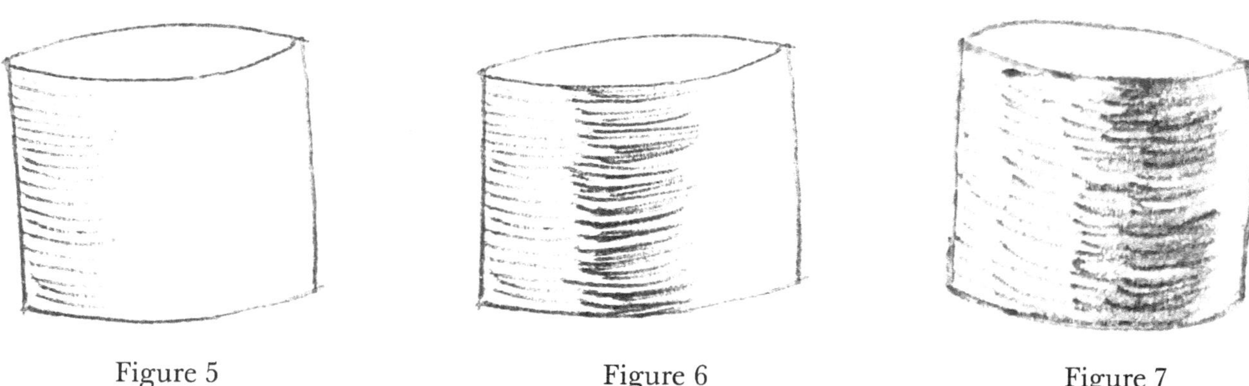

Figure 5   Figure 6   Figure 7

3. Stippling: In this technique, the light and dark areas are created by using dots. You simply apply a greater number of dots and keep them closer to show dark shading, and light and less dots to show areas of lighter shading. Follow the example given in Figures 8, 9, and 10 below.

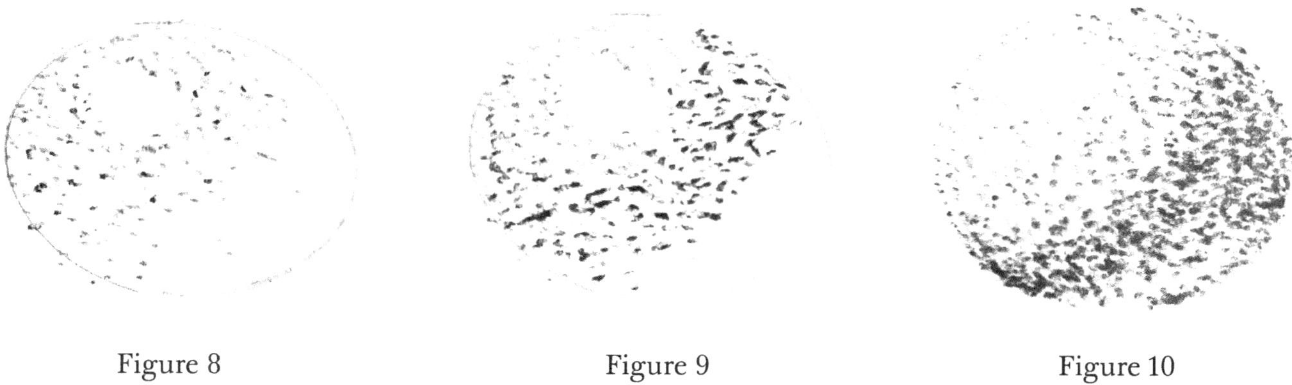

Figure 8   Figure 9   Figure 10

Drawing and shading weapons:

1. Pick two weapons you would like to draw and the shading techniques you want to use. Study the art samples given in Figures 11, 12, 13 of the conch, which uses the stippling method, and the other two weapons (Figures 14 and 15), which use the contour method and the hatching method, before beginning your artwork.

2. You can use the weapon templates given in the resources section at the end of this chapter.

3. Just as you shaded the geometric shapes, shade each weapon beginning with the light shading and ending with the darkest strokes.

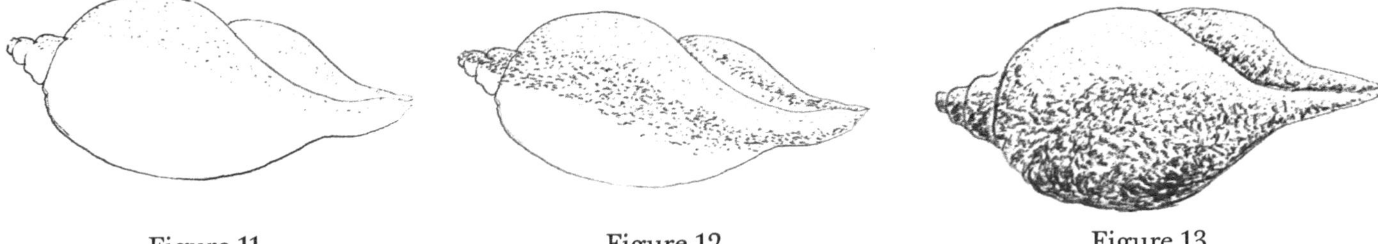

Figure 11   Figure 12   Figure 13

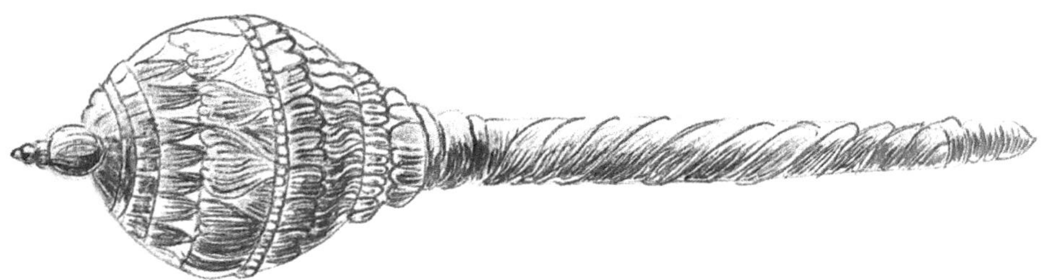

Figure 14: Contour method

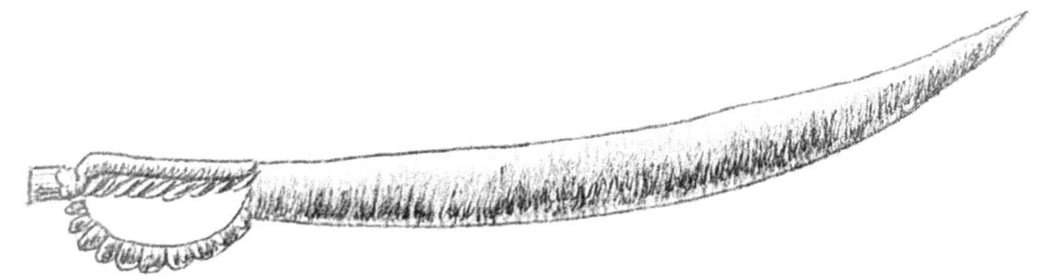

Figure 15: Hatching method

Action Activity

... to get you moving and learning

CHARADES: THE LORD'S EXPANSIONS

In this chapter we learned how the Lord's expansions, like His incarnations, ornaments, and weapons, are omnipotent and identical to His holy name and can provide full protection.

Charades are a fun way to enhance your creative skills and out-of-the-box thinking by acting out a word or a phrase and guessing the word simultaneously.

Play a game of charades by enacting the different incarnations and expansions of the Lord and have your friends guess the correct name of the Lord in that incarnation or expansion. Then encourage your friend to speak a few words on the incarnation of the Lord and the pastime associated with it, especially how the Lord protects His devotees in these incarnations.

Directions:

1. Write words or phrases depicting the different incarnations of the Lord or the different weapons and ornaments of the Lord on individual sheets of paper, e.g., Lord Nṛsiṁhadeva, Lord Varāhadeva, Lord Nārāyaṇa holding the Pāñcajanya conchshell, etc.

2. Place the sheets of paper in a box. Shuffle well.

3. Divide the class into teams or you can play with a partner.

4. Take turns to pick the pieces of paper **one at a time** and act out the Lord's incarnations without using any spoken words. Be creative.

5. Have your opponent team or member guess the incarnation or expansion and speak a few words on it.

Critical-Thinking Activity

... to bring out the spiritual investigator in you

THE QUALITY OF SURRENDER

It is interesting that Indra accepted the Nārāyaṇa-kavaca shield from his *guru* and later chanted it to get his kingdom back, yet when Parīkṣit Mahārāja heard of the Nārāyaṇa-kavaca shield from Śukadeva Gosvāmī, he never thought of using it to protect himself from his impending death. Both Indra and Parīkṣit were devotees of the Lord yet acted differently.

In the pictures on the next page both Lord Indra and Parīkṣit Mahārāja are thinking about their respective situations and the possible solution in the Nārāyaṇa-kavaca. Fill out the thought bubbles.

Would it be fair to judge the actions of these devotees as "good" or "bad" based on their thoughts?

Writing Activities

... to bring out the writer in you

LETTER TO ŚRĪ HARINĀMA PRABHU

In this chapter we see that there are many prerequisites before one can chant the Nārāyaṇa-kavaca. On the other hand, in the second verse of the Śikṣāṣṭakam, Lord Caitanya states that there are no hard and fast rules for chanting the holy name.

In your notebook list all the qualities, benefits, and glories of chanting the holy name described in this chapter and what you've learned so far.

Then write a short personal letter to the holy name, Harināma Prabhu, expressing your appreciation and realizations of the holy name and how you intend to commit to chanting regularly and sincerely. Sign off your letter with your name as you would any other letter.

THE HOLY NAME OFFERS THE BEST PROTECTION

Please complete either activity A or B:

A. FABLE

Through the example of Indra's chanting of the Nārāyaṇa-kavaca in this chapter, we see how the holy name can be the best protection. Let us write a fable to illustrate this theme.

What is a fable? It is a short story that has animal characters with human characteristics. In simple terms, the animals in the story are main characters who behave and act like human beings. The fable has a story plot with an issue/a problem/a complication for the characters, which finally gets resolved due to some action taken. Fables teach the reader a moral lesson through the story.

Based on your understanding that by taking shelter of the Lord's holy names one can receive protection from all evil forces, internally and externally, write a fable to portray the moral that only ***the Lord's holy names can offer protection to an individual.***

Directions for writing the fable:

1. Think of the animal characters and name them.

2. Create a setting (place where the story would take place).

3. Introduce the characters and describe their qualities or nature.

4. Create a storyline with an issue, a problem, or a complication that one or some characters face. You may brainstorm ideas in a group or with your class.

5. Carry forward the story.

6. Show how the problem is resolved by taking shelter of the holy name.

7. Don't forget to add a title to your fable.

B. ADVERTISEMENT

Create an advertisement on how by chanting the different holy names of the Lord, a devotee is thoroughly protected. You may include other names of God for other audiences.

What is an advertisement?

An advertisement is a promotional announcement calling the attention of the people regarding various products, services, or offers through an attractive visual presentation.

How to write an advertisement?
- **Keep it short and simple**: The sentences must be short and simple to grab the maximum attention for the subject. Long sentences are a big NO for advertisements.
- **Have catchy headlines**: The headlines should be attention-grabbing.
- **Be informative**: The contents should be informative and useful for the public to ensure promising benefits.
- **Identify and Channelize**: Always identify the target audience and create the contents to deliver a message efficiently.
- **Use simple language.**

Other tips on presentation:
- Bold out the offers.
- Use proportional fonts.
- Give name, contact, and other details.
- Put the advertisement in a box or decorative border.

Taking the example of the following advertisement, prepare your own advertisement to highlight and announce the benefits of chanting the holy name.

Example: Distribution of Śrīla Prabhupāda's books

Language Activities

... to help you understand better

INTERVIEW: PROCEDURES IN DEITY WORSHIP

Many procedures mentioned in this chapter to successfully chant the Nārāyaṇa-kavaca *mantras* are similar to those used in Gauḍīya Vaiṣṇava Deity worship. Please interview the temple *pūjārī* or a senior devotee in your community and complete the following table:

PROCEDURES FOR RECITING THE NĀRĀYAṆA-KAVACA	CORRESPONDING PROCEDURES IN DEITY WORSHIP
1. Cleanliness – washing hands and legs, chanting *oṁ apavitraḥ pavitro vā* . . .	
2. *ācamana* and *aṅga-nyāsa/kara-nyāsa* – placing the syllables of the *mantra* on various parts of the body and hands	
3. Establishing and becoming fixed in one's spiritual identity as qualitatively one with the Lord (6.8.11).	
4. Meditating on the Lord's various forms/ activities	
5. Meditating on the Lord's carrier and weapons	
6. Taking initiation	

THE SUPREME PROTECTORS

Match the following incarnations with the corresponding request for protection. (Notice how their protection is related to their pastimes.) Then use the underlined 16 letters to answer the question at the end:

1. MATSYA   a. Protect me in difficult places, like the forest and the battlefront.

2. VĀMANA   b. Protect me from rogues on the street.

3. VIŚVARŪPA   c. Protect me in the water from the fierce animals.

4. DATTĀTREYA   d. Protect me on the land.

5. NṚSIṀHA   e. Protect me in the sky.

6. RĀMA   f. Protect me in foreign countries.

7. PARAŚURĀMA   g. Protect me from neglecting to offer respectful obeisances to the Lord.

8. NĀRADA   h. Burn our enemies to ashes.

9. VARĀHA   i. Protect me from falling from the path of *bhakti-yoga*.

10. HAYAGRĪVA   j. Protect me from committing offenses in Deity worship.

11. SUDARŚANA *CAKRA*   k. Protect me on the tops of mountains.

The most merciful of all incarnations:

— — — — — ⁻ — — — — — — — — — — —

(Hint: Locana dāsa Ṭhākura's *bhajana*: *parama karuṇa, pahū dui jana*)

How would you pray to these merciful incarnations for protection?

CHAPTER 8 ANSWERS

How Is the Cause also the Effect?

1. The spiritual world is on the absolute platform – it is transcendental and comes from Kṛṣṇa, so it has the same quality as the Lord. When the quality of one thing is different from the quality of another, they are considered similar; 2. They are all connected to the Lord and "belong" to Him; just like a father may remember the child when he sees the child's shoe, the creation of the Lord helps us remember Him when we see different things in the material world; 3. The Lord's weapons have the potency to give the same benedictions as the Lord; 4. One feels the presence of Kṛṣṇa when chanting His holy name and therefore experiences divine peace and happiness. The holy name also never becomes dull or boring over time, unlike mundane sound; such is the effect of Kṛṣṇa's oneness in His holy name.

4. Since they all have the potency to give the same benedictions of the Lord and one feels the Lord's presence by associating with them, we can derive the same benefits and achieve the Lord's favor by either serving Him in the material or spiritual world, worshiping His weapons, or chanting His holy name. Therefore, they are all nondifferent from the Lord and their worship is as good as the worship of the Lord.

The Quality of Surrender

Indra: I have lost my kingdom because I foolishly disrespected my *guru*. The Lord has been kind to me to give me another chance with Viśvarūpa as my *guru* and the protection of the Nārāyaṇa-kavaca. I am grateful to use these to regain my kingdom.

Parīkṣit: The Nārāyaṇa-kavaca could certainly protect me from my death, but I do not wish to use it to avoid my death. It is by the Lord's will that this has happened, and if the Lord wants, He can protect me as He previously did in the womb. I do not want to go against His will.

It would be wrong to judge one devotee as good and the other as bad because 1). They are both willing to follow the Lord; 2). They are taking shelter of the Lord for whatever desires and mood they have. The *Bhāgavatam* states that one should take shelter of the Lord whether one has no desire, is full of desires, or desires liberation. Indra took shelter of the Lord for material desires, and Parīkṣit had no material desires and took shelter. While the quality of surrender may be different, one cannot judge one as right and the other as wrong.

Procedures in Deity Worship

1. Cleanliness is required before beginning Deity worship. The injunction is to rise early and first clean externally by bathing and internally by reciting *mantras* in remembrance of lotus-eyed Lord Kṛṣṇa: *oṁ apavitraḥ pavitro vā. . .*

2. *ācamana* and *viśeṣa-ācamana*, or complete *ācamana*, is used in Deity worship: Sipping water three times after reciting *mantras* for purification is called simple *ācamana*. Reciting additional *mantras* while touching various sense organs and parts of the body is called *viśeṣa -acamana*.

3. This limb in Deity worship is called *yoga*, which means establishing and becoming fixed in one's spiritual identity. This is done by reciting the following *mantra* from the *Ṛg Veda*: *oṁ tad viṣṇoḥ paramaṁ padaṁ. . .*

4. *Bhūta-śuddhi* is done by identifying oneself as the eternal servant of the servant of Lord Kṛṣṇa by chanting the following *mantra* from *Padyāvalī* (*śloka* 74): *nāhaṁ vipro na ca nara-patir nāpi vaiśyo na śūdro . . .*

5. The Gayatri *mantras* received during the *brāhmaṇa* initiation are meditations on the Lord's various forms and activities. Similarly, verses of glorification used in Deity worship are meditations on the Lord's qualities, opulence, and loving dealings with the devotees.

6. Worship of the Lord's bell, conch, *tulasī*, spiritual master, and *guru-paramparā*, as well as His flute, shoes, and other paraphernalia is done in Vaiṣṇava Deity worship.

7. *Brāhmaṇa-dīkṣā* from a bona fide spiritual master is taken before one begins Deity worship.

The Supreme Protectors

1.c; 2.d; 3.e; 4.i; 5.a; 6.f; 7.k; 8.j; 9.b; 10.g; 11.h

Nitai-Gauracandra: (*Potential answers*) Protect me from falling prey to *māyā*; protect me from forgetting Kṛṣṇa; protect me from lust, greed, anger, etc.

RESOURCES

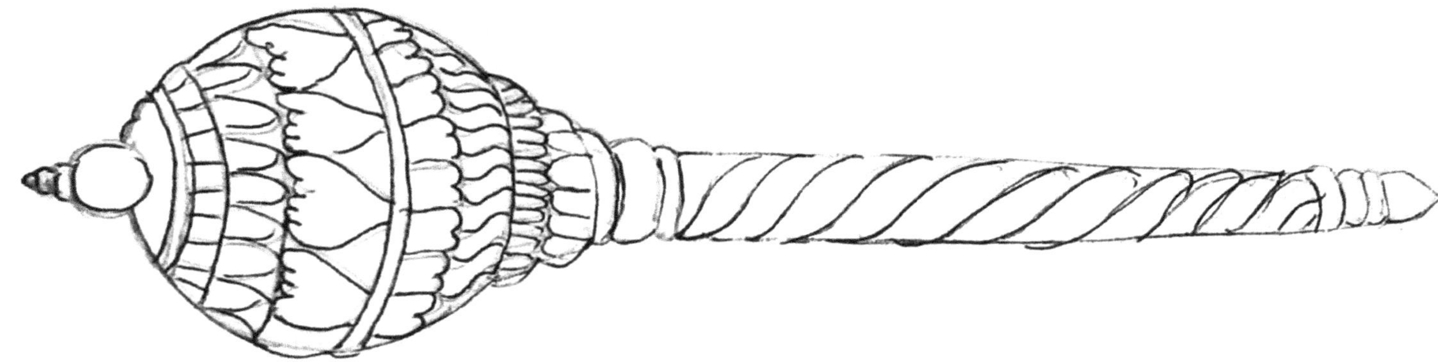

Template 1

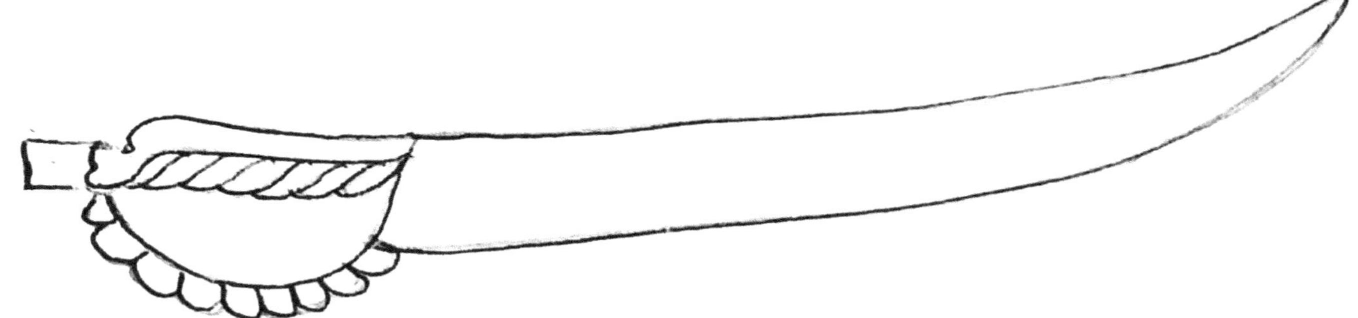

Template 2

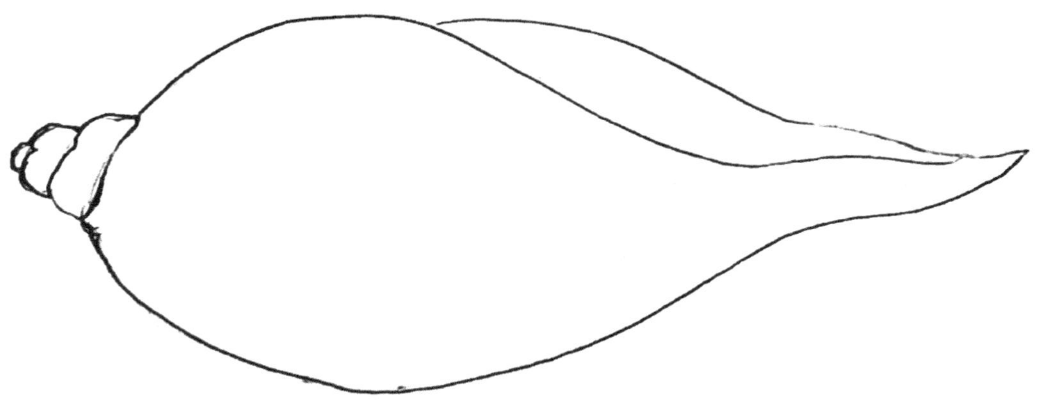

Template 3

9

APPEARANCE OF THE DEMON VṚTRĀSURA

Indra was overjoyed that the demigods were strong again and had regained control under the competent guidance of their priest, Viśvarūpa, until one day . . . Viśvarūpa was loudly chanting *mantras* and offering *ghee* in the sacrificial fire for the demigods, who were related to him from his father's side. Viśvarūpa was also secretly offering oblations in the fire for the benefit of the demons. You see, the demons were also related to him but from his mother's side. And Indra, the king of the demigods, found out! You can imagine how enraged he was. He felt betrayed. He was terrified of being defeated by the demons again because of Viśvarūpa's favoring the demons. So you wouldn't believe what Indra did. He cut off Viśvarūpa's three heads! Yes, Viśvarūpa had three heads: one for drinking *soma-rasa*, one for drinking wine, and one for eating food. And when Indra cut off his heads, each head transformed into a bird, which flew away.

But Indra could not get away from the sinful reactions for killing a *brāhmaṇa*. He had to suffer for one year even though he could have neutralized the sinful reactions. To purify himself he distributed the reactions for his sin among the earth, water, trees, and women. Because the earth accepted one fourth of his sinful reactions, Indra gave the earth the benediction that ditches would fill up automatically. But because of those sinful reactions, we find many deserts on the surface of the earth.

Similarly, Indra gave the trees branches and twigs that grow back for accepting one fourth of the sinful reactions, which we see in the flowing sap from trees. Women too received the benediction from Indra that they enjoy lusty desires continuously for accepting another fourth of the sinful reactions. As a result, women have the menstruation cycle every month. And then, water accepted the last quarter of sinful reactions in return for Indra's benediction that water would increase the volume of other substances with which it is mixed. The sinful reactions took the form of bubbles and foam in water, which should be avoided.

But Indra's troubles were not over. Viśvarūpa's

destroyer of the entire creation. He danced and shouted, making the entire earth tremble as if from an earthquake. As he yawned again and again, it seemed as if he would swallow the whole sky with his cave-like mouth. He seemed to lick the stars with his tongue and eat the universe with his long, sharp teeth. This fearful demon, who became the son of Tvaṣṭā, covered all the planetary systems and was therefore called Vṛtra, or one who covers everything. Terrified, everyone ran in all directions.

The demigods, headed by Indra, charged Vṛtrāsura with their soldiers, striking him with their divine bows and arrows and other weapons, but Vṛtrāsura swallowed all their weapons. The demigods couldn't believe what was happening. Disappointed and beaten by the powerful demon, they fled. They then gathered to please and worship

father, Tvaṣṭā, was infuriated when he heard of his son's death. He performed a ritualistic ceremony to avenge Viśvarūpa. Offering oblations into the fire, he said, "O enemy of Indra, immediately come forth to kill your enemy!" But he made a mistake – he chanted the *mantra* long instead of short, and so the meaning changed. Instead of "the enemy of Indra," it meant "Indra, who is the enemy." Little did Tvaṣṭā know that the personality he was about to invoke was not the enemy of Indra, but of whom Indra was the enemy.

To everyone's horror, a ghastly demon appeared from the fire. Day after day, he grew into a tall and blackish creature with eyes as piercing as the midday sun. With his gigantic form that reached the sky and his copper-like hair, beard, and moustache, he looked like the

the Supreme Personality of Godhead, their only shelter.

They prayed: "O Supreme Lord, You alone can give us full protection. We are afraid of the time factor, which will end our existence, but time himself is scared of You. Therefore, taking shelter of You brings fearlessness.

"O Lord, You are always jubilant and self-satisfied, steady, and detached. You are the only shelter of everyone. Anyone who thinks he can be protected by anyone other than You is like someone who desires to cross the ocean by holding the tail of a dog. What a great fool he is!

"All Your incarnations prove that You are there to protect Your devotees. Lord Matsya saved King Satyavrata from the great danger of the flood. May that same fish incarnation save us from the great and fearful danger caused by the son of Tvaṣṭā.

"Please protect us, O Lord, who protected Lord Brahmā when he fell from his seat on the lotus in the water of devastation.

"O Lord, You have created us, and it is only by Your mercy that we are able to assist in the creation of the universe. You are present before us as the Supersoul, yet we cannot see You. This is because we think that we are separate and independent gods.

"O Lord, You expand into various transcendental bodies to give protection to Your devotees. You came as Vāmana, Paraśurāma,

Nṛsiṁha and Varāha among animals, and Matsya and Kūrma among aquatics. Among humans, You appeared as Lord Rāma and Lord Kṛṣṇa. So we take shelter of You, for we are sure that You will give us Your protection."

Suddenly, the demigods felt the Lord's presence within them. Closing their eyes, they looked inwards and saw Him within their hearts, holding His weapons, conch shell, disc, and club. They then opened their eyes to see the same Lord Nārāyaṇa in the same pose before them. He smiled and looked at them with His lotus-petal eyes. Sixteen personal attendants who looked like

Him were worshiping Him. The demigods fell down like rods, in obeisance, with great ecstasy. They then rose slowly and began to glorify the Lord with more prayers:

"We offer our obeisances to You, dear Lord, who has many varieties of names and who releases the *cakra* to kill the demons. O supreme controller, You control the three destinations, yet You live in Your supreme abode, Vaikuṇṭha. We cannot understand Your activities; therefore we have nothing to offer You but our humble obeisances.

"O Lord, You don't have a material body, and You certainly don't need us. You create, maintain, and destroy this cosmic manifestation by Yourself, but You are transcendental to all material activities, so Your activities are very difficult to understand.

"Like an ordinary human being, do You exist in this world with a material body? Do You enjoy and suffer the results of good and bad actions? Or, on the contrary, are You present here as a neutral witness, who is self-sufficient, free from material desires, and full of spiritual potency? We can't understand Your actual position."

The Lord glanced lovingly at the demigods with a gentle smile on His lips.

"Your unlimited glories are inconceivable to the conditioned souls," they continued, mesmerized by the Lord's beauty and presence. "Modern theologians and philosophers argue about right and wrong, but their arguments are false and their judgments are inconclusive because they have no authorized way to gain knowledge of You. They are confused by the scriptures that have false conclusions, so they are unable to understand You. Because their intention is polluted – they just want to come to the right conclusion – their theories cannot reveal You. But You are transcendental, O Lord. All contradictions can be reconciled in You. In You, contradictions like doing and not doing, happiness and distress are not actually contradictory; because You are so great, You can undo anything as You like. What is impossible for You? You can do everything by Your energies."

The Lord continued smiling, nodding his head gently and listening attentively.

"A bewildered person gets scared of a rope, thinking it to be snake, but an intelligent person knows that it is just a rope. Similarly, devotees who know You do not see contradictions in You, but nondevotees see You as the snakelike source of all fear. For example, when Nṛsiṁhadeva appeared, Prahlāda saw You as the supreme solace whereas his father saw You as ultimate death."

King Indra stepped forward. With tears in his eyes, he kneeled at the Lord's lotus feet. Looking at the Lord's radiant, attractive face, he folded his palms and said, "O Lord, You are the cause of all causes. Without You, everything would be dead. You, as the Supersoul, the supreme controller, are the only one remaining. Therefore, O killer of the Madhu demon, those who have tasted the nectar of your glories are ever blissful. You are the soul and dear friend of such devotees. How could they give up Your devotional service?

"O supremely powerful one, You always appear in various incarnations to punish the demons as soon as they become very powerful and cause distress to Your devotees. Therefore, we pray that You appear today as another incarnation, if You so desire, to kill Vṛtrāsura.

"We are all surrendered to You, O supreme pure, O supreme protector. We are bound to Your lotus feet by chains of love. Please be compassionate to us. By Your loving glance, Your soothing smile, and Your sweet words, remove our anxiety caused by this demon.

"You know everything, O Lord, because You exist everywhere and are the witness of everything. Therefore, we don't need to inform You of anything. You know very well why we've come here and taken shelter of Your lotus feet. Your lotus feet give cooling relief from all material disturbances, so please give us relief from the tribulations of this material world."

Then there was silence. The demigods bowed their heads, trembling in excitement and nervousness at the same time. They still couldn't believe that the Lord of their hearts was right in front of them hearing their pleas.

The Supreme Personality of Godhead smiled and said, "O beloved demigods, I am very pleased with you, for you offered sincere prayers in knowledge. Devotees become liberated by such knowledge and become purified by offering such personal prayers to Me. This is the source of devotional service. In fact, pure devotees, whose minds are exclusively fixed on Me, do not ask Me for anything. All they want is the opportunity to engage in My devotional service."

The demigods looked down, embarrassed. They recognized they weren't such pure devotees, yet they knew that they could not take shelter of anyone other than their Lord.

The Lord continued, "Those who just desire material benefits are called misers, *kṛpaṇa*s. They don't know the ultimate need of the soul. And if someone awards such fools what they want, they are also considered foolish."

The demigods looked at each other, astonished. They hadn't expected the Lord to be so straightforward with them. They understood that they were unintelligent for granting the wishes of their devotees, because such material benefits only increase one's attachment and repetition of birth and death. They knew that their Lord was most intelligent, so why should He fulfill their desires? Yet, they also knew Him to be the protector of His devotees.

Seeing the sincerity and helplessness of His devotees, the Lord said, "O Indra, go to the exalted saint Dadhīci, who is performing severe vows and austerities. Through the head of a horse, he delivered the spiritual science to the Aśvinī-kumāras, who became liberated as a result.

"Sage Dadhīci has a strong body because of reciting the invincible Nārāyaṇa-kavaca. He gave this same protective shield to Tvaṣṭā, who delivered it to Viśvarūpa, and from whom you received it. Therefore, immediately go to Dadhīci and ask him for his body."

King Indra looked confused. What did the Lord mean?

"When Dadhīci awards you his body, Viśvakarmā will prepare a thunderbolt from his bones, which will be invested with My power. This thunderbolt will certainly kill Vṛtrāsura."

For a second Indra smiled and then realized that it won't be so easy to get the sage's body.

"How will he give his body to me?" asked Indra.

"Ask the Aśvinī-kumāras to beg him for his body on your behalf; then he will surely give it because of his affection for them."

King Indra nodded and felt remorse for his previous actions.

"Don't be afraid of Vṛtrāsura," the Lord concluded. "Although he can destroy the three worlds, he is My devotee and will never harm you. He will be killed because of My spiritual strength, and you will regain your strength, weapons, and wealth."

Themes and Key Messages

Please go through this table of themes and key messages, with corresponding verses, and discuss each topic further.

THEMES	REFERENCES	KEY MESSAGES
If we are afraid, we should seek shelter only of the Supreme Personality of Godhead.	6.9.21–27	The Lord is the only real shelter. The demigods, being afraid of death, took shelter of the Supreme Lord, who is feared by everyone, including the demons and time personified. One becomes fearless when one takes shelter of the Lord. Anyone who thinks he can be protected by anyone or anything else is a great fool. He is like someone who wants to cross the ocean by catching hold of a dog's tail. One can only cross the material ocean of birth and death by taking shelter of the Lord's lotus feet, which are like an indestructible boat that can easily cross the material ocean.
The Absolute Truth is very difficult to understand; His activities are apparently contradictory, so people understand Him from different angles of vision.	6.9.34–37	The Lord's activities are inconceivable; therefore devotees and nondevotees see the Lord differently. Nondevotees see the Lord's pastimes and actions as contradictory whereas devotees do not. For example, the Supreme Lord is full of transcendental bliss whether He appears happy or distressed. He is happy to protect His devotees and also kill their enemies. This may seem contradictory, but it is not. Because He is spiritual, material conceptions of happiness and distress do not apply to Him. This also applies to the Lord's pure devotees who experience bliss in the presence of the Lord or in separation from Him. Similarly, devotees see the Lord as a source of bliss whereas the nondevotees see the same Lord as a source of fear. Therefore the Lord is understood differently from different angles of vision. Only devotees can understand the Lord through devotional service.

THEMES	REFERENCES	KEY MESSAGES
The Lord is omnipresent and omniscient – He is present everywhere and knows the necessities of His devotees – so there is no need to worship Him for personal benefit.	6.9.40–42, 48	*Sakāma* devotees, those with material motivations, approach the Lord for relief from difficulty, whereas *akāma* devotees, those with no material desires, never disturb the Lord for material benefits because they know their suffering is due to their past impious activity. They also know that the Lord knows everything, so they don't ask for anything but the opportunity to engage in devotional service. However, *sakāma* devotees like the demigods, immediately pray to the Lord as soon as they are in difficulty, but they are considered pious because they still depend on the Lord's mercy.
All tribulations in the material world can be relieved when one fully surrenders to and takes shelter of Kṛṣṇa's lotus feet.	6.9.43–45	Although the *sakāma* devotees are not pure and approach the Lord with material motives, there is an advantage. When they take shelter of Kṛṣṇa's lotus feet, they can become purified and give up their material desires. At the same time, they are relieved of their suffering when they helplessly surrender to the Lord, like the demigods did in this chapter. On the other hand, a pure devotee surrenders fully, asking the Lord to protect him or destroy him, as the Lord desires. Thus the Lord becomes the property of such a devotee.
If one offers personal prayers to the Supreme Personality of Godhead, one becomes eligible to become a pure devotee and go back to Godhead.	6.9.46–47	The Lord was pleased with the demigods' prayers, which were offered in helplessness. They offered personal prayers, unlike the impersonalists who sometimes offer prayers but are not directed to the Supreme Person. They cannot become purified. Devotees, however, who pray to the personal feature of the Lord become purified and can go back to Godhead.
Devotees never pray for material things, but if someone comes to Kṛṣṇa asking for material benefits, Kṛṣṇa generally does not award him the material things he desires.	6.9.49–50	A *kṛpaṇa* is foolish because he asks the Lord for something material, which is temporary and compared to poison because it increases one's cycle of repeated birth and death. The person who awards the material benedictions is also foolish, but Kṛṣṇa is not foolish like such an unintelligent devotee. He shows special favor by taking away whatever material possessions a devotee has and gradually gives him the intelligence to be satisfied only by rendering service to His lotus feet. Demigods, on the other hand, award material benedictions; therefore generally materialistic people worship the demigods instead of Kṛṣṇa or Viṣṇu.

Higher-Thinking Questions

Now try to deepen your understanding of this chapter by delving into Śrīla Prabhupāda's purports and reflecting on the following questions:

1. In verse 1 purport Śrīla Prabhupāda explains that we cannot perceive the heavenly kingdom, for we cannot go there. How does he suggest we understand things beyond our perception and understanding?

2. Why can't we see the Supreme Lord face to face as Śrīla Prabhupāda explains in verse 25 purport?

3. In Vaikuṇṭha the Supreme Lord and His devotees look very similar. How is the Lord distinguished from His devotees? See verse 30 and purport.

4. How can we understand that the Lord is equal to everyone, that he gives His favor to the devotees and also the demons? Refer to verse 35 purport.

5. What three conclusions about the Lord do the demigods come to in verse 38?

6. What is the difference between *sakāma* and *akāma* devotees as explained by Śrīla Prabhupāda in verse 40 purport? Relate this to *kṛpaṇas* and *brāhmaṇas* mentioned in verse 49 and purport.

7. From this chapter how do you know that the demigods are not pure devotees? Refer to verses 40 and 48 and their purports.

8. Why doesn't Kṛṣṇa award material things to a devotee as explained in verse 49 purport?

9. Why is a *kṛpaṇa*, someone who asks the Lord for material benefit, considered foolish according to verse 49 purport?

10. Why do people generally not worship Kṛṣṇa or Viṣṇu as explained in verse 50 purport? Who do they become devotees of?

11. If the Lord could reciprocate wonderfully with the demigods, who are *sakāma bhaktas*, with mixed devotion, and with Prajāpati Dakṣa (in chapters 4 and 5 of this canto), reflect on the complete reciprocation He offers His pure devotees, like Prahlāda Mahārāja or the Vrajavāsīs.

ACTIVITIES

In this section you will find many exciting things to do. These activities
will get you thinking, moving, drawing, and having loads of fun.

Analogy Activity

... to bring out the scholar in you

THE BOAT OR THE DOG'S TAIL

"That Supreme Personality of Godhead is the only shelter of everyone. Anyone desiring to be protected by others is certainly a great fool who desires to cross the sea by holding the tail of a dog." *SB* 6.9.22

In this verse the demigods are praying to the Lord seeking His protection from the demon Vṛtrāsura. The demigods realize that in the material world only the Lord can give them protection – it is useless to seek protection from any other source although we may feel tempted to do so. They explain this point using the example of a person who tries to cross an ocean by holding on to the tail of a dog. Śrīla Prabhupāda explains how useless and foolish this attempt is.

Further in the purport, Śrīla Prabhupāda gives another analogy to explain how one can cross the ocean of material existence (*SB* 10.14.58): "The Lord's lotus feet are an indestructible boat, and if one takes shelter of that boat he can easily cross the ocean of nescience."

Let us try to understand how to cross the ocean of material existence using these two analogies.

On the next page are five students from Radha mataji's *Bhāgavatam* study group who are trying to understand this analogy. They have a few comments and realizations after they hear the explanation:

Within your own study group, discuss each of these comments and understand them. In the end, summarize your understanding in two to three sentences in your notebooks.

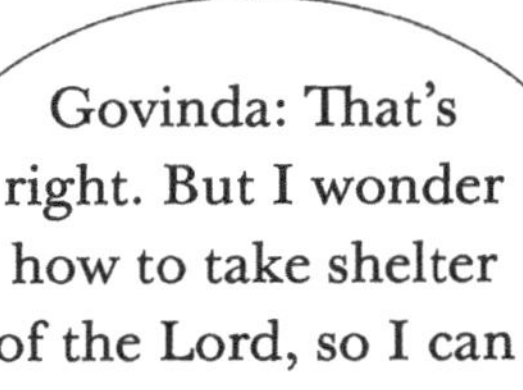

Artistic Activity

HOLY NAME CARDS

Read the verse, synonyms, and translation to verse 33 carefully. It lists several names of Kṛṣṇa you may not have heard of:

bhagavān — O Supreme Personality of Godhead; *nārāyaṇa* — the resort of all living entities, Nārāyaṇa; *vāsudeva* — Lord Vāsudeva, Śrī Kṛṣṇa; *ādi-puruṣa* — the original person; *mahā-puruṣa* — the most exalted personality; *mahā-anubhāva* — the supremely opulent; *parama-*

maṅgala — the most auspicious; *parama-kalyāṇa* — the supreme benediction; *parama-kāruṇika* — the supremely merciful; *kevala* — changeless; *jagat-ādhāra* — the support of the cosmic manifestation; *loka-eka-nātha* — the only proprietor of all the planetary systems; *sarva-īśvara* — the supreme controller; *lakṣmī-nātha* — the husband of the goddess of fortune

Let's try to learn these names and remember them with flash cards:

- Using the template below, photocopy or duplicate at least ten cards on cardboard or writing paper.
- Cut out the cards, color in the borders, or make your own decorative borders. Then write the Sanskrit name of the Lord on top. Draw any other pictures on each card that may remind you of the meaning of the name.
- On the back of the card, write down the meaning of each name and decorate it.
- Finally, put the cards together and make a small Nāma Flip Book!

Template

Action Activity

GROUP DISCUSSION:
THE ABSOLUTE TRUTH IS INCONCEIVABLE

In this chapter the demigods admit that it is very difficult even for them to understand the Absolute Truth, but only through devotional service can one try to understand Him and His activities.
Form groups or partners to discuss this topic further.

Group Discussion:

A group discussion is a discussion between a group of participants on a given topic.
It improves your thinking, listening, and speaking skills. It also boosts your confidence and is an effective tool in providing facts, solutions, or ideas.

Look at the table of questions below. With the help of your teacher and understanding of this chapter, try to discuss and answer each one of them:

START HERE	MOVE YOUR DISCUSSION HERE
1. Why do you think that the Lord's activities are inconceivable?	• Discuss the imperfections of conditioned souls. • Discuss the superiority of the Lord in relation to the soul. • Discuss the transcendental nature and power of the Lord that cannot be perceived by our minute intelligence or vision.
2. Why is the Supreme Lord happy to protect His devotees?	• Discuss examples of how the Lord protected His devotees, such as Indra, Prahlāda Mahārāja, And Dhruva Mahārāja. • Give your viewpoints on why devotees are protected by the Lord. • Discuss why the enemies of the devotees are killed by the Lord. • Discuss why the Lord is so blissful in protecting His devotees.
3. How is the Lord understood from different angles of vision?	• How devotees see the Supreme Lord (with bliss). • How nondevotees see the Lord (with fear). • What makes their vision different? Give your opinion.

Some important directions for group discussion:
• Always have your points planned on a sheet of paper before speaking.

- Unlike a debate, you can present your viewpoints for both situations: where you agree and where you disagree. So feel free to express.
- Listen to a participant without interrupting. No one should interrupt you either.
- Listen actively and with an ear to understanding others' views.
- Allow everyone the chance to speak.
- Criticize ideas, not individuals. We all can learn something from each other, even if your viewpoints don't necessarily align.
- Use polite words and maintain a positive attitude.
- Use encouraging body language and tone of voice.
- Speak sensibly and don't rush your points.

Critical-Thinking Activity

... to bring out the spiritual investigator in you

AKĀMA-BHAKTI VERSUS SAKĀMA-BHAKTI

In the last chapter we saw how Indra and Mahārāja Parīkṣit took shelter of the Lord in different ways. Indra, being a *sakāma* bhakta (a devotee with material desires), approached the Lord for relief from his material problem; on the other hand, Parīkṣit, who was an *akāma* bhakta (a devotee with no material desires), considered his misery the will of the Lord and never prayed for relief. We learned how both categories of people are considered devotees, even though the quality of their devotion may be at different levels.

In verses 48–50 of this chapter, however, the Lord describes devotional service with no expectation of material return as superior to service rendered with the expectation of getting something in return. Let's analyze each perspective and understand how *akāma-bhakti* is superior to *sakāma-bhakti.*

Set up a debate with the following motion: It is better to approach the Lord with material desires than to pretend to have given up all material desires when becoming a devotee of the Lord.

- Read the translations and purports to verses 48 to 50. Complete the discussion board provided below with relevant points for each perspective.
- Divide the class into two groups, one to present each viewpoint.
- Discuss and debate the viewpoints.
- Come to a conclusion that is supported by evidence from Śrīla Prabhupāda's purports.

If you do not have a class to participate in this activity, still fill in the discussion board and discuss with your mentor or friends. Write your conclusion in your notebook.

Based on your conclusion, comment on the following statement: It is better to be a *sakāma-bhakta* (devotee with material desires) of the Supreme Lord than to be an *abhakta* (nondevotee).

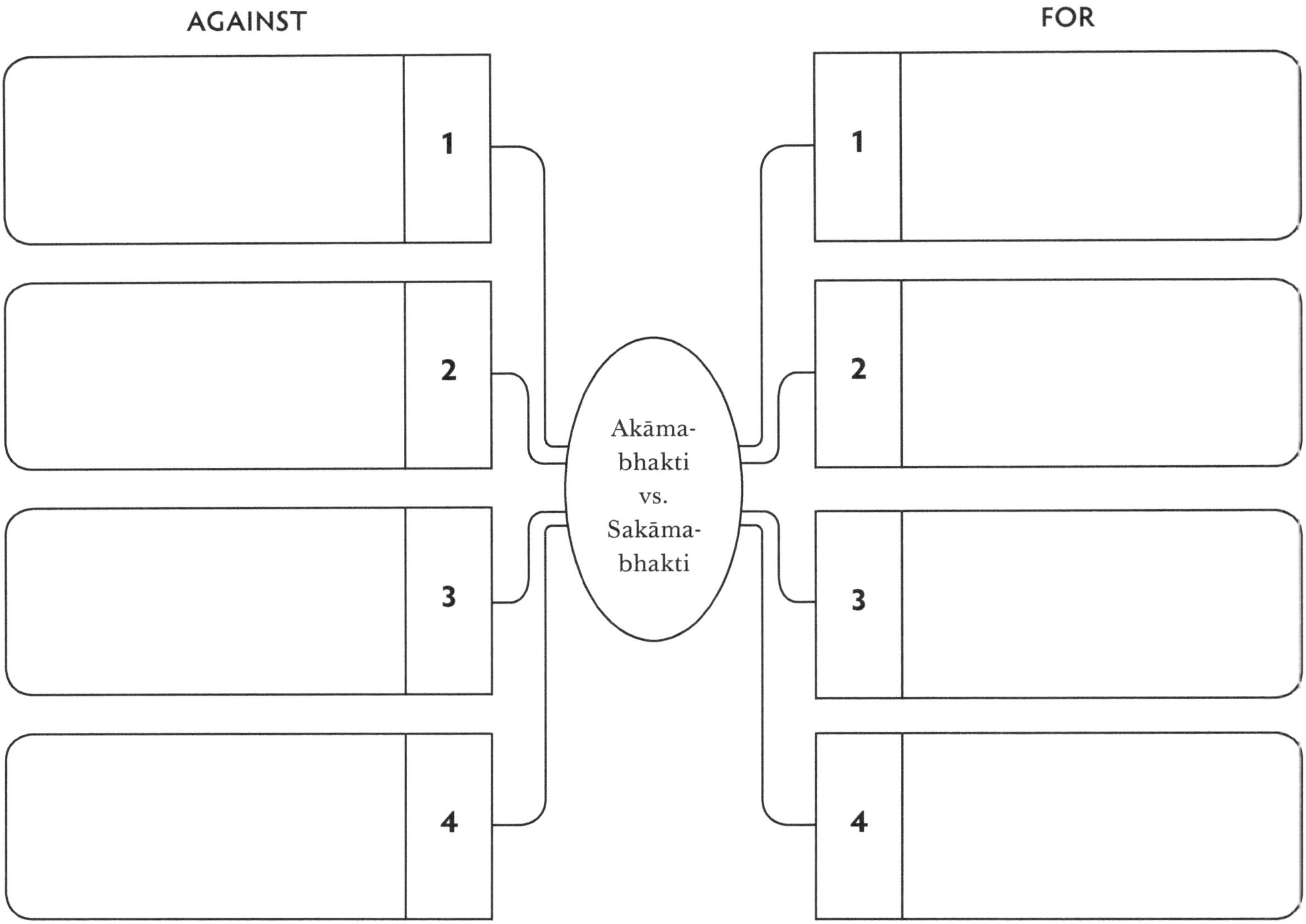

Introspective Activity

... to bring out the reflective devotee in you

PERSONAL PRAYERS

Vandanam, offering choicest prayers to Lord Kṛṣṇa, is one of the nine limbs of *bhakti-yoga*. Lord Kṛṣṇa is most pleased when His devotees pray to Him only for devotional service. The demigods wanted to be free from the material distress caused by Vṛtrāsura, so they prayed to the Lord to help them. Nonetheless, the Lord was pleased by their *sakāma* prayers, which they offered in great knowledge of the Lord's exalted position. The Lord states that such prayers are a source of devotional service to Him.

Reflect on the statements below and compose a short prayer to the Lord. Write the prayer in your notebook, and then in a devotional mood say it to a picture or deity of Kṛṣṇa:

1. Though we might not be *akāma* devotees, we should still offer prayers to the Lord every day. We can take shelter of the Lord in all conditions of life just like the demigods repeatedly approach the Lord's lotus feet in adversity.

2. Lord Kṛṣṇa always reciprocates with sincere, personal prayers. The demigods always address the Lord with His various names and glorify His qualities, pastimes, associates, and paraphernalia. Do we remember to first offer our respects and praise to the Lord before placing our concerns before Him?

3. Do we offer prayers with the understanding that only Kṛṣṇa's will prevails, and are willing to accept whatever Kṛṣṇa desires? Śrīla Prabhupāda taught us how to pray: When Śrīla Prabhupāda was about to leave his body, he told his disciples to pray to Kṛṣṇa to make him better only if Kṛṣṇa desires.

4. In our prayers we can always add our deepest prayer to eventually become pure devotees, to serve Kṛṣṇa exclusively even though we request material benefits, protection, etc.

Guidelines to compose a prayer: First glorify the Lord, thank Him for whatever He's given you, then request Him for what you desire, and then add a prayer for exclusive love and devotion to His lotus feet.

Writing and Language Activities

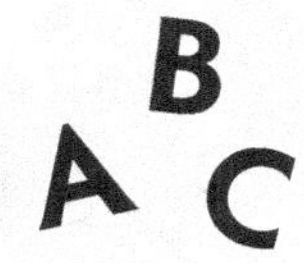

... to help you understand better

AUTOBIOGRAPHY EXTRACT:
WHEN AFRAID, SEEK THE SUPREME SHELTER

In this chapter we learned how by seeking shelter of the Supreme Personality of Godhead, all our fears vanish. Let us explore this topic through an autobiography exercise.

What is an autobiography?
An autobiography is a story of a person's life written by the same person. It contains detailed information of his or her personality, life stories and experiences, personal relationships, career, and achievements. Autobiographies always relate true events of a person's life. There can be numerous events described in an autobiography. They are written in the first-person narrative.

Based on your understanding of the theme in this chapter, think about a time or situation in your life when you were very scared and afraid of something. It could be a fear of doing something new, a fear of beginning a new relationship, a fear of failing a task, or even a fear

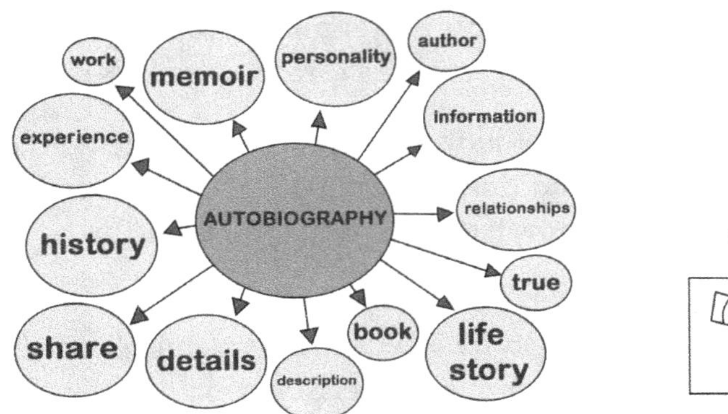

of the dark or any other external factor. Do you think that taking shelter of the Supreme Personality of Godhead helped you at that moment? How? If you haven't gone through such a situation, imagine a scenario you could face in life and describe how taking shelter of Kṛṣṇa helped you overcome fear.

Then write a brief excerpt that could appear in your autobiography.

Directions:

1. Think about the particular incident or situation of fear.

2. Make notes on what happened and how you were affected.

3. Describe the situation and setting; mention characters if needed.

4. Explain how the situation changed by remembering the Supreme Lord and taking His shelter.

5. Use first person narrative to write the autobiography; this means using pronouns like "I," "me," and "my."

6. Make it interesting.

ALL CONTRADICTIONS ARE RESOLVED IN THE SUPREME LORD

In verse 36 the demigods bring out a very important feature of the Supreme Lord:

"O Supreme Personality of Godhead, all contradictions can be reconciled in You."

What do they mean by this? Please study the purport to this verse and discuss with your teacher and class. Discuss how Kṛṣṇa is free from all dualities. What is duality? It is an instance of opposition or contrast between two concepts or two aspects of something; e.g., happiness and distress, birth and death, attachment and repulsion, etc.

Then explain in your notebooks how the following contradictions or dualities are reconciled in the Lord; in other words, explain how they are not actually contradictory in relation to the Lord:

1. Happy/distressed

2. Partial/impartial

3. Infinite/finite

4. Personal/impersonal

PARTS OF SPEECH GAME: BECOME A PURE DEVOTEE OF THE LORD!

In this chapter we learn that one can become a pure devotee of the Supreme Lord and go back to Godhead by worshiping His personal form and attributes.

Frame interesting sentences using one or more parts of speech to explain that a devotee becomes pure by worshiping Kṛṣṇa's personal form and attributes. This game can be played in pairs or in a group.

The eight parts of speech:

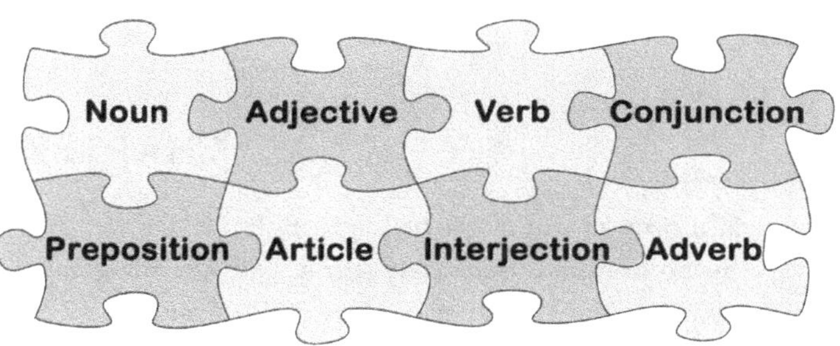

- **NOUN** – person, place, thing, or idea (e.g., common nouns: ball, desk, boy; proper nouns: Kṛṣṇa, Balarāma)
- **PRONOUN** – word that replaces a noun in a sentence (e.g., he, she, it)
- **VERB** – describes or indicates an action (e.g., run, jump, stand, read)
- **ADJECTIVE** – describes a noun, such as what something looks like and what it feels like to touch, taste, or smell (e.g., red, soft, big, old, marvelous, adventurous)
- **ADVERB** – describes an action (verb) or an adjective; usually ends in "ly" (e.g., quickly, carefully, intentionally)
- **PREPOSITION** – a word that shows the relation between a noun or pronoun to other words in a sentence (e.g., in, under, behind, by, to, at)
- **CONJUNCTION** – a word used to connect clauses or sentences or to coordinate words in the same clause (e.g., and, but, if)
- **ARTICLE** – like adjectives, articles modify nouns; "the" is a definite article and "a/an" is an indefinite article.

Based on your understanding of the chapter, use one or more parts of speech to form sentences stating how a devotee of the Supreme Lord only worships His personal form and becomes eligible to perform devotional service and go back home, back to Godhead.

Example: IF A DEVOTEE WORSHIPS KṚṢṆA, HE BECOMES PURE AND EASILY GOES BACK TO GODHEAD.

In this sentence we find all the parts of speech:
DEVOTEE – common noun
A – article (indefinite)
WORSHIPS – verb
KṚṢṆA – proper noun
HE – pronoun
PURE – adjective
AND – conjunction
EASILY – adverb
TO – preposition

Now

Challenge:
Try to use all the parts
of speech in a single
meaningful sentence!

Write your sentence on a sheet of paper and highlight the different parts of speech with different colors! Then indicate which words belong to which part of speech (like example above).

CHAPTER 9 ANSWERS

The Boat or the Dog's Tail

Some points to be clearly discussed: The material world is like an ocean, a place full of unknown dangers. We, the living beings, are being tossed around in the waves and are also facing unexpected and dangerous situations continually, but we have no clue how to protect ourselves in this place. We sometimes find hope in temporary solutions to our problems, which help us get rid of immediate troubles. But these solutions, which are compared to holding on to a dog's tail, will never help us overcome the main problem – to find a way to safely get out of the material ocean and no more be tossed and troubled. Only a boat can rescue us in a stormy ocean; in the same way, only the shelter of the Lord's lotus feet can rescue us. By taking shelter of a bona fide spiritual master and serving his instructions, we can take shelter of the Lord's lotus feet.

Akāma-Bhakti Versus Sakāma-Bhakti

Points in favor of *sakāma-bhakti*: It helps one approach the Lord (44–45); the Lord considers them pious because they choose to approach Him for relief (47); they can get purified because they render some service in return for some favor from the Lord (31–43); they repent for their sins, unlike the demons, because of their association with the Lord (6).

Points in favor of *akāma-bhakti*: It is the purest form of devotional service where there is no expectation of return from the Lord (47); devotees can remain peaceful even in the midst of great crises because they accept it all as the will of the Lord (40); they please the Lord the most (47); they are eligible for immediate liberation (45); they are most dear to the Lord (47); they are sinless and have the 26 divine qualities of pure devotees; they have no material desires and nothing to do with the material world.

Note to teachers: Steer the discussion in a way that the students understand that *akāma-bhakti* is the purest form of devotional service and is advocated in the *Bhāgavatam*. Pure devotees, such as Śrīla Prabhupāda, Parīkṣit, Prahlāda, and the Pāṇḍavas are *akāma-bhaktas*, who can do anything to please the Lord. The demigods, on the other hand, are *sakāma-bhaktas*, who have some material desires to fulfill but who take shelter solely of the Lord. So while they are not considered pure, they are still considered pious and devoted. They will get purified of their material desires by continuing to render service.

They are certainly better than the nondevotees who neither take shelter of the Lord for relief from material distress nor care for dharmic rules and regulations. So while we should always aspire to practice *bhakti* in a pure way taught by the *ācāryas*, we should also guard against artificial display of renunciation. We should also not disrespect any devotee who may approach the Lord out of material motives, understanding that they are pious even though not pure.

All Contradictions are Resolved in the Supreme Lord

Duality is present in the material world, not in the spiritual world. In spiritual existence there is no duality of birth and death, attachment and repulsion, something favorable or unfavorable, etc. Uttara, King Parīkṣit's mother, had prayed that only Kṛṣṇa can protect her in this world of duality.

The experience of happiness and distress is absolute for Kṛṣṇa and His devotees. When the residents of Vṛndāvana experience distress in Kṛṣṇa's separation, it actually gives them happiness because of their intense remembrance of Kṛṣṇa.

Though it seems like the Lord is partial to the demigods and favors them, the truth is that Kṛṣṇa's anger is also His grace. He is fully free to reciprocate with His devotees, and someone's past activities do not disqualify them from seeking protection from Kṛṣṇa. Lord Rāma was willing to forgive Rāvaṇa till Rāvaṇa's last breath. So the Lord is partial to His devotees but impartially allows everyone to come to the platform of devotion and gain His favor.

The Lord is infinite, and we are infinitesimal (minute). Still by His grace, He allows the infinite to be known to the infinitesimal. Kṛṣṇa says, "My *bhakta* knows Me."

The Māyāvādīs do not accept the simultaneous personal and impersonal manifestation of the Lord. But the knower of truth, the devotee, knows that Brahman is the effulgence of Bhagavān, which is the highest form of the Supreme Person.

10

THE BATTLE BETWEEN THE DEMIGODS AND VṚTRĀSURA

The demigods looked on, stupefied. They had seen and spoken to the Supreme Lord face to face! The Lord had instructed them and then disappeared. They needed to find Sage Dadhīci and beg for his body in charity.

They found him meditating in trance. It pained them greatly to ask him for his life, but they had no choice. It was either this or Vṛtrāsura would kill all of them and destroy their entire kingdom.

Reluctantly, the demigods begged the sage to give them his body. He nodded, smiled, and jokingly said, "O elevated demigods, what kind of charity are you asking of me? Don't you know that severe, unbearable pain consumes someone at death? How could you ask this of me?"

The demigods looked at each other, embarrassed.

"O elevated demigods, everyone in this material world is addicted to their material body," the sage said. "Everyone tries to protect it even at the cost of their possessions. Therefore, who would be prepared to deliver his body to anyone, even if Lord Viṣṇu demanded it?"

Lord Indra came forward and folded his palms. "O exalted *brāhmaṇa*," he said, "pious souls like you are praiseworthy and are very kind and affectionate to others. What can't such pious souls give for the benefit of others? They can give everything, including their bodies.

"O great sage, a beggar begs from someone, not knowing his struggles. If the beggar knew, he wouldn't ask for anything. In the same way, if someone who can give charity knows of the beggar's difficulty, he wouldn't refuse the beggar."

Sage Dadhīci smiled and then chuckled and said, "I refused to offer my body to you because I wanted to hear from you about religious principles. I must give up my body for your benefit even though my body is extremely dear to me, for I know that this body will leave me today or tomorrow.

"O demigods, one who has no compassion for suffering humanity and does not sacrifice one's temporary body for a higher cause – to uphold religious principles – is certainly pitied. But if one is unhappy to see the distress of others and happy to see their happiness, one's religious principles are glorified and appreciated by exalted souls."

The demigods glanced at each other, their eyes brimming with tears. They were benefiting from hearing about religious principles from the sage, not the other way around. Their hearts felt heavy, yet they felt enlivened by the selflessness of this exalted personality.

"I am not this body," continued Sage Dadhīci. "This body is eaten by jackals and dogs after death. What good can it do for me, the spirit soul? This body and its possessions should be used for the benefit of others, or else they will cause misery."

Parīkṣit Mahārāja had been listening attentively. He was impressed by the exalted character of the sage.

Śukadeva Gosvāmī said, "Thus Dadhīci Muni, the son of Atharva, decided to give up his body for the service of the demigods. He placed himself, the spirit soul, at the Lord's lotus feet, and absorbed in trance he gave up his material body."

"Jaya!" exclaimed Parīkṣit Mahārāja. "Surely he attained the eternal shelter of the Lord's lotus feet," he thought.

Śukadeva Gosvāmī then described how Viśvakarmā manufactured the thunderbolt from Dadhīci's bones, which were invested with the power of Dadhīci Muni and further charged with the power of the Supreme Personality of Godhead. King Indra was now invincible.

Indra shone brilliantly as he grasped the powerful thunderbolt weapon and rode on the back of his elephant carrier, Airāvata. Surrounded by all the demigods and praised by the sages, Indra charged towards Vṛtrāsura, ready to kill him. The *asuras* on the battlefield, headed by Vṛtrāsura, saw this blinding effulgence approaching them. Realizing that it was the king of the demigods, they gathered their army to retaliate. Thus the war between the demons and the demigods at the end of Satya-yuga, on the banks of the celestial Narmadā, began.

Many hundreds and thousands of demons, including the Yakṣas and Rākṣasas, charged towards King Indra's army, which consisted of the Rudras, Vasus, Ādityas, Aśvinī-kumāras, Maruts, and other celestial beings. Not even death personified could conquer Indra's army, yet the demons were fearless. They stormed ahead and roared like lions, their golden ornaments dazzling in the sun. They attacked with clubs, bludgeons, arrows, darts, and mallets. They hurled lances, tridents, axes, and swords from all directions and scattered the chiefs of the demigod armies. The

demigods were covered by the falling arrows just as the sky is covered by dense clouds.

For a moment, the demons cheered, not seeing the demigods anywhere. Then, in a flash, the demigods emerged and instantly cut the demons' weapons into thousands of pieces in the sky. The demons panicked when their weapons and *mantras* were diminished. They then started throwing mountain peaks, trees, and stones upon the demigod soldiers. But the powerful demigods broke them to pieces in the sky as before.

When the demon soldiers saw that the demigods were not harmed in any way, they trembled in fear. Just as insignificant persons' angry words do not disturb great personalities, the demons' efforts against the demigods were futile because the demigods were protected by the Supreme Personality of Godhead, Kṛṣṇa. The *asuras*, on the other hand, were not devotees of the Lord and thus lost their pride in fighting. They fled for their lives, leaving Vṛtrāsura alone on the battlefield.

Vṛtrāsura had not given up. His gigantic form loomed overhead, obscuring the sun. As he watched his fellow soldiers, even the great heroes,

run away, he frowned and then smiled,
showing his large, jagged teeth.

As he stomped, the ground trembled.
The hero among heroes called out in a
thunderous voice: "O Vipracitti! O Namuci!
O Pulomā! O Maya, Anarvā, and Śambara.
Hear me! Don't run away!"

Everyone stared at the giant, afraid of
what he may do next.

To their surprise, Vṛtrāsura said, "Every
living being who has taken birth must die.
No one has been saved from death. No one
can escape it. So if death is inevitable, you
can be promoted to the higher planets by
dying a suitable death on the battlefield.
What man will not accept such a glorious
death?

"There are two ways to meet a glorious
death, which are recommended in the *śāstra*:
to die as a devotee of the Lord, by controlling
the mind and being absorbed in thoughts
of the Lord; and to die on the battlefield,
leading the army and never giving up."

Themes and Key Messages

Please go through this table of themes and key messages, with corresponding verses,
and discuss each topic further.

THEMES	REFERENCES	KEY MESSAGES
One should sacrifice one's bodily needs and desires for higher religious principles.	6.10.7–9	Sage Dadhīci told the demigods that someone who does not have compassion for suffering humanity and does not sacrifice one's body and other needs for higher causes is pitiable. One should feel the happiness and distress of others as their own and should therefore not inflict pain on other living beings, like the animals. Caitanya Mahāprabhu and the six Gosvāmīs were examples of exalted souls who sacrificed their lives out of compassion for the upliftment of others. Śrīla Prabhupāda also encourages us to give our life to distributing religious principles throughout the world.

THEMES	REFERENCES	KEY MESSAGES
We should act to benefit others.	6.10.10–12	"It is the duty of every living being to perform welfare activities for the benefit of others with his life, wealth, intelligence and words." (*SB* 10.22.35). Sage Dadhīci explains that since one's body perishes at death, it should be used for the benefit of others. The greatest benefit is to give others Kṛṣṇa consciousness. One who has taken a human birth in the land of India (Bhārata-varṣa) should make his life successful by helping others achieve the ultimate goal of life – to please the Supreme Personality of Godhead. Such work is perfect. Humanitarian work without Kṛṣṇa is nothing. Kṛṣṇa must be at the center of all our activities to have any value. Therefore, Dadhīci gave up his body for the demigods' benefit and to please the Lord.
A devotee of the Lord cannot be defeated.	6.10.27–28	When the demons saw that King Indra's soldiers were not being injured by all their weapons, even by the trees, stones, and mountain peaks, they were afraid. Because the demigods were protected by the Lord, the demons' curses and attacks were futile.
Anyone should be prepared to die while performing glorious deeds.	6.10.32–33	Vṛtrāsura told the demons when they fled the battlefield that all living beings must die. Since death is inevitable, one should die in such a way that he can be elevated after death. There are two ways to have a glorious death, which are very rare: One is to die in thought of the Supreme Lord and go back to the spiritual world, and the second is to die on the battlefield and be elevated to the higher planetary systems. Lord Kṛṣṇa gave Arjuna the same advice on the battlefield. A glorious person is not meant to die like cats and dogs.

Higher-Thinking Questions

Now try to deepen your understanding of this chapter by delving into Śrīla Prabhupāda's purports and reflecting on the following questions:

1. Verse 6 describes two kinds of people: one who gives charity and one who begs for it. What should each of them do as described in the purport?

2. Describe how Śrī Caitanya Mahāprabhu and the six Gosvāmīs sacrificed everything for the benefit of others? (See verse 8 purport.)

3. On what principle is the Buddhist religious principle nonviolence based upon? Explain. (Refer to verse 9 and purport.)

4. Verse 11 describes how Dadhīci Muni gave up his body. In the purport Śrīla Prabhupāda compares his death to Dhṛtarāṣṭra's. Refer to the purport and in your own words explain how they both gave up their bodies.

5. What did Sage Dadhīci mean in verse 10 when he said that this body and its possessions should be used for the benefit of others, or else they will cause misery? How do you think selfishness can end in suffering?

6. According to verse 12 purport, how does a perfect *yogī* die? Was Sage Dadhīci then a perfect *yogī*?

ACTIVITIES

In this section you will find many exciting things to do. These activities will get you thinking, moving, drawing, and having loads of fun.

Analogy Activity

TREE OF KINDNESS OR SELFLESS ACTS

"Those who are too self-interested beg something from others, not knowing of others' pain. But if the beggar knew the difficulty of the giver, he would not ask for anything. Similarly, he who is able to give charity does not know the beggar's difficulty, for otherwise he would not refuse to give the beggar anything he might want as charity." (*SB* 6.10.6)

The demigods use this example of a beggar and a charitable person to explain the importance of selfless acts. If one thinks only of one's needs, one becomes selfish and does not think of others' needs. On the other hand, when one thinks of another's need or distress and desires to help, one automatically becomes selfless. Selflessness is glorified here by the demigods, and Dadhīci Muni sets a great example of selflessness.

We can easily perform acts of selflessness in our daily lives. Helping others, being there for a friend in need, performing chores for family, caring for elders or siblings, and especially getting involved in preaching activities to spread the holy name are examples of selfless acts. Let us consciously cultivate this quality and examine our progress.

Directions: Let us construct the "Tree of Kindness" in our hearts.
- Look at the resource at the end of the chapter. It is the Tree of Kindness.
- Using the template of the leaf and flower, make 30 leaves from green paper or regular paper that is colored green. Similarly, make at least five flowers from colored paper or color your flowers yourselves.
- Perform at least one act of selflessness every day for the next month. Every day, add a leaf to the tree with a one-word or one-phrase description of your act. For every spiritual activity related to preaching, add a flower. See the tree flourish at the end of the month. Finally, write a short journal entry about how you feel about performing selfless acts.

Notes to the facilitator: The resource at the end of the chapter is a template. Students may cut it out or make one of their own using craft paper. They can choose to display it if they like. At the end of the month, students gather to discuss their realizations. They can share what they did, display their trees if they like, and have a short reading session from their journals.

Action Activity

... to get you moving and learning

BALDERDASH: ADDING KṚṢṆA TO KINDNESS

Real kindness and compassion means to think of others' spiritual benefit, not their temporary material needs or comforts. We connect them to Kṛṣṇa, who can end their suffering forever in the material world. Therefore humanitarian work without Kṛṣṇa at the center is not really beneficial.

Let's play a fun game of Balderdash and use our imagination to see how we can act with real compassion for others.

Even if you don't have a board and dice, you can still play Balderdash. This game can be played in pairs or in teams.

Directions:
- Write the following words on individual slips of paper related to various Kṛṣṇa conscious welfare activities: laddus, money, truck, japa *mālā*, *mṛdaṅga*, flower, book, happiness, hunger, kind, computer, phone, microphone, etc. (You can also think of your own words.)
- Shuffle the slips of paper and put them in a bowl.
- One team member picks up a slip and calls out the word loudly.
- The other player or team will try to use the word to show how it can be used to show

Vaiṣṇava compassion to others.

For example:

> » FOOD – I can offer laddus to Kṛṣṇa and distribute to people, giving them *kṛṣṇa-prasāda*, food for their souls.
> » COMPUTER – I can use my computer to make a beautiful poster advertising a Kṛṣṇa conscious festival and inviting people to attend.
> » KIND – I can be kind to a guest who visits the temple or my home by offering them welcoming words, *prasāda*, and listening to them.

- Each answer is given a point.
- To make the game more challenging, you can use words which are not much in context.

Now discuss what is the outcome of your compassionate acts. In other words, what result will you achieve and what benefit will others get because of your compassion?

Critical-Thinking Activity

... to bring out the spiritual investigator in you

REAL ADVANCEMENT OF KNOWLEDGE

In his purport to verse 7 Śrīla Prabhupāda writes, "We therefore invite all men and women advanced in knowledge to join the Kṛṣṇa consciousness movement and sacrifice their lives for the great cause of reviving the God consciousness of human society." In the purports that follow, Śrīla Prabhupāda uses the expressions "learned" and "advanced in knowledge" to mean those advanced in spiritual knowledge.

In this world we see many people advanced in different branches of material knowledge, but Śrīla Prabhupāda indicates that those who have spiritual knowledge are truly advanced in knowledge and are able to really benefit everyone. Let us try to understand why this is so.

The *Śrīmad-Bhāgavatam* is full of descriptions of spiritually learned devotees who have benefited the world. Many *ācāryas* in our *guru-paramparā* were also advanced in material knowledge, but they used their lives to spread Kṛṣṇa consciousness because they recognized the importance of spiritual knowledge and sharing it with others.

Below is a list of some of these great personalities:

Śukadeva Gosvāmī, Dadhīci Muni, Prahlāda Mahārāja, Rūpa and Sanātana Gosvāmīs, Raghunātha Dāsa Gosvāmī, Jīva Gosvāmī, Bhaktisiddhānta Sarasvatī Ṭhākura, Bhaktivinoda Ṭhākura, A. C. Bhaktivedānta Swami

In your study group each of you can choose one or two of the above *ācāryas* and research the following about them:

- Their material and spiritual qualifications
- How they used it to spread Kṛṣṇa consciousness
- How it benefited the world

Now have a One-Minute Paper game, in which each of you presents your findings to the group in one minute. At the end of the presentation, write down in one sentence what you conclude about the importance of becoming advanced in spiritual knowledge and propagating it.

Introspective Activities

... to bring out the reflective devotee in you

BENEFITING OURSELVES AND OTHERS

In this chapter Śrīla Prabhupāda emphasized how we should use our life, wealth, intelligence, and words for the benefit of others, and the greatest benefit we can give others is Kṛṣṇa consciousness. Great personalities of the past did the same. Let us now apply this knowledge to our own lives. How can we use our intelligence, wealth, skills, and talents for our spiritual benefit?

- Think about what you'd like to become when you grow up.

- What skills would you need? How do you think your skills would help you? How can you use the career of your choice to benefit others?
- Now think of all the devotional knowledge you are getting through the study of the *Bhāgavatam*. How do you think it will help you later in life? What benefit can you give others through it?
- How do you see yourself balancing your devotional life with your professional life?

You can make a short photo journal with your ideas. Use some pictures of your chosen profession to express your ideas (refer to the first two prompts above); use another set of photos from the lives of the *ācāryas* mentioned in the critical-thinking activity (refer to the second two prompts above); and finally write a short statement about how both your professional and spiritual efforts can be combined to become spiritually beneficial for you and those around you.

BECOMING FEARLESS IN KṚṢṆA'S SERVICE

In this chapter we have two great examples of devotees, Dadhīci and Vṛtrāsura. They are neither afraid of death nor do they lose sight of religious principles despite grave circumstances. Rather they see their challenges as glorious opportunities for service. How are they able to have such unflinching faith in the lotus feet of the Supreme Personality of Godhead? From where does the determination, fearlessness, and detachment come?

Reflect on a time when you were unable to help someone else. What stopped you? Was it because you were afraid of inconvenience or of losing some valuable possession?

Now recall a time when you were able to help someone else even at the cost of personal inconvenience. What was your motivation? What was your experience after the incident – were you pleased or did you regret the endeavor? Write a short paragraph in your notebook.

We see from the example of Dadhīci that he had a history of practicing the principles of spiritual life and thus had gained a deep spiritual disposition and strength. Devotional life naturally gives us knowledge and detachment. By pleasing the Lord and His devotees, we are blessed with great resolve and compassion that help us surpass even the biggest fear and attachments.

Writing and Language Activities

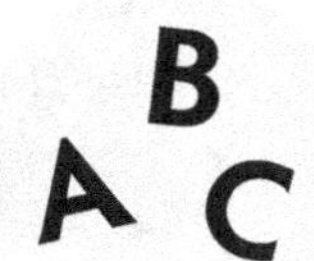

... to help you understand better

NARRATIVE ESSAY: SAVE A SUFFERING LIVING ENTITY!

In this chapter we learn that we should not inflict pain on any living entity but rather feel compassion for suffering humanity by sacrificing bodily desires for higher religious purposes.

Write a narrative to illustrate this theme. Use the following prompt to begin your essay, or any similar scenario.

"I was cycling back home when I saw a lost child, crying beside a busy road . . ."

Plan your narrative as follows:

- Select the main character – (it is you!)
- Select the suffering living entity
- Provide a brief storyline:
  » How does the living entity suffer (problem)?
  » What is the setting and the difficulties the person is facing?
  » How do you go out of your way to help?
  » What is the climax of the story?
  » How does the story end?
- Include some short dialogue

COMPREHENSION PYRAMID: CHARACTER LESSONS

Descripton: In this activity you are given a pair of characters to complete a comprehension pyramid by providing five details associated with these characters. The characters are from chapters 7 to 10.

For example, for Indra and Bṛhaspati the five details would be:

1. <u>Location/timeline in the story:</u> Indra's assembly.

2. <u>Situation:</u> Indra enjoys being the head of the assembly and Bṛhaspati enters.

3. <u>Problem:</u> Indra fails to honor his *guru* and Bṛhaspati disappears. The demigods are defeated by the demons, and they have no one to guide them in performing sacrifices.

4. <u>Solution:</u> They approached Viśvarūpa and accepted him as *guru*.

5. <u>Main idea or lesson:</u> By the mercy of *guru* and the Vaiṣṇavas one can receive all strength, but by offending them one attains all inauspiciousness.

Directions: Use six paper cups to construct the pyramid. You could also play this with a friend. Each child gets a set of characters, writes five details on the cups associated with those characters (as indicated in the example above), and stacks the paper cups to form a pyramid.

Time limit: 8 minutes

Character sets:
1. Indra/demigods and Viśvarūpa
2. Indra/Vṛtrāsura
3. Indra/demigods and Nārāyaṇa
4. Indra/demigods and Dadhīci

Materials needed: 12 paper cups; 4 strips of paper with one character set written on each and folded; 2 pens

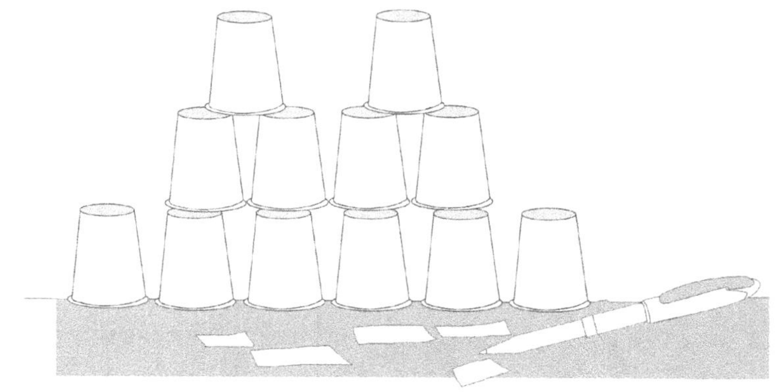

Steps:
- Choose a character set from the folded pieces of paper.
- Write the names of the characters on the first cup. Then write the location/timeline details on the second cup and place it next to the first cup.
- Next, write the situation on the third cup and put it next to the other two. Similarly, add the fourth, fifth, and sixth cup by defining the main problem, solution, and the main idea.
- Then stack the remaining cups in two more rows on top to form a pyramid.
- The winner completes the pyramid in the given time. Take turns reading each other's descriptions.

   Variation for young children: Narrate the details instead of writing them.

   Variation for older children: Reduce the time to four minutes.

LETTER: THE CENTER OF ALL ACTIVITIES

In this chapter we understand the importance of keeping Kṛṣṇa at the center of all our activities and using this material body to help people realize the ultimate goal of life: to please Kṛṣṇa.

With your understanding of this important aspect in your life, write a letter to a friend relating how you study different subjects at school in a Kṛṣṇa conscious way, by keeping Kṛṣṇa in the center of all learning activities.

For example: Instead of learning A for "Apple" and B for "Bat," you study A for "Arjuna," B for "Bhakti," C for "Caitanya," D for "Dāmodara," and so on. When you play games, you like enacting the pastimes of Kṛṣṇa. You can also include other situations and activities in which you are able to remember Kṛṣṇa.

Some directions:

- Think about and note down your activities that teach you about Kṛṣṇa and allow you to keep Him in the center.
- Now structure a letter, mentioning all these activities and how you enjoy them.
- Address your letter to a friend and keep your language informal and friendly. You can use short forms and contractions.
- Make it interesting by explaining that you enjoy the activities very much.
- Explain why it is important and also joyful to keep Kṛṣṇa or God the center of our activities.
- Don't forget to sign out with your name.

BLOGGING: REAL HEROES ARE NEVER DEFEATED

In this chapter Vṛtrāsura mentions that there are two kinds of glorious deaths – to die as a servant of Kṛṣṇa and to die on the battlefield, fighting to protect one's people. In either case, one gets a higher destination. The Lord's devotee is a hero and is protected by the Lord. Let's write a blog post on real heroes.

What is blogging?
Blogging is an online writing activity, including photography and other media, that is self-published. Bloggers write diary-style entries on any theme of their choice. They are responsible for writing, editing, posting, and promoting content in the form of blog posts.

Directions:
Using the example of Vṛtrāsura in contrast to the demons who fled the battlefield, analyze who a real hero is. Think of other characters from the *śāstra*, like Arjuna for example, and write about how he was a perfect hero who followed the instructions of the Lord and fought for the sake of *dharma*.

Write a short blog, using the example of Vṛtrāsura or any other devotee, describing how true heroes are never defeated.

Points to remember:
- Give a catchy title to your blog.
- Write in paragraphs with an introduction and conclusion and a proper structure of ideas. (Get help from your parent or teacher.)
- Feel free to add illustrations or pictures for your readers.
- Then you may self-publish your blog post. (Alternatively, you may do this as a writing exercise in your notebooks.)

CHAPTER 10 ANSWERS

Real Advancement in Knowledge

Potential Answers: Students need to understand the basic importance of spiritual knowledge over material knowledge though examples. Śukadeva Gosvāmī was a liberated soul, learned in the knowledge of Brahman (incomplete knowledge of Absolute Truth). He became attracted to the personal form of the Lord and spoke the *Śrīmad-Bhāgavatam* to Parīkṣit Mahārāja, thus attaining liberation and granting the same to Parīkṣit Mahārāja. Dadhīci Muni was obedient to Lord Viṣṇu, and by personal example taught that one should be selfless and work for higher causes. Prahlāda Mahārāja was a pure devotee king who was dear to Lord Nṛsimha and had nothing to fear from this world; yet he prayed to the Lord for the fallen conditioned souls; Rūpa and Sanātana Gosvāmīs were scholars and rich ministers in the kingdom of Nawab Hussain Shah but preferred to use their intelligence to understand their true identity as a servant of the servant of the Lord. They eventually left everything and joined Lord Caitanya and wrote many books to teach the world these truths. Raghunātha Dāsa Gosvāmī was the son of a rich zamindar (land owner); he was a very good businessman, yet he became a renunciate and great devotee and taught others that devotion gives far more benefit; Jīva Gosvāmī was the greatest scholar of his time, and he chose to establish the conclusions of *bhakti* as the ultimate goal of life with his scholarship and wrote scholarly books on devotion. Bhaktivinoda Ṭhākura was an influential and highly successful magistrate, but he strongly believed that knowledge about Lord Kṛṣṇa is what will save us from the cycle of birth and death – he envisioned that this knowledge would spread all over the world, so amid his busy schedule he wrote many books and sent them to different parts of the world; Bhaktisiddhānta Sarasvatī was a Vedic scholar and great astrologer, but he gave up practicing just to focus on spreading the Kṛṣṇa consciousness movement; A. C Bhaktivedānta Swami was a Vedic scholar and a well-educated gentleman and businessman, but he gave up everything to spread Kṛṣṇa consciousness in pursuance of his *guru's* desire. All these great personalities were learned in material branches of knowledge, but they understood that spiritual knowledge of our relationship with Kṛṣṇa is far superior and worked towards realizing and spreading this higher knowledge.

Benefiting Ourselves and Others

Students own answers. Point of emphasis: Everything in our lives, including our skills and talents, is not separate from our spiritual lives and can be used in Kṛṣṇa's service.

Comprehension Pyramid

Indra/demigods and Viśvarūpa

1. Location/timeline: The demigods are injured and defeated at the hands of demons.
2. Situation: Brahma advises the demigods to honor their *guru* and seek Viśvarūpa's help after their defeat.
3. Problem: Viśvarūpa is younger to the demigods, and they need a more powerful solution to fight the demons.
4. Solution: Persons like Viśvarūpa who are learned and realized in Vedic knowledge are accepted as superiors. Viśvarūpa awards them the Nārāyaṇa-kavaca.
5. Main Idea or lesson: One can become a spiritual master regardless of *varṇa* and *āśrama* if one is advanced in the science of Kṛṣṇa consciousness.

Indra/Vṛtrāsura

1. Location/timeline: Indra beheads Viśvarūpa out of anger and fear of losing his opulence.
2. Situation: Tvaṣṭā is enraged, and he performs a ceremony to kill Indra.
3. Problem: As a result of the sacrifice, the powerful demon, Vṛtrāsura, appears to destroy the demigods.
4. Solution: After losing their weapons and confidence, the demigods headed by Indra pray to Lord Nārāyaṇa.
5. Main idea or lesson: Lord Nārāyaṇa is our only shelter in all conditions of life, and we must approach Him in a prayerful mood.

Indra/demigods and Nārāyaṇa

1. Location/timeline: The demigods offer choicest prayers to Lord Nārāyaṇa.
2. Situation: The Lord is pleased and appears first in their heart and then in front of them.
3. Problem: Vṛtrāsura destroys all their weapons, and they lose their strength for fighting.
4. Solution: Lord Nārāyaṇa asks them to beg for Dadhīci's strong and powerful body from which a thunderbolt to destroy Vṛtrāsura will be prepared from it.
5. Main idea or lesson: The Lord is the source of all strength, whether spiritual or material. Dadhīci's body is spiritually powerful because he recited the Nārāyaṇa-kavaca and followed religious principles.

Indra/demigods and Dadhīci

1. Location/timeline: The Lord instructs the demigods to approach Dadhīci for his bones.
2. Situation: The demigods begged Dadhīci to give up his life.
3. Problem: Everyone is very attached to their body and giving it up is painful.
4. Solution: Dadhīci is selfless and willingly gives up his life for serving the order of Lord Viṣṇu.
5. Main idea or lesson: The greatest attachments can be given up on the strength of pure devotional service.

11

The demons hid, trembling in fear. Their efforts had been futile. They looked at Vṛtrāsura, who loomed overhead unaffected by the attacks of the demigods. As he moved, the ground shook and his voice rumbled like thunder. Their commander-in-chief had instructed them in the principles of religion, but they were so terrified that they couldn't accept his words.

Vṛtrāsura looked around. Most of his army had fled. He was now facing the enemy alone. The demigods took advantage of this moment and attacked the remaining demon soldiers from behind. They were driven away as if they had no leader.

Vṛtrāsura, the best of the *asuras*, could not tolerate the pitiable condition of his soldiers. He howled in fury, injecting terror into his opponents.

"O demigods," he rebuked them, "these demons have a useless birth. They came from their mothers' bodies just like stool. Why do you kill such enemies from behind while they run in fear? How can you consider yourselves heroes

when you're killing your enemies who are afraid of losing their lives? You are not heroes, and such killing can never be glorious. It cannot promote you to the heavenly planets.

"O insignificant demigods, if you are true heroes, stand before me now and show me your prowess!"

Vṛtrāsura roared like a lion, and his roars echoed through the battlefield and through the hearts of everyone. Some of the demigods fainted and fell to the ground as if struck by thunderbolts.

Vṛtrāsura took up his trident and walked towards the demigods, making the earth tremble. As the demigods closed their eyes in fear, he trampled them beneath his feet just as a mad elephant tramples hollow bamboos in the forest.

Indra was furious. He threw an invincible club at Vṛtrāsura, but the demon easily caught it with his left hand. With the same club he angrily struck the head of Indra's elephant, making a tumultuous sound. The elephant Airāvata, with Indra on his back, flew back fourteen yards,

spitting blood from his broken mouth. The soldiers on both sides were astounded. They even glorified Vṛtrāsura's strength and bravery.

When the valorous Vṛtrāsura saw that he had injured Indra's elephant carrier and had made Indra morose because of that, he refrained from striking again, in accordance with religious principles. King Indra seized the moment and touched the elephant with his nectar-producing hand. Miraculously, Airāvata was relieved of his pain and cured of his injuries. Then King Indra and his elephant once again stood in front of Vṛtrāsura silently.

Vṛtrāsura glanced at the thunderbolt in Indra's hand. He laughed sarcastically and said, "He who has killed a *brāhmaṇa*, he who has killed his own spiritual master – indeed, he who has killed my brother – is now standing face to face before me as my enemy! This is my great fortune."

With red eyes, Indra glared at Vṛtrāsura, grinding his teeth yet hesitant to release the most dangerous weapon.

"O most abominable one," Vṛtrāsura's

voice continued to reverberate throughout the battlefield, "when I pierce your stonelike heart with my trident, I shall be freed from my debt to my brother!"

Vṛtrāsura laughed loudly again. "Just look at you! Just for the sake of living in the heavenly planets you killed my elder brother, a self-realized, sinless, qualified *brāhmaṇa*, who was your chief priest. He was your spiritual master to whom you entrusted to perform your sacrifice. Yet you mercilessly severed his heads from his body just like one butchers an animal."

Vṛtrāsura's reddish eyes welled with tears as he spat on the ground. "O Indra, you have no shame; you have no mercy, glory, or good fortune. You are condemned even by the Rākṣasas. Now I shall pierce your body with my trident, and when you die, not even fire will touch you; only the vultures will eat your body. I shall also sever the heads of your soldiers if they dare attack me. With those heads I shall perform a sacrifice to Bhairava."

King Indra hissed in anger. He grasped the thunderbolt tightly between his fingers.

Vṛtrāsura glanced at the thunderbolt again and said, "But if you cut off my head with your thunderbolt and kill my soldiers, I will be happy to offer my body to the jackals and vultures. I will be relieved of the reactions of my *karma*. I will have the fortune of receiving the dust from the lotus feet of great devotees like Nārada Muni."

Indra loosened his grasp on the thunderbolt and started to twirl it in his palm, but he still hesitated to use it.

Vṛtrāsura grinned and continued, "O King of the demigods, why don't you hurl your thunderbolt at me? Unlike your club, the thunderbolt will not be useless. Don't doubt this! It has been empowered by Lord Viṣṇu and by the strength of Dadhīci's austerities. You have come here following Lord Viṣṇu's order, so there is no doubt that you will kill me with your thunderbolt."

Tears now streamed down Vṛtrāsura's rugged cheeks. "Lord Viṣṇu has sided with you, O Indra. Therefore you can be assured of victory and all opulence. As for me, I will be freed of material bondage by the force of your thunderbolt. I will give up this body and this world of material desires. Fixing my mind upon the lotus feet of Lord Saṅkarṣaṇa, I shall attain the destination of great sages like Nārada Muni."

King Indra still glared at the demon, but his heart was racing. "Is this a demon or a devotee I am facing?" he thought.

Vṛtrāsura said, "The Lord recognizes His surrendered devotees who always think of His lotus feet as His dear servants. The Lord never gives such servants the brilliant opulences of

the upper, lower, and middle planetary systems. Why? Material opulence increases one's enmity, anxiety, and pride. And when one works hard to accumulate possessions, he suffers greatly when he loses them."

Vṛtrāsura pointed his large forefinger in the air and said, "Therefore our Lord forbids His devotees to endeavor for material things. Can you see how kind our Lord is! Only His devotees can obtain such mercy, not persons who work for material gain."

King Indra softened his grasp on the thunderbolt. This demon was certainly speaking transcendental knowledge, or was it from transcendental realization?

As if forgetting that he was on the battlefield facing his enemy, Vṛtrāsura closed his eyes and said, "O my Lord, will I again be a servant of Your eternal servants who find shelter only at Your lotus feet? O Lord of my life, may I again become Your servant; may my mind always think of Your divine qualities, my words glorify them, and my body engage in Your loving service.

"O my Lord, I don't desire anything. I don't want to enjoy in Dhruvaloka, Brahmaloka, or any heavenly planet. I don't want to be the ruler of any of the planetary systems. I do not desire mystic *yoga* perfection nor liberation if I have to give up Your lotus feet."

The demigods who held on to their weapons shot glances at one another. Their weapons slackened from their grip as they listened to the prayers of Vṛtrāsura.

"O lotus-eyed Lord, just as baby birds are dependent on their mothers, as calves eagerly await to drink the milk of their mothers, or as a wife who eagerly waits for her husband to return home, I yearn to be with You and serve You.

"O my Lord, I am wandering in this material world because of my fruitive activities. Therefore I simply seek the friendship and association of Your enlightened devotees. I don't want to be attached to my body, family, and home any longer. Let my mind, consciousness, and everything I have be attached only to You."

Themes and Key Messages

Please go through this table of themes and key messages, with corresponding verses, and discuss each topic further.

THEMES	REFERENCES	KEY MESSAGES
Real heroes face their opponents and do not hide or run away in fear.	6.11.4–5	Vṛtrāsura insulted the demon soldiers who were fleeing the battlefield by comparing them to the stool of their mothers. Since both stool and cowardly sons come from the abdomen of the mother, there is no difference between them. Similarly, he insulted the demigods who were attacking the demon soldiers from behind, which is against the *kṣatriya* code of behavior. He challenged them to fight him if they felt they were true heroes.

THEMES	REFERENCES	KEY MESSAGES
Appearances can be deceiving – a devotee is attached to the Lord's service and desire the dust of the lotus feet of great devotees even though he may externally not appear to be a devotee.	6.11.14–21	Vṛtrāsura was a devotee of the Lord and unattached to material wealth or position even though in the body of a demon. He was unafraid and encouraged Indra to use the thunderbolt against him because he knew that the thunderbolt was invested with the power of the Supreme Lord. By dying with the stroke of the thunderbolt with his mind fixed on the lotus feet of Kṛṣṇa, he would immediately go back to Godhead. On the other hand, Indra, a demigod, did not have such faith as Vṛtrāsura and was doubtful to use the thunderbolt, fearing that he will be defeated. He had also performed sinful acts against a *brāhmaṇa* because he was attached to material opulence and position. Yet, Vṛtrāsura was happy to offer his body for the service of the Lord and considered that he will receive all good fortune if he gets the dust from the lotus feet of great devotees, like Nārada Muni.
A surrendered devotee does not desire material opulence, and neither does the Lord award such a devotee material opulence.	6.11.22–23	Vṛtrāsura told Indra that the Lord forbids His devotees to strive for economic gains or sense gratification, for this only increases one's material bondage; one suffers great distress by losing one's possessions. Thus the Lord shows His mercy to His pure devotees by awarding them just enough material opulence to maintain the devotee and facilitate his devotional activities.
A pure devotee only desires and prays for the Lord's eternal service and the association and service of His enlightened devotees.	6.11.24–27	Vṛtrāsura did not desire material opulence or residence in the heavenly planets; he prayed only to serve the Lord and His servants with his body, mind, and words. He prayed to become detached from his family and only attached to the Lord, just as baby birds are dependent on their mothers, as calves eagerly await to drink their mother's milk, or as a wife who eagerly waits for her husband to return home.

Higher-Thinking Questions

Now try to deepen your understanding of this chapter by delving into Śrīla Prabhupāda's purports and reflecting on the following questions:

1. According to the description of a true hero in verse 4 purport, who do you consider a hero – Vṛtrāsura or Indra? Explain.

2. Why did Vṛtrāsura encourage Indra and the demigods to fight and face him? (Refer to verses 19 and 20 and their purports.)

3. Who do you think is more fortunate and is the actual winner? Indra or Vṛtrāsura? Read the verses 20 to 22 and their purports and give a reason for your answer.

4. How are a devotee's possessions different from a *karmī's*, as explained by Śrīla Prabhupāda in verse 22 purport?

5. In the purport to verse 25 Śrīla Prabhupāda explains that a pure devotee never desires to gain anything material from performing devotional service. Why is this? [Hint: What does the devotee gain that is greater and more relishable than material opulence?]

ACTIVITIES

In this section you will find many exciting things to do. These activities will get you thinking, moving, drawing, and having loads of fun.

Analogy Activity

... to bring out the scholar in you

A HEARTFELT EXPRESSION OF LOVE

In verse 26, Vṛtrāsura prays:

"O lotus-eyed Lord, as baby birds that have not yet developed their wings always look for their mother to return and feed them, as small calves tied with ropes await anxiously the time of milking, when they will be allowed to drink the milk of their mothers, or as a morose wife whose husband is away from home always longs for him to return and satisfy her in all respects, I always yearn for the opportunity to render direct service unto You."

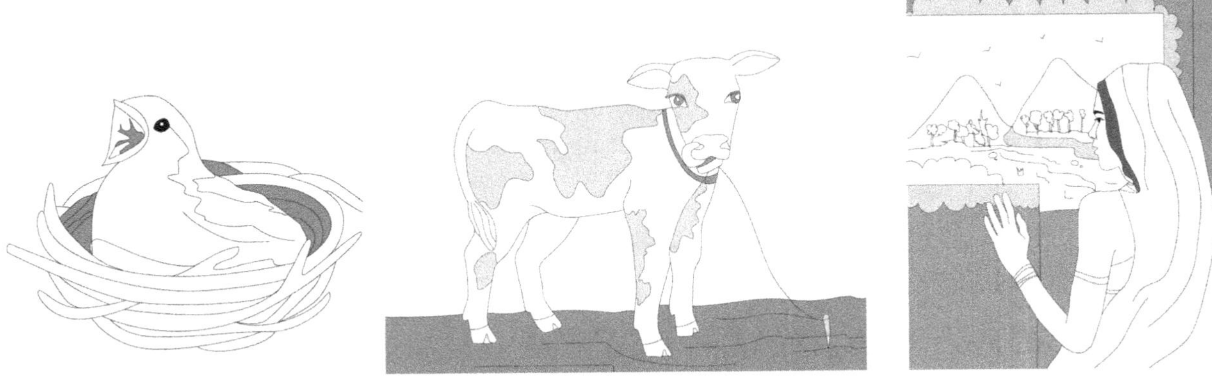

Śrīla Viśvanātha Cakravartī Ṭhākura explains in his commentary to this verse that the order in which Vṛtrāsura presents each example is significant. He starts by describing his yearning to be similar to that of a baby bird for its mother, but he becomes dissatisfied by this example and compares his yearning to the yearning of a calf for its mother. He then recognizes the incompleteness of this description as well, so he finally compares his yearning to a wife for a husband who is away. Let us try to understand his thoughts.

Look at Vṛtrāsura's thought wheel below. Against each example is a clue that helps us understand Vṛtrāsura's thoughts about the example he uses. Analyze each clue and fill out the missing details in the thought note that follows:

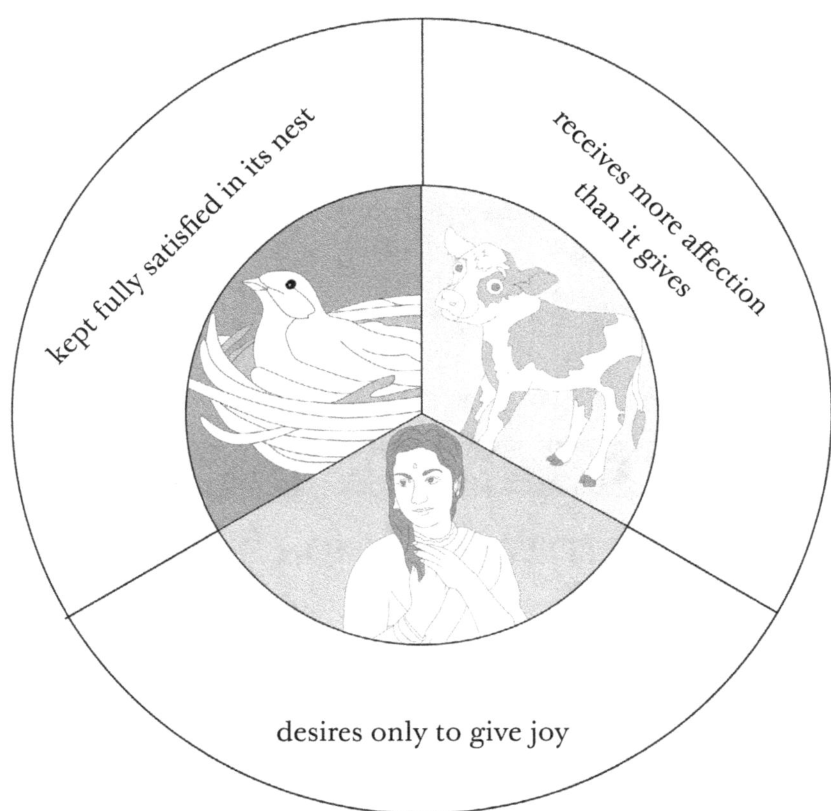

Before moving on to the thought note, think about the following:

a) What connection does Vṛtrāsura draw between the baby bird's remaining in the nest and his own position in the material world?
b) What makes Vṛtrāsura feel that the calf also does not give the right idea about how he is feeling towards the Lord?
c) Why does Vṛtrāsura feel that the wife captures the mood of his desired relationship with the Lord properly?

Once you contemplate the answers, try to complete the thought note below:

I certainly hanker to be in the personal association of the Lord and be fully dependent on His mercy. I feel like a little baby bird in the nest, hankering for my mother's return with some food. But when I describe my yearning like this, the Lord may feel that _______________________________________

____

___________________________. I will therefore clarify to Him that this is not the kind of yearning I feel. I do not desire these things personally, and I do not wish that the Lord thinks I do. I can describe my yearning more accurately with the example of the calf aching for the association of its mother. But then again, the calf ____

____. So I think that the mood of the wife who is hankering to see her husband return best captures my own mood towards the Lord. Just like a wife wants to _______________________________

____

___________________________________, I also want to ____

____

___________________. I hope the Lord grants my wish.

Artistic Activity

NESTED BOXES OR DOLLS: THE HEART OF A VAIṢṆAVA

Though Vṛtrāsura appeared like a fearsome demon, he was a surrendered devotee, longing for the service of the Lord. In this fun activity you will create five layers of Vṛtrāsura's personality, beginning from his external appearance and ending with his deepest aspiration.

You will need: 5 nested cardboard boxes (empty matchboxes, jewelry boxes, or grocery boxes) of varied sizes that fit into each other. Alternatively, you may purchase 5 unpainted nested dolls if they are available in your town (see image 1); 5 light-colored cardstock sheets to cover the surface of the boxes; black pen; pencil; eraser; scissors; glue; plain paper; paints or colored pens or pencils.

Description: The biggest box or doll will be Vṛtrāsura, who externally appears as a demon. Vṛtrāsura desired to regain his original position as a servant of the servants of the Lord, so the second largest box or doll will be Vṛtrāsura as a pure Vaiṣṇava. Verse 26 describes the three levels of his yearning to serve the Lord while feeling totally dependent upon the His mercy. So the third, fourth, and fifth boxes or dolls will represent his three longings:

Box 3 – a baby bird

Box 4 – a calf

Box 5 – a chaste wife

The fifth box will be the smallest one.

Directions for nested boxes:

1. Cut cardstock sheets to size and glue them to the five respective boxes.

2. On plain paper practice the five illustrations in image 2.

3. When you are satisfied, outline the images on the covers of the respective boxes with pencil, then with the black marker.

4. Color the images with paint or colored pencils. Your nested boxes are ready as in image 3.

5. Now nest the boxes in proper order.

6. Present your nested boxes or dolls to your class. When you open the first box, observe how appearances can be deceiving and that you can only know a Vaiṣṇava by seeing the devotion in their heart.

If you are using nested dolls, outline the respective images on the front of the dolls with pencil, then with a black marker, and then use paint or colored pens to color them in.

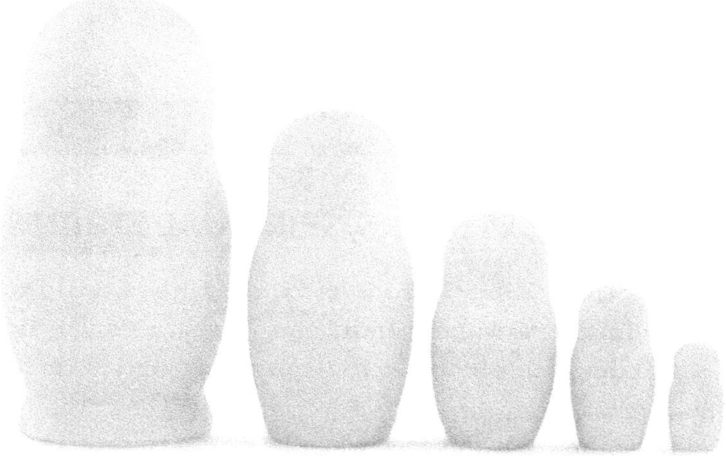

Image 1: Nested doll set

Image 2: Suggested illustrations for nested boxes

Image 3: Nested boxes

Critical-Thinking Activity

MATERIAL SETBACKS, SPIRITUAL STRIDES

In his purport to verse 22, Śrīla Prabhupāda quotes Lord Kṛṣṇa's words from *Bhagavad-gītā* (4.11) to illustrate how the Lord treated both Indra and Vṛtrāsura equally despite appearing partial: "As devotees surrender unto Me, I reward them accordingly. Everyone follows My path in all respects, O son of Pṛthā."

Śrīla Prabhupāda further deepens this idea when he points out the irony of the situation in his purport to verse 20: "By killing Vṛtrāsura, Indra would not actually gain; he would remain in the material world. Vṛtrāsura, however, would go to the spiritual world. Therefore victory was destined for Vṛtrāsura, not for Indra."

It is difficult for an ordinary person to understand the will of the Lord. Pure devotees, however, understand the plan of the Lord by His grace. They are therefore only interested in aligning to the will of the Lord. When one has this mood, he understands how even apparent material setbacks can be spiritual victories by the will of the Lord.

We have come across a few devotees in the *Bhāgavatam* who have faced material setbacks, accepted it as the will of the Lord, and gained great spiritual victories. The following table lists some of these devotees. Fill in the missing information:

	MATERIAL SETBACK	SPIRITUAL FAVOR BY THE LORD	DEVOTEE'S RESPONSE TO SETBACK
Nārada (previous life)			
Parīkṣit Mahārāja			
Vidura			
Dhruva			

MATERIAL SETBACK	SPIRITUAL FAVOR BY THE LORD	DEVOTEE'S RESPONSE TO SETBACK
Vṛtrāsura		

Finally, list at least two lessons you learned about strengthening your own faith from these examples.

Action Activities

... to get you moving and learning

PHOTOJOURNALISM PROJECT: LONGING OF THE SOUL

Our real need as a spirit soul is loving relationship of service with Lord Kṛṣṇa. In the conditioned state, we try to fulfill that primeval need through opulence, position, security, society, and friendship in the material world. But we are never satiated.

Vṛtrāsura did not care for these material things; he only cared to return to his eternal relationship with Lord Saṅkarṣaṇa.

In this activity you will be exploring the above theme through photojournalism. It is a form of journalism in which you use effective photos to tell a visual story and enlighten your audience.

What you will need: Camera, photo printouts, cardboard sheet, color markers, glue

Directions:

1. Reflect on Vṛtrāsura's and Indra's characteristics and understand how the material world can never be perfect or satisfy us completely. Pure devotees like Vṛtrāsura have no other desire than to lovingly serve the Lord; therefore they never want anything material. On the other hand, those who are like Indra are always anxious about maintaining their pride and position.

2. Everyone is looking for Kṛṣṇa; He is our greatest need. He is our shelter and life. Keeping this in mind and remembering the analogies used in this chapter, look for subjects for your photographs. For example: a baby crying for its mother; plants straining to get some sunlight; fish dying without water; someone taking shelter in a storm; a parched land in

want of rain, etc. All your subjects should reflect the soul's need and hankering for Kṛṣṇa, the supreme maintainer and shelter.

3. Then select your favorite photos and print them. On a big cardboard sheet, glue your photos to make a collage. Give a catchy title and make a decorative border. Write a few lines on the theme and display your photojournalism project at home or in your classroom.

ACT IT OUT: HEROES AND COWARDS

In this chapter we learned that real heroes face their opponents and do not run away or hide in fear. Play a fun game with your friends to learn how to become a hero instead of a coward.

This game can be played as teams or in pairs. One team/individual creates four to five imaginary situations which depict a hero or a coward. The other team/individual watches the action and tries to guess the situation.

Please note: This activity is not meant to ridicule or look down upon "cowards" but to distinguish between a heroic act and a cowardly act, so we can try to emulate real heroes.

Examples:
- Hero – Gaura is walking past the playground when he sees a child being bullied by some teens. Gaura goes and stands up against the bullies, without being afraid.
- Coward – Ravi is cycling back home and sees a boy stuck in the mud with his bicycle. He takes a U-turn and avoids the situation, lest he is asked for help!
- Hero – Gaurangi is distributing Śrīla Prabhupāda's books, and someone is rude to her. She ignores the person and happily continues.
- Coward – Gaurangi is distributing books, and someone is rude to her. She cries and runs away, deciding never to distribute books again.

Create similar situations to depict a heroic deed and a cowardly deed. The teams or individuals can take turns to act out a scene. Have the other team or individual guess the situation and narrate the scene to everyone. Guess whether the actor is a hero or a coward.

Introspective Activity

A MATTER OF FAITH

As we saw in the last chapter, Viśvakarmā had made a thunderbolt from the bones of Dadhīci Muni for the demigods. This thunderbolt was infused with the power of Lord Viṣṇu and of Dadhīci Muni's austerities to kill Vṛtrāsura. It is interesting to see how despite knowing this, Indra doubted the effectiveness of the weapon while Vṛtrāsura did not. This is because Vṛtrāsura was a pure devotee and had firm faith that the desire of the Lord will always come to pass. Indra, on the other hand, was not a pure devotee, and therefore his faith was not as strong.

In his *Bhakti-rasāmṛta-sindhu*, Śrīla Rūpa Gosvāmī describes how our progress in Kṛṣṇa consciousness is determined by how our faith in the Lord increases: a devotee has some initial faith (*śraddhā*), which grows by performing devotional practices in the association of devotees. Then one's faith becomes firm faith (*niṣṭhā*), which eventually gives one love of Godhead (*prema*). Faith, therefore, is an essential part of devotional service.

Śrīla Prabhupāda explains that faith in Kṛṣṇa is not blind. It is based on knowledge of the Lord's position and will. We display such reasonable faith in many instances in our daily lives – when we go to the barber, for example, we have faith that he will use the knife to shave and not cut our throats; when we buy a ticket to go to some place, we have faith that the airplane or train will take us to our destination; when we hear news from a trusted news agency, we have faith that the events they are describing really took place, and so on. Similarly, our faith in Kṛṣṇa should not be blind but based on the knowledge that the *ācāryas* have left us.

Before introspecting about our own faith in the Lord, let us consider the following:
- Why was Vṛtrāsura's faith in the Lord so strong?
- Why was Indra's faith not so strong?

Now, consider an instance when you may or may not have put firm faith in the Lord's plan for you. It could be something that didn't go according to your plan or some failure or setback you experienced:
- What kind of dilemma or testing situation were you put in?
- What factors made you trust or doubt the plan of the Lord?
- What lessons have you learned from Vṛtrāsura's and Indra's situation that will help you better deal with a similar incident in the future?

Discuss within your group.

Writing Activities

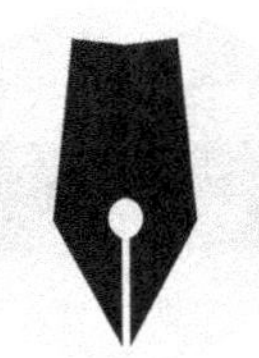

NARRATIVE ESSAY: APPEARANCES CAN BE DECEIVING

We learned in this chapter that a devotee, even if he doesn't appear as one, always desires the dust of the Lord's lotus feet and is surrendered to Him within his heart.

Write a story beginning with the following words:

"A new family came to our neighborhood last week. I never saw them greeting anyone or smiling at anyone…"

In this story narrate how the external appearances or deeds of the family members were deceptive for you at the beginning and how gradually you understood that the persons were nice devotees of the Lord.

How to write a story in five steps:

1. Find inspiration. The first step in writing a story is coming up with an idea or using a theme to write one.

2. Brainstorm. Once you have an idea for a story, brainstorm and note down the key ideas.

3. Outline. Create an outline for your story. Choose characters and build your plot.

4. Write the first draft. It's time to write your story using all your ideas.

5. Revise and edit your story.

DIARY ENTRY: IS THE LORD FAVORING ME?

In this chapter we see that the Lord favors His devotee when He doesn't give the devotee material extravagance or position. Vṛtrāsura was grateful for this because it meant that he would not become proud and he could take full shelter of the Lord and not depend on anything else in this world. It also meant that he would not be attached to this world and it would therefore be easier to go back to Godhead.

Reflect on your situation:
- If you don't have something you want, like the latest iPhone for example, do you complain or do you see it as the Lord's favor on you?
- If so, how is it the Lord's favor on you?
- Are you grateful for whatever the Lord has given you?

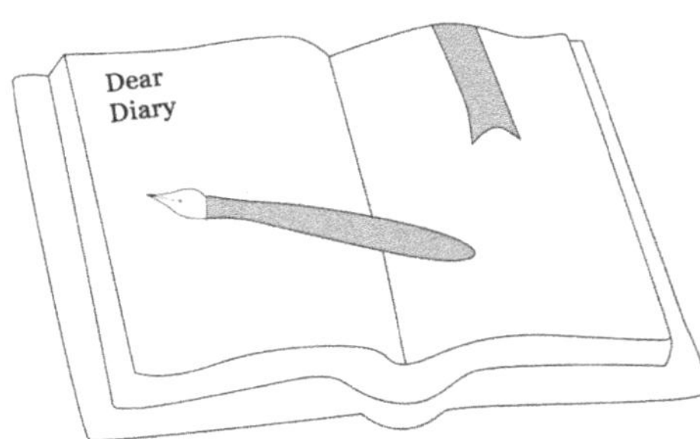

- If you do have everything materially, do you also see that the Lord wants you to use His gifts in His service?
- How can you remember that whatever you have or don't have is best for you?

Then write a diary entry on your realizations.

What is a diary entry?

It is recounting in note form various incidents and experiences from one's life. Each diary entry has contents ranging from thoughts, emotions, reflections, dreams, and so on.

Some tips to write a diary entry:

1. Start by writing the date.

2. Think about the key points on which you would write the entry.

3. Open with "Dear Diary" if you want to.

4. Write in the first person by using "I" statements.

5. Be honest in your entries.

6. Use inspirational quotes or dialogues if you want to state any.

7. Use lots of details to preserve moments in time; for example, "Today I had a similar experience . . ."

8. End with a positive note.

CHAPTER 11 ANSWERS

A Heartfelt Expression of Love
Bird: I want to remain in the material world, enjoying various facilities under the Lord's nurture and protection; b. The calf receives ample affection from its mother but is still too young to reciprocate in the same proportion; c. The wife serves and satisfies her husband with all her senses and mind and derives happiness in return; similarly, Vṛtrāsura wants to serve and satisfy the Lord with all his heart and senses.

Material Setbacks, Spiritual Strides
Nārada: His mother died of a snake bite when he was only five years old, and therefore he had no other caregiver; the Lord freed him from the only material relationship that was binding him to this world; the boy Nārada had faith in the plan of the Lord and left home to achieve spiritual success, trusting that the Lord was present with him and would always protect him;

Parīkṣit: He was cursed by the *brāhmaṇa* boy, Śṛṅgi, to die in seven days; Mahārāja Parīkṣit took it as the Lord's signal to call him back to His own abode; He did not retaliate or neutralize the curse by his own power; he readily gave up his kingdom and got ready to give up his body, trusting that the Lord who had protected him in his mother's womb would protect him even in this situation;

Vidura: He was sent out of the palace by Duryodhana; The Lord gave him the opportunity to associate with saintly people and travel to holy places to purify himself; He followed the Lord's plan, keeping faith that his removal from royal duties was for his own good and that he would gain spiritually and please the Lord;

Dhruva: He was rejected by his father and stepmother and left to the forest to pray to Lord Viṣṇu for a material kingdom greater than his ancestors; the Lord sent him his spiritual master, Nārada Muni, who instructed him on how to achieve the Lord's favor; by getting the audience of the Lord, Dhruva understood that he had gained something much greater – that the Lord's and the devotee's association are more valuable than anything else in this world – and he devoted his life to their service;

Vṛtrāsura: He was to be killed by Indra; the Lord made him understand that all his previous *karma* would be vanquished, that he would become detached from all material relationships and things, and that he would go back to Godhead and serve the Lord; he trusted the plan of the Lord even in the difficult circumstance.

A Matter of Faith
Vṛtrāsura was a pure devotee who always hankered to serve the Lord and His devotees. Through association of great devotees, he progressed on the path of *bhakti* and understood how the will of the Lord never fails. He also had faith that the Lord would take Him back after leaving the body. Indra, on the other hand, was a devotee who approached the Lord with material desires. He also had disrespected his spiritual masters, and therefore was denied the grace to have the same faith as Vṛtrāsura.

12

King Parīkṣit was fascinated with the story so far. "Vṛtrāsura was no demon," he thought, "but certainly a great devotee of the Lord. It seems as if King Indra realized this and so hesitated to use his thunderbolt."

Śukadeva Gosvāmī explained that Vṛtrāsura was not at all interested in victory. He preferred to be killed in the battle and go back to Godhead. So to urge Indra to fight, he violently whirled his trident toward Indra and yelled, "O sinful one, I shall now kill you!"

The points of Vṛtrāsura's trident were like the flames of the raging fire at the end of the millennium. As it flew in the sky, the blazing weapon looked like a brilliant meteor, which almost blinded everyone. Indra acted quickly. Unafraid, he at last launched the thunderbolt, which cut

the trident to pieces and simultaneously cut off one of Vṛtrāsura's arms, which was as thick as the body of Vasuki, the king of the serpents.

The demon hollered, sending waves of terror through the battlefield. But nothing could stop him. He wielded an iron mace with his remaining arm and struck Lord Indra's jaw with it. He then hit Indra's elephant carrier, which sent Indra crashing to the floor and the thunderbolt slipping from his hand.

The demigods, demons, and the Cāraṇas and Siddhas had been watching in awe. They praised Vṛtrāsura's quick retaliation, but when they saw King Indra lying on the ground, dazed, they exclaimed, "Alas! Alas!"

King Indra eyed the thunderbolt a few meters away. He was practically defeated but slowly got up, hanging his head in shame. How could he pick up his weapon again? But Vṛtrāsura encouraged him: "O Indra, take up your thunderbolt and kill your enemy! This is not the time to lament your fate."

Indra looked up, confused yet intrigued by this powerful personality.

Vṛtrāsura's thunderous voice echoed through the battle grounds: "O Indra, no one is guaranteed of victory except the original enjoyer, the Supreme Personality of Godhead. He is the cause of everything, and He knows everything. But we subordinates are sometimes victorious and sometimes defeated.

"Everyone in all the planets of the universe is under the Lord's control. They are like birds caught in a net, who cannot move on their own. Even our sensory and mental power, our bodily strength, and our life or death are under the Lord's control. Only foolish people think that the dull material body is the cause of their activities.

"O King Indra, we are like wooden dolls in the hands of our master. We cannot act independently, but we dance according to the desire of the supreme controller, our Supreme Lord. Even the three *puruṣas* – Kāraṇodakaśāyī

Viṣṇu, Garbhodakaśāyī Viṣṇu, and Kṣīrodakaśāyī-Viṣṇu – and material nature cannot create this material world without the Lord's direction. So no one is independent.

"If one thinks that his body is created by his father and mother or killed by another agent, this is not proper understanding. The Supreme Lord Himself creates and devours living beings through other living beings."

Lord Indra smiled. Yes, this gigantic demon had a hideous body and a severed arm, but the words that were coming from his mouth were powerful truths.

"No one likes to die," Vṛtrāsura continued, "but the Lord forcibly takes everything away from us at the time of death. In the same way, if the Lord desires, He can give us everything. So everything is dependent on the supreme will of the Lord.

"Therefore, we should be equipoised in fame and defamation, victory and defeat, life and death. Through whatever we go through, we should not be anxious. If we know that goodness, passion, and ignorance are not qualities of the soul but qualities of material nature, we won't be bound by these qualities. We are the pure soul who simply observes the actions and reactions of these qualities."

King Indra looked down in embarrassment. His actions and behavior so far had shown quite the contrary. His lips quivered and his hands trembled. He didn't want to pick up the thunderbolt and kill this exalted soul.

"Just look at me, O Indra!" Vṛtrāsura shouted, making Indra look up at him again. "I am already defeated. My weapon and arm have been cut to pieces, but I am not at all morose. Acting as your enemy, I desire to kill you. I will try my best to fight even in these conditions because I want to do my duty. You too should not be morose and should continue fighting!"

King Indra was bewildered. "How is it that this demon is speaking transcendental truths?" he

and endurance. This is because of your devotion. You have overcome the Lord's illusory energy and given up the demoniac mentality, and so you've become a perfect devotee of the Supreme Personality of Godhead, who is the Supersoul and friend of everyone."

Slightly bowing his head, Indra continued, "O Vṛtrāsura, demons are generally in the mode of passion, so how wondrous it is that although you're a demon, you have the mentality of a devotee and have fixed your mind on Vāsudeva, who is in pure goodness. Such a fixed devotee swims in an ocean of nectar. For a devotee like you what is the use of the water in small ditches?"

Vṛtrāsura grinned. Certainly, any material happiness is like water in a ditch, whereas spiritual happiness enjoyed eternally in the spiritual world is like an ocean of nectar.

thought. Then he remembered great devotees like Prahlāda Mahārāja and Bali Mahārāja, who had been born in demon families. He then came to his senses.

"O my enemy," Vṛtrāsura continued, "Consider this battle a gambling match in which our lives are at stake, the arrows are the dice, and our animal carriers are the game board. No one knows who will be victorious and who will be defeated. It all depends on our fate."

Vṛtrāsura's words filled Indra with courage. He picked up the thunderbolt and held it tightly, ready to use it. But first he smiled and said, "O great demon, I can see that even in this dangerous situation you have great knowledge

Śukadeva Gosvāmī continued, "Thus Vṛtrāsura and Indra spoke about devotional service even on the battlefield, and then as a matter of duty they again began fighting. They were both equally powerful and great fighters.

"Vṛtrāsura whirled his iron club in the air and threw it at Indra with his left hand. Quickly bowing his head to Vṛtrāsura and then to the thunderbolt, called Śataparvan, King Indra launched it and cut to pieces Vṛtrāsura's club and his remaining arm."

Parīkṣit Mahārāja wasn't sure he wanted to hear anymore. His heart was heavy at the thought of Vṛtrāsura being slain, but because he knew that the so-called demon's death would be glorious, he urged Śukadeva Gosvāmī to continue.

Śukadeva Gosvāmī described that Vṛtrāsura was covered in blood with his two arms cut off at their roots. He looked beautiful like a flying mountain whose wings had been cut off by Indra.

You would think that by now Vṛtrāsura would give up, but he didn't. His power and strength were unfathomable. He opened his gigantic mouth so wide that his lower jaw reached the ground and his upper jaw the sky. Within his deep mouth, his tongue looked like a large serpent, and his sharp, deathly teeth seemed like they would devour the entire universe. As he walked and crushed the earth's surface, he appeared like the Himālayas.

King Indra was astounded. He tried to hide, but Vṛtrāsura swallowed him and Airāvata in one gulp, just as a python may swallow an elephant.

Lord Brahmā had arrived on the scene to join the other demigods. They gasped and shrieked, fearing for Indra's life. "What a disaster!" they lamented.

Indra struggled in Vṛtrāsura's belly. Then he remembered the Nārāyaṇa armor, which had been protecting him all along. With his mystic power and the power of the Nārāyaṇa-kavaca, Indra was unharmed in the demon's stomach. With his powerful thunderbolt he pierced Vṛtrāsura's abdomen and came out. Not giving Vṛtrāsura any time to retaliate, Indra hurled his thunderbolt and cut off the demon's head, which was as high

as a mountain peak. The thunderbolt rapidly and constantly revolved around Vṛtrāsura's neck, but it took an entire year for his head to fall to the ground.

The Gandharvas and Siddhas played heavenly music and sang Vedic hymns to celebrate King Indra's victory. They showered flowers upon him with great joy. Yet, it was Vṛtrāsura who was the real winner. Everyone saw a fiery spark leave Vṛtrāsura's body and soar into space. They all knew that the great devotee was on his way to the spiritual world to become an associate of Lord Saṅkarṣaṇa.

Themes and Key Messages

Please go through this table of themes and key messages, with corresponding verses, and discuss each topic further.

THEMES	REFERENCES	KEY MESSAGES
Victory or defeat depends on the Supreme Lord, so we should act in a detached way and depend on the Lord.	6.12.7	The illusioned souls think they are the doer of activities, but their activities are carried out by material nature under the direction of the Supreme Lord. Therefore victory and defeat is not actually theirs because these are arrangements of the Supreme Lord through the agency of material nature. Thus one should perform one's prescribed duties not being attached to the fruits of one's actions and depend on the Lord. Victory or defeat is up to Him. We should not be jubilant in victory or morose in failure. Our duty is to work sincerely so that our activities may be recognized by Kṛṣṇa.
The Supreme Lord fully controls all living beings, so no one is independent.	6.12.8–12	Every living being from every part of the universe, including the presiding deities of all planets, are fully under the Lord's control. The power of our senses, our mental and bodily strength, and our life is all dependent on the Lord. Whether we fail or are victorious, the Lord is always victorious because we act under His directions. Even the three *puruṣas* – Kāraṇodakaśāyī Viṣṇu, Garbhodakaśāyī Viṣṇu, and Kṣīrodakaśāyī-Viṣṇu – cannot direct the material manifestation without the Supreme Lord's direction. We are not created by our mother or father but by the Supreme Lord, who dictates to them within the heart. Therefore He is the original cause of our birth, and He is the only independent person.
We become victorious only by Kṛṣṇa's mercy.	6.12.13	We should not be puffed up, thinking that by our own efforts we have become opulent, learned, beautiful, and so on. We achieve all such good fortune by the mercy of the Lord. Similarly, misfortunes and reversals in life are His chastisement and also His mercy. Therefore everyone is dependent on His mercy and chastisement. Sometimes He gives us everything and sometimes He takes away everything; consequently, everything is dependent on His will.

THEMES	REFERENCES	KEY MESSAGES
If we see that everything is dependent on the will of the Lord, we will be undisturbed in happiness and distress.	6.12.14–15	When we are dependent on Kṛṣṇa, we will never be in anxiety because we have confidently placed ourselves in Kṛṣṇa's hands. This is true surrender. We will see happiness and distress external to our real self and therefore not be affected by these dualities. In such a liberated stage, we become an observer of our actions and reactions. So instead of focusing on the modes, which make us swing between joy and sadness and has nothing to do with the self, we can focus our mind on Kṛṣṇa and find relief and true happiness in His shelter.
We should do our duty regardless of the outcome, while depending on the Lord.	6.12.16–17	Even though Vṛtrāsura depended on the Lord, he still did his duty. He told Indra that although he knows that he will be defeated, he will still fight and do his duty. He was not affected by defeat. So acting as a spiritual master to Indra, he encouraged Indra to give up his moroseness and also fight.
Anyone can become purified if one takes shelter of a pure devotee and molds his character according to the pure devotee's direction.	6.12.19–22	King Indra wondered how Vṛtrāsura could've been elevated to the position of a pure devotee, since he was in a demon body. Prahlāda Mahārāja, who was born in a demon family, was initiated by Nārada Muni. So similarly, Vṛtrāsura must have obtained such good fortune previously. Therefore, anyone, in any position, can become purified and become a perfect person, a *mahā-pauruṣya,* by the mercy of Kṛṣṇa and His pure devotees. Such a person does not desire liberation or the happiness of Brahmaloka but simply wants to associate with the Supreme Lord in His spiritual abode.

Higher-Thinking Questions

Now try to deepen your understanding of this chapter by delving into Śrīla Prabhupāda's purports and reflecting on the following questions:

1. Why did Vṛtrāsura prefer to die in the battle than be victorious, as Śukadeva Gosvāmī states in verse 1?

2. Why should we not be concerned about victory or defeat as explained by Śrīla Prabhupāda in his purports to verses 7 and 8?

3. If every being acts under the Lord's control, it seems that we are not responsible for our

actions. But Śrīla Prabhupāda explains in the purport to verse 8 that we act according to our *karma*. So how do you think the Lord is involved in administering our *karma* as the supreme controller? [Hint: Do you think that if you are a devotee of Kṛṣṇa, He has the ability to minimize or change the results of your *karma*?]

4. According to verse 12 purport, how can we understand that our mother and father are not the original cause of our birth?

5. How can we see any distress or reversal in life as Kṛṣṇa's mercy in the form of chastisement? (Refer to verse 13 purport.)

6. From what you read in this chapter, how does Vṛtrāsura's example guide us back to Godhead?

ACTIVITIES

In this section you will find many exciting things to do. These activities will get you thinking, moving, drawing, and having loads of fun.

Artistic Activity

... to reveal your creativity

STRINGED PUPPET

In verse 10, Vṛtrāsura describes how we are controlled by the supreme controller, Lord Kṛṣṇa, just as a wooden puppet is controlled by a puppeteer. We are controlled by our *karma*, time, and the three modes of material nature, which are in turn under the direction and sanction of the Supreme Lord.

In this activity, we will make a puppet and a simple control to direct the puppet's motion.

What you will need: Thick cardboard 8 X 6 inches; scissors, pencil; black markers; string; 2 wide straws; 4 paper clips; color pens or printed paper to decorate the puppet's dress; thick needle; printout of the puppet silhouette given in Resources; glue

Directions:

1. Print the outline of the puppet you prefer to make (See Resources at the end of this chapter).

2. Cut it along the printed outline. Now place the figure on the cardboard, trace around the outline, and cut out the figure.

3. Separate the head, torso, limbs, and lower body as shown in Image 1.

4. Punch holes with the needle to join the limbs, body, and head together using string as shown in Image 2. Do not tie the string tightly as you need to move the different parts of the puppet's body.

5. Lightly draw the face and hair, and when satisfied use the black marker to complete the face. (Image 3)

6. Similarly, add patterns on clothing and shoes with markers, or cut printing paper and glue on the respective part to make your puppet lively and colorful. (Image 4)

7. Make a simple controller by tying two straws with string. (Image 5)

8. Place the four paper clips in the four openings of the straw. Practice inserting a string from below as shown in Image 6 and hook it in the pin as shown in Image 7. This holds the string in place and facilitates easy maneuvering. Remove this string.

9. Make holes in both hands, the shoes, and the head, and tie a string to each of them.

10. Pull the strings attached to each limb and insert them from below in each paper clip. (Image 8)

11. Roll the string attached to the head of the puppet over the center of the straw controller.

12. Practice pulling and releasing all strings to control the puppet's movement. (Image 9)

Image 1

Image 2

Image 3

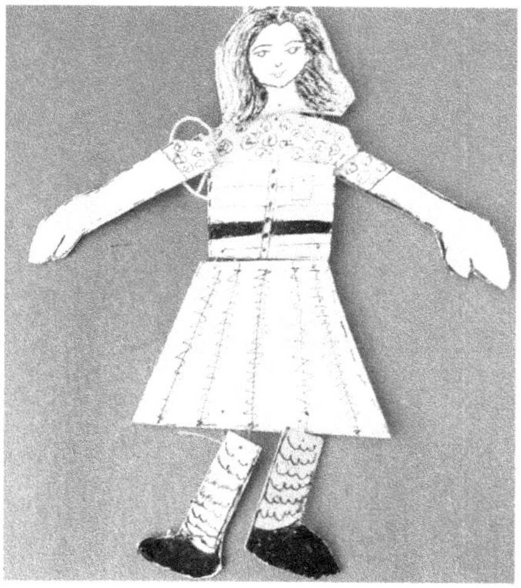

Image 4

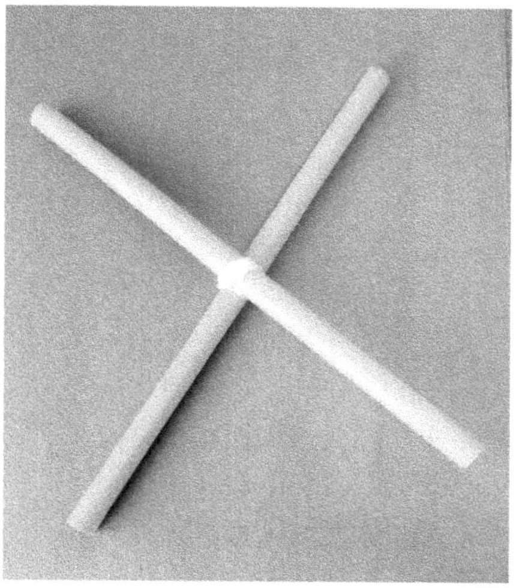

Image 5

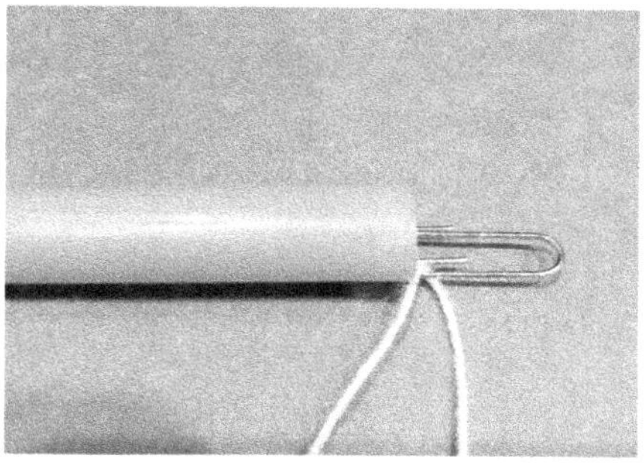

Image 6

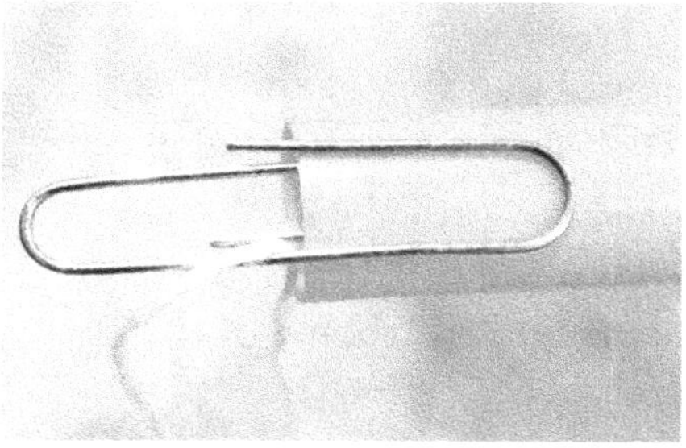

Image 7

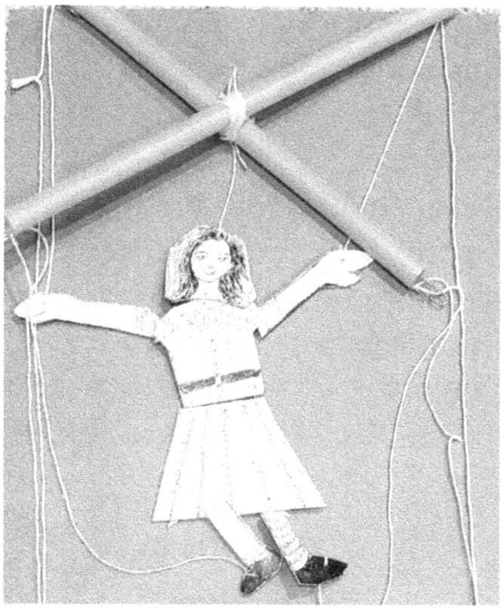

Image 8

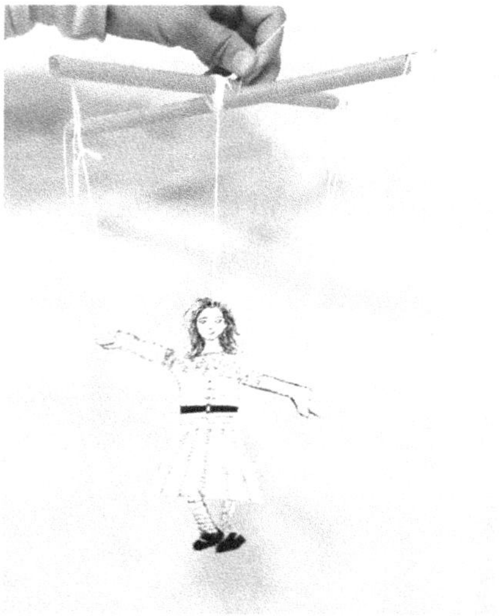

Image 9

Analogy Activity

... to bring out the scholar in you

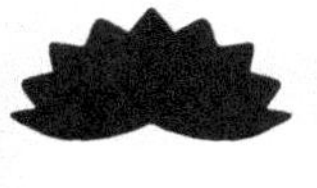

DANCING TO THE DESIRE OF THE SUPREME CONTROLLER

"O King Indra, as a wooden doll that looks like a woman or as an animal made of grass and leaves cannot move or dance independently, but depends fully on the person who handles it, all of us dance according to the desire of the supreme controller, the Personality of Godhead. No one is independent." (*SB* 6.12.10)

Related verse:

"Our sensory prowess, mental power, bodily strength, living force, immortality and mortality are all subject to the superintendence of the Supreme Personality of Godhead. Not knowing this, foolish people think the dull material body to be the cause of their activities." (*SB* 6.12.9)

In these verses Vṛtrāsura describes that every aspect of the living being is under the control of the Supreme Lord. The example of the string puppet beautifully and simply shows us how this is true, although we may not always realize or understand our position.

Using the stringed puppet you created for the art activity in this chapter, try to see how the Lord easily controls everyone just like we easily control a puppet. Let the string puppet represent a living entity in the material world, and the control represent the fingers of the Lord that control the living being.

Can you do any of the following activities with the stringed puppet? Put a tick against any activity in Column A that can be performed. Then read verse 9, and in Column B write down what this implies about the Lord's control. (Please note that in some instances of the analogy below the Lord is not fully responsible for our actions, because He lets us use our free will to make choices, but examples in Column A are used for the sake of illustrating the theme of the Lord's control over our basic faculties of speech and movement.)

COLUMN A   COLUMN B

1. I can make the puppet walk and talk by moving the strings that are attached to the feet.

2. If the puppet performs in a puppet show, I can speak and give an impression that the puppet is thinking or speaking.

3. I can control how sturdy the puppet will be based on the material I choose to make it in.

4. I can tear the puppet and destroy it if I choose.

<table>
<tr><td>COLUMN A</td><td>COLUMN B</td></tr>
<tr><td>5. I can keep the puppet safe if I choose.</td><td></td></tr>
<tr><td>6. I can give the puppet any kind of personality that I want.</td><td></td></tr>
</table>

Now consider: The puppet suddenly comes to life and desires to run its own show without a master manipulating it with the strings. What would you tell such a puppet to convince him about the truth of his position?

How do you think this applies to our position as living entities dependent on the Supreme Lord? How can we constantly remind ourselves of this position?

Introspective Activity

... to bring out the reflective devotee in you

DEPENDING ON KṚṢṆA FOR THE RESULTS

Vṛtrāsura encourages Indra to do his duty well and not be concerned about the results; he should leave the results to Kṛṣṇa, who is the supreme controller and doer.

But this may not be easy for us. We often strive to do things just so we can enjoy the results. For example, we study hard for our school exams so that we can pass to the next grade, or we strive to do well so that we can get some recognition or respect. And often when the results are not satisfactory, we lament and feel bad about ourselves.

Let's try to see how doing one's duty well without becoming stressed about the results can actually work in our favor.

For your next test or exam, try to study and prepare well without thinking too much about the outcome. Become absorbed in the activity of studying. Know that Kṛṣṇa is with you, and by His grace you are able to understand and remember anything. Then leave the results to Him. This is called dependence.

If you are cooking, learning a new skill, playing a sport, or even trying to make friends, think of Vṛtrāsura's story and what a real winner is. Vṛtrāsura may have failed externally, but he was actually victorious. Similarly, you may not get the best results, but the fact that you gave it your all and were detached from the results proves that you are successful.

Therefore, Kṛṣṇa says that He doesn't want or need grand offerings or opulent material achievements from us; simply a leaf, fruit, flower, or a drop of water offered in love will satisfy Him.

So try to do your activities thinking of Kṛṣṇa, offering your activities to Him in love, and depending upon Him for the results.

Below is a leaf, fruit, flower, and a drop of water. Each of these symbols represents one of your activities for the week.

Think of some of your activities in the week that require you to get some kind of result. Above each symbol write down the activity. Then within the symbol write a prayer to Kṛṣṇa to help you see how your activities are dependent on Him, including the result, and offer a heartfelt prayer of surrender and dependence.

See example below:

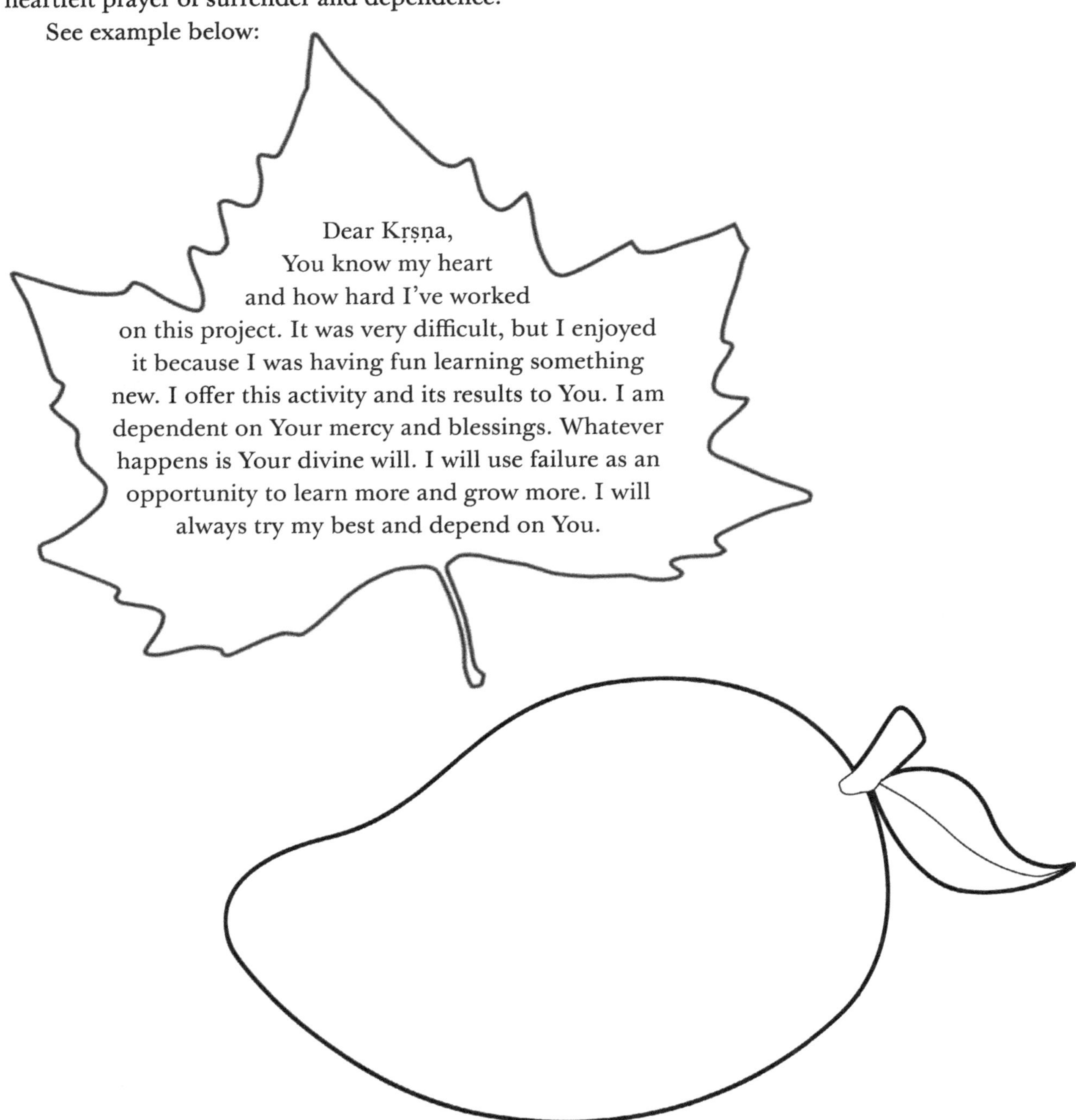

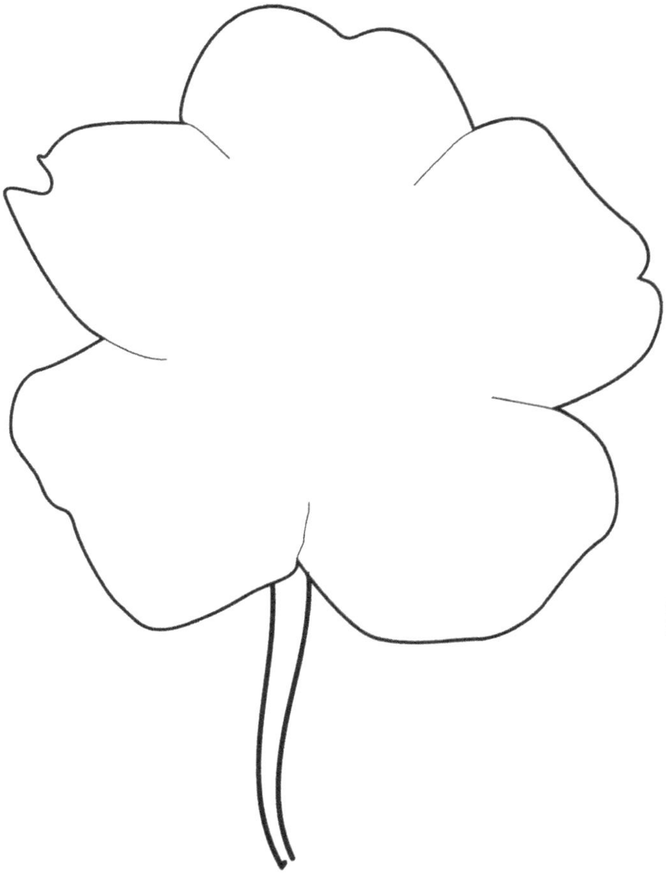

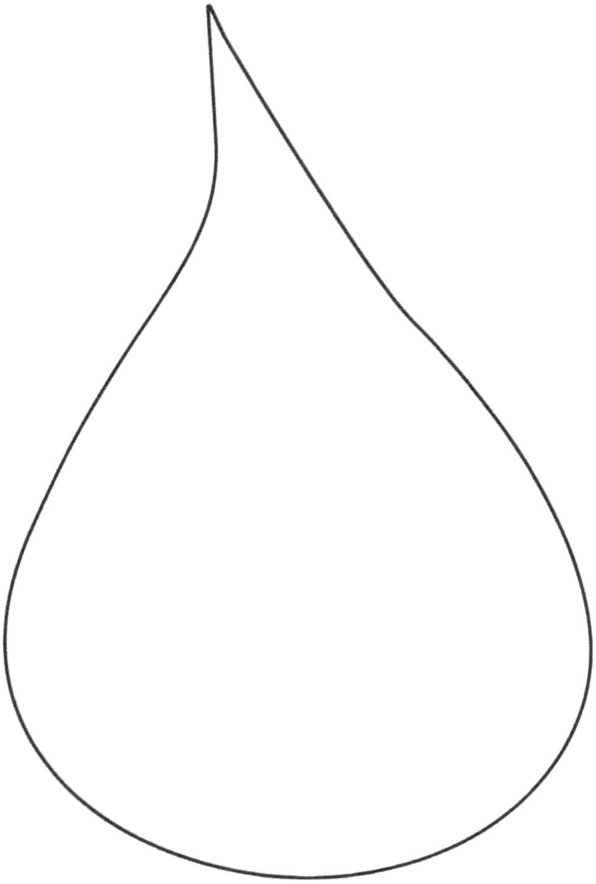

Critical-Thinking Activity

REAL VICTORY

In verse 7 Vṛtrāsura tells Indra, "O Indra, no one is guaranteed of being always victorious but the original enjoyer, the Supreme Personality of Godhead, Bhagavān." In this case, in the fight between Vṛtrāsura and Indra, how is the Lord victorious when He never really fought in the first place? How would Indra not be the actual winner when he killed Vṛtrāsura? Let us understand by studying the purports more deeply.

This chapter teaches us a unique way of looking at victory and defeat. "Victory" meant different things to Vṛtrāsura, Indra, and the Supreme Lord in this case.

Look at the following thoughts about victory. Sort them out into three categories: Indra's idea of victory, Vṛtrāsura's idea of victory, and Kṛṣṇa's idea of victory. Then fill the tables with the correct information.

1 . I want to kill Vṛtrāsura.
2. I want to act according to the will of the Lord for Him.
3. I want to complete my duty successfully.
4. I direct each person fairly according to their desire.
5. I take special care that a pure devotee's desires for unalloyed service are fulfilled.
6. I want to regain sovereignty of the heavenly kingdom.
7. I want to go back to Godhead.
8. I want to understand the plan of the Lord and act according to it, irrespective of victory or defeat.
9. Material nature and a pure devotee act as an instrument to execute My will.
10. I want to win the battle.
11. I accept subordination to the Lord.
12. I direct the situation as the supreme controller of everything.

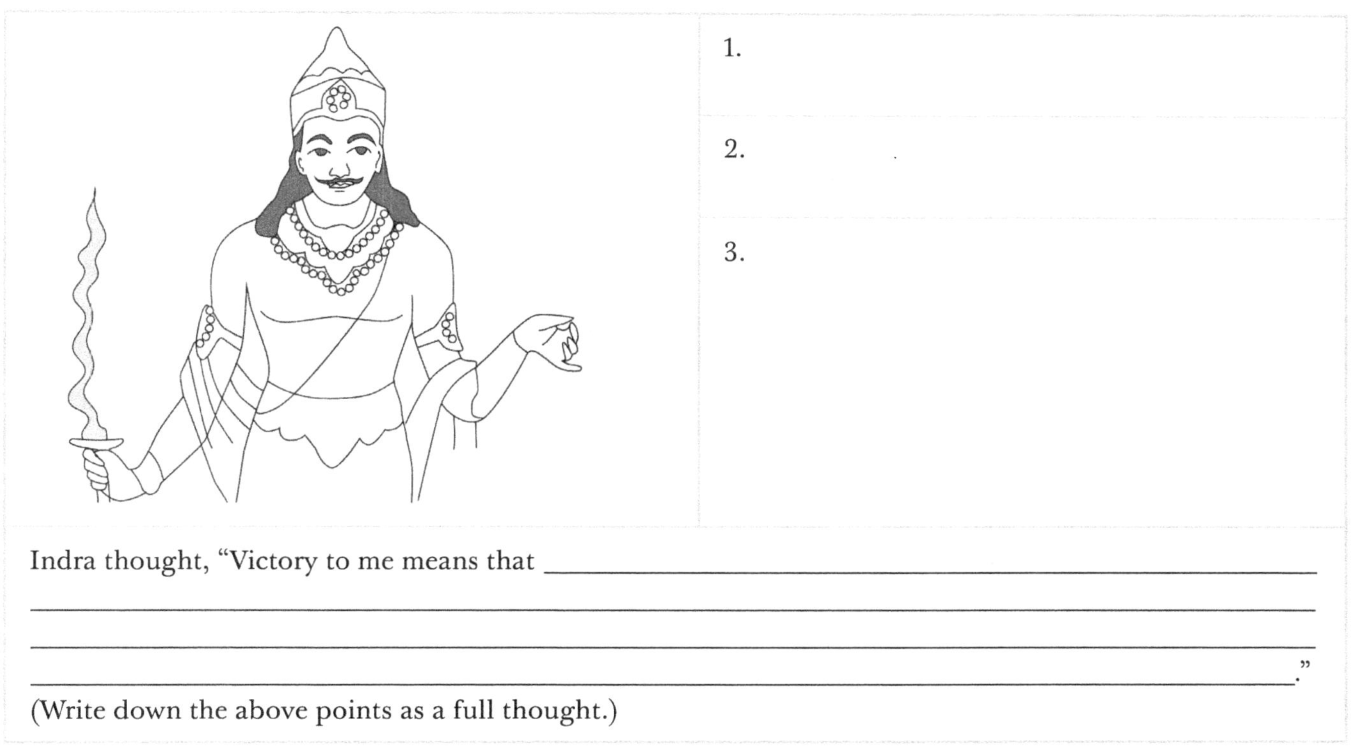

1.

2.

3.

4.

5.

Vṛtrāsura thought, "Victory to me means that ____
____
____
____."

(Write down the above points as a full thought.)

1.

2.

3.

Indra thought, "Victory to me means that ____
____
____
____."

(Write down the above points as a full thought.)

1.

2.

3.

4.

Kṛṣṇa thinks, "Victory to me means that ______________________________
____
____
____."

(Write down the above points as a full thought.)

Now consider:

1. How is the idea of victory different for Vṛtrāsura and Indra?

2. Who finally became victorious out of the two?

3. What interesting things can we learn about victory from this?

4. How does all this show that the Lord is ultimately always victorious?

Action Activity

ROLL AND TELL A STORY:
SINFUL ACTS CANNOT MAKE A MAN HAPPY!

We learn in this chapter that by committing sinful acts we cannot be happy no matter how much material opulence we have.

With the understanding of this theme in this chapter, roll a dice and plan a story to show how by committing a sinful action, a person receives sinful reactions and can never be happy.

Roll your dice once for each category: Character, Plot, and Setting

1. If you roll your dice to 1 for choosing a character, choose the first character in the list below.

2. For the plot, if you roll your dice to 3, choose plot number 3 from the list.

3. In the same way, for setting, if you roll your dice to 6, choose setting number 6.

4. Take turns to roll your dice and be creative in making your story! (See an example below.)

	CHARACTER	**PLOT**	**SETTING**
1.	A domestic helper	Is very jealous of someone	At workplace/school
2.	A doctor who is trusted by many	Steals something	Inside a bank
3.	A classmate sitting beside me	Rudely criticizes and blasphemes someone	Inside a temple
4.	A shopkeeper of our locality	Is greedy for something (position, money, food, etc.)	Inside a friend's house
5.	A close relative	Tells a lie or hides the truth to save himself/herself.	In the residential community
6.	A gatekeeper of a building	Bullies someone badly	On the road

Example of a story by rolling the dice with the following character, plot, and setting:

CHARACTER (5): A close relative
PLOT (2): Steals something
SETTING (4): Inside a friend's house

THE TALKING EARPHONES

It happened last year in the winter. One of my close relatives, Sam, visited his friend's house for a birthday party. There were lots of other guests in the house. He was excited to see all his friends dressed up in fancy clothes. He was also flaunting one of his best outfits. Sam liked to get compliments as he loved attention and good remarks. He always loved to show off his expensive garments, shoes, electronic gadgets, and so on.

During the party, Sam noticed a pair of gorgeous, shiny black earphones lying underneath a chair. There were so many people inside that he thought it futile to go around looking for the owner, so he thought that if he took the earphones for himself, no one would really come to know about it. Sam stealthily sneaked the earphones inside his backpack without caring about the consequences. He behaved normally and went around eating, talking to everyone, and having fun.

Suddenly, something started beeping loudly. No one could understand where it was coming from except one of the guests, who came tracing the path of the beeping sound, which led to Sam's backpack lying beside a rocking chair in the living room. Everyone looked clueless, including Sam, who had no idea that the earphones which he stole were making the beeping noise and that the owner was trying to locate his lost earphones! Sam wasn't updated about the technologically advanced earphones that had a tracking device. The owner gazed sternly at the bag, asking who it belonged to. Sam had no other option than to come forward and claim ownership of the backpack. The guest snatched the backpack from Sam's hand and opened it angrily to take his earphones back. Oh, what an embarrassing moment! As Sam stood there, everyone gaped at him with so many questions on their faces. Sam was thoroughly embarrassed and very unhappy because of his wrong action.

He definitely wanted to leave the place but couldn't move an inch because of the horrible shame he felt for his wrong deed. Sam thought, "I should have just asked everyone about the earphones than feeding the greed of having it for myself!"

Science Activity

PAIN OR NO PAIN?

In this chapter, we see how Vṛtrāsura's arms and head were severed off. When we get cut, we feel pain. Have you ever wondered why?

Lalita has just learned about the death of Vṛtrāsura. Then she accidentally cuts her thumb when she is chopping vegetables for a salad her mother is preparing for the evening offering. She is in a lot of pain.

As she wraps a plaster around the wound, she notices her little brother Sundar trimming his nails. Although he is also cutting a part of his finger, he feels no pain at all.

Lalita decides to investigate why this happens. Here is her notepad. Can you help her complete it?

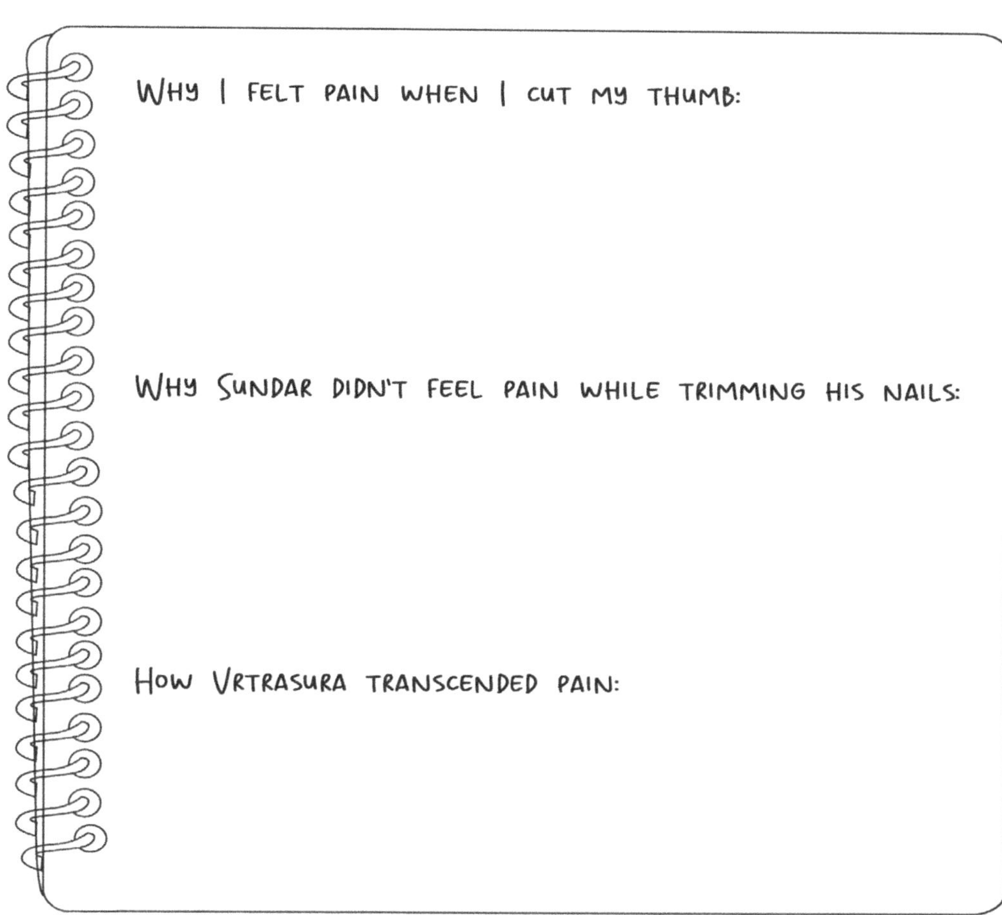

Writing and Language Activities

... to help you understand better

THUMBS UP, THUMBS DOWN: VICTORY OR DEFEAT

In this chapter we learned that victory or defeat depends on the Supreme Lord. Therefore, we should try to focus on performing our prescribed duties rather than thinking about the results.

Try to identify each situation and think whether we must act as mentioned or not. Show a thumbs up for "yes" and a thumbs down for "no".

For each "no" situation, discuss with your teacher or write in your notebook how one could have reacted in that situation to make it a thumbs up.

See example in the first situation:

Situation 1: Sita's mother is sick and she asked Sita to cook for the day. Sita doesn't want to cook because she is worried that it wouldn't taste as good as mum's. Sita asks her neighbor to cook for her family.

 If I were in Sita's place, I could think that this as an opportunity to improve my culinary skills and try to cook something simple, under my mother's instructions. At least I would learn to help, learn a new skill, and be more confident for the next time.

Situation 2: Madhava is preparing for an entrance test to his favorite university. He studies really hard and does his best to prepare. On the day of the test, Madhava doesn't perform well because he got nervous and couldn't remember many of the answers. He comes home demotivated and decides to quit his dream of getting into his favorite university.

Situation 3: There has been a scarcity of rain, and a group of farmers are worried that their crops won't survive. Some of them decide not to sow any crops at all and buy grains from the market. Some farmers, however, make tireless efforts to dig a small canal from a nearby pond to water the crops nicely. They think that if they don't sow crops, whether it rains or not, people in their village wouldn't get to eat.

Situation 4: Two football teams are playing a match against each other. One team plays fair and scores a few goals. The opposing team, however, is quite unfair during the match and somehow wins the match. The fair football team decides to play unfair from the next game because they think it is an easy way to win.

Situation 5: Some young boys see a puppy drowning. They don't know how to swim and are getting late for their games. Except for one boy, they all ignore the pup and leave the place. The boy immediately runs to get help from a man, totally forgetting about his games.

Situation 6: The teacher gives a project to be completed without help at home. Mona asks her elder brother to complete the tasks for her, while she spends time on her favorite game. Her project is better than the rest of the class.

Situation 7: Gaura passes his assessments with flying colors. He is happy and becomes overconfident due to his achievements. He thinks he can manage to study at the last minute and gradually puts less efforts in his studies.

PUPPETRY SCRIPT: THE SUPREME CONTROLLER

What is a puppetry script?

It is a script written for a puppet show and has all the elements of a story: setting, characters, problem/conflict, plot, climax, resolution, and theme. It is written in a dialogue or a narrative format. Puppetry scripts are read out while performing the puppet show to depict the happenings through the characters.

In this chapter we learn that the Lord is the supreme controller of all living entities, just as a wooden doll or puppet is controlled by its master. No one is independent.

Write a puppetry script for the following story, which illustrates this theme of being dependent on the Lord who is our well-wisher, just as children are dependent on their parents, who are their well-wishers.

Simon wants to go on a road trip with his classmates. He needs money as well as permission from his parents to go. Simon's parents don't allow him to go, knowing that it's unsafe to go through an area where it had rained heavily and landslides were a possibility. Simon is angry, upset, and stops speaking to his parents.

Create a puppetry script for a puppet show to depict how Simon's parents are correct in not permitting him to go for the road trip. Think of some mishap that could occur if Simon was allowed to go. Depict how the parents' control over their child's life, in this circumstance, is meant for the child's benefit. At the same time, the child can choose to obey or disobey the parents, just as we can choose to be dependent on or independent of the Lord. In both cases, we have to face the consequences.

Some writing tips:

1. Make a short script and name the characters.

2. Create a problem/conflict and finally a solution.

3. Add a short sentence to the script, comparing the situation with Kṛṣṇa's control over all living beings.
   For example:
   » In the same way, Kṛṣṇa takes control over our lives just as Simon's father took charge over his son's safety by not allowing him to go for the road trip.
   » Even if we are not happy with the results or happenings in our life, we must believe that it is ultimately Kṛṣṇa's will for our benefit.

4. Add a catchy title to the script.

5. You can also use this script to enact a puppet show with the puppet you created in the art activity.

LETTER: SURRENDER TO KRṢṆA IN HAPPINESS OR DISTRESS

If we confidently surrender to Kṛṣṇa by accepting our circumstances, we will remain undisturbed in happiness and distress, because we realize that everything is dependent on Kṛṣṇa's will.

Your friend is quite upset because his or her grandmother is about to leave her body. The doctors have given up hope of her survival and have asked everyone to be mentally prepared for this loss in a few weeks.

You know that your friend is very close to his or her grandmother, and it will be very difficult to bear this loss. Write a letter to console your friend, explaining that everything happens by Kṛṣṇa's will and that it will be better if your friend leaves everything in Kṛṣṇa's hands. Remember not to preach and be insensitive but to encourage your friend to accept that which is inevitable and under the Lord's direction.

Points that can be mentioned in a gentle way:
- When someone is born, they must die; so we must take this as an arrangement of the Supreme Lord.
- Your friend can use this time to read out the Lord's glories to his or her grandmother and to sing or chant the holy name.
- We will all lose our loved ones someday. The only person who would never leave us is Kṛṣṇa.
- Whether we are happy or sad, we must always think that we have no ultimate control over our lives and that we are simply puppets in Kṛṣṇa's hands.
- Your friend must do his or her prescribed duty by looking after his or her grandmother, to provide all comfort, and pray to Kṛṣṇa that she can go back to Godhead or continue in her spiritual journey.

DISCUSSION:
ANYONE CAN BECOME PURIFIED BY THE MERCY OF KṚṢṆA!

In this chapter, we clearly understand that even if one is in a demon body, one can become a perfect person and get elevated to the position of a pure devotee of the Lord, by His causeless mercy.

Discussion is an effective way to involve people in sharing ideas or activities. People in the discussion are connected with one basic idea. Based on that idea or topic, everyone in the group represents his/her perspective.

With the understanding of the theme mentioned above, discuss the following questions with your teacher or with your class group:

1. When Śrīla Prabhupāda preached in the West, he transformed all kinds of people, including hippies, who were engaged in many sinful activities. Why do you think Prabhupāda interacted with all kinds of sinful people, knowing about their impure lifestyles?

2. We all know how fallen Ajāmila had become due to his degraded association with the prostitute. He was about to be snatched away by the Yamadūtas when the Viṣṇudūtas came to his rescue. Why do you think he deserved a second chance?

3. How do you think successful modern-day leaders in society are different from Vṛtrāsura in character? What made Vṛtrāsura stand out, even being in a demon body?

4. Therefore, discuss how one can make a difference in the current society, where we are surrounded by all demonic leaders.

Some tips for effective discussion:

1. Give enough time to everyone while they speak.

2. Take notes of different viewpoints, expressed by different people in the discussion.

3. Try providing real life examples or personal examples during a discussion.

4. Listen intently and keep the content of the discussion relevant to the topic/main idea.

THE 3D'S – DUTY, DETACHMENT, AND DEPENDENCE

In this chapter Vṛtrāsura repeatedly encouraged Indra to fight dutifully, in a detached manner, and to depend on Kṛṣṇa's will, just as Lord Kṛṣṇa spoke *Bhagavad-gītā* when Arjuna was despondent and his Gāṇḍiva bow slipped from his hands on the battlefield. Understanding their instructions can guide us in proper Kṛṣṇa conscious action and attitude in life.

A. Choose the three verses from *Bhagavad- gītā* below which are reflected in Vṛtrāsura's teachings in this chapter:

1. You have a right to perform your prescribed duty, but you are not entitled to the fruits of action. Never consider yourself the cause of the results of your activities, and never be attached to not doing your duty. (*Bg.* 2.47)

2. Never was there a time when I did not exist, nor you, nor all these kings; nor in the future shall any of us cease to be. (*Bg.* 2.12)

3. This individual soul is unbreakable and insoluble and can be neither burned nor dried. He is everlasting, present everywhere, unchangeable, immovable and eternally the same. (*Bg.* 2.24)

4. Perform your duty equipoised, O Arjuna, abandoning all attachment to success or failure. Such equanimity is called *yoga*. (*Bg.* 2.48)

5. Yet in this body there is another, a transcendental enjoyer, who is the Lord, the supreme proprietor, who exists as the overseer and permitter, and who is known as the Supersoul. (*Bg.* 13.23)

B. State whether the following statements are true or false based on verses 7–17. If false, give a reason:

1. We can always be victorious.

2. Kṛṣṇa is the supreme cause of creation, maintenance, and annihilation.

3. We are independent doers.

4. *Suras* understand that nothing can happen without the desire and sanction of the Lord whereas the *asuras* don't.

5. There is no need to acknowledge the supreme position of Lord Kṛṣṇa because He is self-satisfied.

6. Vṛtrāsura said, "We have to be equipoised in fame and defamation, victory and defeat, life and death." He perfectly demonstrated this by his actions.

7. Depending on Kṛṣṇa means not taking responsibility and becoming lazy and passive.

CHAPTER 12 ANSWERS

Dancing to the Desire of the Supreme Controller

(The puppet represents us, and our control over the puppet's strings represents the Lord's control over us.) 1. Our senses are controlled by the Supreme Lord; 2. Our power to think may seem to be our own, but it comes from the Supreme Lord; 3. Our bodily strength is supplied by the Lord; 4. The body is at some point destroyed by the will of the Lord; 5. The Lord can protect us (the soul); 6. The Lord can give us any body or personality we deserve based on the results of our activities.

You cannot do anything on your own strength. You are in illusion if you think that you can do any activity without the help of your master. If you think you can do everything on your own, you will fail. So recognize your master who is pulling the strings and be grateful to him.

In the same way, the *jīva* who thinks that he is capable of acting independently of the Lord's control is under illusion under the external energy and does not understand that the Lord is the real controller and will remain so whether or not the *jīva* acknowledges the Lord's superior position. We can always think of ourselves subordinate and dependent on the Lord to be successful in any activity.

Pain or No Pain?

Pain is a reaction of the human body to any stimulus that may cause damage to it. When there is some tissue damage in the body, our skin contains nerve cells that respond to these stimuli. The nerves send a signal to the brain, which in turn responds to the cause of pain. Therefore, we feel pain, which is nature's way of warning us of danger to the body. This is not true, however, for nails and hair, which are dead cells and do not have any nerve endings to detect pain when we cut them. Vṛtrāsura, on the other hand, transcended pain because he was fully realized in knowledge and deeply absorbed in thoughts of the Lord. This doesn't mean, however, that he didn't feel pain. His pain was minimized when his mind and consciousness transcended bodily suffering. Sometimes, the Lord also removes suffering or pain for a devotee, as in the case of Haridāsa Ṭhākura or Prahlāda Mahārāja, when they were tortured and put in danger.

Real Victory

Vṛtrāsura: 2, 3, 7, 8, 11; Indra: 1, 6, 10; Supreme Lord: 4, 5, 9, 12

1. Indra's idea of victory was material, meant for his personal material gain – he approached the Lord with a desire, and the Lord sanctioned it; Vṛtrāsura's desire, on the other hand, was spiritual – he wanted to act according to the Lord's desire without asking the Lord any material favors; he therefore only tried to align himself with whatever the Lord wanted.

2. As discussed in the last chapter, Vṛtrāsura was the actual winner as he went back to Godhead while Indra had to stay in the material world.

3. Victory is something that is not necessarily material. Material victory awards temporary results whereas spiritual victory has long-term and lasting results. Real victory means spiritual victory, which is to serve and please the Lord. By pleasing the Lord, we become truly fulfilled and happy, like Vṛtrāsura, and we can be reunited with the Lord in the spiritual world.

4. The Lord is understood to be the real winner in all circumstances for the following reasons: 1) He directs everyone, and nobody can do anything without His will; 2) The Lord as Paramātmā directs every living entity to act according to His will to do any activity – the living entity can neither take decisions nor act in ways that are not sanctioned by the Supersoul, (even though he may not realize it); 3) The Lord is equal to everyone and tries to fulfill everyone's desires according to their level of surrender to Him. In this way, only His will is executed in all circumstances. Therefore, in all situations, the Lord is the real winner.

The 3D's

A: Verses 1, 4, and 5

B:

1. False: Only the Supreme Lord is always victorious for He is the supreme controller and the most powerful.

2. True.

3. False: "The bewildered spirit soul, under the influence of the three modes of material nature, thinks himself the doer of activities that are in actuality carried out by nature." (*Bg* 3.27). The Lord gives orders to material nature, and she arranges facilities for the living entities. We are dependent on material nature to carry out our duties and activities.

4. True.

5. False: Such persons are described as foolish and senseless. (*SB* 6.12.12) The Lord wants us to not only acknowledge Him but to have a relationship with Him and serve Him with love.

6. True.

7. False: Dependence on Kṛṣṇa means working sincerely, to the best of our capacity, with the goal of pleasing Kṛṣṇa by our service. We are not attached to success or failure.

RESOURCES

Figure 1

Figure 2

13

Finally, Vṛtrāsura lay dead on the battlefield. The demigods and everyone from the three planetary systems rejoiced. But not Indra. He didn't look at Lord Brahmā and Lord Śiva as they mounted their airplanes and left for their respective abodes. They too didn't speak to King Indra but left him to deal with his emotions. Indra's face was wet with tears. He could not bear to look at the body of the dead demon – whom he had realized was not demonic at all.

"Why was Indra so unhappy?" asked Parīkṣit Mahārāja. "After all, even the demigods were jubilant when Vṛtrāsura was killed."

Śukadeva Gosvāmī replied, "You see, my dear King, when the great sages and demigods were afraid of and disturbed by Vṛtrāsura's extraordinary power, they had urged King Indra to kill the demon, but Indra declined their request at first. Vṛtrāsura, the son of Tvaṣā, was also considered a *brāhmaṇa,* so Indra was afraid of

killing a *brāhmaṇa* for the second time. He
told the demigods, 'When I killed Viśvarūpa
I received great sinful reactions, but the
women, land, trees, and water favored me
and shared my sinful reactions. But now if I
kill Vṛtrāsura, how shall I become free from
the sinful reactions?'

"But the sages encouraged Indra and
told him not to fear, for they would perform
an *aśvamedha* sacrifice on his behalf to
release him of any sin. They told him that by
performing such a sacrifice to please Lord
Nārāyaṇa, anyone could be relieved of the
sinful reactions for even killing the entire
world, what to speak of killing a demon like
Vṛtrāsura.

"They told Indra, 'Simply by chanting
the holy name of Lord Nārāyaṇa anyone
can immediately be freed from all sinful
reactions – from killing a *brāhmaṇa*, cow, or
even one's own mother, father, or spiritual
master. So if you can perform the great
horse sacrifice to please Lord Nārāyaṇa, why
should you be afraid?'"

Śukadeva Gosvāmī explained that King
Indra had been encouraged by their words and
then had killed Vṛtrāsura. Now he regretted his
actions as he looked at the bloody carcass of the
demon strewn across the battlefield. He knew he
could not commit sin on the strength of chanting
the holy name or by performing any kind of
atonement. An overwhelming grief overcame
him; he could not feel any happiness despite
his apparent victory. How could he be happy
committing sinful acts? All his material opulence,
and even his good qualities, could not help him in
his sorrow now.

Then, as he had feared, he saw personified
sin appear in the distance. She was in the form
of an old, wrinkled *caṇḍāla* woman. As her limbs
trembled, she coughed blood, suffering from
tuberculosis.

"Wait! Wait!" she called to Indra in a shrill

voice. Her body and garments were covered in
blood, and she breathed an unbearable fishy odor
that polluted the entire area.

Indra fled. First he flew to the sky, but then
the witch appeared there as well. She followed
him wherever he ran. Indra could not escape.
Then he had an idea. He quickly traveled
northeast to the Mānasa-sarovara Lake, where he
knew he would be protected from the dreadful
witch. The sweet scent of fresh lotuses guided
him, until he saw the lake shimmering like
thousands of diamonds in the sunlight. Lotuses
of every kind captivated the King, as if beckoning
him to enter the water. Indra swam underwater
among the labyrinths of lotus stems, until he saw
the goddess of fortune, Lakṣmīdevī, amid the
lotus clusters. She smiled at him and raised her
hand in a blessing pose. Indra then knew that he
could get shelter there. He wrapped himself in the
stem of one of the lotuses. Invisible, he lived in

that lake for a thousand years, meditating on Lord
Viṣṇu and worshiping Him. But King Indra was
starving. He wondered why the fire-god, Agni,
was not bringing him his share of all *yajñas* even
though he had known about Indra's whereabouts.
Then one day Indra looked up, and through the
lotus clusters on the surface of the water he saw
Agni standing on the lake's bank with a terrified
expression on his face. He had been coming all
along but had been too scared to enter the water.
Nevertheless, Indra was peaceful – he was being
protected by the goddess of fortune and her
husband, Lord Viṣṇu, so he knew that his sins
could not affect him anymore.

In the meanwhile, King Nahuṣa was given
the position of King Indra in the heavenly
kingdom because of his knowledge, austerity,
and mystic power. But it wasn't long before
Nahuṣa became blinded and maddened by
power and opulence. He tried to seduce
King Indra's wife, and so he was cursed by a
brāhmaṇa to become a snake.

King Indra's sins were being diminished
by the influence of Rudra, the demigod of
all directions, and through his strict worship
of Lakṣmī-Nārāyaṇa. Then one day he was
called back to the heavenly planets where
he performed the *aśvamedha-yajña*, the horse
sacrifice, to please the Supreme Lord. Because
he worshiped the Supreme Lord in that sacrifice,
Indra was relieved of all his sins, just as fog is
vanquished by the brilliant sunrise. Thus Indra
regained his exalted position and was again
honored by everyone.

King Parīkṣit smiled as Śukadeva Gosvāmī
ended the narration. He felt blissful having
heard the divine topics of the Lord and His
devotees and knowing that all had ended well.

Śukadeva Gosvāmī also smiled and said,
"O King, learned scholars hear and repeat this
narration on every festival day."

"Why is that?" asked Mahārāja Parīkṣit.

"Oh, this narration is very auspicious.

This great narrative glorifies the Supreme Lord,
Nārāyaṇa, explains about devotional service,
and describes devotees like Indra and Vṛtrāsura.
It also describes Indra's release from sinful
life and his victory in fighting the demons. By
understanding this incident anyone can be freed
of all sinful reactions. Therefore, the learned
always advise everyone to read and hear this
narration. If they do, they will become expert
in all activities, their opulence will increase, and
they will become famous. They will also conquer
all their enemies and live a long life. Such are the
glories of this narration."

Themes and Key Messages

Please go through this table of themes and key messages, with corresponding verses, and discuss each topic further.

THEMES	REFERENCES	KEY MESSAGES
The cleansing power of the Lord's holy name is unlimited, yet one cannot perform sin on the strength of the holy name.	6.13.8–10	The first three chapters of Canto 6 glorified the powerful effects of chanting the Lord's holy names, and this chapter describes that by once chanting the holy names one can be freed from more sins that one can commit. This doesn't mean, however, that we can intentionally commit sin and think ourselves free from sinful reactions because we are chanting the holy name. Ajāmila did not sin on the strength of chanting the holy name, so he was liberated. Indra, on the other hand, killed Vṛtrāsura intentionally and thought he could be excused by performing sinful deeds on the strength of his atonement. Indra had to suffer for his sins, and the sages who had advised him to sin and then atone also had to suffer, when Nahuṣa became king.
One cannot be happy by committing sinful acts.	6.13.11	King Indra was not happy when he killed Vṛtrāsura despite his heavenly material opulence. People began to blaspheme him for killing a *brāhmaṇa*, so he was always unhappy because of their accusations. His mind could not be peaceful, knowing that he had committed a great sin toward a Vaiṣṇava despite the Lord having inspired him to kill Vṛtrāsura. The Lord teaches us through His devotees about the effects of pride and sinful action.
Sinful reactions can only be vanquished by pleasing Lord Viṣṇu.	6.13.12–21	Indra suffered for thousands of years because of his sinful killing. Personified sinful reaction in the form of a low-class woman was chasing him, and he couldn't escape. Eventually, Lakṣmīdevī protected him, and when he worshiped Lord Viṣṇu he was reinstated in his position in the heavenly planets. There he performed an *aśvamedha* sacrifice to please the Lord and was thus relieved of all sinful reactions.

Higher-Thinking Questions

Now try to deepen your understanding of this chapter by delving into Śrīla Prabhupāda's purports and reflecting on the following questions:

1. In verse 3 purport, Śrīla Prabhupāda mentions that a *brāhmaṇa* who is not a Vaiṣṇava cannot be a *guru*. Why do you think this is so?

2. According to verse 10 purport, why was Indra's sin of killing Vṛtrāsura greater than killing his *guru* Viśvarūpa?

3. Why do you think that Indra had to go through so much suffering for killing Vṛtrāsura although the Lord Himself had inspired him to kill Vṛtrāsura and even showed how to do it? [Hint: The Lord instructs through his devotees; who did Indra offend in the beginning, which spiralled into different events?]

4. What lessons do we learn from Indra's and Nahuṣa's behavior? In other words, what qualities shouldn't we imbibe?

5. Verse 17 tells of how Indra was protected. What does this indicate about Kṛṣṇa's devotees who may make mistakes or even temporarily fall down from the pure path due to sinful acts? How do you think you should think about or act towards such devotees?

ACTIVITIES

In this section you will find many exciting things to do. These activities will get you thinking, moving, drawing, and having loads of fun.

Analogy Activity

... to bring out the scholar in you

THE WITCH OF SIN

In verses 12 to15, we see how Indra was chased by the sinful reactions of killing a *brāhmaṇa* in the form of a witch. He had to take shelter in the stem of a lotus flower in Mānasa-sarovara lake to get protection from her.

This pastime can serve as an allegory for us, which means we can learn several lessons from it.

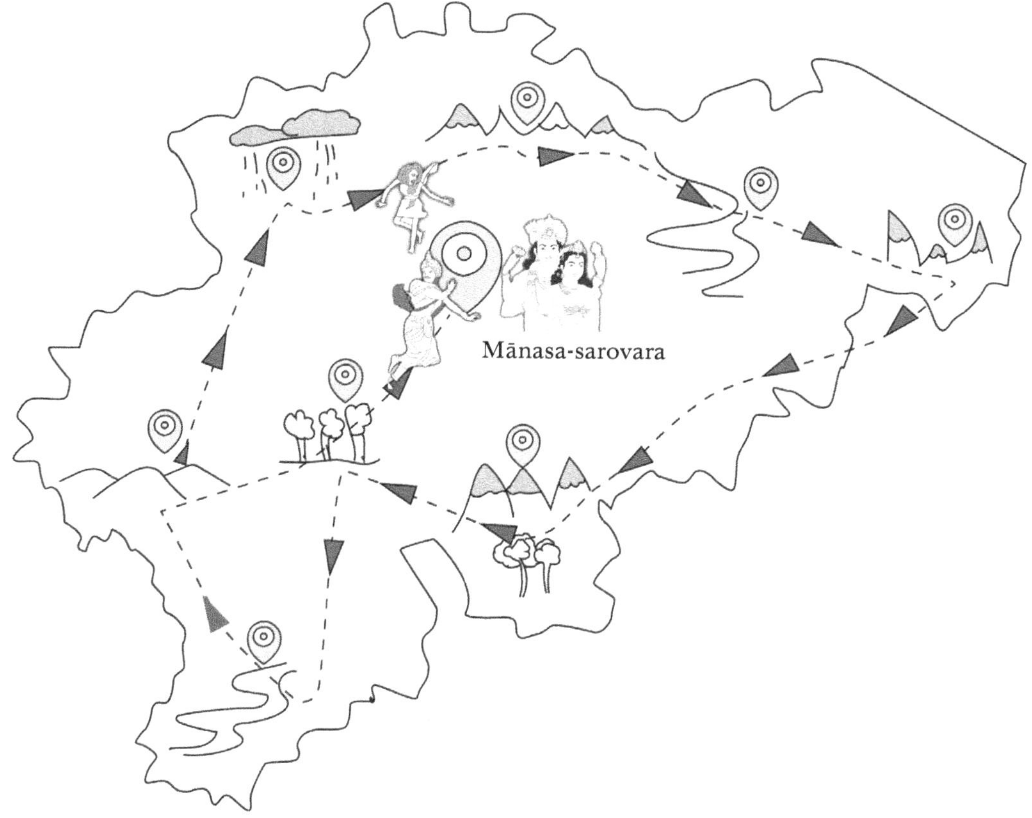

Look at the map above and fill out the following table. In the left column, some of the points are given regarding the pastime. In the right column, fill out what lesson you derive from each point. The first one is done for you.

WHAT THE PICTURE DEPICTS	WHAT WE CAN LEARN FROM IT
1. Indra ran everywhere he could to escape the witch.	We cannot run from our sinful reactions – we have to face the reactions, no matter where we try to go in the universe to avoid them.
2. The witch (personification of sin) had a terrible form.	
3. Indra could see the witch.	
4. The *brāhmaṇas'* promise – that Indra would be protected if he committed the sin and then atone – did not work.	
5. Indra worshiped Lakṣmī-Nārāyaṇa, and the witch could not enter the lake.	

Theatrical Activity

... to bring out the actor in you

LESSONS FROM KING INDRA'S RELEASE

Read the following dialogue with a partner:

Gopal: Wow, what a narrative, Mother! It spans over seven chapters!

Mother: Yes, it began with Indra being honored in his assembly and ends with Indra regaining his position and again being honored by everyone!

Gopal: (laughs) Yes, very interesting and educational as well!

Mother: What are some of your reflections?

Gopal: Well, there are many: First, pride is the cause of offenses to superiors, and then Kṛṣṇa shows His mercy when He destroys the causes of pride, like opulence and status. Second, Kṛṣṇa is the ultimate maintainer of all, the *suras* and the *asuras*, the mixed devotees and the pure devotees, in all conditions of life. Third, Kṛṣṇa is the source of all material and spiritual benedictions. And fourth, I learned about the pure, surrendered heart of devotees and their steadfastness in distressful situations, and many more. But one practical lesson is very prominent in my mind after reading the 13th chapter.

Mother: What is it, dear son?

Gopal: It reminds me of my experiences with the team leader at the temple. Sometimes I used to think that the leader is taking advantage of his position and is partial toward certain members. Also, at times I felt I could do better than him in certain areas!

Mother: Hmm . . . What has changed now?

Gopal: Two things: From a perspective of a leader, I realize that one attains a leadership position because of one's past service and capacity. But ultimately, a leader is responsible for his own attitude and desires. If I ever find myself in a leadership position, I will try to be very careful about my intention to please Kṛṣṇa through the service and see that the devotees working with me are dear to Kṛṣṇa. In the short term, I may have to direct or correct someone, but in the long run, they could end up being way ahead of me in their service to Kṛṣṇa, just as Vṛtrāsura was in relation to Indra.

Mother: That is a very mature reflection! What about your understanding as a team member?

Gopal: From a perspective of a subordinate, I can see that when Nahuṣa gained power for a short time, he ended up committing an offense to Śacīdevī and the exalted sages. I learned that it is not easy to stay humble and restrained in positions of power.

Mother: That is why the *Śrīmad-Bhāgavatam* advises us not to condemn the authority of powerful rulers like Lord Indra and Lord Brahmā for their mistakes.

Gopal: Yes, Mother. Also, when a leader behaves differently from what I expect and treats me in an unfavorable way, I will try to see it as Kṛṣṇa's arrangement for me to serve dutifully without taking things personally.

Mother: Wonderful, son! This attitude can help us resolve so many unwanted conflicts in relationships. It turns such conflicts into opportunities for strengthening our relationship with Lord Kṛṣṇa and His devotees.

Critical-Thinking Activity

... to bring out the spiritual investigator in you

CHANTING TO NULLIFY REACTIONS

In this chapter we see how Indra could not be relieved of sinful reactions even though the *brāhmaṇa* priests had promised him relief from the reactions of killing Vṛtrāsura through the chanting of the holy name of the Lord. In Chapter 2 of this canto, on the other hand, we saw how Ajāmila got relief from his sinful reactions just by chanting the holy name of the Lord.

Sridama is trying to understand how this can be possible. He decided to send a message to his study mates at *Bhāgavatam* study group on WhatsApp. Here is how the chat went:

Now:

1. Comment on why Haridev and Vamsi are not accurate in their understanding.

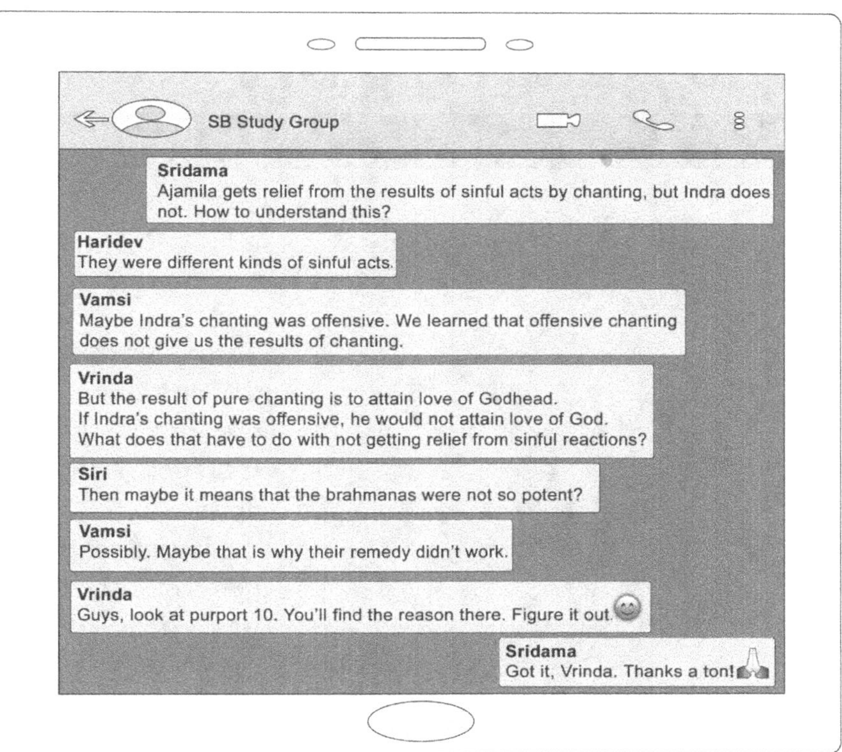

2. How do you understand Siri's comment?

3. What did Vrinda read in purport 10 that convinced Sridama?

Science Activity

HOW DOES WATER PUT OUT FIRE?

In this chapter, we read how Agni was unable to bring Indra's share of offerings to him, because Indra had taken shelter of a lotus stem in the water, which left Indra practically starving.

While we may find it hard to materially analyze how Agnideva wasn't able to enter the water, we can certainly investigate the relationship between fire and water.

Investigate the following:

1. Why does water put out fire?

2. Can all types of fire be put out by water? Why or why not?

3. Why does fire not burn when water is poured on it, although it has both hydrogen and oxygen (both of which promote burning) in it?

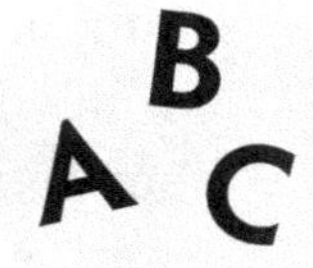

Writing and Language Activities

POEM: PLEASING LORD VIṢṆU VANQUISHES SINFUL REACTIONS

The performance of a poem is a powerful demonstration of a happening through poetry. The poet or actor makes the poem come alive through recitation, actions, voice modulations, and sounds or music.

In this chapter we learn that only when Indra performed the *aśvamedha-yajña* and pleased Lord Viṣṇu was he relieved of all his sins for killing the devotee Vṛtrāsura.

Based on your understanding of this theme, write a short poem to describe how Indra finally got relieved of his sinful reactions by performing devotional service and pleasing Lord Viṣṇu. You can also enact the following poem with actions, voice modulations, and characters, like in a play.

Example:

YOUR SINFUL REACTIONS CAN FLEE!

The scary *caṇḍāla* woman, with blood-stained clothes
Follows Indra here and there, everywhere he goes!

The sin of killing a *brāhmaṇa* is on Indra's head
He better hide himself, or he will be dead.

Vṛtrāsura, the great *brāhmaṇa* demon,
Taught lessons on duty, definitely for a reason!

In his heart, knowing he was sinful,
Indra ran, hopeless in repentance, feeling remorseful.

Hiding himself inside a lotus stem,
Starving for years, his acts he did condemn.

Lakṣmīdevī protected Indra and came to his rescue
Indra left his kingship for Nahuṣa to pursue.

Only by performing the *aśvamedha* sacrifice,
Viṣṇu became pleased and relieved Indra of his vice.

O people of the three worlds, open your hearts and see
Only by pleasing Lord Viṣṇu, your sinful reactions can flee!

Instructions for performing a poem:

1. Present yourself well and be attentive.

2. Use good posture.

3. Be confident and make a direct connection with the audience.

4. Make sure you know how to pronounce every word in your poem.

5. Use actions or props if you want to make it more animated.

6. Do not act out each word of the poem; try enacting just the sense of the sentence.

CROSSWORD PUZZLE

Across

3. Indra went to this lake to escape personified sin.
5. One of the sages who favored Indra.
8. Whom did Vṛtrāsura become an associate of in Vaikuṇṭha?

Down

1. He ruled the heavenly kingdom in absence of Indra.
2. Indra hid in its stems in Mānasa-sarovara.
4. The *brāhmaṇas* initiated King Indra into this sacrifice to please Lord Viṣṇu.
6. When Vṛtrāsura was killed, everyone was satisfied except who?
7. Indra was relieved of all sinful reactions by strictly worshiping Him.

CHAPTER 13 ANSWERS

The Witch of Sin

2. Indra had to face severe reactions for a severe crime; similarly, we have to face our sinful reactions in proportion to the sins we commit. In general, sinful reactions, like the descriptions of the witch, can be foul, undesirable, and can be in the form of disease, old age, and other miserable conditions.

3. If we are introspective and mindful, we can understand and see that negative reactions in our lives are a result of sin.

4. By planning atonement before committing sinful acts, we cannot get relief from sin. Taking shelter of the Lord is the real atonement and relieves us from sinful reactions.

5. If we take full shelter of the Lord, sinful reactions cannot touch us. Our past sinful reactions are vanquished only when we are able to please the Lord by our sincere devotion.

Chanting to Nullify Reactions

1. Haridev: All kinds of sinful reactions are nullified by offenseless chanting; it is not true that the holy name can nullify certain types of reactions but not others. Vamsi: The *brāhmaṇas* advised Indra to perform offensive chanting (offense 7: to commit sinful activities on the strength of chanting the holy name), but release from sinful reactions should not be the purpose of chanting.

2. Siri: While the *brāhmaṇas* may have been potent (they successfully performed the *aśvamedha-yajña* later), they did not have the proper understanding of how to chant purely; therefore they were not able to advise Indra properly.

3. Vrinda read, "The planned execution of sinful deeds on the strength of chanting the holy name of the Lord or undergoing *prāyaścitta*, atonement, cannot give relief to anyone, even to Indra or Nahuṣa." In other words, the reactions of killing a *brāhmaṇa* or Vaiṣṇava purposely are so great that atonement cannot relieve one of the reactions – one needs to undergo suffering, and then atonement. Also, in such situations, offensive chanting is when one purposefully commits sin on the strength of the holy name, thinking that the holy name would eradicate the effects of sin. Such offensive chanting cannot give relief to anyone for an offense as grave as the killing of a Vaiṣṇava.

How Does Water Put Out Fire?

1. Water cools the burning material so that the temperature of the fire goes below ignition temperature. Water also cuts off the oxygen supply from the air to the fire by creating a barrier between the atmosphere and the fire. It thus puts off the fire.

2. Water, however, cannot be used to extinguish electrical fires or fires caused by flammable liquids (sand may be used in a similar way in this case).

3. Although hydrogen and oxygen aid combustion, when they combine to form a water molecule, they create a substance with entirely different properties. Therefore, water does not burn. When poured on fire, water may turn into steam (which is water in a gaseous form), but it remains water and does not split into hydrogen and oxygen.

Crossword Puzzle

Across: 3. Manasasarovara; 5. Marici; 8. Sankarsana
Down: 1. Nahusa; 2. Lotus; 4. Asvamedha; 6. Indra; 7. Visnu

14

Parīkṣit Mahārāja was deep in thought. At last, he asked Śukadeva Gosvāmī, "O learned *brāhmaṇa*, demons are generally sinful, covered by the modes of passion and ignorance. So how is it that Vṛtrāsura could have such great love for the Supreme Personality of Godhead?

"O best of the *brāhmaṇas*, in this world there are as many living beings as atoms, and out of these living beings, a small portion are humans, and among them just a fraction are interested in following religious principles. And among these, only a few desire liberation from material life, and among these a smaller portion may achieve liberation, giving up all attachments. And among many thousands of liberated persons, only one may be a pure devotee of Nārāyaṇa, or Kṛṣṇa. Such *nārāyaṇa-parāyaṇa* devotees, those who are most dear to Lord Nārāyaṇa, are extremely rare."

Śukadeva Gosvāmī smiled and nodded, understanding what the King was implying.

"If such pure devotees are so, so rare," Mahārāja Parīkṣit continued, "then how was it

that Vṛtrāsura, an infamous sinful demon, became so Kṛṣṇa conscious? How was it that he was a *nārāyaṇa-parāyaṇa*, even on the battlefield? I am confused by these contradictions, my lord, so please remove my confusion."

Śukadeva Gosvāmī replied, "O King, I shall tell you the history of Vṛtrāsura that I've heard from the great sages Vyāsadeva, Nārada, and Devala. Please hear carefully."

Parīkṣit Mahārāja leaned in to listen. He was intrigued by the whole story and couldn't wait to hear more.

"O King Parīkṣit," said Śukadeva Gosvāmī, "once, in the Śūrasena province, a king named Citraketu ruled the entire earth. The earth flourished during his reign. King Citraketu had ten million wives. . . ."

"Ten million!" exclaimed Parīkṣit, not believing what he had heard.

"Yes, the King first married one wife, and because she could not bear a child, he married again, and when that wife couldn't bear any children, he chose another wife. Like this, because none of his wives could have children, he ended up marrying millions of wives.

"Citraketu had everything – a beautiful youthful body, a high birth and education, great riches – but he could not have a son. His gorgeous wives, his extravagant opulence, and the many lands that he owned could not make him happy. He was in constant anxiety – who would continue his legacy and offer oblations to him and his forefathers after he left this world?

"One day while the King was sitting on his throne, he heard that the powerful sage Aṅgirā had come to the palace. Citraketu's gloomy expression turned into a wide smile that lit up his face. Excited, he stood up from his throne and welcomed the sage. He offered worship, water, and delicious food to his guest. Then when the sage was seated comfortably, the King sat at his feet with folded palms and head bowed in humility."

Śukadeva Gosvāmī described how Aṅgirā Ṛṣi beamed with appreciation and praised the King for his humility and hospitality. He said, "My dear King, I hope you and your royal associates and possessions are well. When the seven properties of material nature [the total material energy, the ego, and the five objects of sense gratification] are in order, the living entity can be happy. Similarly, when a king is protected by seven elements – his instructor or *guru*, his ministers, his kingdom, his fort, his treasury, his royal order, and his friends – and follows their instructions, he is happy. And when his associates serve the King and follow his orders, they are also happy. This mutual dependence makes everyone happy.

"O King, are you in control of your wives and citizens, secretaries, servants, merchants, and other dependents? But more than this, are you in control of your mind? Only if the King's mind is controlled can he control all his subordinates."

The King looked down, embarrassed. He wished that he could control his mind and that this dreary feeling of not having a son would go away, but he could not restrain his unsteady mind.

"I can see that your mind is not pleased," the sage said with a comforting tone. "It seems that you cannot achieve some goal. Is it because of you yourself or because of others? By your pale face, I can see that you're anxious. What's the matter?"

The King slowly looked up into the kind eyes of the sage. Then humbly bending his head low, he said, "O great lord Aṅgirā, as a perfect *yogī* you understand everything about conditioned souls like us. You know everything, yet you are asking me. So I will tell you what's wrong. Just as a person who is hungry and thirsty is not satisfied with flower garlands or sandalwood pulp, I am not satisfied or happy with my empire and opulence, because I have no son.

"Therefore, O great sage, save me and my forefathers from going to hell. Kindly do something so that I can have a son who will offer oblations to

us when I am gone and deliver us from hellish conditions."

The sage's eyes softened. He could not bear the suffering of the great King. He immediately performed a fire sacrifice by offering sweetrice to Tvaṣṭā. Then, he gave the remnants of the sweetrice to Kṛtadyuti, the first and most perfect among Citraketu's millions of queens.

As Aṅgirā Ṛṣi was about to leave, he told Citraketu, "O great King, now you will have a son who will be the cause of both jubilation and lamentation."

Citraketu did not fully understand what the sage meant, but he was too overjoyed to care. Finally he would have a son; that's all that mattered.

Soon after Kṛtadyuti ate the sweetrice, she became pregnant and appeared as radiant as the moon. And when she finally gave birth to a beautiful son, the entire kingdom rejoiced. You can imagine how thrilled Citraketu was. He immediately made elaborate arrangements for the birth ceremony. To the *brāhmaṇas* who performed the ritualistic ceremony he gave gold, silver, garments, ornaments, villages, horses and elephants, and six hundred million cows! As rain pours indiscriminately on the earth, the King gave in charity to everyone just to increase the reputation, opulence, and longevity of his newborn son.

Śukadeva Gosvāmī described that King Citraketu felt like a poor man who gets money after great difficulty and whose affection for the money increases daily. In a similar manner, having received a son after great difficulty, the King's affection for his son increased day after day. The mother's attention and attraction to her son also increased dramatically as the days passed. When the other wives saw Kṛtadyuti's son, they became agitated as if struck by high fevers with a desire to have sons of their own.

The queens observed the King fondle his son on his lap as he gazed lovingly at Kṛtadyuti. The three had become a close-knit family, and the other queens felt totally excluded. It was obvious that the King was spending more time with Queen Kṛtadyuti and had lost his affection for them.

They burned with envy and lamented their ill fate. One of the queens said in a voice filled with bitterness, "A wife with no son is neglected by her husband and dishonored by her co-wives just as if she were a maidservant. Such a woman is condemned!"

Another queen, with hot tears flowing down her cheeks, responded, "She is worse than a maidservant. At least a maidservant who serves the husband is honored by the husband, so she has no reason to lament. But our position is that we are maidservants of the maidservant. How unfortunate we are!"

The co-wives continued to reveal their minds to each other and cry in anguish. As days passed, the envy in their hearts burned stronger and stronger. They couldn't stand the King's neglect any longer nor tolerate how happy the elder queen was with her precious baby. Their envy became so intense that their hearts filled with hate and their intelligence faded away. Alas, they finally fed poison to the child.

Queen Kṛtadyuti paced her chambers, eager for her baby to get up. She thought that he had been sleeping for a long time, but she didn't want to disturb him. She pictured his beautiful chubby face, his black locks of hair, and his endearing eyes that were always filled with laughter. She couldn't wait any longer. She called for the nurse: "Please bring my son here at once."

The maidservant approached the sleeping child in his crib. "Get up, little boy, your mother wants to see . . ." She gasped as if she would suffocate. The baby's eyes were turned upward, and when she shook him there were no signs of life. Understanding that he was dead, she shouted, "Now I am doomed!" and fell to the ground. She struck her breast with her hands and cried loudly. The Queen heard her loud wailing and ran to her son's side only to find him dead. The Queen let out a shrill scream and also fell to the floor, her hair and dress in disarray. Not able to contain her grief, she became unconscious. All the palace residents heard the loud crying and ran to the Queen's chambers. They also began to cry. The co-wives were beside themselves with sorrow, or so it seemed. They knew well their offense and were just pretending.

King Citraketu was informed of the news. He felt like a blazing fire was consuming him as he ran to see his dead child. He couldn't see anything, and he kept slipping and falling on the ground. When at last he arrived at his son's side, he fell unconscious at the child's feet, his hair and dress scattered. His ministers and the learned *brāhmaṇas* watched in dismay as the aggrieved King regained consciousness and breathed heavily. He started to sob uncontrollably when he realized what had happened, but he could not utter a word. When the Queen, who had also regained consciousness, saw her grief-stricken husband and her dead child, she also wept and wailed hysterically. The flower garland in her hair fell, scattering her hair over her shoulders. Her tears smudged the black ointment in her eyes and moistened her breasts, which were covered with *kuṅkuma* powder. Her loud crying resembled the sweet sound of a *kurarī* bird. When the palace residents, the ministers, and the *brāhmaṇas* saw the state of their beloved King and Queen it increased the pain in their hearts.

The Queen lamented: "Alas, O Providence, O Creator, You are certainly inexperienced in creation because You have caused the death of a son during the lifetime of his father. You are

determined to contradict Your creative laws, so You are certainly the enemy of the living beings and are never merciful."

In between her sobs, she continued, "My Lord, since everyone lives and dies according to their *karma*, what is the need of a God if *karma* controls one's child's birth or death? And if *karma* disturbs the affection between a parent and child, no one will raise their children with affection; everyone will cruelly neglect their children. So since You've cut these bonds, You appear inexperienced and unintelligent."

Everyone looked at each other, shocked. They could understand that her grief was making her angry with the Lord.

The grieving Queen picked up her son and cradled him in her arms. Her tears wet his body as she bent down to kiss him. "My dear son," she said, "I am helpless and heartbroken. Please don't leave me. Just look at your distressed father. Without a son we will have to suffer going to the darkest hellish regions. You are our only hope. So please don't go away with the merciless Yama."

Still rocking him in her arms, she said, "My dear son, you've slept enough; now please get up! Can't you hear! Your friends are calling you to play. You must be very hungry, so get up and suck my breast milk and remove our sorrow."

Realizing that her son wouldn't get up, she

sobbed again and then said, "My dear boy, I am so unfortunate, for I cannot see your smile nor your sweet voice again. You've closed your eyes forever. You've been taken from this planet to another, from which you will never return."

Śukadeva Gosvāmī said, "My dear King Parīkṣit, King Citraketu wept profuse tears with his inconsolable wife. He cried loudly and piteously with his mouth open wide. All their followers cried with them, and when the citizens heard of the sudden tragedy, they were almost unconscious with grief. When Aṅgirā Ṛṣi heard that the King was almost dead in an ocean of lamentation, he rushed there with Nārada Muni."

Themes and Key Messages

Please go through this table of themes and key messages, with corresponding verses, and discuss each topic further.

THEMES	REFERENCES	KEY MESSAGES
It is extremely rare to be a devotee of Kṛṣṇa.	6.14.2–6	Among millions of liberated souls or those seeking liberation, a pure devotee is hardly to be found. Unless the dirt within one's heart is cleansed one cannot become a pure devotee; therefore, such devotees are *su-durlabhaḥ*, very rare.

THEMES	REFERENCES	KEY MESSAGES
Bhakti is transcendental to the mode of goodness.	6.14.6–7	Mahārāja Parīkṣit wanted to know why Vṛtrāsura's consciousness was so exalted despite his demonic birth and enmity toward Indra. Śrīla Jīva Gosvāmī comments in the *Bhakti Sandarbha* that Vṛtrāsura was not in the mode of goodness, so this means that *bhakti* does not come from *sattva-guṇa*. *Bhakti* is transcendental to the mode of goodness. Therefore the devotees are the best even among the liberated souls and *yogīs*.
An interdependent relationship between the king and his dependents, with a connection to the Supreme Lord, will make everyone happy.	6.14.17–20	Aṅgirā Ṛṣi gave managerial advice to King Citraketu. He explained that a king is protected by seven elements: the *guru*, the ministers, his friends, the treasury, his people, his fort, and his military strength, so the well-being of the king is dependent on them just as they are dependent on the king. The king should not simply give orders to his dependents; sometimes he must follow their instructions. This mutual dependence will make everyone happy. He also explained that if the king has a controlled mind, his kingdom will run successfully.
Envy makes the heart hard and makes one lose one's intelligence.	6.14.37–43	When the co-wives saw the Queen's intimate relationship with her son and the King, they burned with envy knowing that they could not have sons nor be the object of the King's affection. This envy made them so cruel and foolish that they killed the baby prince. Therefore, envy should be curbed.
We should not condemn the Supreme Lord when we go through reverses; rather we should see everything as the Lord's mercy.	6.14.52–55	The Queen criticized the Lord for causing the death of her son during his father's lifetime. She said what is the need of a God if *karma* controls one's child's birth or death. She condemned the Lord for having improperly made a creation that allows elders to live while their child dies. Although her reaction was natural because of her grief, it was not devotional. A devotee who suffers from reversals sees suffering as the Lord's mercy and supreme will and surrenders to the Lord, just as Vṛtrāsura had done. In this way he becomes entitled to reach the Lord's supreme abode. (*SB* 10.14.8)

Higher-Thinking Questions

Now try to deepen your understanding of this chapter by delving into Śrīla Prabhupāda's purports and reflecting on the following questions:

1. Why do you think that *jñānīs*, *yogīs*, and *karmīs* without devotional service are considered offenders as mentioned by Śrīla Prabhupāda in verse 5 purport?

2. What do you think could be the cause of Vṛtrāsura's being an exalted devotee? Try to think of how others in *Śrīmad-Bhāgavatam* became pure devotees.

3. Aṅgirā Ṛṣi explains to King Citraketu in verse 20 that if a king's mind is controlled he will be able to manage his dependents and his kingdom well. Why do you think this is so?

4. Why did King Citraketu want a son so much according to verse 26 and purport? How would he and his forefathers suffer without an heir?

5. How did King Citraketu interpret the sage's words when he said that his son would be a cause of both jubilation and lamentation? (See verse 29 and purport.)

6. In verse 55 purport Śrīla Prabhupāda explains that the subtle laws of *karma* cannot be understood by ordinary souls. Only a devotee can understand the Lord and how He is acting. What happens to such a devotee's past *karma*?

7. How would you defeat Queen Kṛtadyuti's arguments against the Lord in verse 55? What do you think is the Lord's purpose behind cutting the bonds of affection in this case?

ACTIVITIES

In this section you will find many exciting things to do. These activities will get you thinking, moving, drawing, and having loads of fun.

Analogy Activity

... to bring out the scholar in you

HUSKING PADDY FOR REAL GRAIN

* Paddy – grain in the husk before threshing
* Husk – outer shell or covering of the grain

"Impersonalists generally undergo great endeavor for no tangible benefit, and therefore it is said that they are husking paddy that has no grain (*sthūla-tuṣāvaghātinaḥ*)." (*SB* 6.14.5, purport)

In this purport, Śrīla Prabhupāda comments about *karmīs*, *jñānīs*, and *yogīs* who may be on the spiritual path but are not considered devotees because they don't accept the Lord's supremacy over them. The austerity they perform for spiritual perfection is compared here to a person husking paddy with no grain – that is, it is an attempt that does not yield the desired result. Let us try to understand why.

Look at the paddy field in the resource at the end of this chapter. It has husked grain zoomed up close. Not all the husk, however, contains paddy.

Photocopy the resource and cut up each individual paddy grain. Divide the grains into two piles – the pile with the paddy in it, and the pile without.

Look at the messages printed on the grains in your piles, and answer the following questions:

HUSK WITH PADDY

1. What is the main message from the pile that has the paddy inside the husk?

2. What kind of people would choose to hear this message and work according to it?

3. Why are they compared to a person husking paddy with the grain in it?

EMPTY HUSK

1. What is the main message from the pile that has only husk, but no paddy inside?

2. What kind of people would choose to hear this message and work according to it?

3. Why are they compared to a person husking paddy without the grain in it?

Śrīla Prabhupāda concludes his discussion to verse 5 as follows: "Not only among hundreds and thousands, but among millions of perfectly liberated souls, a pure devotee is hardly ever found." Based on the above analysis, how do you understand this conclusion?

Artistic Activity

... to reveal your creativity

ONE IN A MILLION

Humans form a fraction of the population among all living entities. Among humans, a few are interested in following religious principles (*karmīs*). Even fewer are those desiring liberation from material entanglement (*jñānīs*). Out of many such *jñānīs*, one may achieve liberation, and among thousands of such liberated personalities, only one may be a pure devotee of the Lord.

Such *nārāyaṇa-parāyaṇa* devotees, whose hearts have fully blossomed in love of Godhead, are extremely rare.

In this activity, we will acknowledge and appreciate how rare a devotee is by making a "one in a million" card and then presenting it to a devotee. Kṛṣṇa says in *Bhagavad-gītā* (7.3), "Out of many thousands among men, one may endeavor for perfection, and of those who have achieved perfection, hardly one knows Me in truth."

What you will need: Card stock paper, pencil, eraser, black ink pen, watercolors or colored pencils

Directions:

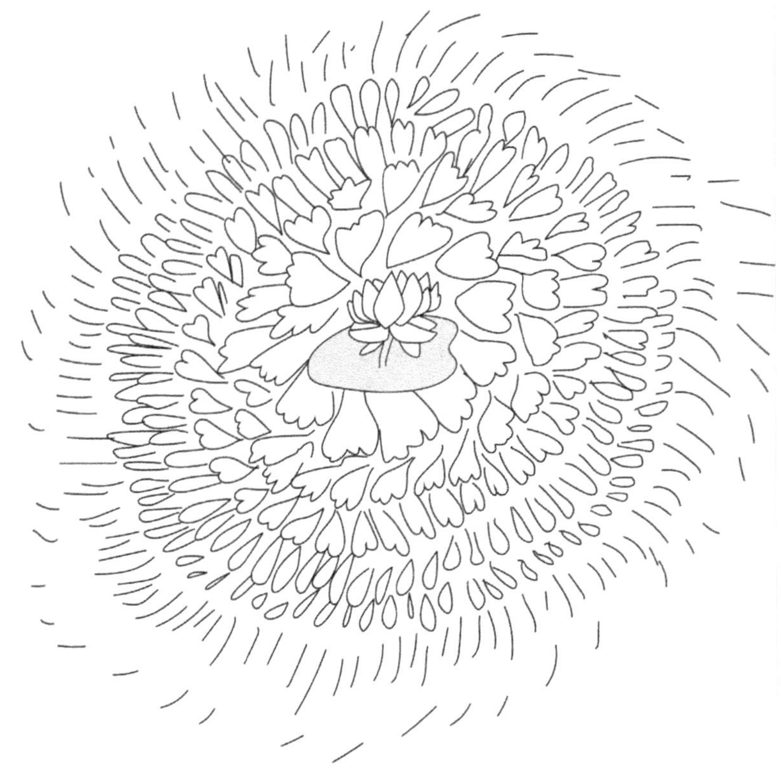

1. Study the illustration to the right. Observe how the lotus is the center of the artwork, highlighted by its full-blown form and beauty. This represents a rare pure devotee in full love for Kṛṣṇa.

2. Notice how the lotus is surrounded by circles of buds; the larger buds represent liberated souls.

3. The humans not interested in following *dharma* are indicated by simple lines. Dots indicate other living entities.

4. Fold the card stock paper in half. The drawing will be on the top, and the message will go inside.

5. Begin your illustration by drawing the lotus in the center of the card. Add circles of lotus buds around the lotus.

6. When satisfied with the drawing, you can outline your marks with black ink. Erase any visible pencil marks once the ink dries.

7. Now paint or color in your drawing. You can use dark colors for your lotus and the leaf. Use lighter colors for the subsequent blooming buds. This will bring the lotus into focus. Above or below the drawing you can write in fancy print: "You are One in a Million."

8. Think of a devotee who you would like to present the card to, remembering that anyone who is trying to surrender to Kṛṣṇa and serve Him is very rare. Inside the card, address the devotee and write a few lines appreciating him or her.

Introspective Activity

THE FIRE OF ENVY

Envy is like a fire that destroys one's intelligence and good sense. The co-wives poisoned the child because they were envious. This act eventually made them more miserable than happy.

Envy is a feeling of discontentment or resentment that arises when we see someone else having something (possession, quality, success, etc.) that we wish to have. Here are the stages one passes through when one is envious:

1. We desire something strongly.

2. We do not get what we desire, sometimes despite trying hard.

3. We see someone else possessing that same thing, and we become unhappy about it.

4. We either work to also gain possession of the same thing, or we work to deprive the other person of the possession. This makes us lose our intelligence and act in shameful ways.

5. If we fail, we become more miserable. If we succeed, we feel some sense of victory – but only till we find someone or something else to become envious of.

In your notebooks, write down the acts of Citraketu's wives for each of the steps given on the right.

The main characteristic of the residents of the spiritual world, however, is freedom from envy. In the spiritual world, Lord Kṛṣṇa gives most attention to Śrīmatī Rādhārāṇī. Rather than feeling envy and trying to harm their relationship, the other *gopīs* rejoice in the situation and joyfully try to unite them. They feel genuinely happy that one among them has conquered Kṛṣṇa and serves Him the best. In this way, not only do they make Rādhā and Kṛṣṇa happy, but they also become happy.

If we become envious of anyone who is serving Kṛṣṇa better, we should remember that Kṛṣṇa is happy with their service and if we are envious it means that we do not want Kṛṣṇa to be happy and enjoy their superior service or facilities they have to serve.

Think of a time when you may have been envious of someone. Write a short paragraph of your experience. How did you deal with it? What would you change if you were faced with the same situation now?

Critical-Thinking Activity

MATERIAL AUTOCRACY VERSUS SPIRITUAL AUTOCRACY

An autocracy is a system of government in which one ruler has absolute control and decision-making power. Vedic governments used to be autocratic, and citizens were happy with their king. The *Bhāgavatam* and other Vedic histories also describe that Vedic kingdoms under autocratic rulers flourished and prospered.

Autocracies in modern times, however, have often led to public unrest and have often been characterized by little progress or prosperity for the country. What did the Vedic kings do from which modern autocrats can learn?

A Vedic autocracy is usually based on spiritual principles whereas modern autocracy is usually materially motivated.

Look at the two diagrams below. They list the characteristics of Vedic and modern autocracies. Study each diagram carefully.

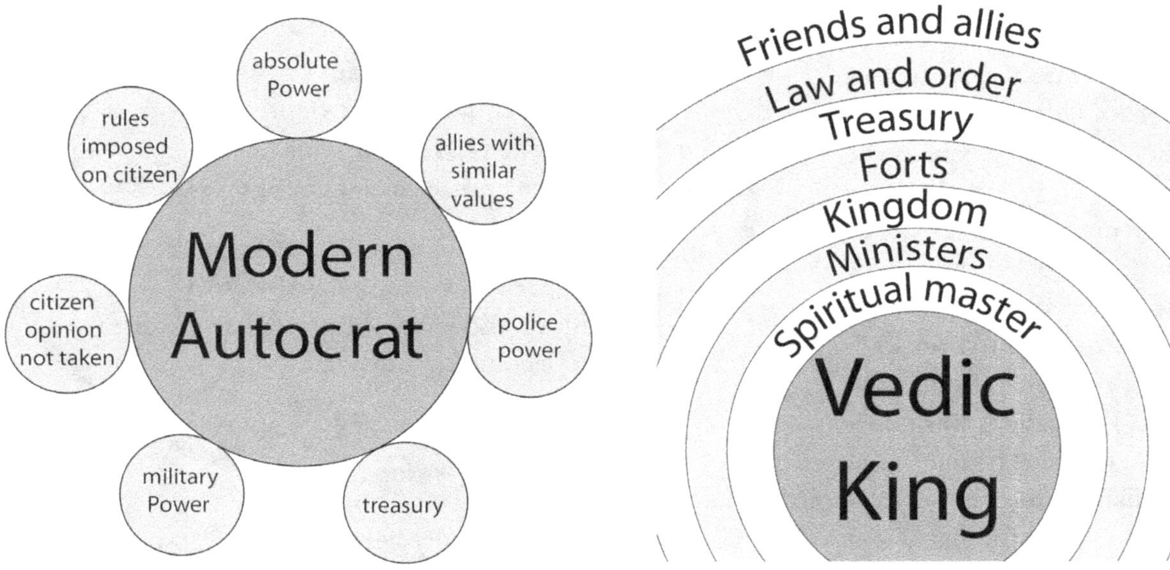

Characteristics of a modern autocrat   Characteristics of a Vedic autocrat

Now consider:

1. What do you understand about Vedic autocracy according to the diagram design? Give an example of a Vedic autocracy.

2. What do you understand about modern autocracy according to the diagram design? Give an example of modern autocracy.

3. Is there something a Vedic autocrat can learn from a modern autocrat?

4. Is there something a modern autocrat can learn from a Vedic autocrat?

5. Why do you think people in a Vedic kingdom were happier than in modern society?

Make short notes based on the above prompts.

Finally, use your notes to contribute to a discussion on the following topic: An ideal autocracy in which a God-conscious leader and God-conscious citizens are interdependent is beneficial for all.

Record your group's responses on a display board.

Action Activity

... to get you moving and learning

INTERVIEW: EFFECTIVE LEADERSHIP

Aṅgirā Ṛṣi advised King Citraketu on mutual dependence between the king and his dependents and the need for mind control. In this activity, you will interview leaders in at least three areas: family, work, and temple administration. You can also interview a government or political leader. This will help you understand the dynamics of teamwork, efficient leadership, and mutual dependence between group members. After you review their responses, present your findings for each leader in an essay or a speech. Compare their viewpoints with the *Bhāgavatam's* viewpoints and then write a conclusion on this topic.

Some questions and guidelines for your interview:

1. What is your role in your environment of control?

2. What are your rights and responsibilities?

3. What is your relationship with your dependents? Do you expect them to follow your directions, or do you invite discussions and suggestions periodically?

4. Do you foresee your dependents becoming future leaders? If yes, how are you facilitating the leadership potential of your dependents?

5. What gives you more pleasure: when you are praised or when your subordinates are flourishing and being praised?

6. Do you think a leader needs to control his mind?

7. Share a challenging situation you overcame with a calm mind and focused intelligence.

8. What is your advice to other leaders?

Writing and Language Activities

... to help you understand better

WHO IS ELIGIBLE FOR LIBERATION?

Though the grief of Kṛtadyuti and Citraketu was natural due to parental affection, advanced devotees have a different vision. They see reversals or miseries differently from that of a conditioned soul. Lord Brahmā in *Śrīmad-Bhāgavatam* (10.14.8) tells us how such devotees facing difficulties respond and what is their destination:

tat te 'nukampāṁ su-samīkṣamāṇo
bhuñjāna evātma-kṛtaṁ vipākam
hṛd-vāg-vapurbhir vidadhan namas te
jīveta yo mukti-pade sa dāya-bhāk

Translation
My dear Lord, one who earnestly waits for You to bestow Your causeless mercy upon him, all the while patiently suffering the reactions of his past misdeeds and offering You respectful obeisances with his heart, words, and body, is surely eligible for liberation, for it has become his rightful claim.

Memorize this wonderful verse and its translation.

In *Caitanya-līlā*, we see that when Śrīvāsa Ṭhākura's son died, he forbade the family members to cry lest it disturb Lord Caitanya's happiness in *kīrtana*. Śrīvāsa Ṭhākura, an intimate associate of Śrī Caitanya, told his family members that as the child left his body in the presence of Lord Caitanya's performing *nāma-saṅkīrtana*, the child returned to the spiritual world.

Here we see three different perspectives: that of a conditioned soul, an advanced devotee, and a *mahā-bhāgavata*. A conditioned soul does not have accurate knowledge about the law of *karma*, material nature, and the supreme benevolence of the Lord and is therefore moved by happiness and sorrow. An advanced devotee sees the personal hand of the Lord and regards both happiness and distress as the mercy of Kṛṣṇa. He therefore responds from the spiritual platform of knowledge and continues serving the Lord. A *mahā-bhāgavata* like Śrīvāsa Ṭhākura is only concerned with the Lord's happiness and distress, not caring about himself.

Most of us may not react to difficulties like the advanced devotees, but we can try to learn from them as exemplified in this verse. In your notebooks, explain in your own words the essence of this verse, or how advanced devotees see reversals. How do they see all their difficulties as Kṛṣṇa's mercy? What of their qualities are highlighted in this verse? Why are such devotees eligible for liberation? And what is their ultimate destination?

BHAKTI CAUSES BHAKTI

Mahārāja Parīkṣit had eagerly inquired from Śukadeva Gosvāmī the reason for Vṛtrāsura's exalted love for the Lord despite being in a demon's body. Śrīla Viśvanātha Cakravartī Ṭhākura, in his book *Mādhurya Kaḍambinī*, has established that just as Lord Kṛṣṇa appears in the material world out of His sweet will, *bhakti* is self-manifesting and is not dependent on any material cause. He states that chance, *karma*, piety, *jñāna*,

goodness, and purity are not causes for the appearance of *bhakti*. *Bhakti* arises in the heart of a living entity due to the mercy of devotees. So the cause of the mercy in the heart of a devotee is devotion itself. Lord Kṛṣṇa becomes subservient to His devotees and gives them independent power to bestow mercy on others. Then Kṛṣṇa's mercy follows His devotee's mercy.

For example, when a pure devotee prays to the Lord for a person's advancement in Kṛṣṇa consciousness, the Lord hears that prayer and gives His mercy to the person.

Based on the above paragraph, please answer the following questions:

1. *Bhakti* is independent of charity, *yoga*, austerity, study of the *Vedas*, etc. Which of the following support/s this statement: a, b, or both?
   a) Lord Caitanya commanded everyone: *yāre dekha, tāre kaha 'kṛṣṇa'-upadeśa āmāra ājñāya guru hañā tāra' ei deśa* – "Instruct everyone to follow the orders of Lord Śrī Kṛṣṇa as they are given in the *Bhagavad-gītā* and *Śrīmad-Bhāgavatam*. In this way become a spiritual master and try to liberate everyone in this land." (*CC Madhya-līlā* 7.128)
   b) The Lord says, "Even though one engages with great endeavor in the mystic *yoga* system, philosophical speculation, charity, vows, penances, ritualistic sacrifices, teaching of Vedic *mantras* to others, personal study of the *Vedas*, or the renounced order of life, still one cannot achieve Me." (*SB* 11.12.09)

2. Purity of place of worship and proper time are absolutely needed for the proper execution of devotional service. Does the following verse support or refute this statement?

   nāmnām akāri bahudhā nija-sarva-śaktistatrārpitā niyamitaḥ smaraṇe na kālaḥ – "My Lord, O Supreme Personality of Godhead, in Your holy name there is all good fortune for the living entity, and therefore You have many names, such as 'Kṛṣṇa' and 'Govinda,' by which You expand Yourself. You have invested all Your potencies in those names, and there are no hard and fast rules for remembering them." (*Śikṣāṣṭakam* verse 2)

3. *Niṣkāma karma yoga* is not a prerequisite for *bhakti* to arise in the heart of someone. Does the example of Mṛgāri support this statement?

4. Does *bhakti* depend on knowledge and detachment, or does *bhakti* cause knowledge and detachment?

5. Do factors like age, gender, social position, caste, creed, etc., disqualify one from practicing the process of *bhakti*?

CHAPTER 14 ANSWERS

Husking Paddy for Real Grain (*Potential answers*)

A. Pile containing paddy inside the husk: personal form, holy name, Bhagavān feature, Kṛṣṇa, transcendental, Nārāyaṇa. 1. It indicates that the Lord is a person whose highest transcendental feature is known as Bhagavān. The Lord manifests in multiple forms, of which Nārāyaṇa, the four-handed form, and Kṛṣṇa, the two-handed form, are commonly known and worshiped; 2. Those who are devotees of the Lord and have received and accepted knowledge about Him through the *guru-paramparā* worship the Lord in these forms; 3. They are compared to those who find paddy inside the husk because they find the real worshipable object, the Supreme Lord, and attain Him by His causeless mercy. This is the real goal of life.

B. Pile containing no paddy inside the husk: Brahman feature, impersonal form, material form of God, mental speculation, effulgence, merging into God. 1. It indicates that the impersonalists consider God to have no form, and they reach this conclusion through their speculative methods. They consider that Brahman, or impersonal non-existence, to be the highest feature of God and desire to merge into it so they can become God; 2. Impersonalists, or Māyāvādīs; 3. The Brahman feature is the effulgence of the Lord's body, which covers his real form, but the impersonalists do not understand this. They can never reach the real substance; therefore, their attempt is compared to husking empty paddy.

Śrīla Prabhupāda's statement reveals that most people who are searching for the Absolute Truth husk empty paddy, that is, they follow processes other than bona fide *bhakti* and therefore rarely attain the shelter of the Supreme Lord.

Material Autocracy Versus Spiritual Autocracy

1. In a Vedic autocracy the king is never alone in ruling the kingdom; he has the spiritual master to guide him, and then the opinion of his ministers, citizens, friends, and allies, which he seriously considers. The king protects his kingdom with his military strength, forts, and treasury. The system of law and order is present to govern the citizens. They therefore have an interdependent

relationship. The concentric circles in the diagram are meant to indicate that all these factors help the king govern the citizens.

2. The modern autocrat is usually characterized as one ruler with absolute power and decision-making authority. The disconnected semi-circles indicate that the autocrat does not use his citizens or ministers as a support system to govern fairly but uses them for his own selfish motives. He almost never consults the people or Vedic authorities when making rules for the citizens, neither does he consider their opinion. He may use the military, the police, or the state's treasury for his own motives. His allies are people who have similar ideas, and he makes enemies with others.

3. There is little a Vedic autocrat can learn from the modern autocrat, since the latter barely follows God-conscious life or rules (even in Vedic culture, such autocrats like Kaṁsa may be found).

4. The true Vedic autocrat ruler, however, has a lot to teach the modern autocrat. He shows by example how the citizen-ruler relationship is an interdependent one and that kings should consider the welfare of the citizens.

5. Leaders in Vedic society are God-conscious. God-conscious leaders follow spiritual principles and God's laws and therefore genuinely care for their followers and people. They inspire their followers by their godly qualities and teach how to live harmoniously with God in the center. Therefore people in Vedic kingdoms were generally happier and more peaceful.

Students may discuss in the end how such God-conscious interdependence helps all involved.

Bhakti Causes Bhakti

1. Both a and b.

2. Refutes. Lord Caitanya emphasizes that there are no hard and fast rules for chanting the holy name.

3. Yes. Mṛgāri was not performing *niṣkāma-karma* (activities without a desire for the results); on the contrary, he was breaking the principles of religion by committing violence against animals. Nārada Muni was merciful to him, and by Mṛgāri's deep faith in Nārada Muni, he advanced quickly.

4. *Bhakti* is the mother of knowledge and detachment. ("By rendering devotional service to Lord Kṛṣṇa, one immediately acquires causeless knowledge and detachment from the world." *SB* 1.2.7)

5. No. We see many examples of all kinds of humans and living beings who became great devotees: Prahlāda (who was hearing from within the womb), Dhruva, Kuntīdevī, Śabarī, the Niṣādas, Gajendra, Vṛtrāsura, etc. In current times, we have seen people from all walks of life taking to the process of *bhakti-yoga* after coming in touch with devotees and Śrīla Prabhupāda's books.

personal form
impersonal form
Bhagavān feature
mental speculation
transcendental
merging into God
Brahman feature
holy name
material form of God
Kṛṣṇa
effulgence
Nārāyaṇa

15

NĀRADA AND AṄGIRĀ INSTRUCT KING CITRAKETU

Śukadeva Gosvāmī described how Nārada and Aṅgirā Ṛṣis had found King Citraketu lying like a dead body beside the dead body of his son. One of the palace residents shook the King awake. King Citraketu, his clothes drenched in tears, slowly got onto his knees and bowed his head to the venerable sages.

Looking at the dead son and then the mourning King and Queen, Aṅgirā Ṛṣi said, "O King, what relationship do you have with this dead body for which you lament so much? You may say that you are related as father and son, but do you think that this relationship existed before? Does it truly exist now, and will it continue in future?"

The King wiped the tears from his eyes and looked up at Aṅgirā Ṛṣi, still dazed.

"O King, as small particles of sea sand sometimes come together and then separate because of the force of the waves, living entities with material bodies sometimes come together and sometimes separate by the force of time. Sometimes a prospective father can beget a child and sometimes not. Conception only takes place by the potency of the Lord. Therefore, do not lament over the artificial relationship of parenthood."

King Citraketu's lips stopped quivering and his tears lessened.

"Look around you, O King. We all are in a temporary situation. Before our birth this situation did not exist, and after our death this situation will also not exist. Therefore, our situations are temporary, although they are not false."

King Citraketu looked at his grieving queen and followers, who were also listening attentively, sobered by the words of the sage. Certainly, what he was saying was true, thought the King.

Nārada Muni came forward and said, "The Supreme Lord is not interested in this temporary world, yet He keeps everything under His control. He creates by allowing a father to beget a son, He maintains by engaging a King in the public's welfare, and He annihilates through the agents of killing, such as snakes. All these are simply agents

The King sat up straight and again wiped the tears from his shriveled face. In a meek voice, he said, "O revered sages, you have come here dressed as *avadhūtas* just to cover your identities, but you are actually most elevated of all great personalities. Vaiṣṇavas like you wander the earth to remove our ignorance. I am like a foolish village animal, in the darkness of ignorance. You can give me real knowledge. So please save me with the torch of knowledge."

Aṅgirā Ṛṣi smiled and said, "My dear King, I am that same Aṅgirā Ṛṣi who gave you this son, and this is the great sage Nārada, the direct son of Lord Brahmā."

The King fell flat on the floor in obeisance. He was ready to do whatever was needed to become enlightened by these great personalities.

"My dear King," said Aṅgirā Ṛṣi, placing his hand on the King's head. "You are an advanced devotee of the Supreme Personality of Godhead, so it's not fitting for someone like you to be lamenting for something material. Someone advanced in spiritual knowledge should not be affected by material loss and gain. So we've both come to relieve you from this false lamentation.

"When I first came to your home, I could've given you the same supreme knowledge, but when I saw that your mind was absorbed in material things, I gave you a son who caused you great joy and sorrow. Now you're experiencing the misery of being a parent.

"O King of Śūrasena, your wife, palace, kingdom, and other opulences are all temporary.

for creation, maintenance, and annihilation; they have no independent potency. But under the spell of *māyā*, illusion, they think that they are the doers."

Pointing to the dead body of the son, Nārada continued, "This body is generated from the body of the mother and father, but it is the soul that gives life to the body. The soul is eternal, and the material elements of the body are also eternal because they exist eternally as the Lord's potencies. But because the conditioned soul has forgotten his original identity, he accepts different material bodies and thinks that he belongs to a certain nationality, species, or society. This is just the imagination of ignorant persons without spiritual knowledge."

these things, and then you'll be able to give up your material attachment. You will also see that anything not in touch with Kṛṣṇa and Kṛṣṇa's service is temporary. Then only will you be peaceful."

The King's eyes again filled with tears, but this time they were of gratitude, not sorrow.

Nārada continued, "My dear King, I will give you a most auspicious *mantra*. Accept it from me, and after seven nights you will see the Lord face to face."

The King gasped, not believing what he had just heard. Tears trickled down his cheeks. The Queen and onlookers also stared at Nārada Muni in disbelief.

"O King," Nārada Muni said, "a long time ago Lord Śiva and other demigods took shelter of Lord Saṅkarṣaṇa's lotus feet and immediately became free from illusion. Such is the glory of devotional service! Very soon you will also attain that position."

The King again fell flat in full obeisance, feeling the knot of attachment in his heart being loosened by the words and blessings of the wise sages.

Your military power, treasury, servants, ministers, relatives, and friends can cause great fear, lamentation, and distress. Because they are all temporary, they are no better than illusions, dreams, and mental concoctions. Sometimes you can see them and sometimes not. We create such mental concoctions because of our past actions, which lead us to perform further activities.

"A materialistic person is absorbed in the body, and through the mind suffers the three kinds of tribulations – *adhibhautika*, *adhidaivika*, and *adhyātmika*. So the body is the source of all miseries."

The King nodded, his eyes now bright and face aglow with this divine knowledge.

"Therefore, O King," said Nārada Muni, "try to understand who you are. Are you the body, mind, or soul? Where have you come from? Where are you going to after death? And why are you suffering? Try to understand

Themes and Key Messages

Please go through this table of themes and key messages, with corresponding verses, and discuss each topic further.

THEMES	REFERENCES	KEY MESSAGES
The so-called relationships in the material world are illusions, so one should not lament for the temporary material body or material situations.	6.15.2–5, 7–8	This world is temporary with temporary relationships, which are all finished at death. Just like a dream, they did not exist in the past nor will they exist in future. By Kṛṣṇa's time energy, they are just like particles of sand that come together for some time and then are separated. These relationships, like father and son, are illusory because one identifies the body with the self. The soul, which is eternal, doesn't have anything to do with the temporary nature of the body, relationships, or material situations. Therefore, those in knowledge do not accept bodily designations as real.
The Supreme Personality of Godhead is the indirect controller, creator, and maintainer, yet in illusion the living entity thinks that he is the creator and maintainer.	6.15.6–7	Kṛṣṇa is the ultimate doer, but the conditioned soul thinks that he is the doer. Rather we should think that we are the agents of the supreme doer, the Supreme Lord. Leaders have forgotten that they've been appointed to act by the Supreme Lord; their duty is to consult the Lord and His teachings in the *Bhagavad-gītā* and act accordingly. However, the living entities, not the Lord, should take responsibility for their condition. Since living beings desire to enjoy the material world, the Lord gives them a chance to accept different material bodies to enjoy and suffer in different material conditions.
We should not approach the *guru* for material benefits; taking shelter of temporary things awards a mixture of happiness and distress and entangles us more in the material world.	6.15.16–20	One should not approach the *guru* to fulfill one's material desires but to receive transcendental knowledge, which can save one from the darkness of the material world. Aṅgirā Ṛṣi awarded a son to King Citraketu because the King had approached him with this desire, but the sage only wanted to give him divine knowledge. So when the King was lamenting, Aṅgirā Ṛṣi took the opportunity to enlighten him and free him from his lamentation. Therefore, we should always aspire to engage in the service of advanced devotees and hear from them. We should realize that all our material possessions and relationships can make us fearful, illusioned, and distressed – not permanently happy. We should therefore not take shelter of these things but of the pure devotees.

THEMES	REFERENCES	KEY MESSAGES
Material pleasure comes from the mental platform, which is temporary and actually causes us suffering.	6.15.21–25	Everything material is like a dream because it has no permanent existence. At night one dreams of tigers and snakes, and while dreaming sees them, but as soon as one wakes up, they no longer exist. Similarly, the material world is created out of our mental concoctions. According to these mental concoctions, we work in various ways, desire various achievements, and then get the resultant pleasures we desire, which are all temporary. Our mind and body actually cause us suffering in the end.
We can only give up material attachments and become peaceful when we understand who we are, where we came from, where we are going to after death, and why we are suffering. However, only *bhakti* can permanently remove our material attachments.	6.15.26–28	The purpose of the Kṛṣṇa consciousness movement is to make people understand that one is not the body but the soul within the body. Receiving this knowledge, they can go toward the goal of life. By understanding the goal of life, they can become detached from material things and become sober and peaceful. But ultimately, *bhakti* (taking shelter of Kṛṣṇa), not *jñāna* (the knowledge of the body and the soul) will make us free from illusion and attachments and achieve success in spiritual life.

Higher-Thinking Questions

Now try to deepen your understanding of this chapter by delving into Śrīla Prabhupāda's purports and reflecting on the following questions:

1. In verse 4 purport, Śrīla Prabhupāda discusses why some people who are fertile cannot have children while some who are sterile end up having children. What reason does he give for the ultimate cause of these unexpected happenings? Therefore, why shouldn't we desire anything material?

2. How does the Lord arrange what happens to us? Does He want us to suffer? (See verse 4 purport.)

3. Why are nationality and other bodily designations the imaginations of foolish persons as described in verse 8? [Hint: Who are we in reality and what should our vision be?]

4. Why shouldn't we approach a *guru* for material benefits? Who is eligible to approach a *guru*? (See verse 16 purport.)

5. Describe how our mental concoctions trick us into thinking we can enjoy in the material world. (Refer to the examples Śrīla Prabhupāda uses in verse 25 purport.) How can one become free from these mental concoctions?

6. Why are people not peaceful as Śrīla Prabhupāda describes in verse 26 purport? How does material attachment make one not peaceful? How do you think one can give up material attachments and become peaceful? Why is this more effective than just knowing we are not the body? (See also verse 28.)

ACTIVITIES

In this section you will find many exciting things to do. These activities will get you thinking, moving, drawing, and having loads of fun.

Analogy Activity

... to bring out the scholar in you

THE DREAM OF MATERIAL REALITY

The Oxford Dictionary defines a dream as "a series of images, events, and feelings that happen in your mind while you are asleep." A dream is considered an impermanent state because it does not occur in the world that we know, but inside the mind, and produces no tangible change (good or bad) in our lives as soon as we wake up from it. Despite this, a dream is considered powerful because it can create a strong, and sometimes lasting, experience for us.

Śrīla Prabhupāda compares material life – along with our relationships, hopes, wealth, fears, emotions, power, and everything else – to a dream. Since the living being is "asleep" to his real identity as a servant of Kṛṣṇa, he "dreams" of being different beings in various bodies. These dreams create powerful experiences for him, but he forgets these experiences when his dream "breaks" – that is, when he moves to a different body.

Śrīla Prabhupāda draws two important lessons about material life using the analogy of the dream:

- The feature of impermanence: In his purport to verse 5, Śrīla Prabhupāda points out that material life is impermanent (temporary), and therefore illusory.

- The feature of extended misery: In his purport to verse 24, he points out that these "dreams" of material situations create more material situations for us, and these lead to our suffering.

The Feature of Impermanence
Let us first understand how dreams, as well as material situations, are impermanent through an activity.

Directions:

1. Work in pairs. One of you should narrate a dream you had that you either fondly remember or had a strong impact on you.

2. As you narrate, your partner should carefully listen and look for clues that prove that the dream was not real but only a creation of your mind when you were asleep.

3. At the end of your narration, your partner will list out the events/signs he or she identified to prove your dream story wasn't real.

4. Remaining in pairs, next try to analyze how our waking material life is also a dream. To do this, we have to understand that the "waking" state is also a "dream" state – the soul, whose real identity and life is that of a loving servant of Kṛṣṇa is "dreaming" that he is a certain person in a certain body with certain relationships and situations.

5. Remember to apply some of the typical signs of a dream that you deduced in the previous part to complete this part of the discussion.

6. So, while identifying (thinking of) yourself as a servant of Kṛṣṇa, rather than as someone of a particular family, country, race or place, consider the following:
   » 5.1. How can I understand that my current identity is a dream?
   » 5.2. How can I actually "wake up" from it?

7. Write down your answers to the above questions in your notebooks.

8. Also write a short statement of understanding about how material identity is a dream by completing the following statement:
   » My identity as _________________ is temporary because _____________________. My real identity is that of ___________________.

The Feature of Extended Suffering
This will be dealt with in the critical-thinking activity.

Critical-Thinking Activity

WEB OF MENTAL CONCOCTIONS

The Feature of Extended Suffering (continued from Analogy activity)

As already mentioned, in his purport to verse 24 Prabhupāda points out that the material world is a result of our mental concoctions. In other words, we are pure spirit souls whose only business is to serve Lord Kṛṣṇa. But in the material world, we take on many false identities and create many false situations. These situations give many experiences, each leading to further experiences. We finally get caught in the web of these experiences and are unable to free ourselves of their effects. We thus bring suffering upon ourselves.

Let us do a simple activity to try and re-create what happens to us as a result of mental concoctions.

Directions:

1. Photocopy, trace, or draw the image given in resources at the end of this activity. Cut along the outer lines and fold it up into a dice that can be rolled.

2. Take a big chart paper and some pens. On the chart paper, you will draw the path of the living being in a web. Draw the outer web strand, and in it write the first step the living being takes in this world; for example, "A man has forgotten his identity in the world." (You may use the template on the next page and fill it in.)

3. Then draw another strand and in it write down one desire the man may have when in this world; for example, "He wants to eat a palatable dish today."

4. On the third strand write down what the man needs to fulfill this desire; for example, "He gets the ingredients to cook the dish – rice, meat, spices, etc." (You can choose the resources that could lead him to sin or piety.)

5. Once you have completed these three strands of the web, roll the dice. Follow the instruction that faces upwards when the dice is rolled and create a path on the web for the living being in this world. For example, if the dice shows "A reaction," then on the next strand in the web state the reaction the man would get – if he eats meat, he will get a negative reaction (give an example). If the dice shows "A new desire," then come up with another desire to write on the web.

6. In this way, add one strand to the man's web at a time. Roll the dice again and continue. If working in a group, each can take turns to roll the dice and add on to the web in the chart.

7. Stop the game once you have finished three to six rounds (depending on how many are playing), or when the situation gets too complicated to continue.

8. Once you have completed this, discuss:
   » How did the living being get caught in his own desires?
   » Why does Nārada and Aṅgirā call these desires illusion?
   » How can the living being realize this?

Template

Introspective Activity

SHOULD WE IGNORE ILLUSORY RELATIONSHIPS?

In verses 2 and 3, the sages Aṅgirā and Nārada explain to Mahārāja Citraketu that the King's relationship with his son was temporary and therefore illusory – it did not exist before, it existed for some time, and it ceased to exist once the son left his body. They tell him not to give importance to temporary relationships but instead focus on his eternal relationship with the Supreme Lord.

1. Now that you've learned that relationships in this world are temporary, how do you think your parents should relate to you, and you to your parents?

2. Since material relationships are illusory, does this mean that we ignore or neglect relationships in many aspects of our life?

3. How can we understand relationships better, which can help us relate to parents, friends, and people in general?

Science Activity

DETECTING THE SOUL

The body of Mahārāja Citraketu's son was lying before him, yet the King was lamenting the loss of his son. Nārada and Aṅgirā explained to Mahārāja Citraketu that the actual son was the soul within the body. Can we detect the soul, and if so, how?

Research the internet and find out:

1. Has anyone been able to see the soul?

2. What kind of an instrument would someone have to make to detect the soul?

The *Bhagavad-gītā* says that we will not be able to detect the soul despite our best efforts.

1. Can you find out why we cannot "see" the soul with our eyes?

2. Can you think of a simple observation we can make to detect the presence or absence of a soul?

3. Just by studying the scriptures, we understand the characteristics of the soul. Referring to *Bhagavad-gītā* chapter 2, list some of these characteristics.

What can you conclude about the soul from the above study?

Writing and Language Activities

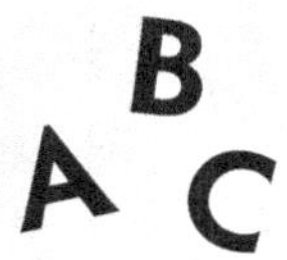

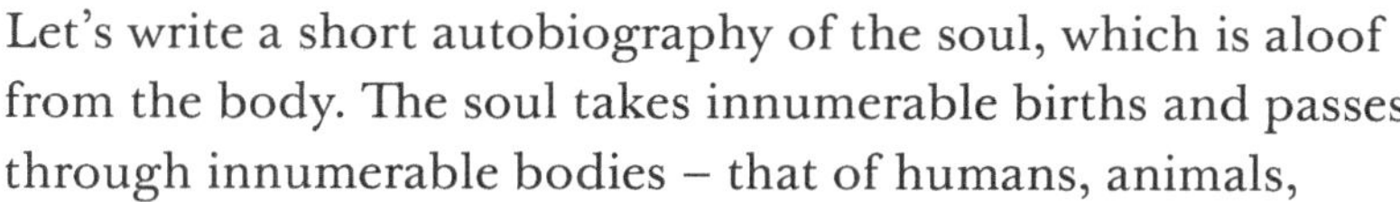

AUTOBIOGRAPHY OF A SOUL

An autobiography is the story of a person's life, written by the person himself. Autobiographical works can take many forms, from one's intimate realizations during life or simply an account of one's entire life.
Autobiographies are predominantly written in the first-person narrative.

Let's write a short autobiography of the soul, which is aloof from the body. The soul takes innumerable births and passes through innumerable bodies – that of humans, animals, insects, plants, and so on. No matter how many bodies it may change, the soul is eternal, having no death. In other words, no matter what situations it passes through in different lives, the soul remains the same. Only the body and mind enjoy or suffer according to the type of body the soul receives. Therefore, we must relate ourselves to that soul, which is unchangeable and unaffected by any material body or situation.

With this understanding, think of yourself as a "soul" (like an individual), who passes through three or four different bodies. For example, first in the body of a boy, then a cow, and finally a Vaiṣṇavī (a female devotee). This soul goes through a range of experiences in all the lives, and its actions determines the next body.

Write an autobiography of this soul who witnesses all three births and the enjoyment and sufferings it experiences in each lifetime. Knit a story together and narrate on behalf of the soul, to show that the soul understands its true position and how it stays unaffected by any kind of disturbing situations during its stay in the mentioned bodies.

Points that can be discussed:

1. You, the soul, are just a silent witness to all the happenings while on your journey through different bodies.

2. You, the conditioned soul, feel pain or happiness in varied circumstances in the different lifetimes due to contact with the modes of material nature and the body and mind, but ultimately you can console yourself by remembering that the situations are all temporary and that you would soon move into a different body.

3. In a different body it is again a new adventure and journey in which you might be happier, or maybe not. You experience different relationships, meet other souls who are in different bodies, and have conversations about happiness and distress. Yet, you are unaffected, knowing that the body is temporary.

4. You share your lessons in self-realization, that no matter how much you traveled through different bodies, you are eternal, unchanged, and unaffected.

NARRATIVE ESSAY: MATERIAL ILLUSION CAN LEAD TO SUFFERING

In this chapter we see that everything material is like a dream and breaks as soon as the sleep breaks. These material desires and pleasures therefore are temporary and only bring us suffering in the end.

With the understanding of this theme, read the following topic as an example, think about a similar story, and then write your own to show how material desires and pleasures are temporary and breaks like a dream.

Your neighbor is very attached to material pleasures and desires to have a very expensive house with many cars, technical gadgets, and other luxury goods. To fulfill this desire, he takes huge bank loans and purchases an expensive house and some cars. He lives "happily" with his family for some time. Instead of working hard to repay his loans, he gets more and more entangled in enjoying his material pleasures; he eats all kinds of food, sleeps a lot, drinks alcohol, and gambles with his friends. In a sudden unfortunate event, he suffers from a life-threatening disease, unable to work or earn money and leaves his helpless family in heavy debt. Being unable to repay his debts, the bank forfeits all his property (house, valuables, and cars), leaving the family like paupers.

Points to think about and frame your narrative storyline:

1. How can this situation be termed as a non-permanent situation, like a dream?

2. How did the material attachments become a cause of suffering for the person?

3. What could he have done instead of desiring for things beyond his capacity to possess?

4. You can also show that a pious person had a very wonderful life with good relationships and all material facilities, but at death he still needed to leave everything behind.

5. Try to emphasize that even if we don't want suffering, material illusion, which is like dreams, ultimately brings us suffering in some way or the other.

POEM: BHAKTI IS YOUR ŚAKTI (POWER)

In this chapter we learn that it is essential to know who we are and our ultimate goal in life to become free from material illusion, but by performing *bhakti* it is easier to become free from illusion and material attachments.

Read and recite the following poem and try to summarize its primary theme in your own words.

BHAKTI IS YOUR REAL ŚAKTI

Come, let me tell you who you are
Knowing this your fears will run away far!
The ultimate knowledge Kṛṣṇa gave
of self-realization was meant to save.

The root cause of all sufferings, it's plain to see,
emerged from attachments to the mind and body!
Can you cut away these ropes of attachment?
Which have made you paralyzed and discontent?

Lower desires make you crippled and weary,
Spiritually blind, weak, and dreary!
Endless sufferings they bring along,
Making us fall or do something wrong!

Kṛṣṇa gives knowledge sublime, our life's goal,
You are not your body, but the eternal soul;
You came as a ray from Kṛṣṇa's shimmering body,
His parts and parcels are you, me, and everybody!

> Give up your material desires, right now!
> There's no way to escape its consequences somehow.
> Knowing the truth, you will be more peaceful,
> Practicing devotion you'll be more joyful!
>
> This material world is but a dream, not real
> It's like a hollow, in passing time's wheel.
> Nothing is permanent, except your *bhakti*
> Surrender to Kṛṣṇa, 'cause that's your *śakti*

Some points for summarizing:

1. A summary is not a rewrite – it's a short summation of the original piece.

2. A summary paragraph is usually around five to eight sentences.

3. Keep it short and to the point.

4. Identify the main theme of the poem.

5. Briefly describe what the poem is about.

6. Explain if you find any figurative language or unusual terms in the poem.

7. What is the symbolism of these unusual terms and how can you relate it to the theme of the activity?

CHAPTER 15 ANSWERS

The Dream of Material Reality (*Potential Answers*)
3. The listener could identify some of these tell-tale signs of a dream: people in the dream are unknown or behave differently; the dreamer is in an unusual place or situation; the dreamer's fears are being played out; people look different and have unusual powers; something unreal happens, and so on.

5. Some of the tell-tale signs of souls living in a "dream" in material life: the material body looks different from our original selves; we behave not as servants of the Lord but as independent entities; our hopes, interests, aspirations, etc., may be different from that of a realized soul, etc. (If you find it a little challenging to understand how souls act in their identities purely as servants of the Lord, think about how Śrīla Prabhupāda thought or acted.)

5.1. Similar to answers in 5 above.

5.2. By understanding that the soul in its pure state is a servant of Kṛṣṇa and acting in that relationship with Him. (In other words, receiving transcendental knowledge and acting on the knowledge.) We can awaken that dormant relationship by connecting with the Lord through the holy name, reading His teachings from the *śāstras*, imbibing His instructions, performing practical devotional service, etc.

Web of Mental Concoctions
The desire web may vary. Students need to appreciate how a living being can get caught in complicated situations without actually "doing" much other than desiring to enjoy false things. 1. Living beings get caught by being engrossed in sense enjoyment and

by developing many desires to enjoy themselves;
2. Nārada and Aṅgirā call these an illusion because
the enjoyment is like one in dreams – done with a false
identity and is temporary and unsatisfying to a soul
that seeks permanent and lasting enjoyment; 3. A living
being who understands the useless material cycle he is
going through can try to get out of this by the mercy of
the spiritual master.

Should we Ignore Illusory Relationships?
(Potential Answers)

Learners' own answers. Learners should understand
that while relationships may be temporary and thus
illusory, we still work within the material framework
and need to have relationships in accordance with
the rules of society. Relationships are integral to the
soul and cannot be ignored or rejected. But we can
spiritualize our relationships by seeing everyone in
relation to Kṛṣṇa; e.g., parents love and raise their
children as a service to Kṛṣṇa, and children reciprocate
with their parents respectfully as elder Vaiṣṇavas. They
treat their friends and others as devotees or parts of
Kṛṣṇa and thus give everyone the respect they deserve.
In this way, what is seemingly material illusion can be
converted into meaningful interactions with the Lord
and His energies.

Detecting the Soul

1. Nobody has been able to prove that they have
"seen" the soul with their naked eyes; 2. Science
has not been able to prove the presence of the soul;
therefore scientists have not been able to construct any
instrument to detect the soul – unless we can make
an estimation of the characteristics of something, we
will not be able to understand how to detect it; 3. We
cannot see the soul because the eyes have no ability to
see spiritual substance, which the soul is made of; 4.
The soul is all pervading within the body and animates
the body. It can therefore be detected by the presence
of consciousness in the body. When the soul leaves
the body, bodily consciousness ceases, and therefore
the body is lifeless; 5. The soul is eternal (has neither
birth nor death), cannot be cut to pieces, cannot
be burned, cannot be wet, cannot be withered; it is
unchangeable, immovable, and eternally the same; it is
invisible, inconceivable, and immutable. Conclusion:
The soul gives life to matter; therefore it is the essential
element of life, and without it material bodies would
not function; although it is inconceivable with the
naked eye, its presence can be observed, just as we can
differentiate between a dead and a living body.

RESOURCE: DICE FOR CRITICAL-THINKING ACTIVITY

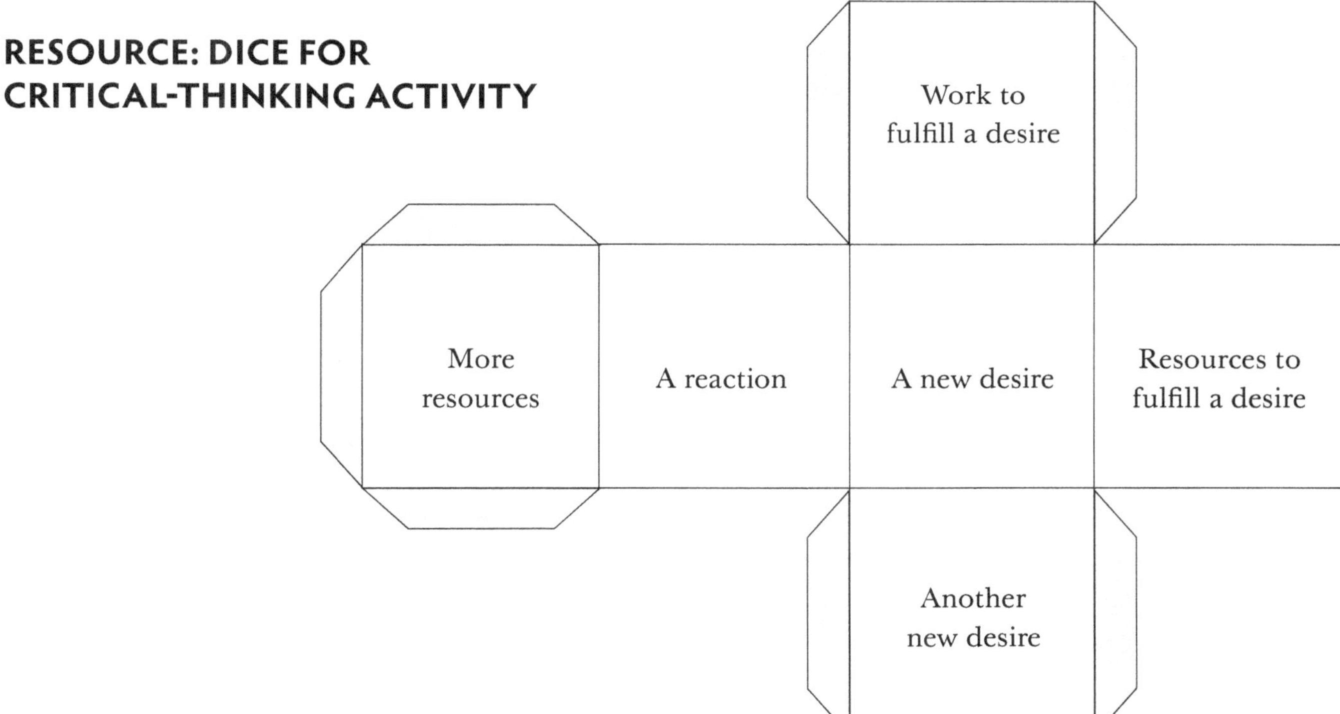

16

KING CITRAKETU MEETS THE LORD

Nārada Muni closed his eyes as the grieving King and Queen knelt beside their son's golden crib. A bright light emerged and hovered above the dead body. Everyone stared at the golden spark and then at Nārada who seemed deep in meditation. He opened his eyes slowly and said to the light, "O soul, good fortune to you. Just look at your mother and father, relatives, and friends overwhelmed with grief because of your death. But you can still live out the balance of your life since you died before your time. So reenter your body and enjoy the remainder of your life. Accept the throne given to you by your father."

The spark twirled and entered the child's dead body. Everyone gasped. The boy opened his eyes and slowly sat up. The King's jaw dropped, and the Queen shrieked in astonishment. "O my boy!" the Queen cried out, her eyes raining tears again. "Oh, you've come back!" Laughing amid her sobs, she sat up to pick up her son, but Nārada lifted his hand to stop her. The baby gurgled and giggled and then said, "My father? My mother?

I, the soul, have no mother or father. I've been traveling from one body to another, sometimes to the demigod species, sometimes to the lower animal species, sometimes plant species, and also to the human species." Looking at the King and Queen, he asked, "So, in which birth were you my mother and father? How can I accept you as my parents?"

The palace residents looked at each other astounded.

"This material world is like a river that carries away the soul," said the child. "People become friends, relatives, and even enemies in different lifetimes. The soul ends up having so many relationships, sometimes loving one another and sometimes despising one another. But all these relationships are temporary! They are like gold traded from buyer to seller, or the relationship between an animal and its owner after the owner sells the animal. The living being, because of his fruitive actions, wanders throughout the universe, injected into various bodies in different species of life by one kind of father after another.

quality. But because you are so small, you are prone to become illusioned by the material energy. So you create various bodies, life after life, according to your desires."

The Queen wiped her eyes and swallowed hard. She knew that these enlightening words were meant to make her see reality, but she couldn't let go of the rope of attachment that bound her to her son.

"The soul doesn't distinguish between what is its own or what belongs to someone else. Just like the Lord is not affected by friends and enemies, the soul, being a tiny fragment of the Supreme Lord, is also not affected by anyone or anything because he has no material body. The soul, like the Supersoul, is just an observer, a witness of the different qualities of men, such as friends, enemies, and relatives. So why lament for anything!"

As the boy said these final words, his life force again left his body, which then fell and lay limp on the bed. The Queen sobbed again, but this time she knew she had to give up her attachment and let her son go.

"All these relationships are based on the body. The body is perishable, but the soul within is eternal; it is never born nor dies. The soul has no relationship with so-called mothers and fathers. It becomes connected to the body given by the mother and father, and the conditioned soul falsely accepts itself as their son. But when the son or parents die, the relationship is finished. So there is no reason to rejoice or lament."

King Citraketu's eyes filled with tears. The truth of his son's words began to soothe his aching heart.

Looking at his mother who gazed at him with tear-filled eyes, the boy continued, "You, the soul, are so sublime that you are equal to the Lord in

As the King and Queen and relatives burned the dead child's body, their remembrance of their son's instructions burned the attachment, illusion, lamentation, fear, and pain in their hearts.

Queen Kṛtadyuti's co-wives had also observed and heard everything. Crying piteously out of shame and remorse, they appeared pale from lamentation. They gave up their desire to have children and went to the banks of the Yamunā to bathe there and atone for their sins.

King Citraketu also went to the Yamunā. A huge weight had been lifted from his heart. Controlling his mind and senses, he offered

oblations of water to the forefathers and
demigods, and then he offered his obeisances to
the sons of Brahmā – Aṅgirā and Nārada – who
had come there to give more inspiration and
guidance.

Nārada was pleased with his disciple and
touched his head. This most powerful sage, self-
controlled devotee, and surrendered soul was the
perfect person to transmit divine instructions and
the *mantra* that he had promised the King.

The words of the *mantra* emanated from
Nārada's mouth and went deep into the heart of
the enlightened King:

O my Lords Vāsudeva, Pradyumna, Aniruddha,
    and Saṅkarṣaṇa
Obeisances to You, reservoirs of spiritual potency
    and bliss
You are realized as Brahman, Paramātmā, and
    Bhagavān
You're the ultimate truth and abode of
    peacefulness

You are the greatest, O Lord, while we are the
    smallest
You are the master of the senses, while we are
    their slaves
Your forms are unlimited, impersonal Brahman
    also
Please protect us, O Lord who's beyond *māyā's*
    waves

Obeisances to You, O cause of all causes,
the origin of Brahman that expands so much
As iron cannot burn unless heated by fire
the body and mind can't work without Your touch

You live in the topmost planet in the spiritual sky
The best devotees' lotus hands serve Your lotus
    feet
O most perfect master of all mystic power
Obeisances to You, O Bhagavān, with six
    opulences complete

Śukadeva Gosvāmī fell silent, closing his eyes and
meditating on the Lord.

"Then what happened?" asked Parīkṣit
Mahārāja excitedly. "Did Citraketu Mahārāja
recite these prayers and receive the Lord's *darśana*
as Nārada had promised?"

"O King, Nārada was very pleased with his
disciple and instructed him with this prayer
because Citraketu was fully surrendered," said
Śukadeva Gosvāmī. "After Aṅgirā and Nārada
left to Brahmaloka, Mahārāja Citraketu fasted
and drank only water, continuously chanting
the *mantra* with great care and attention. After
only one week, he became the master of the
Vidyādharas, just as a by-product of his spiritual
advancement."

"Amazing!" exclaimed Mahārāja Parīkṣit.
"Please tell me more!"

Śukadeva Gosvāmī explained that Citraketu's
mind became increasingly enlightened as he
chanted the *mantra*, until he saw Lord Anantadeva
face to face and received His shelter.

Mahārāja Citraketu was stunned to see the Lord's dazzling form, which was as white as the fibers of a lotus. Lord Ananta smiled at the King and glanced at him with His reddish eyes. His bluish garments and glittering helmet and jewelry enchanted the mind of Mahārāja Citraketu.

By the sight of the Lord, his heart was completely purified. He stood with folded palms, silent and grave, while drinking in the beauty of his Lord. His heart erupted with love, and tears fell down his cheeks and wet the ground at the Lord's lotus feet. His hairs stood on end as he fell to the ground in obeisance. Finally, he got up, and still not believing that the Supreme Personality of Godhead was right before him, he tried to speak and offer prayers, but his voice was choked in ecstasy. Nothing could come out. Still trembling, he closed his eyes and went inward, focusing his mind and intelligence on the Lord. And then he found suitable prayers, which flowed from his mouth:

O Lord, who cannot be conquered
You are conquered by Your devotees true
They keep You under their control
For they don't ask anything of You

Indeed, You give yourselves to such
    devotees
And so You have full control over them too
Whereas those creators who think they're
    independent
are covered in false prestige, as tiny
    portions of a portion of You

You have no beginning or end
Yet in the beginning, middle, and end of
    everything You are
You are the original potency, permanent
    and unlimited
In You reside countless universes, moving
    like atoms, gigantic by far

Those worshiping demigods are like animals
For they thirst for sense enjoyment and fail to
    worship Your Divinity
The demigods are small sparks of Your glory
Whose benedictions vanish like a king no longer
    in authority

Those who worship You are not subject to rebirth
They follow *bhāgavata-dharma*, the pure religious
    system
This eternal *dharma* gives the shelter of your lotus
    feet
Such is the glory of those endowed with real
    wisdom

What's the use of any other religious system
That only benefits one's self esteem
Full of envy and passion, such systems are
	irreligious
Their sins in the name of religion are hard to
	redeem

Just by seeing You my heart is cleansed of lust
Anyone can be purified by hearing your holy
	name
I'm seeing you only by the mercy of Nārada
Who trained me and predicted that Your *darśana*
	I'll attain

Materialists don't have the eyes to see You
Nor understand Your real position
They say this world is independent of Your
	opulence
So they're always under the greatest illusion

Lord Brahma and Indra act only after You direct
	them
The senses perceive only after You've perceived
Obeisances to You, O Lord with thousands of
	hoods
On them You hold the universes like mustard
	seeds

When Citraketu saw Anantadeva's smile, he
started to tremble in ecstasy again. The four
Kumāras who sat around Him also beamed at the
King.

The Lord said, "O King, you are now
completely perfect because you've received divine
knowledge from the great sages Nārada and
Aṅgirā. Because you are now educated in the
spiritual science, you can see Me face to face.

"All living beings are My expansions. I live as
the Supersoul within their hearts. They only exist
because I've created them. I have two forms – the
transcendental sound of My name and the blissful
spiritual form of the Deity. They are eternal and
are in no way material.

"This material world and the living beings
are expansions of My energies; I am their source
and they rest in Me. The three states of a living
entity's consciousness – waking, dreaming, and
dreamless sleep – are also My energies. So one
should always remember Me, who is unaffected by
these states.

"The conditioned living beings, who
can observe these three changing states of
consciousness, can perceive the self as different
from these states. The fact that they *can*
know means that they have consciousness.
Consciousness is a quality of Brahman, so they are
equal to Brahman in quality.

"But because they don't cause these three
states of consciousness, they are not quantitatively
one with the Supreme Brahman, the Supersoul,
who is the supreme observer and knower. They
forget that they are qualitatively one with Me
in eternity, bliss, and knowledge, so instead of
thinking of My interest, they think of their own
and pursue things that have no meaning or value.
In this way, they suffer repeated birth and death.

"Human beings, especially those born in the
pious land of Bhārata-varṣa, India, can achieve
perfection by understanding the self, according
to the directions given in the *Vedas*. But if such
a person with such a pious birth doesn't try to
understand the self, he cannot attain this highest
perfection.

"So such conditioned souls should remember
that fruitive work for enjoyment have caused them
misery instead. They should stop trying to satisfy
their material desires and engage in devotional
activities, which will free them from misery. They
should understand that the soul is above material
happiness and distress, and that the soul is a part
of the Supersoul, the whole. There is no truth
greater than this.

"O King, accept My conclusion, detach
yourself from material enjoyment, and adhere to
Me with great faith. If you become aware of this
knowledge and practically apply it in life, you

will achieve the highest perfection: you will attain Me!"

As Lord Saṅkarṣaṇa said these words, He left. Citraketu looked on, still reeling from the divine experience of seeing the Lord and hearing His perfect instructions.

Themes and Key Messages

Please go through this table of themes and key messages, with corresponding verses, and discuss each topic further.

THEMES	REFERENCES	KEY MESSAGES
Material relationships are temporary because they are based on the material body; yet the soul is eternal and aloof from material relationships.	6.16.4–11	The soul continually transmigrates from one material body to another. Therefore the relationships one has through many lifetimes are all temporary. Yet despite the temporary nature of the material body and the relationships based on it, the soul is eternal and part and parcel of the Supreme Lord. The soul has the qualities of the Lord in minute quantity. Just as the Lord is aloof from material relationships and acts as a neutral observer and witness, so does the soul. But because the soul becomes illusioned, it takes on different material bodies. In one life someone may be your enemy and in another life a friend; thus all relationships end or change when the body dies. However, because we are conditioned, it is very difficult, or even impossible, to be neutral when we lose a loved one. So the best course is to depend upon the Lord and do our duty in devotional service, which will help us overcome grief and delusion in the face of personal loss.
When we hear transcendental knowledge from great souls and follow their guidance, we can give up our illusion and material attachments and experience Kṛṣṇa's presence.	6.16.12–15, 28–31, 50	The King and Queen gave up their lamentation and illusion when they heard transcendental knowledge from their son and from the wise sages; they were thus able to become detached from family life. The co-wives also became purified by hearing Aṅgirā Ṛṣi's instructions. And when Mahārāja Citraketu took shelter of Nārada and chanted the *mantra*, he was able to see the Lord. (He was also able to attain great material opulence as a by-product of his devotion.) Similarly, our hearts can become purified by hearing the scriptures, taking shelter of exalted souls, and seeing the Deity in the temple. In this way we can make steady progress in Kṛṣṇa consciousness and one day see Kṛṣṇa as Citraketu did.

THEMES	REFERENCES	KEY MESSAGES
The Supreme Personality of Godhead is the unparalleled object of worship. Anyone who solely worships Him attains all success.	6.16.21–25 35–39	The Supreme Brahman and Paramātmā infuse and enliven the material senses, mind, and intellect, which are dull matter. Just as iron can burn only when in the association of fire, so the body, senses, mind, and intelligence can only function when the Lord infuses them with His potency. Yet, the Supreme Lord in His personal feature is the origin of impersonal Brahman and the Supersoul. He is also the origin of the demigods. Therefore, one should worship the unlimited, omniscient, and omnipotent Supreme Lord, the cause of all causes, instead of His other features or the demigods. A devotee who approaches the Lord without any material desire conquers the Lord. However, even if one worships the Lord with material desires, one's life eventually becomes successful and one no longer is subjected to repeated birth and death.
Those who practice *bhāgavata-dharma* – the system of religion taught by the Lord Himself – associate with the Lord and attain Him.	6.16.40–48	Those who practice *bhāgavata-dharma* – pure religion taught by the Lord – act only in devotional service for His pleasure. Pure service is not contaminated by self-interest, irreligion, or envy. The *Bhagavad-gītā* and *Śrīmad-Bhāgavatam* teach *bhāgavata-dharma*, which purify us and guide us to the highest goal of life, devotion to the Supreme Lord. Simply chanting His holy names even once we become free from material contamination. Therefore there is only one true religion: *bhāgavata-dharma*, which are actions only meant to please the Lord. It is not a sectarian religion.
When we do not identify with the Lord's interests but our own, we become illusioned and continue in the cycle of birth and death.	6.16.56–62	When we forget our constitutional position as a servant of God, that we are His parts and are therefore eternal, knowledgeable, and blissful, we become illusioned and think of ourselves as supreme. Instead of identifying with the Lord's interest, we only become interested in our bodily expansions, like wife, children, and material possessions. As a result, we are forced to take repeated birth and death in different bodies. We are also never happy trying to enjoy separately from the Lord. One can come out of this illusion by transcendental knowledge and following the instructions of the *Vedas*. One should give up the desire for fruitive results and become a devotee of the Lord.

Higher-Thinking Questions

Now try to deepen your understanding of this chapter by delving into Śrīla Prabhupāda's purports and reflecting on the following questions:

1. Why did Citraketu's son deny that Mahārāja Citraketu and his wife were his mother and father? (Refer to verse 4 and purport.)

2. What does Śrīla Prabhupāda suggest in verse 5 purport that Citraketu could've thought of to prevent his lamentation? Do you think this is a valid question to ask ourselves when we are faced with such a situation?

3. Since the soul is part of the Supreme Lord, the soul has similar qualities as the Lord. How should the pure soul then behave and see others? (See verse 10 and purport.)

4. Verse 10 describes that the Lord is neutral in His relation to the conditioned souls. Do you think He is like this to everyone? Give a reason for your answer. (Refer to purport.)

5. Does being neutral, like the Lord, mean that one doesn't act? What does neutrality mean as described in verse 11 purport?

6. In his purport to verse 20 Śrīla Prabhupāda compares the Lord to the living entities to show the Lord's greatness. Describe at least three ways that they are different.

7. Why did Aṅgirā Muni instruct the King in spiritual knowledge only after the King's son had died? What do you think is sometimes a prerequisite for hearing and imbibing transcendental knowledge as demonstrated in the case of Mahārāja Citraketu? (See verse 26 and purport.)

8. How is a *karmī's* and a devotee's material opulence different as described in verse 29 purport? [Hint: Opulence is the same, but what is different in their relationship with it?]

9. According to verse 35 purport, why should we give credit to the Lord for our so-called creations?

10. From verse 50 what can you conclude about receiving transcendental knowledge from the spiritual master or the scriptures?

ACTIVITIES

In this section you will find many exciting things to do. These activities will get you thinking, moving, drawing, and having loads of fun.

Analogy Activity

... to bring out the scholar in you

SHAPING A FALSE IDENTITY

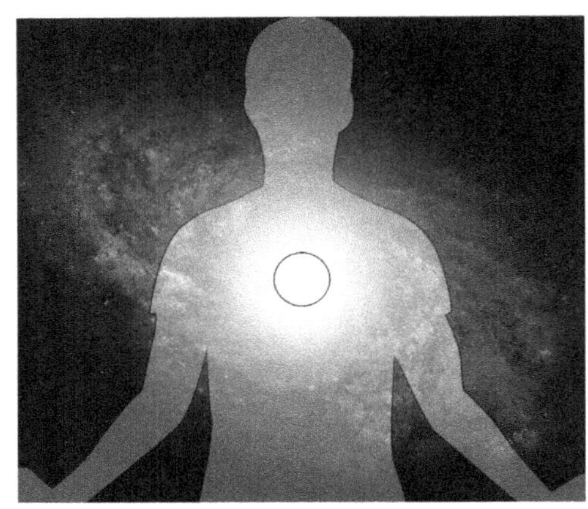

"Just as gold and other commodities are continually transferred from one place to another in due course of purchase and sale, so the living entity, as a result of his fruitive activities, wanders throughout the entire universe, being injected into various bodies in different species of life by one kind of father after another." *SB* 6.16.6

In essence, this verse states that the living being is completely different from the body. To illustrate this point in an easily understandable way, the verse compares the living being to gold, and the owners in which it changes hands to the bodies it can take on.

Let us try to test this analogy. Perform this activity as a group.

Take a lump of molding clay. Each person in the group gets a specified time limit, say two minutes, to mold the clay into something of his or her choice. If you wish, you could agree on a theme (animals, objects, etc.) and mold accordingly. Once the clay is molded by one person, everyone else should guess what it is. Then, the person who molded the clay fills out one column in the following table, writing a sentence or two about why he chose to mold the clay that way. Take turns to mold the clay. At the end, all the responses in the table are read out.

Object the clay was molded into	Reason for molding into the object

Object the clay was molded into	Reason for molding into the object

Finally, discuss:

1. What was common to all the objects that were molded?

2. What was different about the objects that were molded?

3. Once the clay was molded, did you tend to think of it as that object rather than as clay?

4. As the clay was passed around and re-molded, did your perspective change or did you think of it as just clay?

5. Use this activity to say what you understand about the following:
   a) The soul changing identities with changing bodies.
   b) The soul's real identity not changing with changing bodies.

Introspective Activity

... to bring out the reflective devotee in you

TRANSFORMED BY KNOWLEDGE

By the mercy of Aṅgirā and Nārada Munis, Mahārāja Citraketu and his wives were able to understand the temporary nature of material relationships and the trouble that attachment to such relationships bring. Their confusions were cleared, which allowed them to progress in different ways.

Look at the pictures below. The left column shows the confused state of Mahārāja Citraketu, Kṛtadyuti, and the other wives through a Confusion Cloud. The right column shows the clearing of the confusion and how it freed them to take a Progress Path. Can you fill out the Confusion Cloud and Progress Path for each to understand how they transformed?

Confusion Clouds of Bhāgavatam Personalities	Progress Path
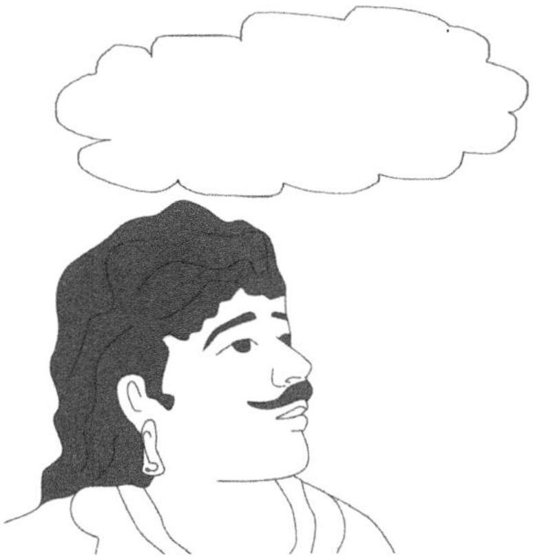 Mahārāja Citraketu	
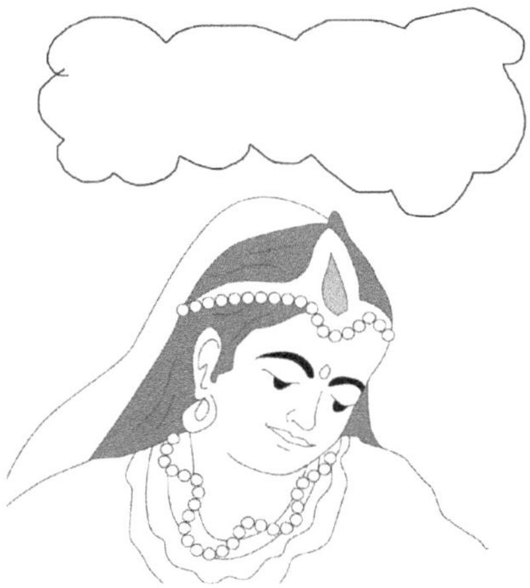 Kṛtadyuti	
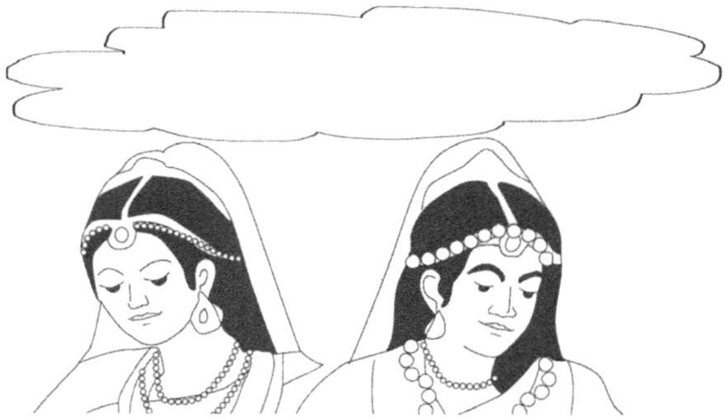 Co-wives of Kṛtadyuti	

Often, we are also attacked by Confusion Clouds in our daily lives, especially when it comes to relationships. We have to apply what we often hear in the *Bhāgavatam* to clear these clouds and find our Progress Path. In the table below, think of two Confusion Clouds that have been troubling you. How did you or do you plan to go on the Progress Path to clear these clouds?

Note to facilitators: To fill personal Confusion Clouds, encourage students to think of dilemmas or conflicts they've had with parents, siblings, peers, authority figures, etc., in their daily relationships. To fill their Progress Paths, encourage them to think about how such relationship dilemmas were resolved or how they could be resolved, and how this can help them.

MY CONFUSION CLOUDS	PROGRESS PATH

Critical-Thinking Activity

... to bring out the spiritual investigator in you

BHĀGAVATA-DHARMA IS THE BEST

In verse 47 Citraketu Mahārāja says to the Lord, "My dear Lord, You are the creator, maintainer, and annihilator of this cosmic manifestation, but persons who are too materialistic and who always see separateness do not have eyes with which to see You."

Let us try to understand what he means by people who are "too materialistic" and who "see separateness" cannot understand Kṛṣṇa. And let us try to understand how people who are not materialistic and who "see oneness" can understand the Lord.

In his purport to the verse, Śrīla Prabhupāda describes how material scientists, atheists, and materialistic philosophers try to understand the world in their own ways. Their system does not include what they cannot see or experience, and since the Lord cannot be seen or experienced by material means, they tend to conclude that this world is not caused by the Lord.

Devotees, on the other hand, know that the Lord is the original cause of the world, and that this world is caused by the will of the Lord and a play of His energies. They understand that not everything in the Lord's creation can be experienced through our limited senses, and therefore, they rely on the process of *śabda* (hearing from authoritative sources) to accept higher truths. They follow *bhāgavata-dharma*, the true religion propounded by the authorized scriptures, which evokes our devotion to God and pleases Him.

These are two widely different ways of thinking, and the results are thus very different.

Perform this group activity to understand the difference. Divide yourselves into groups of two. One group represents the thinking of atheists, scientists, and philosophers; and the other represents the devotees. Choose at least three of the prompts below (you can make up your own prompts if you like). Then, the first group explains the phenomenon with the materialistic way of thinking (e.g., your own guess, what science says, logical analysis based on what you observe); and the other tries to analyze it from a *śāstric* viewpoint. You can record the responses on a chart, writing only the key terms or words.

- How did the world get created?
- How did humans come to exist?
- Why are there so many types of life?
- Does life exist on other planets?
- Can we go to the other planets somehow?
- Can we create life?
- Can we lead better lives by working harder?
- Is there life after death?
- Is what we see of the universe all there is, or is there more to this creation?

After you have discussed these topics, talk about:

1. How are the two ways of thinking different?

2. As a student of the *Bhāgavatam* and a follower of *bhāgavata-dharma*, what do you think is more complete about the Vedic explanations?

3. How do the mundane scholars see separateness and how do the followers of *bhāgavata-dharma* see oneness in this world?

4. Why is *bhāgavata-dharma* considered non-sectarian, meaning that any kind of person or religion can follow it?

5. Why is *bhāgavata-dharma* the best?

Science Activity

OUT-OF-BODY EXPERIENCES

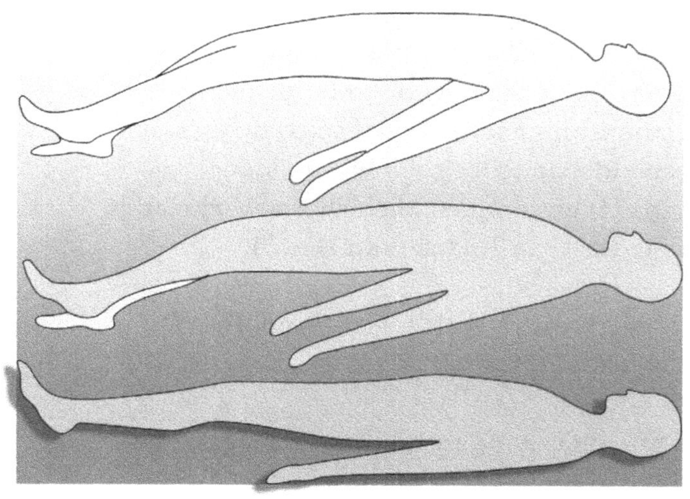

Mahārāja Citraketu's son came back to life for some time and instructed Mahārāja Citraketu and his wives about the temporary nature of material relationships. The son came back to life by the power of Nārada Muni, not of his own accord, for a particular purpose. However, is it possible for someone to re-enter the body after leaving it? If so, what does this prove?

In modern scientific circles, the term Out-of-Body Experience (OBE) is used to refer to someone who reports going out of the body and returning to it. There are many reports of people having such experiences especially closer to the time of death, which are called Near-Death Experiences (NDEs). Since modern science relies on methods of study that involve direct experience, these phenomena are still not very well understood.

Directions:

Research some cases of OBEs or NDEs from reliable sources on the internet or from your local library. Use the following prompts to guide you:

1. What are the prominent common factors you find in each of them?

2. How different are they from the descriptions you read in the *Bhāgavatam*?

3. As a devotee, how can you explain OBEs or NDEs to someone who wants to understand them from a Vedic perspective?

Note to facilitators and students: The research should be carefully guided by the mentor, and only case studies from reliable sources should be chosen. Books such as *Māyā: The World as Virtual Reality* written by Sadāpūta Dāsa also lists some of such cases.

Theatrical Activity

WHAT IS TEMPORARY AND WHAT IS NOT

In this chapter we learn that all material relationships are temporary, whereas the soul is eternal, part and parcel of the Supreme Lord, and therefore has an eternal relationship with Him. Knowing this, we should develop our forgotten relationship with the Lord, and by so doing we can become detached from mundane relationships and be less affected by them.

Read the following dialogue that encourages an old man to let go of his mundane attachment to his son and become attached to Kṛṣṇa. Then complete the dialogue and read it out loud with a partner. (For a female change "Jñāna Dāsa" to "Jñāna-śakti Dāsī.")

Jñāna Dāsa: (sighing in exhaustion) It's been a rough day with such a heavy bag of books! I just hope I can distribute at least one book and talk about Kṛṣṇa!

Old man: (talking to himself from a distance) I don't understand this nuisance of a boy! No time for his old father, who gave birth to him and raised him to be what he is today!

Jñāna Dāsa: (approaching the old man) Seems like someone is quite annoyed! Hare Kṛṣṇa. Is everything alright, Mr . . .?

Old man: (frowning) I am Mr. Chintamukta. Who are you and what do you want?

Jñāna Dāsa: Good to meet you, Mr. Chintamukta. Can I listen to your worries? I heard you complaining about someone, and you seem to be very upset now.

Mr. Chintamukta: My son, my only son, who is supposed to be mine and taking care of me is now sitting at work, earning money to raise his family and children. He has no time for me, to accompany me to the market . . .! What a rascal!

Jñāna Dāsa: You seem to be very attached to your son. What if he goes to a different city and you don't see him for days and months?

Mr. Chintamukta: I would never allow that! He is obliged to look after me and stay with me forever because I gave birth to him.

Jñāna Dāsa: Let's walk to the market; I have time to accompany you today, Sir! I would also like to tell you some stories, which will relieve you from this pain and these complaints.

Mr. Chintamukta: Oh, what's that? You have a solution?

Jñāna Dāsa: (smiling) An excellent one!

Mr. Chintamukta: What are you going to tell me?

Jñāna Dāsa: I am going to reveal to you your real identity, Sir, and help you know who you are and how you can stay happy!

Continue the dialogue in which Jñāna Dāsa enlightens Mr. Chintamukta about the transmigration of the soul and how his relationship with his son as well as his son's relationship with his children, wife, and jobs are all temporary. Conclude by saying what a soul should do instead.

Writing and Language Activities

... to help you understand better

ADVERT: YOU CAN SEE KṚṢṆA TOO!

From this chapter's story we understand that we can also experience Kṛṣṇa's presence and eventually see Him if we hear transcendental knowledge from exalted devotees and follow their guidance.

Imagine that Śrīla Prabhupāda is coming to your town for five days. He will conduct a *bhāgavata-kathā*, speaking about the glories of the Supreme Lord. Śrīla Prabhupāda is able to purify the consciousness of anyone who sincerely hears him and follows his teachings. In this way, in time our illusion and material attachments vanish and we can thus experience Kṛṣṇa's presence!

Design an advertisement (online or offline) for this news to spread far and wide, so that everyone can get this rare opportunity to associate with Śrīla Prabhupāda and become enlightened in *bhāgavata-dharma*, the pure religion taught by the Supreme Lord.

Some tips for designing an effective advertisement:

- Connect with the general public.
- Convince people to accept the opportunity advertised.
- Focus on feel-good moments and thoughts.
- Ask yourself what your reader wants and be emotionally appealing.
- Use interesting visuals (for online content).
- Use catchy headlines, phrases, pictures, or colorful content (for magazines or news ads).
- Keep your message clear, brief, and attractive.
- Talk about the demand of the opportunity and the urgency to reserve their place.

Example:

Come and grab your seats! Come and grab your seats! Come and grab your seats!

ŚRĪLA PRABHUPĀDA IS COMING!

The most exalted devotee, spiritual master,

and

reservoir of transcendental knowledge

will be with you for five days. Come and see Kṛṣṇa in his association!

Date: _______________________

Venue: _____________________________________

Limited seats! Register now!
[Registration details]

[Brief content of what one would receive]: These five days can turn out to be the most eventful in your life! Experience Kṛṣṇa's presence in the presence of Kṛṣṇa's pure devotee.

[Add images or video/music (suitable for online advertisements).]

[Add colorful content for magazine or newspaper advert.]

REFLECTIVE LETTER: BHĀGAVATA-DHARMA GETS RID OF ENVY, IRRELIGION, AND SELF-INTEREST

In this chapter, we understand that those who practice *bhāgavata-dharma* eventually associate with Kṛṣṇa and attain Him. *Bhāgavata-dharma* is the path of pure devotional service, which frees one from irreligion, envy, and all material contamination. Let us try to understand this more by writing a reflective letter.

Reflection allows us to make sense of our experiences in relation to ourselves and helps us learn from a particular practical experience. It gives you an opportunity to think deeper with a calm mind and have realizations that are very useful for future. Reflective writing can also help you develop a better understanding of a topic and can enable you to review your progress.

Write a letter to yourself, reflecting on the following potential situation. Express how you would feel in the situation and how by practicing unalloyed devotional service, you could prevent envy, irreligion, and self-interest arising from this situation. (First discuss with your class and teacher what envy, irreligion, and self-interest mean.)

You have a friend in school that comes from a rich family and loves to show off his or her wealth and status. He or she has always been kind to you, showered you with gifts and material things, until a new student joined your class who has more expensive things, like phones, gadgets, clothes, and a lot of money!

Gradually, they both become close friends and keep away from you, stop sharing their things, and sometimes even humiliating you or speaking badly about you. You feel jealous and terrible and feel like screaming at them or perhaps even crying bitterly. You then remember what you learned from Śrīmad-Bhāgavatam – that by trying to get rid of material attachments, envy, and irreligion, you can attain Kṛṣṇa, Who is the highest of all!

In your notebook complete the scenario (what could have happened), and then in a short reflective letter, share your personal experience in context to this situation and how you've attained Kṛṣṇa's loving presence in your life by avoiding material attachments, irreligion, and feelings of jealousy and envy. How has this potential incident shaped your personality as a devotee and how will you always use this experience in your path of *bhāgavata-dharma*?

Some tips for writing reflective letters:

1. Address the letter to yourself and write as if having a conversation with yourself.

2. Examine the experience – integrate personal viewpoints on the above context.

3. How do you feel about what happened? What did you learn from the experience? (Note down the points.)

4. Clarify how the situation or the experience will be useful for you in future.

FROM IGNORANCE TO KNOWLEDGE TO BHAKTI

Through the instructions of Aṅgirā and Nārada Muni, King Citraketu overcame ignorance and became detached from material identity and relationships, and eventually developed attachment to Lord Kṛṣṇa.

The first table below has five features of ignorance in the first column (fill in the missing ones): 1. Ignorance of one spiritual identity; 2. Absorption in the bodily conception; 3. False possessiveness of enjoyable objects; 4. Anger upon frustration; 5. Sense of death (*SB* 3.12.2).

In the second column are the corresponding situations of King Citraketu and his wives. This table helps us practically understand the term ignorance, the root cause of misidentification.

Please study and complete the following table number 1:

	IGNORANCE	EXAMPLES
1		King Citraketu and his wives were ignorant of their true identity as spirit souls, part and parcel of Supreme Lord.
2		King Citraketu was worried about his ancestors and himself as he had no son. He did not understand that by performing devotional service, he could attain all perfection and need not worry about going to hell.
3	False possessiveness	
4		Kṛtadyuti criticized providence, and her co-wives burned in envy and anger when the King neglected them.
5	Sense of death	

We see many changes in King Citraketu and his wives after they heard Aṅgirā Muni's instructions and the astonishing words of the son who was brought back to life by Nārada Muni.

Please complete table number 2 to understand their transformation in consciousness:

1	Illusion	
2	Lamentation	The royal family understood that for the soul there is neither lamentation nor happiness, as it is a part of the Supreme Soul who is always neutral. (*SB* 6.16.11)
3	Fear	
4	Pain	
5	Purification	King Citraketu was purified of all doubts and illusion, and the queens admitted their crime and atoned. They gave up the desire to bear sons.

Aṅgirā Muni helped Citraketu become detached from material relationships by giving him knowledge. This is helpful to practice devotional service. But the soul's nature is to have relationships. So only when Nārada Muni showed him practically how to develop a deep relationship with Kṛṣṇa by chanting the *mantra* did the Lord appear to Citraketu, which made the King truly satisfied and happy.

Match the following:

a. Citraketu's practice	1. Citraketu attains shelter at the lotus feet of Anantadeva.
b. Intermediate result of his practice	2. The Lord tells Citraketu that he has become perfect and if he follows the teachings, he will attain Him at the end of life.
c. Primary result	3. With a completely spotless mind, Citraketu offers beautiful prayers glorifying the Lord with tears of love.
d. Lord's *darśana* (form)	4. He has *darśana* of the beautiful form of Lord Śeṣa.
e. Citraketu's ecstasy and prayers	5. Rulership of the Vidyādhara planet
f. Lord's response to his prayers	6. Citraketu fasts and attentively and continuously chants the *mantra* given by Nārada.

CHAPTER 16 ANSWERS

Shaping a False Identity

1. The clay was the common raw material from which all objects were molded; 2. Each object molded was different, with a different "story" behind it; 3. Learner's own answer. (Once molded, each object developed an identity of its own; it was no more just "moulded clay." It could be identified as a certain animal or object with a function or use of its own, although, in essence, it was just molded clay.) 4. Learner's own answer, but it should be backed up with some reasoning; 5.a. In essence, we are spirit souls, just like raw clay (or the gold in the analogy). But when we are "molded" by material nature to assume a certain body, we assume the identity of that body, just like clay assumes the identity of what it is molded into. Nature supplies these bodies based on its laws, just like we supplied shapes to the clay based on our motivation; 5.b. The clay never loses its original identity no matter what it is shaped into, just like the soul never loses its nature no matter what body it takes – but just like the clay may no longer be called as such by one who has forgotten what the object is molded out of, a living being may forget his real identity as a soul once he is provided a certain type of material body.

Transformed by Knowledge

Confusion Clouds: Mahārāja Citraketu – a longing for a son to be his heir; thinking that his son was his main source of joy and thus being attached to him; Kṛtadyuti – seeing her son as her main source of joy and means to be her husband's favorite queen; Co-wives – taking Kṛtadyuti's son to be their main source of misery and thus being envious of the Queen; Progress Paths: Mahārāja Citraketu – he chanted the *mantra* continuously and surrendered fully to the Lord in devotion and thus became a pure devotee; Kṛtadyuti – she gave up material attachment and became situated in knowledge; Co-wives – gave up envy, regretted their behavior, atoned for their sin.

Bhāgavata-dharma is the Best

The guided discussion is meant to bring out the differences in thinking between the two groups. The first group should be able to come up with a "reasonable" mundane explanation, and the second group should be able to explain how everything happens by the Lord's energy or system, which is described in the *śāstra*.

1. The mundane philosophers tend to think that everything in the world can be explained through what they can see or experience. But there are instances when this does not work. The devotees, however, are able to trace everything to the Lord and His energies; 2. Students of the *Bhāgavatam* are able to understand phenomena not as they experience it but in a way that explains both what they can directly experience and what is beyond their understanding. They understand that everything within this world cannot be directly experienced through the senses and mind, and needs higher intelligence. Thus they accept the presence of a higher power and understand phenomena in a way that we fail to understand through imperfect observation; 3. The mundane scholars see the creation separate or independent from any superior creator, and the followers of *Bhāgavata-dharma* see everything as one – as God's creation – rather than as separate sets of phenomena happening at its own accord. They also see themselves as one in quality with the Lord, of eternity, knowledge, and bliss; 4. *Bhāgavata-dharma* is the true eternal religion of the soul. The *Śrīmad-Bhāgavatam* and *bhakti śāstras* discuss existential truths that are common to all human beings, irrespective of religion, race, background, or culture. Topics of our true identity and the goal of life pertain to all kinds of people, not just a particular religion; 5. *Bhāgavata-dharma* teaches us perfect knowledge coming from higher sources that are not subject to human error; it purifies us and guides us to the highest goal of life, devotion to the Supreme Lord; it encourages actions only meant to please the Lord and have a personal relationship with Him; in this way one can end the cycle of birth and death in the material world and go back home, back to Godhead.

Out-of-Body Experiences

1. Most subjects in these studies report being able to see from a plane different from their body, and they can provide details of things they would not have been aware of, such as details of an operation they

are undergoing while unconscious. Some, who claim to travel to other realms, may also report seeing dead friends or relatives and/or experience a peaceful light; 2. These descriptions correlate in some respects to the *Bhāgavatam*, which accepts that we are different from the body and that we change bodies. The scriptures also state that by yogic power, one can get out of the body and transfer himself to any place one likes. While the *Bhāgavatam* clearly differentiates between the body (as material) and the soul (as spiritual), modern science is unable to make this distinction; 3. From a Vedic perspective, we can understand that the soul is different from the body. The soul is spiritual, while the body is material. The soul can leave one body and move on (to another). So NDEs or OBEs are not considered unusual phenomena.

Reflective Letter

Potential end to scenario: You decide to focus on your prescribed duty, to study and perform well in school, along with serving the Supreme Lord and performing your spiritual practices: taking care of your Deities, chanting Kṛṣṇa's holy name, reading *Śrīmad-Bhāgavatam*, and so on.

A day arrives when you pass your final assessments with flying colors and get a scholarship to study in your favorite high school/university. Everyone applauds you for your efforts and success, including the two classmates. This time, you don't feel any pain in your heart because you have realized the true essence of *bhāgavata-dharma*. You always felt Kṛṣṇa's presence in your life, while performing your prescribed duties and being immersed in devotional service.

From Ignorance to Knowledge to Bhakti

Table 1: 1. Ignorance of one's spiritual identity; 2. Absorption in the bodily conception; 3. Thinking oneself the enjoyer and the proprietor of one's possessions leads to great attachment to the objects of pleasure and negligence of duties to others and to the Lord. Citraketu and Kṛtadyuti were deeply attached to their son and neglected the other queens; 4. Anger upon frustration; 5. When his son died, Citraketu lamented so much that he appeared to have no life; Kṛtadyuti also seemed dead in great lamentation.

Table 2: 1. Citraketu and his wife became free of the illusion that they were the parents and gave up ties of affection; 3. Citraketu had no more fear of going to hell or of losing the object of his affection; 4. Citraketu, his wife, and co-wives were freed from emotional pain and suffering due to loss and envy.

Matching: a. 6; b. 5; c. 1; d. 4; e. 3; f. 2

17

Citraketu soared through space in his dazzling celestial airplane. He couldn't believe what had just happened. He marveled at his strong muscular body and its beautiful golden form. After he had seen the Lord, he was transformed into a Vidyādhara, a celestial being with powerful mystic abilities and sharpened senses. But he was no ordinary Vidyādhara – he was the king! In his brilliant airplane, which was also a gift from Lord Viṣṇu, he traveled for millions of years within the valleys of Sumeru Mountain. The exquisite Vidyādhara women accompanied him. It would be easy for anyone to become distracted by these heavenly damsels, whose beauty rivaled the stars – but not King Citraketu. In their company, he constantly chanted "Hari! Hari!" enjoying life glorifying the Lord.

Once, from outer space Mahārāja Citraketu saw Lord Śiva sitting in an assembly of Siddhas and Cāraṇas. "I can't believe this!" King Citraketu thought. "Is that Lord Śiva embracing Mother Pārvatī on his lap in front of these saintly persons?" He flew closer to have a better look, and yes, indeed, there was Pārvatī on his lap with Lord Śiva's arm around her.

Without thinking, Citraketu laughed loudly

and said, "Lord Śiva is the spiritual master of everyone and the best of all beings. He is the upholder of religion, yet how wonderful it is to see him embracing his wife in the midst of this saintly assembly.

"Lord Śiva, whose hair is matted from great austerities and penances, is the leader amongst strict followers of Vedic principles, but he is holding his wife as if he were a shameless, ordinary being."

"It is incredible how such a great personality can act like an ordinary human," the King thought. Maybe he should have kept his thoughts to himself, but it was too late. Mother Pārvatī heard his words and took it wrongly. Lord Śiva simply smiled while the others remained silent.

Mother Pārvatī's eyes turned red, and she spoke sarcastically as if emitting fire: "Oh, does this nobody think he's now in a position to punish shameless persons like us? Is he the appointed ruler, the only master of everything, who carries the rod of punishment?"

Laughing mockingly, while glancing at the august assembly, she spat words of sarcasm: "Alas, Lord Brahmā, who was born from the lotus, doesn't know the principles of religion, nor do Bhṛgu and Nārada, nor the four Kumāras. Manu and Kapila have also forgotten religious principles. Maybe that's why they didn't try to stop Lord Śiva from behaving improperly."

Mahārāja Citraketu frowned in disbelief. Had he done something wrong? Had he thought himself better than Lord Śiva in controlling the senses? Perhaps there was some pride there, but he hadn't intended to offend this great devotee. In fact, he had tried to protect Lord Śiva. He knew that Lord Śiva's character could never be tainted even when he was behaving like an ordinary person, but just so that others wouldn't criticize him and follow his example, he was somewhat harsh towards the venerable Lord Śiva.

Seeing Pārvatī's fiery eyes, Citraketu

understood that he had committed a grave mistake.

"O, lowest of *kṣatriyas*," Pārvatī continued, "By insulting my lord, you are impudent to think you could override Lord Brahmā and the other demigods who didn't say anything. They meditate on Lord Śiva's lotus feet. My lord is religion personified and the spiritual master of the entire world, and therefore this Citraketu must be punished!

"O impudent one, my dear son, now take birth in a low, sinful family of demons so that you won't commit such an offense toward an exalted personality again!"

"Oh no!" exclaimed Mahārāja Parīkṣit after hearing the narration from Śukadeva Gosvāmī.

Śukadeva Gosvāmī explained that when Citraketu was cursed by Mother Pārvatī, he descended from his airplane and bowed before her in great humility. With folded hands he said, "My dear mother, I accept your curse, for happiness and distress are given by the demigods due to one's past deeds."

Looking at Mother Pārvatī's crestfallen face, he continued, "Because of ignorance the living

Lord is neutral to everyone and simply awards happiness and distress according to the living being's actions.

"O mother, you are unnecessarily angry, but because happiness and distress are a result of my past activities, I accept your curse and do not ask to be excused from your curse. Although what I've said is not wrong, please forgive me for whatever you think is wrong."

being wanders in the forest of the material world, enjoying and suffering the reactions to his past deeds. So my dear mother, neither you nor I are to be blamed for this incident. Actually, everything is done under the Lord's direction.

"This material world is like a constantly flowing river. Therefore, what is a curse and what is a benediction? What are the heavenly planets, and what are the hellish planets? What is actually happiness and what is distress? Because the waves flow constantly, all of them are temporary.

"The Lord is unaffected by this material world. He is equal to everyone. He doesn't care for so-called happiness and distress of this material world because they are relative. For Him there is no question of distress because He is always happy.

"But He creates happiness and distress, good fortune and bad, bondage and liberation, birth and death because of our good and bad actions. Just as a judge is not responsible for putting someone in prison and is therefore not responsible for their happiness and distress, similarly the

Pārvatī stared in disbelief as Citraketu bowed down and then boarded his airplane. As the great saintly people, including Nārada Muni, the inhabitants of Siddhaloka, and Lord Śiva's personal associates, watched the celestial plane disappear into the clouds, Lord Śiva and Pārvatī smiled.

In everyone's presence, Lord Śiva looked at Pārvatī and said in a grave voice, "My dear Pārvatī, now can you see the greatness of the Vaiṣṇavas? They are servants of the servants of the Supreme Personality of Godhead. They are great souls and are not interested in material happiness.

"Such devotees who always serve the Lord in love are not afraid of any condition of life. For them the heavenly planets, liberation, and the hellish planets are all the same, for they are only interested in serving the Lord. Because they fix their minds on the lotus feet of the Lord and His holy names, they do not feel the so-called pains and pleasures caused by the dualities of this world."

"Just see, although you cursed the King, he was not at all afraid or sorry. Rather, he offered respect to you, called you mother, and accepted your curse. This is the excellence of a devotee." Lord Śiva chuckled and said, "He has defeated you and your beauty and excellence by becoming a pure devotee of the Lord."

Pārvatī looked down, ashamed. Her anger had caused her to misjudge the King.

Lord Śiva continued, "In this world we consider one thing good and the other bad, just as one mistakenly considers a flower garland to be a snake or experiences happiness or sadness in a dream. This is illusion, but a devotee who is engaged in Lord Kṛṣṇa's devotional service is detached from this material world, is in full knowledge, and therefore free from this illusion.

"Neither I, nor Brahmā, the other demigods, nor Nārada and all the other great sages can understand the pastimes of the Lord. Although we are part of Him, we consider ourselves independent and separate controllers. So naturally we cannot understand Him.

"But this magnanimous Citraketu is a dear devotee of the Lord. I am also very dear to Lord Nārāyaṇa. Therefore it is not surprising to see the activities of the most exalted devotees of Nārāyaṇa, for they are free from attachment and envy. They are always peaceful and equal to everyone."

Mother Pārvatī,

realizing her mistake, covered her face with the skirt of her sari in embarrassment. The wise words of her husband had removed her doubts and ignorance.

Śukadeva Gosvāmī said, "The great devotee Citraketu was so powerful that he could've easily counteracted the curse, but instead he very humbly accepted it. This is greatly appreciated as the standard behavior of a Vaiṣṇava.

"Thus Citraketu accepted birth in a demoniac species and appeared from Tvaṣṭā's fire sacrifice. But his mind was still fixed in transcendental knowledge and devotion to the Lord.

"My dear King Parīkṣit, you asked me how Vṛtrāsura, a *mahātmā*, took birth as a demon, so now I've explained this to you. Anyone who hears about him from a pure devotee will be free from all contamination in material life. One who rises early in the morning and recites this history of Citraketu, controlling one's words and mind and remembering the Supreme Lord, will return back home, back to Godhead, very easily."

Themes and Key Messages

Please go through this table of themes and key messages, with corresponding verses, and discuss each topic further.

THEMES	REFERENCES	KEY MESSAGES
A devotee should chant the holy name in a humble state of mind and not commit offenses to the Vaiṣṇavas.	6.17.9–15	Although Citraketu's purpose in criticizing Lord Śiva cannot be understood by ordinary persons and was never meant to insult Lord Śiva, still he shouldn't have criticized a great devotee like Śiva. One should therefore be very humble, as Caitanya Mahāprabhu teaches in his Śikṣāṣṭakam, without any desire for false prestige, and should offer all respects to others. This will prevent one from committing offenses to Vaiṣṇavas, which is considered the "mad elephant" offense. Just as a mad elephant destroys an entire garden, a person who offends a Vaiṣṇava destroys his spiritual life. If one is puffed up, he is unfit to get shelter at the Lord's lotus feet. Only when one is humble and meek can he qualify to sit at the Lord's lotus feet.
A devotee is so meek and humble that he accepts punishment, in the form of suffering, as the mercy of the Lord.	6.17.17	Since Citraketu was a devotee, he wasn't disturbed by Mother Pārvatī's curse because he knew that whatever was happening was due to his past misdeeds, and so he didn't blame anyone. He was humble and accepted his suffering as purification and a blessing from the Lord. Such a devotee, while tolerating suffering and at the same time offering the Lord his obeisances from the core of his heart, is eligible for liberation. (*SB* 10.14.8)
To get free from the *karma-cakra*, the wheel of the results of one's actions, one should take to *bhakti-yoga*.	6.17.18	King Citraketu understood that everyone is subject to suffer and enjoy according to the results of one's past *karma*. Therefore, a conditioned soul is under the control of material nature. The only way to get free from the results of one's *karma* is to take to devotional service and surrender to the Lord with love.
Although the Supreme Lord is the ultimate doer, He is not responsible for the happiness and distress of the conditioned souls.	6.17.21–23	The Supreme Lord is unaffected by the material world and is equal to everyone. He is unattached to the material world and therefore he doesn't care about so-called happiness and distress. The Lord is always happy, but He creates happiness and distress, good fortune and bad, bondage and liberation, birth and death because of the conditioned soul's good and bad actions. Just as a judge is not responsible for putting someone in prison and is therefore not responsible for their happiness and distress, similarly the Lord is neutral to everyone and simply awards happiness and distress according to the living being's actions.

THEMES	REFERENCES	KEY MESSAGES
The Lord's devotees are not interested in happiness and distress and therefore never fear any situation. They are only interested in the service of the Lord.	6.17.27–31	King Citraketu was not afraid of the curse and instead offered respect to Pārvatī and accepted the curse. The Lord's pure devotees are not affected by happiness and distress because so-called happiness and distress are just created by the mind, as in dreams. Therefore The Lord's pure devotees have perfect knowledge and detachment from the material world and are not interested in any kind of material happiness. For them the heavenly and hellish planets are all the same, because they are only interested in the Lord's service. In the service of the Lord they have learned to tolerate all hardships and are never distressed because they are constantly chanting the Lord's holy names and focusing on the Lord's lotus feet. In any condition of life one can be happy by chanting the holy names.

Higher-Thinking Questions

Now try to deepen your understanding of this chapter by delving into Śrīla Prabhupāda's purports and reflecting on the following questions:

1. Why do you think that the Lord arranged for this pastime of Citraketu Mahārāja being cursed if he was a pure devotee? (Refer to verse 4–5 purport.)

2. How was Citraketu's behavior toward Śiva different from Dakṣa's in Canto 4. (See verse 7 purport.)

3. What was Mahārāja Citraketu's actual reason for criticizing Lord Śiva as Śrīla Prabhupāda explains in verse 9 purport?

4. Why should Citraketu have refrained from criticizing Śiva as indicated in verse 10 purport? What did his critical behavior indicate about him, and what should he have done instead?

5. Śrīla Prabhupāda describes Mother Pārvatī, or Mother Durgā, as not an ordinary mother. Why is this so? How was Pārvatī acting like a mother to Citraketu? (See verse 15 purport.)

6. How was Mother Pārvatī's curse actually a boon to Citraketu as described in verse 15 purport?

7. According to verse 17 and purport, why wasn't Citraketu disturbed by the curse?

8. How was King Citraketu's power greater than Pārvatī's as indicated by Lord Śiva's statement to her in verse 27? (Refer to purport.)

9. What is the secret to real happiness as indicated in verse 30 purport?

10. What is the advantage of being a devotee even if one falls from the *bhakti* path? (See verse 38 purport.) Give at least three examples of devotees you've studied about in the *Bhāgavatam* so far which this applies to.

ACTIVITIES

In this section you will find many exciting things to do. These activities will get you thinking, moving, drawing, and having loads of fun.

Analogy Activity

... to bring out the scholar in you

EVER-CHANGING WAVES

"This material world resembles the waves of a constantly flowing river. Therefore, what is a curse and what is a favor? What are the heavenly planets, and what are the hellish planets? What is actually happiness, and what is actually distress? Because the waves flow constantly, none of them has an eternal effect." (*SB* 6.17.20)

Here Citraketu compares the material world to a river, which has waves that flow constantly. This indicates that the river's nature is as good as the waves that compose it. Similarly, the nature of the material world is also the same as the nature of its "waves," which are the modes of material nature. Let us try to understand the nature of the material world with the help of this analogy.

First, consider the nature of the river itself:

» It has sweet water, and you can taste sweet water anywhere along the length and breadth of the river.

Next, let us consider the nature of the river's waves:

» They come and go; that is, they are not permanent.
» They change in their strength without notice; that is, a big wave can lose momentum and turn into a small one, and a smaller wave can gain momentum and turn big as it hits the shore.
» They can be harnessed for our use in the form of providing hydro energy, as a medium for swimming or boating, etc., or they can cause harm (during a flood or, in the case of the ocean, a tsunami).

Now, let us see how this can be applied to the material world.

Look at the diagram on the following page. It represents the material world as a physical entity (like a river), which has its own waves and currents. Within each wave, one aspect of the river has been listed. Use an example of an incident, a personality, or a lesson from the *Bhāgavatam* to show each aspect in the material world. One example has been done for you.

Nature of the material world (refer to purport 20).

Wave 1: Changing river current: Good becomes bad or bad becomes good.
Answer: Dhruva considered gaining a kingdom an obstacle to his service;
Citraketu considered gaining a demon's body a blessing.

Wave 2: Can be used to our benefit.

Wave 3: Can cause us some harm.

Wave 4: Both good and harm are temporary.

Artistic Activity

STYLIZED DRAWING:
TEMPORARY WAVES OF HAPPINESS AND SORROW

As we learned from the analogy activity, Citraketu describes this material world as the waves of a constantly flowing river; the waves have no permanent effect. Similarly, happiness and distress have no permanent effect; all are sorrow when we don't serve and love Kṛṣṇa.

In this activity, you will design a poster illustrating the position of a devotee like King Citraketu. The idea is to represent the material world as the waves of a moving river. The heart of a devotee can be represented by birds flying above the river, or deep-sea aquatic animals who are not affected by the waves. You can also use a mountain as an example of steadiness in service or a ship sailing smoothly because the captain is expert.

The art form we will use is stylized drawing, which is not strictly realistic but more dramatic and dynamic. For example, you can draw the waves, water droplets, and other elements in your art in a way that conveys movement but is not really realistic.

What you will need: Off-white/white cardstock paper, black ink pen, paper, pencil, eraser, scissors

Steps:

1. Study the stylized drawing given below. Notice how the waves are many and add to the feeling of movement and rough action, whereas the sailboat is stable.

2. On a rough piece of paper, make some quick sketches of waves and other elements you would like to include.

3. Practice drawing the curvy lines freely.

4. Choose a focus point in your piece. For example, if you are using the flying birds to represent the devotee, then bring attention to it by using contrasting features like size, shape, variety in design, etc., compared to the waves.

5. Pick your best composition. With a pencil, draw it lightly on the cardstock paper. Use your pen to darken the lines and create movement, variety, and attention to the focus point.

6. Once the ink dries, trim the edges of the cardstock if needed and frame it or hang it up.

Theatrical Activity

... to bring out the actor in you

VAIṢṆAVA ETIQUETTE

With a partner, read or enact the following dialogue:

Class teacher: Mohan, what practical lesson did you learn from the story of Citraketu being cursed by Mother Pārvatī?

Mohan: From Citraketu's mistake, I learnt that we have to be very careful in pointing out the faults of an advanced devotee. Best would be to mind my own business and stay fixed in my work. But should we always keep silent if we see incorrect behavior?

Class teacher: Sometimes it is difficult to understand the behavior of different personalities. Even if you see something that puzzles you, it's better to approach the senior devotee in private and inquire humbly rather than speaking aloud in public or social media. Or you can also speak in confidence to another senior devotee or authority.

Mohan: Haha! Right! There is a right way to be right, and there is a wrong way to be right. I like your point here!

Class teacher: What else did you learn?

Mohan: I was also thinking that the Lord doesn't tolerate pride in His devotees. Doesn't the urge to speak negatively stem from pride?

Class teacher: Yes, here we see Mother Pārvatī referring to Citraketu being puffed up. Of course, Citraketu had no intention of looking down upon Lord Śiva, but we have to be very careful about not becoming proud of our achievements or getting some special attention or mercy from the Lord or His devotees.

Mohan: Finally, I was thinking about how everything is ultimately sanctioned by Lord Kṛṣṇa, either due to our *karma* or due to His special mercy. How can we blame anyone for our distress?

Class teacher: Wonderful! As Śrīla Prabhupāda writes, it is always better to tolerate while remaining connected to Kṛṣṇa in a mood of prayer and gratitude.

Mohan: *Śrīmad-Bhāgavatam* is full of wonderful instructions that help us move forward in the path of *bhakti* easily!

Critical-Thinking Activity

... to bring out the spiritual investigator in you

DOES THE LORD LOVE MAKING HIS DEVOTEES SUFFER?

In verse 24 Citraketu says to Mother Pārvatī, "O mother, you are now unnecessarily angry, but since all my happiness and distress are destined by my past activities, I do not plead to be excused or relieved from your curse. Although what I have said is not wrong, please let whatever you think is wrong be pardoned."

In other words, Citraketu accepted Mother Pārvatī's curse although he felt he didn't do anything wrong.

In the *Bhāgavatam* we often see devotees considering "unfair reversals" as the mercy of the Lord and accepting it. Sometimes it looks like these surrendered devotees voluntarily take on great trouble or harm even when they have the power to avoid the suffering.

In the table below let us look at some devotees and the choices they made to receive the mercy of the Lord rather than choosing a different option that could have brought them out of the situation easily. Then we will analyze why they made these choices. (Fill in the table on the next page. The first one is done for you.)

DEVOTEE	INCIDENT	HE/SHE COULD HAVE...	BUT INSTEAD CHOSE TO...	AND SO...
Parīkṣit	Was cursed by Śṛṅgi	Countered the curse and remained safe	Accept the curse	Had to leave his body in seven days at a young age
Citraketu				
Pāṇḍavas				
Prahlāda				
Haridāsa Ṭhākura				

In groups, analyze the following:

1. Why did each devotee accept suffering over an easy way to get out of the problem?

2. How could they think that accepting suffering was the will of the Lord for them?

3. How could the Lord, who loves His devotees, see their suffering and still allow it?

Each group should present their understanding to the class as a short one-minute presentation. Then, write a small journal entry summarizing what you have understood.

Writing and Language Activities

HUMILITY MEANS NO OFFENSES

We are encouraged to follow Caitanya Mahāprabhu's teachings of being tolerant like a tree and humble like a blade of grass, offering all respects to others. In this way we will not offend Vaiṣṇavas and always be wonderful examples to others.

Let's learn to apply this behavior in different situations.

Directions:
Read the following situations based on this theme. Note down how you think one usually reacts in the situation and then how a devotee reacts. Discuss in a group and then share your viewpoints with your class.

Situation 1:
You are standing in a long queue in a shop for a long time, and suddenly some people come from nowhere and jump the queue. The shopkeeper serves them immediately. It seems that he is favoring some of his friends. (There is no authority around to complain to.) How would one usually react? How would a devotee ideally react?

(Draw reference from the principle of being patient and thinking everything to be Kṛṣṇa's plan.)

Situation 2:
You are at a friend's house and a poor *brāhmaṇa* comes to your friend's door begging for alms. Your friend's father speaks harshly to the poor *brāhmaṇa* beggar and chases him off the premises. How could a devotee deal with this situation?

(Keep in mind what you learned about being humble and not committing offenses to Vaiṣṇavas or *brāhmaṇas*.)

Situation 3:
Your father is a devotee and he goes to the temple every Sunday to do some service for the Deities. He takes the local bus to the temple. After he finds a seat, some teenage boys board the bus and start mocking your father's devotee dress, *śikhā*, *tilaka*, etc. How would an ordinary person react to being mocked? How would a devotee respond?

(Draw reference from Mahāprabhu's teachings of being more tolerant than a tree and more humble than a blade of grass.)

1. From the above examples, do you think that it is only beneficial to be tolerant and humble toward devotees? Explain your answer.

2. Explain how being humble means not committing Vaiṣṇava-aparādha.

3. Does this mean that in all situations we should be humble and tolerant? Explain.

PAMPHLET: FREE YOURSELF FROM THE KARMA-CAKRA!

In this chapter we learn that a conditioned soul performs activities under the control of material nature and produces good and bad results. The only way to get free from the results of one's *karma* is to practice devotional service and surrender to the Lord with love.

With your understanding of this theme, create a pamphlet to inform people about the wheel of *karma*, or the *karma-cakra*. Explain through an illustration of a *karma* wheel, using the template below, that what we send out comes back to us! Use the boomerang theory to explain the concept of the *karma-cakra*. A conditioned soul falls under this theory: whatever he does – good or bad – is bound to come back to him in future. Therefore one must always try to do good *karma*, or actions, or better still, devotional service that doesn't produce good or bad *karma* but transcendental reactions. In your pamphlet explain how a devotee who practices *bhakti-yoga* is therefore no longer subject to happiness or distress under the laws of *karma*. Indeed, he is beyond *karma*.

A pamphlet, sometimes called a leaflet, is a small, unbound booklet used to advertise or provide information on a single subject. It is mainly used for informing rather than for selling something. It is usually printed on a single sheet of paper with the text of the pamphlet on one page and an image or illustration on the opposite side. Use your creativity.

You can add illustrations of good activities and bad activities along with your explanation. Then show through illustrations how a devotee is not affected by the wheel of *karma* due to the presence of the Supreme Lord in his life.

Template

INSTRUCTIONAL WRITING: KṚṢṆA IS NOT RESPONSIBLE FOR YOUR HAPPINESS OR DISTRESS!

In this chapter we studied that the conditioned souls experience happiness and distress only because of their own past good or bad actions. Even though Kṛṣṇa is the supreme doer, He is unattached to the material world. Therefore we must not hold Him responsible for our happiness or distress.

Instructional writing, as the name suggests, **provides instructions on how to do something**. Whether they are instructions on making a dish, assembling furniture, operating a machine, or providing information on what to do and how to do something are the basics of instructional writing. An effective set of instruction requires the following: **Clear, precise, and simple writing**. The ability to put yourself in the reader's position (the person trying to use your instructions) will guide you to give clear instructions.

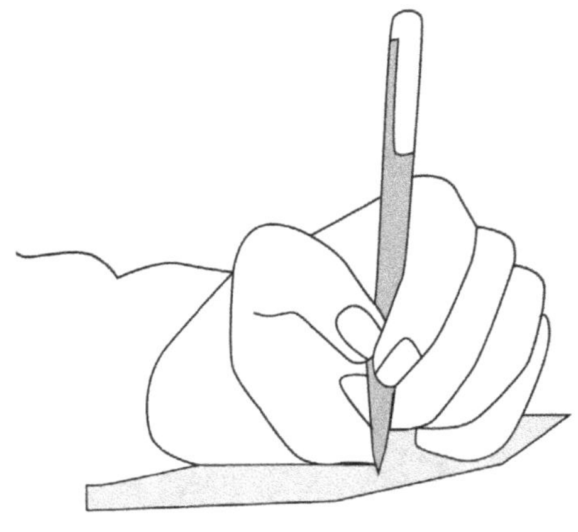

With your understanding of the theme in this chapter, write a set of instructions or guidelines to teach people how to react in situations of happiness or distress. See the sample on the next page and then frame a set of instructions for the two situations in the table:

Sample situation:

Sunita has been waiting for six years to get initiated by her spiritual master. Another devotee girl who is new to Kṛṣṇa consciousness gets accepted for initiation by her spiritual master before Sunita.

"How is that possible?" exclaims Sunita, and her heart fills with envy and anger. She starts blaming the Lord for her ill fortune. She starts feeling that she's unnecessarily wasting her time waiting for her turn and the Lord doesn't want her to get initiated.

Instructions/Guidelines:

1. The way Sunita acted was improper. She could have been more positive in this situation.

2. Even though it is a distressful situation, Sunita must understand that there is a reason why she has not yet been called and it is for her good.

3. The Lord is unattached to any of our bad or good happenings.

4. The Supreme Lord is always our best friend and well-wisher. Even though He sanctions everything, He is not responsible for what reactions we face – good or bad.

5. Therefore, the best way to deal with this is to surrender to the Supreme Lord. Know that everything happens according to the laws of *karma*. Because we are His devotees, the Lord uses our *karma* to purify us and teach many lessons.

6. Follow the instructions of the Lord and keep practicing devotional service and your prescribed duties.

7. Sunita must clean her heart of all envy and pride by regularly chanting the holy names of the Lord and by consciously trying to become a humble servant.

A HAPPY SITUATION

Shyam recently won a badminton tournament in school and has been awarded a first-place trophy and some award money!
He is simply in the clouds, in happiness.
He decides to take a break from his studies and other scheduled lessons because he thinks that the Lord has given him the opportunity to enjoy the money on some leisure activities and fun with his friends.

- What is the best way to act in this situation?
- How can we keep in mind our actions in these times of sudden happiness?
- Do you think that taking a break from your scheduled routine for enjoying is a suitable thing to do at this time?
- How can we use the understanding that *"we should not hold the Lord responsible for our happiness or distress"* to act more wisely in this situation, thinking ourselves to be just conditioned souls who are bound by the *karma-cakra*?
- Write a set of instructions to show how an individual who is aware of this theme would act in such a situation.

A DISTRESSFUL SITUATION

Raman has been practicing day and night to get selected for the final badminton team to play a tournament in an international event. He qualifies for the semi-finals, but he does not win on the final selection day. He is distressed and frustrated. He blames the Lord for giving him a bad fate on that day! He even says that it was not his fault but the Lord's fault.

- In your understanding, is this a good way to deal with this situation?
- What can you understand about the mood of Raman?
- How could he have better dealt with this situation?
- Do you think that surrendering to the Lord and thinking everything to be for one's good could be helpful to him?
- How can Raman use the understanding of this theme to act more sensibly in this situation? Do you think moving on and putting more effort for future would give him motivation and positivity?
- How can he be more thankful to the Lord, instead of holding Him responsible for his failure?
- Write a set of instructions to show how one should act in similar distressful situations and not hold the Lord responsible.

GLORIES OF KING CITRAKETU

In this chapter Lord Śiva glorified King Citraketu's great tolerance. He points out the source of Citraketu's power: pure devotion to Lord Viṣṇu.

Please read verses 27 to 31 and their purports and write a paragraph explaining how Citraketu was able to rise above happiness and distress and remain fixed in service to the Lord.

You may use the mind map below to guide your writing. A mind map is a tool to organize information.

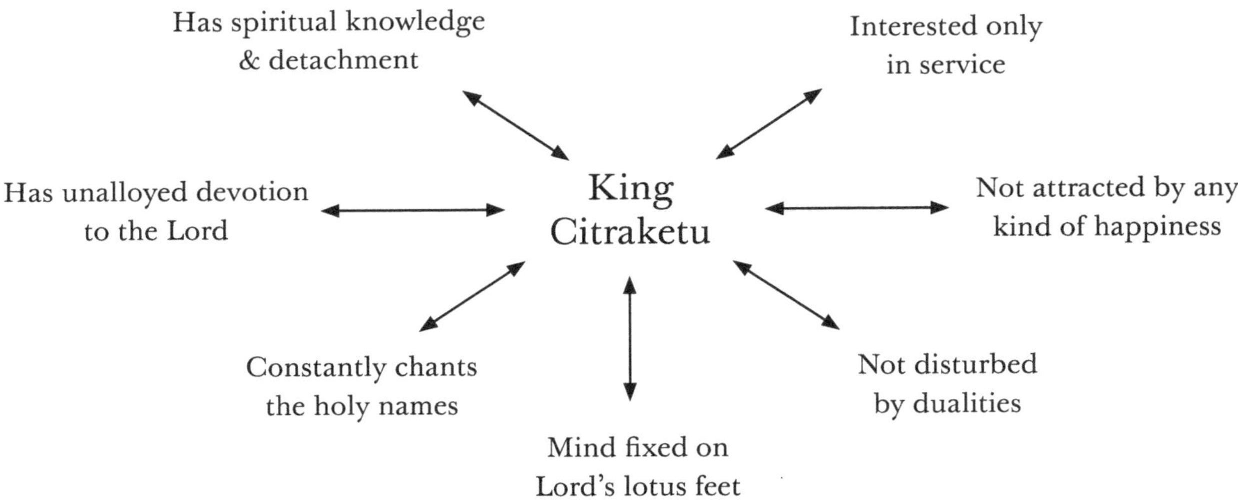

CROSSWORD

Across

1. This material world resembles what of a constantly flowing river?
4. Lord Śiva's position in the assembly of strict followers of Vedic principles (according to verse 7).
5. Citraketu's *guru* who was present in the assembly of Lord Śiva.
7. Citraketu traveled in the valleys of this mountain.
8. He has taken his birth from the lotus.
9. Devotees are interested in only this.
11. Deluded by this, the living entity wanders in the forest of the material world.

Down

2. Citraketu traveled in outer space as head of which celestial beings?
3. Lord Śiva was sitting in the assembly of saintly persons and embracing whom?
6. Citraketu appeared as a demon in whose fire sacrifice?
10. The plane in which Citraketu traveled was given by whom?

CHAPTER 17 ANSWERS

Ever-changing Waves

1. Śrīla Viśvanātha Cakravartī Ṭhākura compares the material world's nature to a mine of salt – one tastes only salt wherever one goes. Similarly, this material world is full of miseries; everything, even so-called happiness we experience, is not beneficial for us, and is in that sense a misery. So the nature of the material world is that there is misery everywhere.; 2. Wave 1: answer given; 3. Wave 2: Devotees like Nārada, Prahlāda, Citraketu, and others used their adverse circumstances to become devotees. 4. Wave 3: Demons like Rāvaṇa, Kaṁsa, and Hiraṇyakaśipu can ride on high material "waves" (have material success) and still degrade themselves; 5. Wave 4: The *Mahābhārata*, through the examples of the Pāṇḍavas and the Kauravas, shows how material benedictions of wealth, power, kingdom, etc., are not permanent for anyone, irrespective of whether they are good or evil.

Does the Lord Love Making His Devotees Suffer?

Citraketu: He was cursed by Pārvatī to become a demon. He could have counteracted that curse, but he chose to accept it and therefore got a demon's body and went through the apparent suffering of being killed by Indra; Pāṇḍavas: They were unfairly deprived of their kingdom; they could have immediately fought the Kauravas to regain it but instead chose to wait for Kṛṣṇa's plans to unfold for them. As a result, they went through multiple reversals, culminating in a war in which they lost almost all their relatives; Prahlāda: He was put through multiple difficulties by his father, Hiraṇyakaśipu. He could have chosen to "listen" to him or seek someone's help to retaliate against him but instead chose to go through the suffering. As a result, he had to face multiple attempts on his life, with apparently nobody to protect him or stop his father; Haridāsa Ṭhākura: He was beaten in 21 market places; he was never disturbed; instead, he tolerated the beating. Because his mind was fixed on the lotus feet of the Lord, he did not feel the so-called pains and pleasures caused by the dualities of this material world.

1. What feels like a material remedy may not always be a spiritual remedy; in the same way, what feels like material suffering may not always be suffering on the spiritual platform. An ordinary person, who is thinking materially, sees a situation as suffering, but a saintly person, who sees things spiritually, tries to see things from the Lord's perspective, that suffering may be purifying and meant for growth in Kṛṣṇa consciousness; 2. Parīkṣit and Citraketu saw their situations as signals from the Lord to return to Him far quicker than expected, while Haridāsa, Prahlāda, and the Pāṇḍavas saw that the Lord was using them as instruments to teach lessons to millions of suffering souls. They therefore accepted so-called unfavorable situations because they saw themselves as servants of the Lord; 3. Both the Lord and the servant act, based on a relationship of love – the servant understands why he has to take on a certain austerity, and the Lord protects the devotee while he takes on this austerity. Because of the faith in this protection, the devotee remains fearless. He is therefore able to see things in a way that others can't and take on situations that others wouldn't – all for the service of the Lord.

Humility Means No Offenses

1. No. To imbibe real humility we need to be humble and tolerant towards everyone. Śrī Caitanya Mahāprabhu emphasized that we should also show respect to everyone. By being humble and tolerant and respecting everyone as part of Kṛṣṇa, we can chant the holy names constantly and set a good example as devotees.

2. When we are humble we see ourselves as a servant of the Vaiṣṇavas, meant to give them pleasure. By being humble servants, we don't find fault with them but glorify their good qualities. In this way there is little room to find faults and commit offenses.

3. No. For our sake or inconvenience we should be humble and tolerant, but for the sake of the Lord or His devotees, we should not. For example, we should not tolerate blasphemy of the Lord or His devotees, but we can tolerate offenses to ourselves.

Crossword

Across: 1. Waves; 4. President; 5. Narada; 7. Sumeru; 8. Brahma; 9. service; 11. ignorance

Down: 2. Vidyadharas; 3. Parvati; 6. Tvasta; 10. Visnu

18

DITI VOWS TO KILL KING INDRA

The sixth chapter of the Sixth Canto discussed the descendants of Dakṣa's sixty daughters. Seventeen of those daughters married Kaśyapa Muni, and two were prominent – Aditi, the mother of the demigods, and Diti, the mother of the demons. Śukadeva Gosvāmī had described the dynasties of Aditi's twelve sons, which led to the history of Indra's killing Viśvarūpa, the son of Aditi's fourth son, Tvaṣṭā.

Now Śukadeva Gosvāmī continued to describe the descendants of Aditi's fifth son, Savitā. Then he discussed the progeny of all twelve of Aditi's sons. The famous of these sons were Soma, the moon god; Bhṛgu, son of Brahmā; Varuṇa; Vālmīki; Agastya Muni; Vasiṣṭha Ṛṣi; and Lord Vāmanadeva.

"Later I shall describe how Urukrama, Lord Vāmanadeva, appeared as the son of Kaśyapa and Aditi and how he covered the three worlds with three steps," said Śukadeva Gosvāmī.

"Now let me describe the sons of Diti, whose father was also Kaśyapa but who became demons. These demons were called Daityas because they came from the womb of Diti. However, there was one great devotee in this family – Prahlāda

Mahārāja – and his grandson Bali Mahārāja, who also surrendered his life fully to the Lord."

As we've learned before (in the Third Canto), Diti's first sons were Hiraṇyākṣa and Hiraṇyakaśipu, powerful demons worshiped by the Daityas and Dānavas. Hiraṇyakaśipu's wife, Kayādhu, gave birth to four sons – Saṁhlāda, Anuhlāda, Hlāda, and Prahlāda – and a daughter named Siṁhikā. Siṁhikā married the demon Vipracit and gave birth to another demon, Rāhu. While Rahu, in disguise, drank nectar among the demigods, the Supreme Personality of Godhead severed his head. The sons of Hlāda were Vātāpi and Ilvala. Anuhlāda had two sons, and Prahlāda had one son, named Virocana, whose son was Bali Mahārāja. Thereafter, Bali Mahārāja had one hundred sons, of whom Bāṇa was the eldest and a great devotee of Lord Śiva.

Śukadeva Gosvāmī said, "Then the 49 Maruts were born from Diti, and none of them had sons. Even though they were born from Diti, Indra gave them the position of demigods."

"How did that happen?" asked Parīkṣit Mahārāja. "Did they perform any rituals or pious activities? Please tell me."

"As I've explained before," continued Śukadeva Gosvāmī, "when Lord Viṣṇu killed the two brothers Hiraṇyākṣa and Hiraṇyakaśipu, Diti was overwhelmed with grief. She thought, 'Through Lord Viṣṇu, Lord Indra has killed my sons. How cruel and hardhearted he is! I'll only be peaceful when I kill him!'

" 'Indra thinks he'll live forever! All dead bodies are transformed into worms, stool, or ashes. If someone kills another just to protect such a body, he doesn't know the purpose of life. He is envious and goes to hell. I want to have a son who will remove Indra's madness. Let me think of a plan.'

"Thinking in this way, Diti was determined to have a son to kill Indra. She tried to satisfy Kaśyapa Muni and served him faithfully and humbly, speaking sweet words and glancing at him just to attract his mind and bring him under her control.

"Kaśyapa Muni was a learned scholar, but he was captivated by Diti's behavior. He promised her that he would fulfill her desires.

"You see, my dear King, from the beginning of creation Lord Brahmā created women from the better half of a man's body to increase the population. A woman's behavior can carry away a man's mind. So it is not surprising that the powerful sage Kaśyapa became enamored by the sweet mannerisms of his wife."

Śukadeva Gosvāmī explained that Kaśyapa Muni approached Diti and smiled sweetly. He said, "O beautiful, faultless lady, I'm so pleased with you. Tell me what you want. If a husband is pleased, there is nothing in this world or in the next that a wife cannot obtain.

"For a woman, her husband is the supreme demigod. If she is attached to material enjoyment, it is recommended that she worship the demigods or her husband. Such a wife should be chaste and obey the orders of the husband as a representative of Vāsudeva."

Kaśyapa Muni came closer to his wife, looking at her affectionately and gently placing his hand on her cheek. In a soft voice he said, "O beautiful, chaste lady, because you've worshiped me with great devotion as a representative of the Supreme Lord, I shall reward you with whatever you desire."

Diti looked away and pushed aside his hand. Turning her back to her husband, she said in a bitter voice, "O great soul, I've lost my sons because of Indra. Indra used Viṣṇu to kill them.

So I ask of only one benediction. I ask you for an immortal son who will kill Indra!"

Kaśyapa Muni flinched. "What!" he exclaimed. "Do you want me to suffer for the sin of killing Indra?"

The exalted sage paced back and forth as Diti watched, his heart racing and his mind disturbed.

"I've become attached to material enjoyment," he thought. "My mind has become attracted by the Lord's illusory energy in the form of a woman. How wretched I am! I will surely go to hell!"

His mind continued to reel: "My wife is not to blame; she is just following her nature. But I am a man. I am condemned. I couldn't control my senses. A woman's face is as attractive as a fully blossomed lotus. Her sweet words are pleasing to the ears, but her heart is as sharp as a razor. In these circumstances, who can understand the dealings of a woman? Women are supposed to be saintly, but sometimes materialistic women can kill even their husbands or sons for their own interests."

Kaśyapa shot a side glance at Diti, who was standing nearby looking down and waiting apprehensively. "I promised to give her a benediction, so I cannot violate my word," he thought. "What shall I do? Indra doesn't deserve to be killed."

Kaśyapa continued to pace the floor, his mind racing. "Aha! I have just the idea!" he thought.

Kaśyapa approached Diti. She tried to avoid her husband's eyes. Was he angry? Or did he have a slight grin on his lips? She could not tell.

"My dear wife," he said, "you will surely get a son to kill Indra, but first you must follow a vow for one year."

Diti's face lit up.

"But!" Kaśyapa said sternly, "If you deviate even a tiny bit from this vow, you will get a son who will be a friend to Indra."

Diti swallowed hard and said, "My dear *brāhmaṇa*, I accept your advice and I must follow your vow. Tell me what I should do, what is forbidden, and what will break the vow."

"To follow the vow, do not be violent or harm anyone. Do not curse anyone, and don't lie," instructed her husband. "Do not cut your nails and hair, do not touch impure things, never be angry, and do not speak or associate with wicked people. Wear only clean, washed clothes and fresh garlands. Eat fresh food. Do not eat the *prasāda* of goddess Kālī, anything contaminated by flesh or fish, or any food touched by a *śūdra*.

"Before breakfast, wear clean clothes and adorn yourself with turmeric, sandalwood pulp, and other auspicious items. Then worship the cows, the *brāhmaṇas*, the goddess of fortune, and the Supreme Lord Acyuta. . . ."

Like this, Kaśyapa Muni gave Diti a list of instructions, including when and how to lie down, how to dress when going outside, and how to worship mothers with sons.

Finally he said, "When you become pregnant, worship your husband by offering him prayers and meditating on him, thinking of him as if he is the embryo within your womb.

"If you perform this vow, called *puṁsavana*, adhering to it for one year with faith, you will give birth to a son destined to kill Indra. If, however, there is any discrepancy in following this vow, the son will be Indra's friend."

"Oh yes, my lord!" Diti exclaimed, her face beaming with happiness. "I will strictly follow your instructions." She touched her husband's feet to receive his blessings, and he gently touched her head. He smiled to himself, knowing well that all these rules and regulations were meant to cleanse her heart of all contamination.

When Diti became pregnant, she felt as if her heart would burst with joy. She faithfully began discharging the vow.

"Was she able to fulfill the vow till the end? Did she really give birth to a son who killed Indra?" asked an impatient King Parīkṣit.

"O King," Śukadeva smiled and said, "Indra knew of the vow, so he hoped that his aunt Diti would somehow break it. And he wanted to make sure that he would be the one to spot any fault in her observance of the vow. Secretly, Indra faithfully served Diti in her *āśrama*. Every day at the same time he brought her forest fruits and flowers for her *yajñas*, *kuśa* grass, leaves, sprouts, earth, and water. And all the time he would sneakily watch if there was any fault in her ritualistic ceremony. But Diti did everything perfectly. As the days passed, Indra became desperate and anxious.

"Day after day, Diti continued to strictly execute all the principles of the vow. She did not notice that devotion to the Lord was growing in her heart and cleansing it at the same time. Eventually, she became weak and thin because of her strictness, and one day she neglected to wash her mouth, hands, and feet after eating and went to sleep during the evening twilight, which was forbidden.

"Indra was there and spotted the fault! He couldn't lose such an opportunity. Using his mystic power, he entered Diti's womb while she was fast asleep. With his thunderbolt he cut her glowing embryo into seven pieces. Other souls entered into the new pieces and began to cry. 'Don't cry!' shouted Indra, and then he cut each of them into seven pieces again. There were now

49 new bodies in which more new entities entered. Folding their hands they cried, 'O Indra, we are your brothers, the Maruts. Why are you trying to kill us?'

"Indra was taken aback. He realized that they were his devoted followers and said, 'If you are my brothers, then don't be afraid.'

"My dear King Parīkṣit, just as you were protected in your mother's womb by the Supreme Lord when you were burning from Aśvatthāmā's *brahmāstra*, similarly when Diti's embryo was cut into 49 pieces by Indra's thunderbolt, they were saved by the Lord's mercy.

"If one worships the Supreme Personality of Godhead even once, he gets the greatest benefit. And what is that? He is promoted to the spiritual world and gets the same bodily features of Lord Viṣṇu. Diti worshiped Lord Viṣṇu for almost a year, observing the sacred *puṁsavana* vow, so she naturally got great spiritual strength and gave birth to the 49 Maruts. So it is no wonder that the Maruts became equal to the demigods by the Lord's mercy."

Śukadeva Gosvāmī narrated how when Diti woke up and saw her 49 sons in front of her with Indra, she was astonished. But she wasn't angry or disturbed anymore. She smiled from ear to ear, seeing that her brilliantly effulgent sons were now friends with King Indra. Such is the power of devotional service – all hatred and envy are completely vanquished from the heart.

Diti looked at Indra, her eyes laden with tears. "My dear son," she said softly, "just imagine, I adhered to this difficult vow just so I could get a son to kill you. I prayed for one son, but instead I got 49! My dear son Indra, how did this happen? Please don't lie to me. Please tell me."

Indra's voice was choked with emotion: "My dear mother, I lost sight of religion because I was blinded with selfish interest. When I found out that you were performing this strict spiritual vow, I wanted to find fault in you, and when I did find such a fault, I entered your womb and cut your embryo into seven pieces. Then I cut each of those pieces into seven pieces again. However, by the grace of the Supreme Lord, none of them died. I was shocked to see them all alive. But then I realized that this was only the secondary result of your devotional service to Lord Viṣṇu.

"Although devotees who worship the Lord do not desire anything material, even liberation, Lord Kṛṣṇa fulfills all their desires.

"O mother, what a fool I've been. Please forgive me for my offenses." Indra bowed his head and his voice trembled. "Your 49 sons were unharmed because of your devotional service to the Lord. As an enemy I cut them to pieces, but they didn't die, because of your devotion. All glories to you, mother." With this, Indra respectfully bowed down to his aunt, and with her permission and blessings, he went back to the heavenly planets with his brothers, the Maruts.

Themes and Key Messages

Please go through this table of themes and key messages, with corresponding verses, and discuss each topic further.

THEMES	REFERENCES	KEY MESSAGES
This material world is going on under the spell of sexual desire between man and woman.	6.18.29–30	Even though Kaśyapa Muni was an exalted, learned soul, he was overcome with sexual attraction, which made him illusioned. This entire universe is going on under the spell of sexual attachment, which was created by Brahmā to increase the population of the universe. By this attraction a man becomes involved in the materialistic way of life. Sexual desire is so powerful that if one is with a woman in a solitary place, his desires can increase.
If a husband and wife are attached to each other for advancement in Kṛṣṇa consciousness, their relationship is very effective for this advancement.	6.18.33–34	It is recommended that if a woman is very materially attached, she can worship the demigods or her husband to progress. If women, who are usually attached to their husbands, serve their husbands as representatives of the Lord, the women benefit, just as Ajāmila benefited by calling for Nārāyaṇa, his son. The husband can be considered the *pati-guru*, the husband spiritual master. However, if both husband and wife are attached to one another for advancement in Kṛṣṇa consciousness, their relationship is favorable and supports their advancement.
Household life in Kali-yuga is extremely dangerous unless both husband and wife are trained in Kṛṣṇa consciousness.	6.18.40–41	In general, women who are materialistic want to enjoy by satisfying the husband. Therefore household life is very risky unless both husband and wife are trained in Kṛṣṇa consciousness or the wife follows her devotee husband. Such a husband should be trained in Kṛṣṇa consciousness from the beginning of life, so that he can deliver his dependents. A relationship without spiritual consciousness but only for sense gratification is dangerous because it entangles one more in material consciousness and binds one to the material world. Kaśyapa Muni directed his wife in such a way that she became purified.

Themes	References	Key Messages
Devotional service can purify anyone regardless of one's motives.	6.18.65–68	If one approaches the Lord with material desire, or even sinful desire, one becomes purified from the desire, just as Diti became purified by performing the *puṁsavana* ceremony to have a son to kill Indra. Everyone, pure or impure, is an eternal soul meant to serve the Supreme Lord, so no one is too impure to become purified, even if they have material motives. Whether one has many material desires, no material desires, or desires liberation, one must worship the Supreme Personality of Godhead. (*SB* 2.3.10)
The fruit of pure devotional service is greater than mixed devotion.	6.18.69–77	When one approaches the Lord with material desires, the Lord fulfills the desire and at the same time purifies the devotee of the desire, just as the Lord purified Dhruva and gave him the polestar planet even though he didn't desire it anymore. Nothing is too wonderful for the Lord. Similarly, He gave Diti not just one son but 49 sons who became Indra's friends. Both Indra and Diti became friends as a result of being purified. However, when a devotee only desires to be a servant of Kṛṣṇa without any material motives he is the most intelligent, because the Lord gives Himself to such a devotee. The pure devotee therefore does not aspire for material happiness because he gets the greatest happiness by loving Kṛṣṇa.

Higher-Thinking Questions

Now try to deepen your understanding of this chapter by delving into Śrīla Prabhupāda's purports and reflecting on the following questions:

1. In this chapter Śrīla Prabhupāda refers to women as "less intelligent" and having the tendency to enjoy. This is often misinterpreted to mean all women. What kind of women is Prabhupāda referring to here? Explain.

2. Verse 47 describes one good quality of a woman. What is it? How can this quality give her immense benefit unlike striving to be independent as encouraged in the modern world?

3. In verse 40 purport, Śrīla Prabhupāda expresses that householder life can be dangerous for a husband and wife who don't take to Kṛṣṇa consciousness. How is this so as indicated in the story of Diti and Kaśyapa?

4. What was Kaśyapa Muni's first instruction to his wife in verse 47? According to Śrīla Prabhupāda why is it important to curb this tendency?

5. In this canto we learned how the fallen Ajāmila got the mercy of the Lord by chanting

His holy names, how Dakṣa with mixed devotion got the *darśana* of the Lord, and how Citraketu with mixed desire also became purified, and then as Vṛtrāsura he achieved perfection and went back to Godhead. According to verses 74 and 75, why did Vṛtrāsura achieve such a destination? [Hint: What are the advantages of pure devotional service?]

6. Why doesn't a devotee desire material happiness as explained in verse 75 and purport?

ACTIVITIES

In this section you will find many exciting things to do. These activities will get you thinking, moving, drawing, and having loads of fun.

Artistic Activity

CLEANING THE HEART

In this fun activity, we will illustrate the impure heart being transformed by devotional service. We will begin by drawing a heart shape and adding some dirt on it. The dirt represents impure desires. Then we will create two hearts on the canvas: one will represent a bright clean heart after performing devotional service and the other will represent the radiance of a purified heart that enlivens and benefits others, just as Indra was positively affected by Diti's devotional service and the appearance of the 49 Maruts.

What you will need:
2 white canvases or thick card stock paper (6x8 inches); old canvas or cardboard (same size or smaller); contact paper (same size as the canvas) – also known as kitchen shelf liner, with a sticky side when the backing paper is removed; scissors; bright acrylic colors; 2 teaspoonful dirt or sand; water; 4 earbuds; old, expired credit card or similar hard surface

Steps:

1. First create the impure heart representation. Draw a heart on an old canvas or cardboard and paint it with some dull color paint. Sprinkle some dirt or sand on the wet paint and allow to dry. This heart reflects some of the heart's common impurities, such as selfishness, anger, greed, lust, etc.

2. Now keep the two canvases side by side. Cut the contact sheet to the size of the canvas and fold it in half as shown in Image 1. Draw the half heart on the contact sheet.

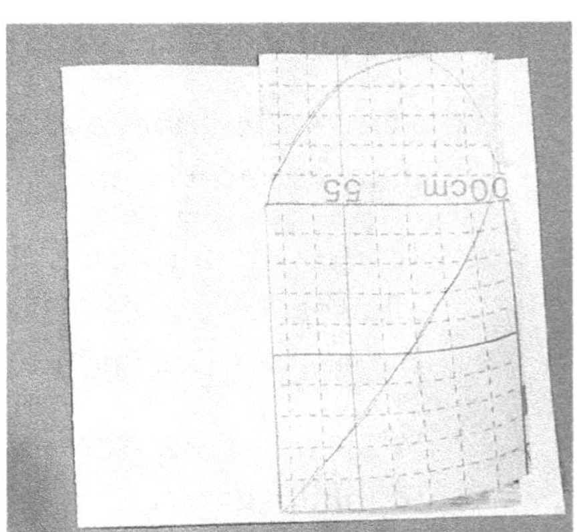

Image 1

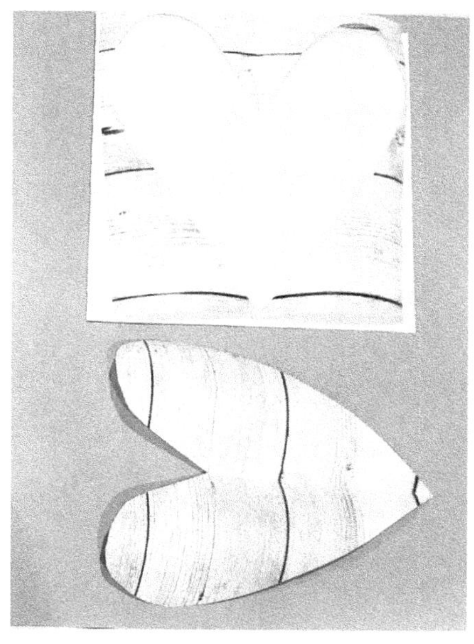

Image 2

3. Cut along the lines, and when you open it, you will have two stencils: the heart stencil and the negative space stencil as shown in Image 2.

4. Peel the backing of the negative space stencil and place the stencil on the first canvas (Image 3).

5. On the second canvas, place the heart stencil (Image 7).

6. Squeeze pea-size bright paints on to the top of the white heart on Canvas 1 (Image 4).

7. Using the credit card, drag the colors downwards to mix them together in an abstract pattern (Image 5). When the paint dries, peel the contact paper or the negative space stencil.

8. Our first bright and beautiful heart is ready (Image 6).

Image 3

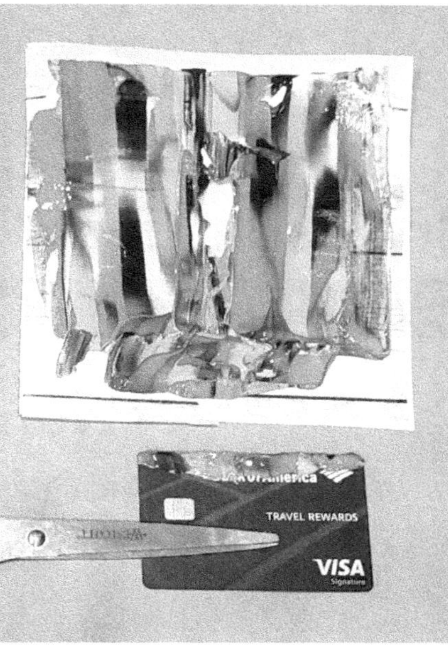

Image 4

Image 5

Image 6

Image 7

9. Now dip earbuds into different colors, beginning with red, magenta, and green, and press them on to the canvas on the outline of the heart stencil. Add lighter colors like yellow and pink toward the end (Image 8).

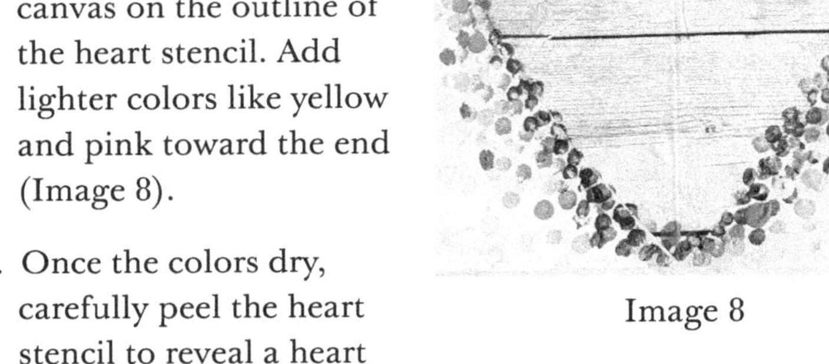

Image 8

Image 9

10. Once the colors dry, carefully peel the heart stencil to reveal a heart radiating joy and devotion (Image 9).

11. If you like, you can draw and paint a picture of Kṛṣṇa, or His lotus feet, in the white space of the heart.

You may also glue all three hearts onto a larger sheet of canvas or board and create a collage. Label them, showing how a dirty heart can become clean, bright, and colorful with love and devotion through *bhakti-yoga*.

Introspective Activity

... to bring out the reflective devotee in you

DEVOTIONAL SERVICE PURIFIES THE HEART

This chapter brings out the process and power of devotional service. Devotional service has the power to purify, and the following are examples of how devotional service purified everyone involved:

Process: Diti

1. Diti accepted her husband as her spiritual master.
2. Diti followed his instructions.
3. Diti served him and the Lord faithfully.

Process: Indra

1. Indra served Diti faithfully.

Result

1. Indra became purified of his desire to harm Diti's son.
2. Diti became purified of the desire to avenge the deaths of Hiraṇyākṣa and Hiraṇyakaśipu.
3. Diti and Indra were honest with each other.
4. Diti forgave Indra.

Have you ever experienced the power of devotional service in this way in your relationships? Can you think of any situation in which you were able to tell the truth to someone or forgive someone for a mistake just because you realized that it is important to behave that way? Did you find it hard? Did you find it satisfying once you did it? How did it change your relationship? Do you think that your practice of devotional service helped you in the situation or you had to consciously endeavor to behave in the proper way? Or do you think both – devotional service and trying to inculcate good behavior and qualities – are necessary?

Try to compare your situation to Diti's. Discuss as a class.

Critical-Thinking Activity

... to bring out the spiritual investigator in you

DEVOTION PURIFIES EVERYONE

In this chapter we see how Indra, Diti, and the Maruts got purified by devotional service. In the *Bhāgavatam* we've learned of many others becoming purified by the process of devotional service.

But how exactly does the process work? Why is it that those who take to devotional service transform their hearts? Given below are some reasons:

1. They realize that they are not alone but the Supreme Lord is their creator and feel a sense of belonging to Him.

2. They understand that the Lord loves them and start behaving in a way that pleases Him.

3. They experience the protection of the Lord and want to remain in that protection.

4. They understand the plan of the Lord and want to act according to that plan.

5. They realize that the Lord is always present in their lives, fulfilling all their desires (including material desires), and they feel grateful for that.

Now, below are some devotees we've read about so far in Canto 6. Each of them took shelter of the Lord in their own way and got purified:

Ajāmila   Diti   Citraketu   Indra   Vṛtrāsura

Split the class into five groups or have five individuals do this activity. Each group or individual researches how one of the above devotees got purified and what motivated them to change. Make notes. Then, each group should select one member to play the chosen character. This person should deliver a short monologue to the rest of the class, explaining the reasons they took to devotional service, how they got purified, and why they chose to remain a devotee of the Lord.

Note: Students should come up with their own understanding and realization of the pastimes based on what they have read. The mentor should guide them to think of different qualities that drive a devotee: love, faith, fearlessness, knowledge, austerity, etc. Students should also be encouraged to understand how the process is personal and it is human nature to want to please a person whom we love, or who loves us. Kṛṣṇa consciousness is thus driven by this personal element, and since Kṛṣṇa is a perfect person, the devotee trying to align to His will/personality also become perfect.

Action Activity

... to get you moving and learning

DEITY WORSHIP IS PURIFYING

This chapter presents the glories of performing worship of Lord Viṣṇu. Śrīla Prabhupāda established Deity worship so that we can become purified by following the rules of cleanliness, punctuality, austerity, recitation of *mantras*, and meditation on the Lord's form and activities.

In this activity, you will explore the above principles in detail and assist your parent or a senior devotee in their Deity worship.

Choose one from the following two Deity worship activities: Doing *ārati* or offering *bhoga*.

Then assist one of your elders in the service of your choice regularly, at least once a week.

In your notebook, write down the steps of the service. Please include the rules, the *mantras* used, and the mood of doing the service. Then try doing the service on your own to your Deities or the pictures on your altar.

Writing and Language Activities

... to help you understand better

NARRATIVE ESSAY: DEVOTIONAL SERVICE CAN PURIFY ANYONE

In this chapter we learned that even if one has material desires or motives, one can get purified by devotional service to Kṛṣṇa. Everyone, pure or impure, is an eternal soul meant to serve the Supreme Lord.

Write a story on one of the following topics to show how anyone can be transformed by the mercy of a devotee and devotional service:

1. A prisoner receives a *Bhagavad-gītā* in jail.

2. A homeless man receives regular *prasādam* from a devotee.

3. A skeptical teenager sees the *harināma* party on the street and is given a book.

4. A *yoga* student comes to the temple and learns about *bhakti-yoga*.

5. A university science graduate attends a scientific presentation of Kṛṣṇa consciousness.

TRUE OR FALSE: INSPIRING QUALITIES OF KAŚYAPA MUNI

Kaśyapa Muni became captivated by Diti's behavior and gave her a boon that he would fulfill her desire. When she asked for an immortal son who would kill Indra, Kaśyapa Muni was taken aback. Despite the provoking situation, Kaśyapa did not lose his sense of discrimination. Please read verses 39 to 45 and answer the following with a True or False. If false, give a reason for your answer:

1. When Kaśyapa Muni heard Diti's desire, he immediately condemned her.

2. Kaśyapa broke his promise to Diti to protect Indra.

3. Kaśyapa ordered Diti to first become purified and then begin worship of Lakṣmī-Nārāyaṇa.

4. The sign of advanced devotees is that they try to raise the consciousness of everyone around them, including someone who has cheated or harmed them.

5. We can learn from Kaśyapa's example of how to reflect upon our own weakness in a conflict and overcome it instead of defending ourselves by putting the blame on the other

party. Devotees are always ready to learn and purify themselves and work for the welfare of others.

INTERVIEW: MARRIAGE ADVICE

In this chapter we learned that Lord Brahmā created sexual attachment between a man and a woman to increase the population. When this attachment becomes too strong, a person automatically gets bound in material life. Therefore, a husband and wife must be attached in Kṛṣṇa consciousness, and the *vivāha-saṁskāra*, Kṛṣṇa conscious marriage, is recommended.

Conduct an interview with three devotee couples in your community to understand practically how a Kṛṣṇa conscious marriage is beneficial. Use the following prompts to guide your interview:

6. For how long have you been married?

7. How did you meet? Was yours an arranged marriage?

8. Why did you decide to live in a Kṛṣṇa conscious marriage? How is it beneficial to you?

9. What are the challenges you face in your relationship and in performing devotional service?

10. How do you think you can overcome these challenges?

11. Does making Kṛṣṇa the center of your relationship help resolve conflicts and bring you closer?

12. How do you balance your family duties with other devotional activities and practices?

13. What is your advice to other householders?

Jot down your answers from each interview and then write a paragraph with the overall conclusions of your interview. Do these conclusions align with the conclusions about householder life in this chapter?

CHAPTER 18 ANSWERS

True or False

1. False: On the contrary he condemned himself for his attachment to material enjoyment.

2. False: He did not want to break his promise nor did he think that Indra deserved to die.

3. False: Devotional service to the Lord will purify everyone regardless of their contamination.

4. True: Kaśyapa Muni directed his wife in such a way that she became purified. He did not give up his responsibility of delivering his dependent wife, though she served him with a cheating tendency.

5. True.

19

THE PUṀSAVANA RITUALISTIC CEREMONY

Mahārāja Parīkṣit could understand the power and purpose of the *puṁsavana* vow. He asked, "My dear lord, I want to hear the details of this vow, for by observing it one can please the Supreme Lord, Viṣṇu."

Śukadeva Gosvāmī nodded and said, "This vow can fulfill all one's desires. On the bright fortnight of the month of Agrahāyaṇa [November–December], a woman should begin this regulated devotional service with a vow of penance. Before worshiping Lord Viṣṇu she should hear the story of the Maruts' birth. In the morning she should clean her teeth, bathe, dress herself with white cloth and ornaments, and before breakfast worship Viṣṇu with Lakṣmī.

"She should then pray to the Lord: 'My dear Lord, You are full in all opulences, but I don't ask You for opulence. I simply offer my obeisances to You. You are the husband and master of Lakṣmīdevī, the goddess of fortune, who also has all opulences. O Lord, You are the master of everyone. You are the Supreme Personality of Godhead because You have all opulences, causeless mercy, strength, and divine qualities.'

"Then she should offer obeisances to Mother Lakṣmī and pray to her: 'O internal energy of Lord Viṣṇu, you are as good as Lord Viṣṇu Himself. O goddess of fortune, please be kind to me.'

"Next, she should recite this *mantra* to Lord Viṣṇu: '*oṁ namo bhagavate mahā-puruṣāya. . .* My Lord Viṣṇu, You are most powerful, full in six opulences, and are the best of all enjoyers. O husband of Mother Lakṣmī, I offer my respects to You. You are accompanied by many associates, such as Viśvaksena. I offer all paraphernalia for Your worship.'

"In this way, one should chant this *mantra* every day with great attention while worshiping Lord Viṣṇu with all paraphernalia, such as water for washing His feet and for His bath. One should also offer Him garments, a sacred thread, ornaments, beautiful scents, flowers, incense, and lamps. Then one should offer ghee to the sacred fire and chant the mantra *oṁ namo bhagavate mahā-puruṣāya mahāvibhūti-pataye svāhā*."

"Hmmm . . ." interrupted Parīkṣit Mahārāja, "It is amazing how Kaśyapa Muni engaged his wife in worshiping Lord Viṣṇu. But not just Viṣṇu, Lakṣmī also!"

"Oh yes," said Śukadeva Gosvāmī, smiling. "Lord Viṣṇu and Lakṣmī are a powerful combination. Lord Viṣṇu is not alone in the heart. He is always with Lakṣmīdevī. They are never separated. They can bestow all benedictions and good fortune. So if one desires all opulences, one should worship Lakṣmī-Nārāyaṇa with great devotion following the process I mentioned. The duty of everyone is to worship Lakṣmī-Nārāyaṇa!"

Mahārāja Parīkṣit bowed his head in obeisance to Lakṣmī-Nārāyaṇa, envisioning the divine couple within his heart. He knew that to worship Lakṣmī-Nārāyaṇa even with material desires would purify the heart and elevate the consciousness to pure Kṛṣṇa consciousness.

"Chant this *mantra* ten times while offering *daṇḍavats*," Śukadeva Gosvāmī continued. "In this way, fall like a rod on the ground with your mind humbled in devotion. Then, you should chant this prayer, 'My Lord Viṣṇu and Mother Lakṣmī, you own the entire creation, and you are the cause of the creation. Mother Lakṣmī, you are very difficult to understand because in the material world you appear as the Lord's external energy, but actually you are always the Lord's internal energy.'

'My dear Lord Viṣṇu, You are the Supreme Person, the master of all energies, and the personified enjoyer of all sacrifices. Lakṣmī embodies all spiritual activities and is the original form of worship that is offered to You. Lakṣmī is the reservoir of all spiritual qualities, and You are the enjoyer of those qualities, because You, Lord Viṣṇu, are the enjoyer of everything! You live as the Supersoul in all living beings, and the goddess of fortune, as the external energy, manifests as their bodies, minds, and senses. She also has a holy name and form, but You are the origin of all such names and forms.

'O Lord Nārāyaṇa and Mother Lakṣmī, you are the supreme rulers of the three worlds. Therefore, may my ambitions be fulfilled by your grace.' "

Śukadeva Gosvāmī sighed and then paused. He looked into the bright eyes of Parīkṣit Mahārāja who had now forgotten the ill fate that would soon befall him. For him, hearing these narrations were giving him real life.

"You see, my dear Parīkṣit, Lakṣmīdevī is the Lord's powerful energy, His *māyā-śakti*, the mother of the universe," Śukadeva Gosvāmī said. "Thus one should worship Lord Viṣṇu, who is known as Śrīnivāsa, along with Mother Lakṣmī, by offering prayers as I mentioned.

"After removing the paraphernalia for worship, one should offer Lakṣmī-Nārāyaṇa water to wash their hands and mouths and then worship them again. One should smell the remnants of the food offered to them and again worship them.

"My dear Parīkṣit Mahārāja, in this way a wife should offer the Lord's *prasāda* to her husband and worship him with devotion as the representative of the Lord. The husband, being pleased with his wife, should look after his family."

"So, should only a wife perform such a vow of devotional service?" asked Mahārāja Parīkṣit.

"No, between the husband and wife, either can execute this devotional service. Because of their good relationship, both will enjoy the result. If the wife is unable to perform this process, the husband should, and the faithful wife will share the result.

"One should just focus on this vow of devotional service without being deviated to anything else. One should offer the remnants of *prasāda*, flower garlands, sandalwood pulp, and ornaments to the *brāhmaṇas* and the women who live with their husbands and children. Most importantly, one must follow all the regulative principles to worship Lord Viṣṇu with great devotion.

"Then after Lord Viṣṇu is laid in His bed, one should take *prasāda.* In this way, husband and wife will become purified and all their desires will be fulfilled.

"For one year this vow should be observed, and after the one year, one should fast on the full-moon day in the month of Kārttika [October–November].

"On the morning of the next day, one should worship Lord Kṛṣṇa as before and cook a grand feast as done on festival days. Sweet rice should be cooked with ghee, and the husband should offer it into the sacred fire twelve times.

"Thereafter, he should satisfy the *brāhmaṇas* and receive their blessings. Then only he should take *prasāda*. But before taking his meal, he should first offer *prasāda* to the *guru*. The wife should then eat the remnants of sweet rice, which will ensure that she gets a learned, devoted son and all good fortune.

"Both husband and wife will get everything they desire from following this ritualistic ceremony – good fortune, opulence, sons, good reputation, and a good home. A Kṛṣṇa conscious husband and wife will thus be happy in this material world and eventually be promoted to the spiritual world.

"By following this vow, an unmarried girl will get a husband, a mother who has lost her child after birth can get another child with long

life and can become wealthy, an ugly woman can become beautiful, and a diseased man can become healthy. Those who recite this narration while offering oblations to the *pitās* and demigods will get the favor of the demigods. And when one performs this ritualistic ceremony, Lord Viṣṇu and Lakṣmī are very pleased with the devotee.

"O King Parīkṣit, I have now fully described how Diti performed this ceremony and as a result had a happy life and good children, the Maruts. I've tried to explain this to you as elaborately as I could."

Mahārāja Parīkṣit bowed his head to his spiritual master. His heart was full and his mind peaceful. He knew there was more to come, more wonderful truths and narrations from the realized sage, Śrīla Śukadeva Gosvāmī.

Themes and Key Messages

Please go through this table of themes and key messages, with corresponding verses, and discuss each topic further.

THEMES	REFERENCES	KEY MESSAGES
The devotee appreciates the Lord by offering whatever he can to worship the Lord, and the Lord blesses the devotee with all opulences.	6.19.4	The Lord is perfect and complete, full in all opulences (wealth, strength, beauty, knowledge, fame, and renunciation); therefore we only need to take shelter of Him. By worshiping the Lord with whatever we have – even a leaf, flower, fruit, or water – with devotion, the Lord is pleased and blesses us with all opulences. However, a pure devotee does not ask anything material from the Lord.
The Lord is the master of everyone, yet He extends His causeless mercy to His devotees by becoming dependent on them.	6.19.5	The Lord is quite competent to do everything on His own, yet He depends on His devotees to perform certain tasks. This indicates the confidential relationship between the Lord and His devotees. He gives them His special mercy to perform certain tasks or activities on His behalf so they can become glorious. He also acts in a dependent or subordinate relationship as a son or a chariot driver to increase the love of His devotees and to interact in this loving relationship.
If one has material desires, one can worship Lakṣmī-Nārāyaṇa but not Lakṣmī on her own.	6.19.6, 9	Lakṣmī and Nārāyaṇa are always situated in everyone's heart. Lord Viṣṇu always stays with his eternal consort, Lakṣmī, His internal energy. One cannot receive any opulence or blessings by worshiping Lakṣmī alone; one should worship Lakṣmī and Nārāyaṇa together if one wants to elevate one's consciousness and free one's heart from material contamination. Therefore, a Vaiṣṇava serves the Lord along with His spiritual energy (*śakti*), including Rādhā-Kṛṣṇa, Sītā-Rāma, Lakṣmī-Nārāyaṇa, and Rukmiṇī- Dvārakādhīśa.

Just as the Supreme Personality of Godhead is spiritual, Lakṣmīdevī is also spiritual; she is His internal energy. The Lord never engages in pleasure pastimes with the external, material energy.	6.19.11–14	The Lord's internal energy, His spiritual energy, is meant directly for His pleasure; the Lord does not have pastimes with the material energy. According to the followers of Caitanya Mahāprabhu, Lakṣmī is in the category of *viṣṇu-tattva*, not *jīva-tattva*. In other words, she is not an ordinary living entity but has the same potencies as Lord Viṣṇu. From Lakṣmīdevī the material energy expands; therefore she is addressed as the mother of all creation. As the puṁsavana vrata demonstrates, everything in the world should be seen in relation to Kṛṣṇa and should be used in His service.
When the husband and wife cooperate in service to the Lord, they can have a harmonious relationship and receive great spiritual results.	6.19.17–28	When a wife is chaste and the husband is sincere, they can have a solid relationship. And when they serve the Lord together, making Him the center of their relationship and lives, they receive all benedictions from the Lord. They can be happy in the material world and be promoted to the spiritual world. This is the result of pleasing the Lord and His consort, Lakṣmīdevī.

Higher-Thinking Questions

Now try to deepen your understanding of this chapter by delving into Śrīla Prabhupāda's purports and reflecting on the following questions:

1. Although the Lord is quite competent to perform any task on His own, why does He depend on His devotees for a particular work? (See verse 5 purport.)

2. According to verse 6 purport, why can't one keep Lakṣmī in one's home without Lord Viṣṇu? What does Lakṣmī become for someone without the service of the Lord?

3. Some people address a poor man as *daridra-nārāyaṇa*. Why does Śrīla Prabhupāda emphasize in verse 9 purport that this is wrong?

4. Can you see the relation of the *puṁsavana* vow to the Deity worship that Śrīla Prabhupāda has introduced in ISKCON temples worldwide? From verses 7, 15, and 16, choose at least three processes of worship that are similar. How do you think that doing these activities can increase our Kṛṣṇa consciousness?

5. Verse 13 purport explains why Śrī Caitanya Mahāprabhu considered Lakṣmīdevī identical with the *viṣṇu-tattva*. Explain in your own words His reasoning. When can Lakṣmī be described as different from Viṣṇu?

6. How can a husband and wife be happy together according to verse 25 purport?

ACTIVITIES

In this section you will find many exciting things to do. These activities
will get you thinking, moving, drawing, and having loads of fun.

Artistic Activity

... to reveal your creativity

ADORNING LAKṢMĪ-NĀRĀYAṆA

Our ISKCON society is well known for its high standard of Deity worship and for meticulous
deity dressing. Although most temples have Rādhā-Kṛṣṇa Deities, Śrīla Prabhupāda guided us
to worship Them in the mood and opulence of Lakṣmī-Nārāyaṇa.

For this art activity choose the Deities you are most attracted to, either at your home, your
local temple, in the holy *dhāmas*, or any ISKCON temple in the world. If it's at your local
temple, take a photo of the dressing for easy reference.

What you will need: One photo or picture of your favorite *darśana* and *śṛṅgāra* (dress and
decorations); the template of Lakṣmī-Nārāyaṇa given in the Resources; pencils; coloring
material of your choice: watercolors, color pencils, or crayons, etc.; decorations (optional)

Directions:
- Study the photo or picture for a few minutes and note what makes the dressing pleasing.
  What color scheme did the *pūjārīs* use? Did they use the principles of art, like harmony,
  symmetry, variety of shapes and colors, focal point of interest, etc.
- On the template, draw the details of the ornaments and clothing lightly with pencil. Note:
  Viṣṇu doesn't hold a flute but holds four items in four hands; He also wears a crown instead
  of a turban. Lakṣmīdevī stands in a blessing pose and also wears a crown.
- Add color, beginning with the head and gradually moving downwards. Try to include
  various textures and contrasting colors (with shadows and light areas) to make your
  drawing look as real as possible.
- Glue on decorative beads or sequins for jewelry or dress enhancements.
- Share your art with the *pūjārīs* of your local temple and express your appreciation for their
  devotion and expertise.

Action Activity

SANKALPA: A VOW FOR A WEEK

In this chapter we learned of the *puṁsavana* vow to please Lord Viṣṇu. In this age, the method to please the Lord the most is the *yuga-dharma*, or *harināma-saṅkīrtana*. Let us follow a vow for a week to improve our chanting of the holy names and thereby please the Lord.

Please request your teacher or parent to give you a few practical guidelines that will nourish your chanting in *japa* or *kīrtana*. The goal is to develop discipline and perseverance and consciously remember to do *japa* or *kīrtana* for Kṛṣṇa's pleasure.

In your notebook write all the guidelines you intend to follow.

Examples: 1. Not using cell phones or having cell phones around during chanting; 2. Sleeping early and rising early to chant during the *brāhma-muhūrta* hours; 3. Practicing no fault-finding; 4. Practicing good posture while chanting; 5. Pronouncing the syllables of the holy names clearly; 6. Not expecting attention for oneself; 7. Endeavoring to chant sincerely from the heart; 8. Reading about the holy name, etc.

Then try to follow them diligently for at least a week. After a week, note your observations, and if you like the result, continue and further your practices.

Tip: Do not make resolutions that are too hard to maintain; at the same time, they should be more than what you usually do.

Critical-Thinking Activity

A CONTRADICTION: DEPENDENT INDEPENDENCE

In purport 5 Śrīla Prabhupāda writes, "Even though the Supreme Personality of Godhead is endowed with all possessions and is self-sufficient, He depends on His devotees."

Toward the end of the purport, Śrīla Prabhupāda continues, "The most important aspect of the Supreme Lord's self-sufficiency is that He depends on His devotees. This is called

His causeless mercy. The devotee who has perceived this causeless mercy of the Supreme Personality of Godhead by realization can understand the master and the servant."

Let us understand what this means. Śrīla Prabhupāda is bringing out an apparent contradiction here. A contradiction is a combination of statements, ideas, or features which are opposed to one another.

Śrīla Prabhupāda states the contradiction in the first statement:

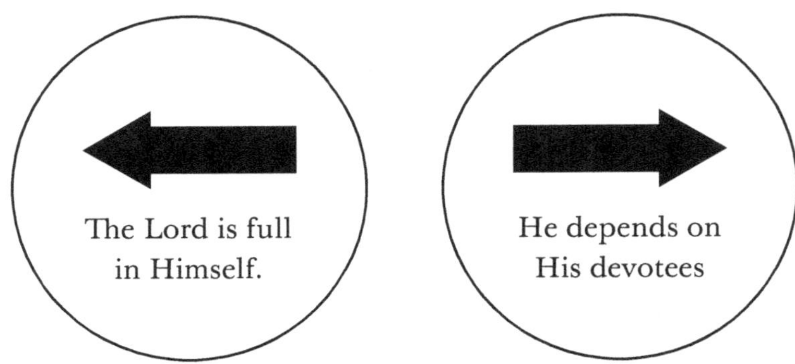

- Fact 1: The Supreme Lord is full in Himself; that is, He does not need anything from outside of Himself to be happy.
- Fact 2: He depends on His devotees for many things.

Contradiction: If the Lord depends on someone else, how can He still be called self-sufficient (or full in Himself)?

To resolve the contradiction, Śrīla Prabhupāda presents several case studies (examples) to show how the Lord depends on His devotees:

Example 1 (*Bhagavad-gītā*):
He asks His devotees to make Him an offering of *patram puṣpaṁ phalaṁ toyam* – a leaf, flower, fruit or water – in devotion, although He is in no need of these things.

Example 2 (*Śrīmad Bhagavatam*):
As the child of mother Yaśodā, He requests His mother for some food as if He were very hungry.

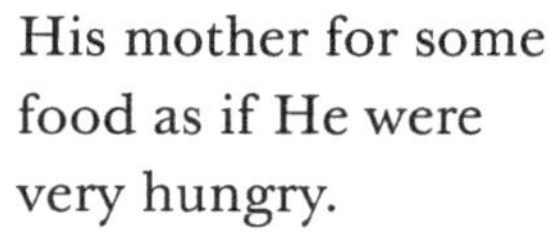

Example 3 (*Bhagavad-gītā*):
He becomes the chariot driver of Arjuna although He is the enjoyer and creator of the three worlds.

Example 4 (Śrīnāthji):
He tells His devotee that He is buried in the earth, and, as if unable to come out Himself, He requests His devotee to rescue Him.

Example 5 (Śrīla Prabhupāda):
He requests Śrīla Prabhupāda to preach His glories all over the world, although He alone is quite competent to perform this task.

Set up a discussion to resolve the contradiction stated above, using the examples mentioned and any others you may be able to present.

Resolving a contradiction involves:
- Checking if Fact 1 is true on its own.
- Checking if Fact 2 is true on its own.
- Checking if Fact 1 and Fact 2 can be true when put together, at least under certain conditions.
- Supplying any additional information/understanding needed for Fact 1 and Fact 2 to become true together, at least under certain conditions.

Once the discussion is completed, note down how you resolved the above contradiction.

Writing and Language Activities

... to help you understand better

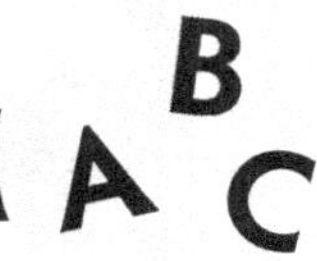

ARTICLE: LAKṢMĪ WORSHIP IS ONLY COMPLETE WITH NĀRĀYAṆA WORSHIP

It is a general practice among the Hindu community to worship Lakṣmīdevī. Often, though, worshipers do not understand that Mother Lakṣmī should be worshiped alongside Lord Nārāyaṇa, not on her own.

Look at some of the statements Śrīla Prabhupāda makes about Lakṣmīdevī in this chapter (verse number in brackets):

1. She is the mother of all creation. (13)

2. She is represented in the material world as the external energy, but she is always the internal energy of the Lord. (11)

3. Mother Lakṣmī is the constant companion of Lord Viṣṇu. It is said, *śakti śaktimān abheda*: the power and the powerful are identical. Therefore, they remain together constantly. One cannot keep Lakṣmī in one's home without Lord Viṣṇu. (6)

4. Lakṣmī is the spiritual energy when she is with Lord Viṣṇu. To keep Lakṣmī, or the riches of the Lord, without the service of the Lord is always dangerous, for then Lakṣmī becomes the illusory energy. (6) Rāvaṇa took Sītā away from Rāma, because he wanted to enjoy Sītā separately from Rāma. This is considered demonic. In the same way, if we worship Lakṣmī without Viṣṇu, just because we want material benefits, we become under the influence of the illusory energy.

Assume that you are writing a simple article on Lakṣmī-puja for a Hindu magazine, *The Hindu Times*. Use some of the above facts and write a simple article describing the proper way to worship Lakṣmīdevī. Your write-up should have a proper structure (beginning, middle, and end) and should have simple persuasive language.

SPEAKING ACTIVITY: LAKṢMĪ-NĀRĀYAṆA AWARD ALL VICTORY AND FORTUNE

Kṛṣṇa possesses all opulence in full, and when He is pleased by our devotion, He can award us material and spiritual opulence. Lord Kṛṣṇa is addressed as Mādhava, the husband of the goddess of fortune, in *Bhagavad-gītā* (1.14), and in the purport Śrīla Prabhupāda says: "Victory is always with persons like the sons of Pāṇḍu because Lord Kṛṣṇa is associated with them. And whenever and wherever the Lord is present, the goddess of fortune is also there because the goddess of fortune never lives alone without her husband. Therefore, victory and fortune were awaiting Arjuna, as indicated by the transcendental sound produced by the conchshell of Viṣṇu, or Lord Kṛṣṇa."

In purport to *SB* 6.19.4, Śrīla Prabhupāda quotes *Bhagavad-gītā* (9.22) in which Lord Kṛṣṇa promises to protect what his devotees have and carry what they lack. The activities of devotional service are all auspicious and full of spiritual potency, which make the devotee perfect in self-realization; the devotee thus only desires to achieve the association of the Supreme Personality of Godhead.

In your own words explain to your class or teacher how a devotee can be fully satisfied and protected by rendering sincere devotional service to Rādhā-Kṛṣṇa, or in this case, Lakṣmī-Nārāyaṇa. Explain how and why they are "a powerful combination" as explained in verse

9. (Also refer to verses 4 to 6 and verses 13 and 14.) Include any examples of their material or spiritual blessings that you may have experienced in your life or heard about from other devotees.

THE TRIANGLE METAPHOR: HARMONY IN MARRIED LIFE

A Kṛṣṇa conscious family life is like the three sides of a triangle. Let's see how.

In your notebook draw an equilateral triangle. Put Kṛṣṇa on the topmost point of the triangle as shown in the diagram below. The bottom two points depict the position of the husband and the wife. Draw arrows pointing towards Kṛṣṇa.

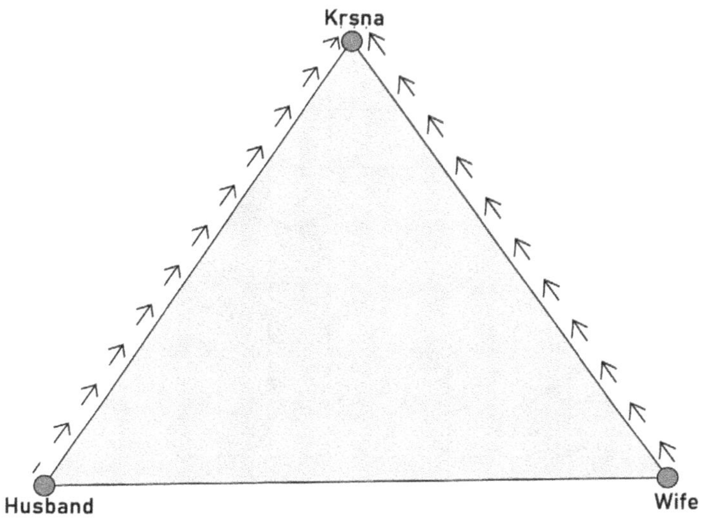

Study the diagram and answer the following questions based on your observations and the theme of how to have a happy married life:

1. As the husband and wife walk upward toward Kṛṣṇa, what happens? Similarly, what happens when the husband and wife come closer to Kṛṣṇa by serving Him together?

2. If the husband and wife had to walk backwards returning to their own positions, what do you think would happen in their relationship? Their own positions at the bottom represent "I" and "mine" – their selfish desires.

3. According to this chapter, what benedictions would they receive when they reach Kṛṣṇa?

4. Explain the importance of cooperation in Kṛṣṇa conscious married life according to this chapter.

CROSSWORD

Across

3. Who is sacrifice personified?

4. The most important aspect of the Supreme Lord's self-sufficiency is that he depends on His ___________.

6. One should offer obeisances unto the Lord with a mind humbled through what?

8. Lakṣmī without the service of the Lord becomes this energy.

11. Mother Lakṣmī is represented in the material world as this energy.

Down

1. The Lord is completely able to bless the devotee with what?

2. Mother Lakṣmī, the wife of Lord Viṣṇu, is this energy of the Lord.

5. Another name of Lord Viṣṇu.

7. Offering *daṇḍavats* means to fall on the ground like a what?

9. The Lord is full in how many opulences?

10. Before beginning the worship of Lord Viṣṇu for the Puṁsavana-vrata, women should hear whose story?

CHAPTER 19 ANSWERS

A Contradiction: Dependent Independence

SB 2.9.33, purport, states: "This means that the transcendental Lord with all His name, fame, quality and paraphernalia exists eternally . . . Even the devotees of the Personality of Godhead are not annihilated during the period of the entire annihilation of the material world." This means that the Lord, His name, fame, qualities, paraphernalia, and associates exist together as one self-sufficient unit – they are not meant to, and do not, exist independent of each other. The energies and associates of the Lord emanate from Himself, meant for His own pleasure. The Lord is self-sufficient in this sense also.

Finally, in the purport to this verse, Śrīla Prabhupāda mentions that when the Lord is dependent on His devotees, it's His way of showing mercy to them. He also shows that His activities and activities carried out on His behalf through His devotees are the same. Self-sufficiency is shown in this way also. Moreover, the love between the Lord and His devotees reconciles all contradictions; because of His devotees' love and devotion, the Lord becomes subservient to them. These points need to be brought out in the discussion, especially points that "fill the gap" to resolve the contradiction.

The Triangle Metaphor

1. The husband and wife come closer to Kṛṣṇa as they walk towards the same goal of pleasing and serving Kṛṣṇa. As a result, they become closer to each other.

2. They would be further apart from each other, taking care of their own selfish interests.

3. They receive material benedictions in the form of wealth, nice home and children, prosperity, and other opulences. They also receive spiritual benedictions in the form of receiving taste for hearing and chanting, developing deeper desires to serve Kṛṣṇa and His devotees, and ultimately developing their love for Kṛṣṇa and returning to the spiritual world.

4. If the husband is sincere and the wife is chaste, they can practice Kṛṣṇa consciousness in a favorable atmosphere. When they cooperate to satisfy Kṛṣṇa, making Him the goal and center of their relationship, they become happier and progress toward Kṛṣṇa. Kṛṣṇa awards them everything favorable to have a harmonious married and family life and eventually takes them back to Godhead.

Crossword

Across: 3. Viṣṇu; 4. devotees; 6. devotion; 8. illusory; 11. external

Down: 1. opulences; 2. internal; 5. Śrīnivāsa; 7. rod; 9. six; 10. Maruts

www.ingramcontent.com/pod-product-compliance
Lightning Source LLC
Chambersburg PA
CBHW080357030726
47598CB00010B/2779